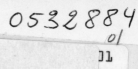

CHINA AFTER THE CULTURAL REVOLUTION

JÜRGEN DOMES

China after the Cultural Revolution

Politics between Two Party Congresses

With a contribution by Marie-Luise Näth

Translated from the German by
Annette Berg and David Goodman

UNIVERSITY OF CALIFORNIA PRESS
Berkeley and Los Angeles

University of California Press
Berkeley and Los Angeles, California

First published in German as *China
nach der Kulturrevolution: Politik zwischen
zwei Parteitagen*
© 1975 Wilhelm Fink Verlag, München

First American edition, 1977
© 1977 C. Hurst & Co. (Publishers) Ltd.

ISBN 0-520-03064-8

Printed in Great Britain

Dedicated to the memory of

DR. ERIK VON GROELING

Preface

Although hardly anyone disputes any longer the significance of the People's Republic of China (PRC) on the stage of world politics, our knowledge of that country is still very limited indeed. There are, in particular, common misunderstandings and misinterpretations of the political development of the world's most densely populated country, with a ruling Party that comprises 31% of all the world's organized Communists, and which attempts to find solutions to the developmental problems of the largest underdeveloped country in the world. For more than a decade it was fashionable to belittle China, while now the propaganda of the Chinese Communist leadership is blindly accepted by some observers. In our attempt to understand China it is important to find a middle course between these two extremes. Some of the western journalists who have managed to visit China during the last couple of years have certainly been able to do this. However, their reports are necessarily limited to short-term impressions. Consequently, they have to be supplemented by further attempts at a more systematic and coherent explanation of China's political development.

This study aims to make such a contribution. It will concentrate on the field of political decision-making and the resulting activities in domestic and foreign policy during the period from the Spring of 1969 to the Autumn of 1973. It is therefore a limited exercise. This study will not attempt to present a sociology of contemporary China, nor an ideological discussion of Mao Tse-tung's, and his followers' versions of Marxism–Leninism. The focus will rather be on practical policies and their relationship to effective power within the leadership of the Communist Party of China (CCP).

To this end I aim to present, as far as is possible, carefully selected information, and at the same time to contribute to an understanding of the political process in Communist-ruled countries.

In this preface I must particularly thank Dr. Marie-Luise Näth of the Research Unit on Chinese and East Asian Politics, Berlin, who has kindly provided, with her specialized knowledge, the account of Chinese foreign policy which is Part 4 of this book.

The exchange of ideas with German China specialists, Wolfgang Bauer, Roland Felber, Herbert Franke, Joachim Glaubitz, Tilemann Grimm, Dieter Heinzig, Gottfried-Karl Kindermann, Hans

Steininger and Udo Weiss, and journalist Harry Hamm has been an important stimulant to this study.

I also owe much to continuous critical discussions with my foreign colleagues, for China studies can only exist through such international contacts. My particular thanks go to W. A. C. Adie, Audrey Donnithorne, Daniel Ellegiers, Harold Hinton, Ellis Joffe, Donald Klein, Roderick MacFarquhar, Ladislao La Dany, Franz Michael, Michel Oksenberg, Dwight Perkins, Ralph Powell, Lucian Pye, Thomas Robinson, Robert Scalapino, Stuart Schram, Benjamin Schwartz, Richard Thornton, Ezra Vogel, Richard Walker, William Whitson and David C. Wilson.

Of great value to my studies was the continuous exchange of ideas with Chinese academics, particularly in Hong Kong and Taiwan. At the top of this list I must mention the late Huang Chen-hsia who died in January of this year at much too early an age, and Chu Wen-lin, Fang Chün-kuei, Hai Feng, Hsiang Nai-kuang, Hsü Tung-pin, Liu Chieh, Lo Wan-sheng and Ting Wang.

While thanking all those who have contributed to this study with their advice and criticisms, I want to state that I alone am responsible for the results of the first three parts of this book. Dr. Näth is responsible for Part 4.

I wish to express especial gratitude to the Ernst-Reuter-Gesellschaft, Berlin, whose generous financial grant made the English translation of this book possible. Christian Koziol kindly assisted in correcting the English manuscript.

Chinese names and terms have been transcribed according to the Wade-Giles system, in general use throughout international political science. The only exception to this rule is that all well-known place names are given according to the World Postal Union's transcription.

This book is dedicated to the memory of Dr. Erik von Groeling. The death on 10 January 1973 of this young German China specialist whose work promised high achievement has hit my colleagues and myself very hard indeed. He was torn from much promising work in which he had elucidated some of the relationships described in this book. May this dedication ensure that he is not forgotten.

Berlin, 1974/Saarbrücken, 1976   JÜRGEN DOMES

P.S. The proofs of the German edition had been passed for press by the time the 4th National People's Congress met in January 1975. Consequently, no consideration was given in the biographical information to personnel changes that resulted from this Congress. Such consideration remains outside our frame of reference in the English edition also.

Contents

Tables

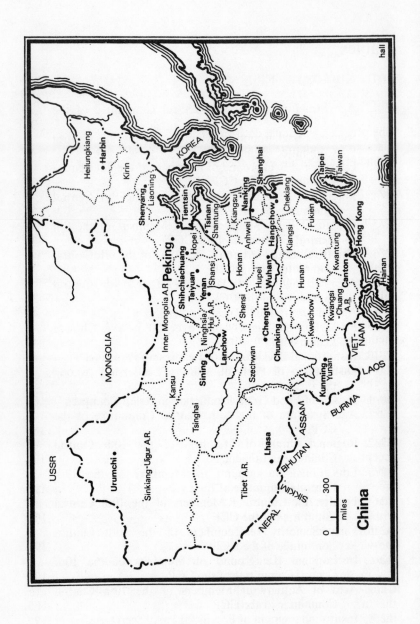

China

Introduction

The process of political decision-making in the PRC does not take place in a framework of open discussion before a well informed public. It takes place in the context of a system unwilling to inform. This makes it almost impenetrable even to the Chinese-speaking foreign observer. Consequently, a different set of rules has to apply for the study of this and similar political systems than for the description and analysis of open societies.

Since the second decade of this century political science has developed a particular methodology in the observation of Soviet politics. This combines the examination of the content of communications, and a long-term and repetitive comparison of official news with a close knowledge of personnel, as well as with the observation of continuity and change in the terms used in political communication. Even the derogatory description of this methodology as 'Kremlin-astrology' cannot disguise the fact that without it there would be no possibility of even a vague understanding of political events in the USSR.

This is true for China at least to the same extent as it is for the Soviet Union. The observer is forced, frequently if not for the most part, to speculate in a similar way. This pressure to be speculative does not only presuppose intellectual flexibility and imagination; it also demands intellectual self-discipline and the willingness to accept the constraining influence of criticism by others.

Even if all this is the case, misinterpretations of political events are still not impossible: for example, this author argued elsewhere that even after the Cultural Revolution new conflicts would arise within the Chinese political élite.[1] But, like other China-watchers, he little expected that these conflicts were going to culminate in the violent downfall of the second man at the top, Marshal Lin Piao. The crisis over Lin Piao, which is the focus of this analysis, has in this way become a crisis of self-confidence in academic China-watching. It has taught us to develop our projections into the future even more carefully. However, with the help of our methodology we were in the position to understand the background to the crisis in China during 1971, and to develop (with some circumspection) perspectives on the not too distant future of

Chinese politics. These in turn may give some indication of and for international relations with China.

Far from what might be expected the observation of Chinese politics suffers not from a lack of sources, but from an excess. In spite of the fact that serious and intensive research within the country is still prohibited, there is such a vast amount of sources available that the sorting and evaluation of these sources is more difficult than their discovery.

Experience has shown that a clear scale of importance can be drawn up for the data-content of the various sources. At the top there are the provincial radio broadcasts that are copy-taped outside the country, and which include articles taken from the provincial press. This is where the leadership speaks directly to the people. This is where details are made public that are seldom mentioned by central organs like the central Peking Radio; the daily newspaper *Jen-min jih-pao (People's Daily; JMJP)* and the monthly theoretical Communist Party journal *Hung-ch'i (HC)*. These sources are only of secondary value in terms of the value of their data. Third in importance are the reports in foreign languages put out by the PRC. The data-content of these sources is reduced considerably because of the propaganda interest of the media. Finally, there are travellers' reports, the reports from Peking correspondents of the foreign news media, and remarks made by refugees from China. This scale does not include the internal communications of the Chinese leadership, which only rarely get abroad. These, of course, are particularly valuable, but they are not regularly available to us and cannot therefore offer a complete picture.[2]

The observer of Chinese politics, therefore, does not only have to be aware of methodological difficulties and dangers resulting from the object of his studies, but he also has to be aware that his most important source of information is in the nature of an official gazetteer. Hardly anyone would think of studying the political, social or economic development of Iran only on the basis of publications from an Iranian Embassy. However, in the case of the PRC we are forced to accept such methods. For this reason we have to apply the techniques of comparative evaluation of these sources with particular care. Revelations of success or failure through the Chinese media in most cases provide a picture of political trends rather than of hard data. If this is forgotten one is in danger of replacing scholarly analysis and description with the unquestioned repetition of official propaganda.

This change has become apparent in some of the literature on China that has been published in Germany in recent years. In the interests of academic integrity and serious scholarship, one therefore has to attempt to reconsider and, where possible, revise both the tentative and the established knowledge of research into Chinese politics.

Since the 1950s the majority of observers of Chinese politics have been influenced by two successive trends. Until the early 1960s a number of writers tended to highlight particularly the more negative aspects of the political system and political behaviour in China.[3] At times this tendency approached unthinking anti-Communism, which obscured not only the emerging Sino-Soviet dispute but also the extensive social changes that were taking place in China in the 1950s. This was followed by a totally revised picture of China. However, for its part this revision resulted in an exaggeration of the more positive aspects of Chinese politics by a number of authors so that an unthinking pro-Communist approach emerged.[4] However, some of the pre-eminent contemporary China scholars have defended the view that without critical academic inquiry an adequate evaluation and presentation of the Chinese political system was impossible.[5]

These scholars have argued for a new revision of these previous attitudes towards China, which would display neither pro- nor anti-Communist prejudices.

The demand for a second revision of our view of China, which would reduce rather than replace our prejudices, is the basic starting point for the following study. I start from the basic premise that one can extract data from propaganda, but that one should not take such propaganda for fact. The significance of the ideology of the Chinese Communist Party (CCP), as the verbalization of the view of the future of the Chinese leadership and as the basis of the behavioural norms brought forward by them to the population, should not be underestimated. However, more than two decades of continuous China-watching have taught us that ideology ought to be seen as the manipulative instrument for the justification of power politics. The ideology may give some indication of political events, but it is not the most effective key to the understanding of these events.

This particular study recognizes this fact and therefore chooses to concentrate on political practice in the People's Republic of China.

Furthermore, this study is based on the assumption that the periods preceding and following the Cultural Revolution call for a new approach to the study of Chinese politics. Richard C. Thornton has correctly pointed out that the majority of China scholars have so far started from the assumption of a united political decision-making process—a process which, if not determined by him, has at least been dominated by a single historical figure, Mac Tse-tung.[6] As Thornton points out, this is the approach used universally by advocates of the most diverse schools of thought. It is of little importance whether one regards Mao Tse-tung as the benevolent dictator of Benjamin Schwarz,[7] the radical humanist of Stuart Schram,[8] the able social engineer of Tang Tsou,[9] the terrifying tyrant of Richard Walker, or even—one might add—the 'Great Teacher' of the newly emerging, underdeveloped nations of so many members of the Left.[10] The common denominator of all these views is an individualized and monolithic concept. Within the last five years such an approach has been shown to be invalid by the findings of a number of detailed and intensive studies of the political élite and of research into the relationships between the various groups in the Chinese power complex.[11] It has, furthermore, become obsolete with the death of Mao on 9 September 1976.

Furthermore, while it may be pointed out that some categories of research into totalitarianism have, in revised form, added to an understanding of the claims to power of the Chinese leadership, they were nonetheless ill-equipped to explain the relationship *within* the leadership. Although claims to power and the mechanisms of leadership can be analysed in such terms, our insight into the 'allocative processes'[12] since the CCP's assumption of power in 1949 leads us to accept that a more detailed analysis is required. Within the last two decades, intra-Party conflict has been the rule while an easily established consensus increasingly became the exception.

This intra-party conflict, however, did not follow an easily identifiable trend. There were always particular aspects to each individual case. Nonetheless, a look at the decision-making process reveals two congruent and basic trends in the form of the conflict:
(1) Two distinct types of groups can be identified in the intra-Party conflict in China since the middle of the 1950s:
— *opinion groups,* existing in the short and middle term, initially formed on the basis of conflict between individuals within clearly defined limits; and
— *factions,* existing on a long-term basis, based on an alternative programme and demanding exclusive access to leadership.[13]
The transformation of the first type of grouping into the second signifies change from intra-Party conflict to an extensive crisis.
(2) Two distinct types of decision-making processes are also distinguishable:
— *majority construction* through the Party Leader who initially failed to gain for his concepts the support of the majority in the official decision-making bodies of the CCP; and
— *majority formation* arrived at through a coalition of opinion groups within the Party, which presented its political ideas so persistently to the Party Leader that resistance was impossible.[14]
The course of Chinese domestic politics during the last two

decades does not therefore substantiate the widespread assumption that the key to an understanding of Chinese politics is to be found only in the concept and actions of a single charismatic leader.

This is not brought into question by the undoubtedly correct acknowledgment of Mao's final and lasting authority over any political interpretation and formulation made by the leadership group.

On the basis of this definition an attempt will be made to provide an overview of the development of the PRC's domestic and foreign policy since the end of the Cultural Revolution. Within China studies there are several arguments about the correct point of time marking the end of the Cultural Revolution. Over the last few years, however, a consensus has largely been reached which dates the end of the Cultural Revolution as April 1969, with the 9th Party Congress of the CCP and the establishment of a new leadership group and the resurrection of the civilian party organization. This study will therefore start by illustrating the period preceding, and the results of, this Party Congress.

Since this Congress, three phases in Chinese domestic policy are clearly distinguishable. In the first phase, between April 1969 and the autumn of 1970, China's internal politics were decisively influenced by the ideas of the then designated successor to Mao—Marshal Lin Piao. Lin's attempt to restore the concept of development through mass mobilization, formulated by Mao in 1958, within a framework of military discipline, was opposed by an emerging coalition of regional military commanders and civilian cadres. This conflict marked the second phase, which ended with the fall, and probably the death, of Lin on the night of 12 September 1971. The third phase was marked by a new course in China's domestic politics which is somewhat similar to the 'politics of readjustment' of the early 1960s. It ended with the 10th Party Congress of the CCP in August 1973, when the beginnings of a new dispute within the Party became noticeable. This new dispute—through the bewildering ups and downs of the campaign to criticize Lin Piao and Confucius and through Teng Hsiao-p'ing's attempt at a wholesale revision of the CCP's theory and practice—led finally to a new all-out confrontation, which reached its first but by no means last climax in the dramatic events of April 1976.

Description and analysis of the development of China's internal politics during the period between April 1969 and August 1973 will therefore be carried out in three parts. The fourth section of this book deals with the developments in the PRC's foreign policy since 1968-9 in order to round off this discussion of China's development since the Cultural Revolution.

The following questions underlie this work:

— How did the character of leadership change when compared to the period before the Cultural Revolution?

— What relationships existed between the Party organization, the military, and the civilian administration?

— What were the ideas about the future of China's development that lay at the bottom of the central conflict of the period under investigation, namely the Lin Piao crisis?

— What types of intra-Party groups and allocative processes are discernible in the period from April 1969 to August 1973?

— In which ways did the sociological and political structure of leadership groups change?

— How did the conflicts of the period under discussion influence the political system?

— What are the fundamental decisions and the international processes which have a determining influence on the PRC's foreign policy? What is China's position in today's international power structure?

— What perspectives on the future development of domestic and foreign policy can be drawn from this analysis of China's politics since the Cultural Revolution?

Finally, an attempt will be made to compare the development of that part of the Chinese Revolution that was determined by the Communists with the course of other revolutionary movements. Apart from explaining the interrelationships and development of Chinese politics after the Cultural Revolution, this is to be an empirical contribution to the understanding of continuity and change in revolutionary leadership. However, this contribution will only be of limited importance as there is too little certainty to be able to view the conclusions that have been drawn here as historically reliable. If, however, this study is able to convey to the reader an impression of the development of China's domestic and foreign policies between the 9th and 10th Party Congresses of the CCP, and of the processes of political decision-making in the PRC, then it will have fulfilled its intention.

REFERENCES

1. Jürgen Domes, *The Internal Politics of China 1949–71*, London, 1972 (hereafter referred to as *Internal Politics*), Ch. XIV.

2. Important collections of such documents include: Union Research Institute, Hong Kong (URI), *CCP Documents of the Great Proletarian Cultural Revolution, 1966–67*, Hong Kong, 1968; *Mao Tse-tung t'ung-chih shih tang-tai tsui wei-ta-te ma-k'ê-ssu-lieh-ning-chu-yi chê* (Comrade Mao Tse-tung is the greatest Marxist-Leninist of the Modern Era) and Mao Tse-tung *ssu-hsiang wen-sui* (Long live the Thoughts of Mao Tse-

tung!), Peking, 1967 and 1969 (four collections of Mao Tse-tung's unpublished speeches, sayings and articles, which were collected for the benefit of cadres in 1967 and after and reached T'aiwan in 1973 and 1974 where they were reproduced in facsimile): and Yüan Yüeh (ed.), *Lin Piao shih-chien yüan-shih wên-chien hui-pien* (collection of original documents on the Lin Piao Incident), T'aipei, 1973.

3. For example see: Jean Monsterleet, *Wird der gelbe Mann rot?* Freiburg, 1956; Richard L. Walker, *China under Communism: The first five years,* Yale University Press, 1955; and Peter S. H. Tang, *Communist China Today: Domestic and Foreign Policies,* New York, 1957 (1st edition).

4. Particularly clearly in: John W. Lewis, *Leadership in Communist China,* Ithaca NY, 1963; Franz Schurmann, *Ideology and Organization in Communist China,* Berkeley, 1968 (2nd edition); James R. Townsend, *Political Participation in Communist China,* Berkeley, 1967.

5. To mention only a few among a great number of works: Richard H. Solomon, *Mao's Revolution and the Chinese Political Culture,* Berkeley, 1967; Lucian W. Pye, *The Spirit of Chinese Politics,* Cambridge, Mass., 1968; William W. Whitson (with Huang Chen-hsia), *The Chinese High Command: a History of Communist Military Politics, 1927-1971,* New York, 1973; Stuart R. Schram, *The Political Thought of Mao Tse-tung,* New York, 1969; Benjamin Schwartz, *Communism and China: Ideology in Flux,* Cambridge, Mass., 1968; A. Doak Barnett, *Uncertain Passage,* Washington DC., 1974; and Adrian Hsia, *Die chinesische Kulturrevolution: Zur Entwicklung der Widersprüche in der chinesischen Gesellschaft,* Sammlung Luchterhand No. 23, Neuwied-Berlin, 1971.

6. Richard C. Thornton, 'The Structure of Communist Politics', in: *World Politics,* Vol. 24, No. 4, July 1972, pp. 498-517. The examples quoted from this article are given in footnotes 7-9.

Thornton's position is represented by: Harold C. Hinton, *An Introduction to Chinese Politics,* New York, 1973, pp. 6-12; and William W. Whitson, *The Succession Question in China: Problems and Prospects for the 1970s,* Rand Corporation Paper, No. E-2847, Washington DC, 1973, pp. 54-75.

The individual-monolithic premise is convincingly developed, although with some limitations by: Michel C. Oksenberg, 'Policy Making under Mao, 1949-68: an Overview', in John M. Lindbeck (ed.), *China: Management of a Revolutionary Society,* Seattle, 1971, pp. 79-115.

For a similar discussion in Sovietology see, for example; Sidney J. Ploss (ed.), *The Soviet Political Process: Aims, Techniques, and Examples of Analysis,* Waltham, Mass., 1971.

7. Benjamin J. Schwartz, 'The Reign of Virtue: Some Broad Perspectives on Leader and Party in the Cultural Revolution', in *China Quarterly (CQ),* No. 35, July-September 1968, pp. 1-17.

8. Stuart R. Schram, 'The Man and his Doctrines', in *Problems of Communism,* Vol. 15, September-October 1966, pp. 1-7.

9. Tang Tsou (Tsou Tang), 'Revolution, Reintegration and Crisis in Communist China: A Framework for Analysis', in Ping-ti Ho and Tang Tsou (ed.), *China in Crisis,* Chicago, 1968, Vol. 1, Book 1, pp. 277-347.

10. Others include Jan Myrdal, *Report from a Chinese Village,* London,

1965; and *China: the Revolution Continued,* London 1971; Joachim Schickel, *Grosse Mauer—Grosse Methode: Annäherungen an China,* Stuttgart, 1968; and—particularly unquestioning and propagandist: Hans Heinz Holz, *Widerspruch in China: Politisch-philosophische Erläuterungen zu Mao Tse-tung,* München, 1970; and: Dietmar Albrecht (ed.), *China 1972: Ökonomie, Betrieb und Erziehung seit der Kulturrevolution,* Berlin, 1972.

11. The following should be mentioned here: Lindbeck, op. cit., passim; Whitson, *High Command,* op. cit., passim; A. Doak Barnett (ed.), *Chinese Communist Politics in Action,* Seattle, 1969; Robert A. Scalapino (ed.), *Elites in the People's Republic of China,* Seattle, 1972; and Parris H. Chang, 'Research Notes on the Changing Loci of Decision in the CCP', in *CQ,* No. 44, October–December 1970, pp. 169-94.

12. The term "allocative process" refers to a political process, in the course of which leading positions and the right to promote policies was distributed amongst members and groups of members of political elites on the basis of the formation of coalitions and other power-political manipulations.

13. Compare the author's definition in Domes, *The Internal Politics of China,* op. cit., London, 1973, pp. 236 ff.

14. Compare Jürgen Domes, 'Die innenpolitischen Voraussetzungen: Aspekte der Organisation und Führung' in *Die Aussenpolitik Chinas: Entscheidungsstrukturen, Stellung in der Welt und Beziehungen zu Deutschland,* published by the German Society for Foreign Policy, München-Wien, 1975 (pp. 83-137), pp. 100-3.

PART ONE

THE ERA OF LIN PIAO: THE ATTEMPT TO ESTABLISH A BONAPARTIST STATE

1. The Last Phase of the Cultural Revolution and the 9th Party Congress

Mao's attempt in 1958 to launch the policy of 'The Three Red banners'[1]—a wide-ranging experiment aimed at implementing a concept of development based on labour-intensive and mobilizatory techniques—against the opposition of leadership cadres of the Party Centre, was the most decisive turning-point in the country's internal politics after 1949. This experiment led China into a deep economic crisis, which was worsened by three consecutive poor harvests.[2] The majority of the Chinese leadership, grouped around the First Vice-Chairman of the Central Committee of the CCP (CC), Liu Shao-ch'i, were impressed by the substantial problems in the provision of food supplies in the Winter of 1961-2 that brought many parts of the country close to starvation, and by the decline in industrial production. Consequently, they carried through a fundamental revision of the Maoist approach against the will of the Chairman—or at least without his active participation.[3] This is how the period of the 'policy of readjustment'—*T'iao-cheng*, as it has since become known in China—began.

Ever since, consecutive attempts by Mao and his closest colleagues and followers in the CCP to return to the ideas of 1958 have been at the centre of the country's internal political developments.

The first of these attempts, in the years 1962 to 1965, resulted in the crystallization of opinion groups within the central Party leadership and the emergence of clearly identifiable factions.[4] After the more pragmatic and growth-oriented followers of Liu Shao-ch'i had succeeded in undermining Mao's attempt to mobilize the Party organization in the 'Socialist Education Movement' *(Shê-hui chu-yi chiao-yü yün-tung)*,[5] and when in the summer of 1965 there were increasing signs of an impending general revision of Maoist policy, the Chairman tried in September 1965 to win over the Party leadership for a new rectification campaign. This campaign was to be directed initially at the intellectual critics of his policies, and at the same time to close the period of readjustment. The experience of having the majority of the intra-Party core openly criticizing Mao's suggestions,[6] made the Chairman take the following momentous decision. He decided to carry through a return to the policies of 1958 against the party *apparat*, depending instead on the majority of the armed forces and on the spontaneous organization of secondary school pupils and students. China thereby entered the crisis of the 'Great Proletarian Cultural Revolution'.

This crisis, which was to shatter the basis of the political system and which, as Mao was to say in 1970, had led the country 'to the brink of chaos,'[7] had begun as an intellectual dispute. During its course the majority of the Party leadership tried to present the dispute between Mao's followers and the intellectual critics of his policies as a 'non-antagonistic contradiction within the people'.[8] However, the Maoist faction, within which Mao's wife Chiang Ch'ing and the Minister of Defence Lin Piao were becoming increasingly influential, intended to have it defined as an 'antagonistic contradiction' between friend and foe.[9] The crisis became public when the Maoists, supported by demonstrations of military power in the capital, successfully removed two of the most important leaders of the opposition, P'eng Chen, Mayor of Peking and a Member of the Politburo, and Lu Ting-yi, the Director of the Propaganda Department of the Central Committee, a Deputy Prime Minister, Minister of Culture and an Alternate Member of the Politburo. At the same time *ad hoc* organizations of secondary school pupils and students, supported by the Political Department of the People's Liberation Army *(Jen-min chieh-fang chün; PLA)*, emerged. These became the strike-force of the Maoist counter-offensive, with their extensive campaigns of terror against teachers and intellectuals.[10] After the Maoist faction gained control over the situation in Peking and succeeded in obtaining a majority in the Politburo through military action at the 11th Plenum of the 8th Central Committee of the CCP in August 1966,[11] these organizations became known as 'Red Guards'.

Between 18 August and 25 November 1966 they celebrated Mao and Lin Piao (Who had in the meantime gained the Deputy Party leadership) at eight mass rallies in Peking attended by one to two million youngsters and soldiers.[12] Between the middle of August and the end of October 1966 the Red Guards ruled not only most of the schools and universities but also the streets in most Chinese towns. They destroyed temples and churches, and most museums had to be safeguarded by sections of the People's Liberation Army. They carried out house investigations through which, in many instances, 'bourgeois luxury articles' like clocks, fish tanks, musical instruments and so on were hunted out and destroyed. Critics and opponents of the Chairman were dragged through the streets, beaten, humiliated and tortured, and one can certainly say that some people were even killed or driven to suicide.[13]

However, these activities of the Left *avant garde* soon encountered opposition. In some provinces the Party organization, which was itself under attack, organized some groups, and after the beginning of October the movement split into a very large number of rival factions.[14] Even so all the attempts made in November and December by Liu Shao-chi's faction in the Centre to stop the movement were in vain. At the end of December the Cultural Revolutionary Left asserted itself. A direct attack on the leaders of the anti-Maoist faction began. By the middle of March 1967 they had been removed from office and in many cases arrested. The 'Cultural Revolution' was now to be carried into industrial plants and into the rural people's communes. The Left immediately went on the offensive against the Party leadership in the provinces, which until then had resisted the movement.

On 4 January 1967 the Maoist mass movement, under the leadership of some of Chiang Ch'ing's close collaborators, overthrew the Municipal Party Committee and the Municipal Government of Shanghai.[15] In a similar manner the Left turned against most of the other provincial party leaderships, but only in a few of the provinces were they equally successful.

The population at large reacted to the new offensive by Mao and his followers with a wave of resistance. In twenty-six of the country's twenty-nine provinces strikes broke out among the industrial and transport workers. In twenty-one provinces there were peasant uprisings in the course of which banks and granaries were ransacked and in a few cases the land of the people's communes was divided up among the peasants.[16] The Party machine was no longer functioning and substantial sections of the population were slipping beyond Central control; it seemed that the Communist government was severely threatened.

In this situation there was only one way out for the Maoists—an appeal to the military. On the night of January 17-18 and on 23 January 1967 the leader of the Party called upon the People's Liberation Army to intervene all over the country in the conflict, and to support the Maoist organization against their opponents.[17] However, there was an uneven reaction to this appeal with the PLA. Only in a few of the provinces did it clearly stand by the Left. Elsehwere it created its own groups to fight against the Maoists and in many parts of the country the armed forces remained neutral in the conflict.[18] On the other hand, the generals almost everywhere forced the provincial Party leaders to resign and made themselves heads of the provisional governing bodies. As

'Military Control Commissions' they took over the leadership of the Party and state *apparats*, and as 'Provisional Production Headquarters' they took control over the economic system.

The Cultural Revolutionary Left felt robbed of the fruits of its victory. It therefore attempted to remove the regional military rulers from their positions,[19] or at least to bring them under control in a second offensive during the spring and summer of 1967. Because these attempts were in many instances resisted by the PLA and their mass organizations, the struggle between these groups became more severe and after May 1967 it frequently led to armed clashes between rival factions. It reached its first climax in an open revolt against the Central Maoist leadership group by the Commander of the Wuhan Military Region (in Central China), General Ch'en Tsai-tao and his First Political Commissar, General Chung Han-hua.[20] Even though this localized military revolt was put down by parachutists and a fleet of gunboats, it did prove that the Centre could no longer completely rely on the loyalty of the regional commanders if it was not prepared to make concessions to their growing concern about the need for a return to law and order.

At an enlarged session of the CCP's Military Committee in August, Lin Piao managed to negotiate a compromise with the regional commanders. They were to declare their willingness to establish the new leadership organs of the Party and Government *apparats*—the 'Revolutionary Committees' (*Kê-ming wei-yüan-hui*; RC)—in all the provinces; while the Centre was to transfer to them the authority to discipline the Red Guard movement and was to agree to military leadership over the RCs.[21]

This in fact meant a drastic change of course in the Cultural Revolution. From now on the Central leadership and the regional military were to join forces against the Left. The winter of 1967-8 started with the closest collaborators of Chiang Ch'ing in the leadership of the Cultural Revolutionary Left—'The Central Cultural Revolution Group of the Central Committee'—being purged as 'Enemies of the Party' and as 'Agents of the Kuomintang' and with the reintroduction of disciplinary measures against the 'Red Guards'.[22] Finally, an opposition group of commanders of military regions succeeded in forcing Lin Piao in March 1968 to remove one of his closest collaborators, General Yang Ch'eng-wu, then Chief-of-Staff of the PLA, from office and to replace him with one of their own number, the Commander of the Canton Military Region, General Huang Yung-sheng.[23]

Thus the failure of Mao's first major attempt to return to the politics of mass mobilization of 1958 was ensured. The Maoist organizations completely lost their effectiveness as an instrument of a Left-offensive. At the centre of events in the last stage of the Cultural Revolution (which began in April 1968) was the elimina-

tion of the 'Red Guards', whose desperate resistance had at times
to be broken with military force in many cities.

In October 1967 the leadership groups of the Party, state and
military *apparats* had, together with the 'Central Cultural
Revolution Group', jointly released a circular which ordered the
immediate return to teaching in schools and universities.[24] Even
though sections of the PLA in most of China's towns had started,
shortly after this release, 'to support students and school pupils to
return to their schools' (as it was put by the PRC's media),[25] it was
really only the primary and secondary schools that managed to
re-open. The first of the universities and colleges to re-open only
started work again after a break of four years in the autumn of
1970. The re-opening of schools was accompanied by disciplinary
measures directed mainly at the Red Guards. In the face of these
measures, opposition to the Peking leadership grew after the
autumn of 1967 among the ranks of Red Guards.[26] Particularly in
the provinces of Hunan, Kiangsi, Honan and Anhui, there
appeared to be resistance to the PLA from the Maoist youth
organizations in the last months of 1967.[27] In January 1968 the
Cultural Revolutionary Left in Canton proclaimed that the city
needed an 'even greater disturbance' since the old power-holders
had returned.[28] The ranks of the Red Guards began to speak
increasingly of a 'New Trend' (*Hsin Ssu-ch'ao*). Since, in Chinese,
the word 'trend' (*Ssu-ch'ao*) is a dynamic concept, the Left-
opposition were in fact putting up an antithesis to the official
Maoist and more static concept of 'idea' (*ssu-hsiang*). The 'New
Trend' was represented most clearly in two documents published
in December 1967 and January 1968 by the 'Committee of the
Great Proletarian Revolutionary Alliance in Hunan Province'
(*Hunan shêng wu-ch'an chieh-chi kê-ming ta-lien-hê wei-yüan-hui*;
abbreviated as *Shêng-wu-lien*).[29] Even though there may be doubts
about those versions of these documents which have circulated
outside the PRC, the main thesis is quoted with so much force in
other more reliable sources[30] that their existence and essential
content can certainly be accepted as genuine.

The young 'Rebels' from Hunan complained that despite the
fact that the 'Storm of the January Revolution' (1967) had demonstrated to the people that 'China was well on its way to a
bureaucracy-less society', military intervention had resulted in 'a
return of the fallen bureaucrats'. Again, they complained that
although the masses were eventually armed in August 1967, it was
at this point that Chairman Mao had 'unfortunately sounded the
retreat'; for these reasons they claimed that the masses could no
longer expect very much at all from the Party, which would always
be a 'Party of bourgeois reformism'. The Socialist Revolution
would only be realized when an 'All-China Commune' (*Chung-hua*

kung shê) was established, based on an essentially rulerless and communal system.

With these and similar proclamations the Left wing of the Red Guard Movement gave the Army the opportunity to take even harsher measures against the new Left-opposition. In May 1968 the PLA consequently began an extensive campaign against the Red Guards. In this campaign the military made particular use of those Red Workers who in January 1967 had in many provinces offered the strongest resistance to the Left's offensive. Together with military cadres, these 'Red Workers' Teams' took over control of the colleges. So it was that at the end of July 1968 Tsinghua University in Peking, where the Red Guard movement had begun in 1966, was occupied by mixed work-teams of the PLA and the Red Workers. In the course of these events a number of students died and many more were wounded. In spite of this, Mao even gave his blessing to this event.[31] In Canton the regional military, together with the so-called 'conservative' mass organizations and workers' militia, fought a relentless campaign of liquidation against the Left from May until August 1968, in the course of which several hundred Red Guards were shot dead.[32] But the most serious confrontation between Maoists and local troops (strengthened by members of erstwhile anti-Maoist organizations) developed during the period from February to September 1968 in the Chuang Autonomous Region, previously the South China province of Kwangsi.[33] It was here that a 'civil war'-like confrontation developed, in the course of which both sides brought heavy weapons into action. The towns of Wuchou and Liuchou were almost totally destroyed and more than 50,000 people were killed in four months.[34] Appeals for help to the Centre in Peking from the 'Revolutionary Rebels' and Red Guards from Kwangtung and Kwangsi were left unanswered, and the autumn of 1968 saw the crumbling of the Left's final stand against the seizure of power by the Regional Commanders and their followers. At the same time in four other administrative units it was officially declared that the Red Guard organizations were to be officially disbanded and replaced by four other kinds of mass organization.[35]

In order to bring the organizations of the 'early Maoists' completely under their control, the new leadership groups started (in August 1968) to force the former Red Guards to undergo manual labour in the villages (*Hsia-fang*), so that they should 'learn from the poor and lower-middle peasants' and learn how to submit themselves to 'revolutionary discipline'. Where these methods proved inadequate they resorted to public executions of the 'anarchists, vagabonds and agents of the Kuomintang', as the former members of the Leftist organizations were now called.[36] Thus by the end of 1968 the Cultural Revolutionary Left was defeated and its fate sealed. Although the Red Guards were mentioned subsequently, the new provincial leaders did not hesitate to point out that while the Red Guards 'did have their merits in the Cultural Revolution', their real worth now had to be tested by 'their current attitude to the Centre of the Revolution'—'Centre' in this context meaning the PLA.[37]

The final phase of the Cultural Revolution led in most of China's provinces to the consolidation of the military's political power and the elimination of the organizations of the Cultural Revolutionary Left.

The task now was to reconstruct the party machine which had crumbled under the assault of the Maoist groups, and thereby to put an end to the Cultural Revolution. Already in October 1967 the Centre had decided to start the reconstruction from above. The 9th Party Congress of the CCP was to be convened; this had been due since 1961. A first directive said that the Party Congress was to be convened before 1 October 1968.[38] From two sources we have become aware of the conceptualization and expectations that the Centre originally entertained in connection with the calling of the Party Congress.

In a speech to Peking mass organizations on 26 October 1967 the Minister of Public Security, General Hsieh Fu-chih, declared that 'the method of electing delegates from the bottom upwards' was 'only seemingly democratic'. For this reason the lists of delegates to the Party Congress were to be put together by the Central Committee. Hsieh was of the opinion that the Party Congress should include 8,000 to 10,000 delegates, as this was the only way to avoid 'a Congress of old men with approximately 1,000 delegates'. The majority at the Congress were to be the 'younger forces', particularly representatives of the mass organizations.[39]

A circular from the Party Centre and the 'Cultural Revolution Group' of the Central Committee on 27 November 1967 laid down that some of the best-known representatives of the anti-Maoist opposition, in particular Liu Shao-ch'i, Teng Hsiao-p'ing, T'ao Chu, Marshal P'eng Tê-huai, Marshal Ho Lung, P'eng Chen, General Lo Jui-Ch'ing, Lu Ting-i and Yang Shang-k'un, were under no circumstances to be delegates to the Party Congress. From now on only the 'real Marxist-Leninists' were to be members of the Party, persons who had demonstrated their 'loyalty to Chairman Mao, to the ideas of Mao Tse-tung and to the revolutionary line of Chairman Mao'.[40]

However, the Party Congress started later than the declaration in the autumn of 1967 had intended. It first required action by the PLA against the Cultural Revolutionary Left and accepteance by the army of responsibility over large parts of society before the Party Congress could announce the start of the reconstruction of the Party machine. Whole battalions and regiments were put into action in the administration[41] and, according to the Chinese public media, soldiers played their parts in 'factories, enterprises, firms, colleges, schools, literature, the arts, the health services, newspapers, publishing, etc.'.[42]

Putting this massive military workforce into action finally caused a stabilization of the Chinese political scene to begin in the autumn and winter of 1968-9. The 12th Plenum of the 8th Central Committee—which, although not having the full quota for statutory decision-making, did comprise almost all the regional commanders and many representatives of the provincial Revolutionary Committees, and sat from 13 to 31 October 1968 in Peking—was in a position to start serious preparations for the Party Congress. The Plenum decided to expel Liu Shao-ch'i 'for all time' from the CCP and to relieve him of all his offices, contrary to all the regulations of the Constitution which makes this power the reserve of the National People's Congress.[43] Although it decided that the party Congress was to convene at 'a certain suitable date', at the same time it passed the draft of a new Party Constitution which had been drawn up under the leadership of Ch'en Po-ta (Chairman of the Central Cultural Revolution Group and a member of the Standing Committee of the Politburo) and Chiang Ch'ing's closest colleagues Chang Ch'un-ch'iao and Yao Wên-yuan, and which was to be put to the Party Congress for ratification.[44] As a result the leaders of the Cultural Revolutionary Left had an opportunity to influence the formulation of the new Party Constitution.

The choice of Party delegates was to rest with the regional leadership groups, contrary to what Hsieh Fu-chih had said. There are reports at hand for eight of the twenty-nine administrative units in China during November 1968 to March 1969 which held conferences of party members in the RC.[45] But there was only one such conference at which it was reported that it had 'discussed' the selection of Party delegates.[46] There cannot therefore be any doubt that delegates to the Party Congress were chosen without any 'discussion'.

The '8,000 to 10,000' delegates was also no longer mentioned, when the 9th Party Congress of the CCP finally did meet in Peking, under a veil of the strictest secrecy, on 1 April 1969.[47] Furthermore the number of 1,512 delegates corresponded to the size of the 8th Party Congress in 1956, and therefore resembled just that 'Congress of old men' which Hsieh had warned against in October 1967. Almost three-quarters of the delegates were wearing the uniform of the PLA.[48] Mao Tse-tung himself opened the Party Congress with a short speech, hailed in the first press communiqué as 'extraordinarily significant'.[49] The Chairman reminded his audience of previous Party Congresses, criticized Liu Shao-ch'i, 'a certain P'eng Chen' and other leaders of the opposition and previous 'deviants', and called for the preservation of unity. He concluded his speech by saying that the Party Congress was to be 'a Party Congress of unity and victory'.[50]

According to a press communiqué of 2 April 1969 the following were to be considered at the Party Congress; in order of importance, the 'Political Report of the 8th Central Committee' given by Lin Piao, the new Party Constitution, and the election of the members and alternate members of the 9th Central Committee.[51] A second press communiqué on 14 April publicized the acceptance of the Political Report and of the Party Constitution.[52] A third press communiqué of 24 April finally made it known that the delegates had elected the new Central Committee on 15 April.[53] Together with the publication of the name-list of the 9th Central Committee on 27 April,[54] the Political Report and the Party Constitution, these press communiqués are the only officially published documents of the Party Congress. Unlike the 8th Party Congress of September 1956, the discussions were not at this time published in the public media. However, the second press communiqué did include a list of those delegates who had participated in the discussion. Here the names of Chiang Ch'ing, Chang Ch'un-ch'iao and Yao Wên-yüan, were missing. This seemed to point to the fact that the leadership of the Cultural Revolutionary Left had disappeared further into the background.

As reported by Chou En-lai at the 10th Party Congress in August 1973,[55] the leadership had had considerable arguments over the content of Lin Piao's Political Report.[56] The original draft of the report, to which Ch'en Po-ta had also contributed, had been subjected to substantial changes by the leadership group, to which according to Chou, Lin 'had only reluctantly consented'. Already then, it seems, differences of opinion had emerged between the Prime Minister and Mao's only ever deputy and designated successor, which set the scene for the disputes of 1970-1.

The published version of the report concentrated the criticism of the Party leadership on Liu Shao-ch'i. It celebrated the 'all-encompassing victory of the Cultural Revolution' and called for unity within the Party, as well as for continuous criticism and self-criticism of its members. Lin praised the reforms of the Peking Opera that had been ministrated by Chiang Ch'ing. However he omitted to mention the wife of the Party leader by name.

The new Party Constitution[57] was phrased in considerably more general terms than that of 1956—thereby giving the leadership more room to manoeuvre than the old constitution. The 'Thought of Mao Tse-tung' was now explicitly recognized as being, next to Marxism-Leninism, the theoretical base of the Party. The constitution provided for Mao personally to be the Chairman of the Party, which amounted to his appointment for life. Contrary to previous practice in all Communist parties, his successor (*Chieh pan-jen*) was also named: Vice-Chairman Lin. Though it was considered that a Party Congress should be called every five years, it did not make any provision, contrary to the 1956 constitution, for an annual Plenum of the Party Congress. It was mentioned, however, that meetings of the Party Congress could be 'advanced or postponed'. The Central Committee was from now on to meet only once a year, but here too the Politburo could postpone its meetings. Neither a Secretariat of the Central Committee nor a Central Control Commission is mentioned in the Constitution. The previously applicable formal rules of Party procedure were also omitted. But, most important, the new Constitution explicitly mentioned the PLA's own party organization which was in future only to be amalgamated with civilian organizations at the central and not at local levels.

The resolutions of the 9th Party Congress formally set the seal on the victory of the Mao and Lin Piao faction in the crisis of the Cultural Revolution. A more detailed analysis of the outcome of the Cultural Revolution suggests the conclusion that this victory was indeed phyrrhic.

One could attempt to apply the Maoist formula of 'Unity—criticism—unity' to the course of the Cultural Revolutionary crisis; this would mean that the development of the crisis had followed a pattern conceived by someone 'in the know'.

Starting out from such an assumption it is possible to argue that in the early stages of the movement Mao and his followers had arrived at the double aim of creating new revolutionary experiences for a generation which had gown up after the Communist take-over, and re-energizing the stagnant structures of the Party and State *apparats*. The Chairman intended to overcome, with the help of the youthful rebellion, the revisionist and bureaucratic tendencies within the Party. He wanted to remove the opponents of his policies from the decision-making bodies, to fill the political system with new revolutionary enthusiasm, thereby raising the political consciousness of the masses to a new and higher level. A new power structure would have been created on the basis of the extensive participation of the majority of the people.

In arguing this case one would, however, have to accept that the original unity excluded the young 'rebels'. A 'contradiction' would have developed not only between them and the 'Revisionists' and the Party bureaucrats, but just as much between the military and the civilian party apparatus, and finally also between the 'Rebels' and the People's Liberation Army. The new 'unity' would therefore exclude not only Mao's opponents in the Party *apparat*, but also the most active forces of the Maoist movement in 1966-7. This unity would instead have been embodied in the armed forces. It is thus apparent that the leadership utilized Mao's Theory of Contradictions to rationalize any desired political change as a necessary historical development. Such an explanation clearly shows the way that a clever and power-conscious élite can use a myth that legitimizes its leadership. But it does not provide a theoretical framework for helping to understand the crisis in the PRC from 1965 to 1969.

The real contradiction was in fact that between theory and practice. If the political programme of the Cultural Revolution is to be seen, as such an explanation suggests, as being concerned with both political control and the direction of the policies to be implemented, then the end result of the Cultural Revolution must have meant a setback for Mao Tse-tung. If it did have this function then one can only speak of a partial success for the Party's leader. The application of the Theory of Contradictions would in this case (to return to our hypothetical argument) have emerged from an assessment of the situation which had led to the mobilization of the masses in order to defend the military and Mao's followers in the Party machine. The way in which the masses misunderstood the basically utilitarian character of the Theory of Contradictions—their enthusiasms were not to be liberated but only channelled in a particular direction—had to lead inevitably to the Chairman's renunciation of his original programme.

The real results of the 'Cultural Revolution', however, can best be examined by looking at the aims (either articulated or implied) of the two leftist groups (the Cultural Revolutionary Left led by the Central Cultural Revolution Group, on the one hand, and the military around Lin Piao on the other) which they set themselves when they started their counter-attack against the 'New Right' in 1965-6. Both of these Left-wing groups had wanted to carry through changes in three areas:
(1) They wanted to halt the growth of the trend to revise Mao's developmental ideas of 1958.

If one believes the party propaganda since 1966, then this goal was achieved. However, the practical political decisions taken in China's provinces since the spring of 1969 lead one to conclude that the leadership groups there were hardly about to renunciate the major results of the 'readjustment' policy of the early 1960s. For this reason the Centre under Lin Piao's influence soon felt compelled to make another attempt to return to the Maoist ideas of 1958, only this time through an extensive militarization of society, with the help of the PLA. This attempt was to lead, as we shall see, directly to the next big internal political crisis in China.

(2) They wanted to silence the intellectual opposition and to halt the dispersal of non-conformist ideas.

In relation to art, literature and public discussion this did certainly initially succeed. It remains to be seen, however, whether the consequent isolation of China from the intellectual world and its own cultural history can be maintained.

(3) In the area of power politics, they were planning the downfall of the majority of the civilian party leadership which under the leadership of Liu Shao-ch'i had rejected Mao's policy of mass mobilization or had at least been sceptical towards it.

It was here that the Left had its greatest successes. Seven of the seventeen members of the Politburo who had been active in 1965[58] and four of the six alternate members[59] were deprived of office and declared Party enemies. On the other hand, three further Politburo members did manage to return to the Central Committee in April 1969 although excluded from the Politburo.[60] Six of the ten members and all three alternate members of the Secretariat of the Central Committee were removed from office.[61] The purge affected fifty-three of the ninety-seven members of the Central Committee.[62] Furthermore, four of the six First Secretaries of the Regional Bureaux and twenty-three of the twenty-eight First Secretaries of the Provincial Party Committees were similarly affected. Finally eight of the fifteen Vice-Premiers of the State Council, the General Secretary, and twenty of the forty-eight Ministers and Chairmen of Commissions were declared 'party enemies'. Four other Ministers did not appear again in public after 1965. These purges eliminated Liu's faction from the political decision-making process.

Besides these goals of the whole faction the 'Cultural Revolution Group' under Ch'en Po-ta and Chiang Ch'ing certainly pursued three further objectives:

(1) In the context of recruiting cadres it wanted to promote 'revolutionary successors' whose experiences were to match the experiences of the old leadership during the Civil War.

In the period between May 1966 and August 1967 this strategy seemed to succeed. But the revolutionary experiences of the generation of the 'Long March' had ended with the triumphant victory of 1949, whereas the experiences of the Red Guards and 'Revolutionary Rebels' ended in the winding-up of these organizations, with their deportation to the villages poorly covered as *Hsia-fang* and with other massive disciplinary measures by the PLA and the Workers' Militia.

(2) In the area of education, (an integral part of mobilization)—they tried to create a fundamental revolution in the educational system, to shorten dramatically the length of training, to introduce manual labour as a form of education and considerably to expand political instruction.

Here the PRC media occasionally reported spectacular successes. However, already by the summer of 1970 one document that went further into the details of a discussion held on 2 June 1970 on the educational revolution in Shanghai,[63] painted a less optimistic picture. It became clear from this document that in only nine of the forty-nine Shanghai high schools had measures for an educational revolution been implemented, that workers were not willing to work in teams, and that the administration had little interest in change. Even by the spring of 1971 only 187 rural communes had reported on the success, and in some cases on the failure, of the educational revolution. Until then 73,800 communes, containing about 80% of the total population, had remained silent. After mid-1971, and particularly in 1972, a growing tendency to return to the educational concepts and symptoms of the early 1960s became quite obvious—and these were to become once again the centre of discussions in the summer of 1973.[64] This is why here too the total picture remained blurred. However, the cost of this obviously not fully concluded change in the educational system was the loss of at least four years of college education.

(3) They wanted to arrive at a fundamental rejuvenation of the central leadership, from which the Chairman himself was to be excluded. Without doubt this goal was not attained.

There is hardly any documentation of the particular aims of Lin Piao and of the other Generals of his old 4th Field Army System. Four of these aims, however, are easily identifiable by this group's particular behaviour:

(1) Lin Piao was to replace Liu Shao-ch'i as Mao's deputy and designated successor. This goal was achieved.

(2) The share of the members of the 4th Field Army in the central and regional leadership groups of the People's Liberation Army was to be enlarged. This process had already begun in 1959, but was accelerated in the 'Cultural Revolution' with control over the positions of Chief of Staff and Commander in the Ch'engtu and Sinkiang Military Regions especially.

(3) The State security system was to be brought under the control of the People's Liberation Army. This was in the beginning also fully achieved.

(4) In the Military Regions and Districts, these cadres who had originally come from the civilian Party system to serve in the PLA's Political Department were to be removed and replaced by personnel from the Political Department itself or from the PLA's own leadership groups. In 1965 about forty-one of the fifty-three Political Commissars in the Military Regions and Districts were in this sense civilians. By 1970, thirty-six out of the known forty-three Political Commissars at these levels were members of the PLA. This is where the military under Lin Piao gained a further success.

One can conclude from this that the aims of the 'Cultural Revolution' had been at least partly achieved in two out of the three areas over which there was some agreement in 1965-6 between the two groups of the Left. The military group fully achieved most of its aims. However, that part of the Maoist Left led by the 'Cultural Revolution Group' had to give up some of its particular goals for the moment. Apart from these its results remained ambivalent. From this one forms the impression that the Mao faction's counter-offensive had failed to achieve its intended goals, but that it had achieved some success in terms of power politics.

These results apart, the internal political crisis had results which had never been anticipated, even by the initiators of the Cultural Revolution, and in particular by the Party Leader. These included the transfer of essential decision-making powers to the military, the increasing influence of regional leadership groups in the top bodies of the CCP, and the remarkable expansion of the economic and administrative autonomy of the Regions, within which the regional Commanders now constituted a determinant political power. Of particular importance were those experiences which a young generation—and in this case the young intellectuals—had gained during the Cultural Revolution. In the early phase of the crisis it had discovered the power to organize outside the limits of the Party and the official occupational associations. This, however, was only possible before the army intervened in the crisis. As a result the younger generation learned another lesson: that the organized uprising of youth against the Party machine and their innovatory enthusiasm had been used as a device to be manipulated in the context for power within the Party and the State by the élite around Mao and Lin Piao.

When the uprising threatened to move beyond the control of this élite, the army managed to assert itself by use of force against the Red Guards and the 'Revolutionary Rebels'. Neither the Party Leader nor the 'Cultural Revolution Group' wanted, or were in the position, to come to the rescue of the rebelling youths when they were under attack from the military. In the face of these experiences it seems doubtful that this generation will again be prepared to put themselves out for Mao and his concept of China's development with the same involvement that they showed in 1966-7.

REFERENCES

1. See among others: Cheng Chi-yüan, *The People's Communes*, Hong Kong, 1959, passim; Max Biehl, *Die chinesische Volkskommune im 'Grossen Sprung' und danach*, Hamburg, 1965, passim; Franz Schurmann,

op. cit., pp. 464-500; Charles Bettelheim, Jacques Charrière and Hélène Marchisio, *La construction du socialisme en Chine*, Paris, 1965, pp. 57-68; Peter S. H. Tang and Joan M. Maloney, *Communist China: the Domestic Scene 1949-1967*, South Orange, NJ, 1967, pp. 374-83; and Domes, *Internal Politics*, op. cit., pp. 94-105.

2. See: Owen L. Dawson, *A Constraint on Chicom Foreign Policy: Agricultural Output 1966-1975*, Stanford, 1967, p. 71; Wu Yüan-li (Yüan-li Wu), 'The Economy after Twenty Years' Chapter 6 in Frank N. Trager and William Henderson (ed.), *Communist China 1949-1969: a Twenty-Year Appraisal*, pp. 123-51; Kung Mien-jen, 'Natural Calamities on the Chinese Mainland 1960', in Union Research Institute, Hong Kong (URI), *Communist China 1960*, Hong Kong, 1962, Vol. I, pp. 41-58; Li Ch'ang-yen, 'Agriculture' in URI, *Communist China 1961*, Hong Kong, 1962, Vol. II, pp. 75-109; Ch'en Hsüeh-wen, 'Natural Calamities in Communist China', ibid., pp. 171-89; Jürgen Domes, *Von der Volkskommune zur Krise in China*, Duisdorf-Bonn, 1964, pp. 41-53; and Domes, *Internal Politics*, op. cit., pp. 113-17.

3. See Schurmann, op. cit., pp. 491 ff; Li, loc. cit., pp. 83-93; and Domes, *Volkskommune*, op. cit., pp. 55-77.

4. See among others: Joachim Glaubitz, *Opposition gegen Mao: Abendgespräche am Yenshan und andere Dokumente*, Olten-Freiburg, 1969, pp. 26-43; Dieter Heinzig, *Mao contra Liu*, Berichte des Bundesinstituts für ostwissenschaftliche und internationale Studien, No. 48 1967, passim; Dieter Heinzig, *Von Lushan zur Kulturrevolution*, Berichte des Bundesinstituts ..., No. 5 1968, passim; Erik v. Groeling, *Der Fraktionkampf in China*, Berichte des Bundesinstituts, No. 37 1970, passim; Erik v. Groeling, *China's Langer Marsch—wohin?*, Stuttgart, 1972, pp. 49-65; Domes, *Internal Politics*, op. cit., pp. 123-47 and pp. 236 ff; Charles B. Neuhauser, 'The Chinese Communist Party in the 1960's: Prelude to the Cultural Revolution', in *CQ*, No. 32, October-December 1967, pp. 3-36; and: Parris H. Chang, loc. cit., passim.

5. See: Richard Baum and Frederick C. Teiwes, *Ssu-ch'ing: the Socialist Education Movement 1962-1966*, Berkeley, 1968, passim; Baum and Teiwes, 'Liu Shao-ch'i and the Cadre Question', in *Asian Survey (AS)*, Vol. VIII, No. 4, April 1968, pp. 323-45; Richard Baum, 'Revolution and Reaction in the Countryside: The Socialist Education Movement in Cultural Revolutionary Perspective', in *CQ*, No. 38, April-June 1969, pp. 92-119; Neuhauser, loc. cit., passim; and Erik v. Groeling, 'Widerstand und Säuberungen in der Grossen Proletarischen Kultur-revolution', unpublished Ph.D. dissertation, Berlin, 1969, pp. 325-44.

6. *Hung-ch'i* (Red Flag), Peking (*HC*), No. 7 and 9, 1967. See: Domes, *Internal Politics*, op. cit., pp. 141-2 ff; Franz Michael, 'Moscow and the Current Chinese Crisis', in *Current History* (New York), Vol. 53, No. 313, September 1967, p. 147; and Philip Bridgham, 'Mao's Cultural Revolution: Origin and Development', in *CQ*, No. 29, January-March 1967, p. 16.

7. Mao Tse-tung in an interview with Edgar Snow in December 1970; in *New Republic* (New York), 10 April 1971.

8. 'Outline Report Concerning the Current Academic Discussion of the Group of Five in Charge of the Cultural Revolution', 7 February 1966, in URI Documents, op. cit., pp. 3-12. See also *I-chiu-liu-pa fei-ch'ing*

nien-pao: 1968 Yearbook on Chinese Communism, T'aipei, 1968, p. 573; and Domes, *Internal Politics*, op. cit., pp. 154 ff.

9. 'Minutes of the Forum on Literature and Art in the Armed Forces Convened by Comrade Chiang Ch'ing on Comrade Lin Piao's Request' (Shanghai), 2-20 October 1966; translated in *Survey of the China Mainland Press* (SCMP), Hong Kong, No. 3956, 9 June 1967; and in *Jen-min jih-pao* (Peking: *JMJP*), 29 May 1967.

10. See among others: Ken Ling, *The Revenge of Heaven: Journal of a Young Chinese*, New York, 1972, particularly pp. 24-53; 'A "Foreign Expert", Eyewitness of the Cultural Revolution' in *CQ*, No. 28, October-December 1966, pp. 4-7; John Israel, 'The Red Guards in Historical Perspective: Continuity and Change in the Chinese Youth Movement', ibid., No. 30, April-June 1967, pp. 1-32; Giovanni Blumer, *Die chinesische Kulturrevolution, 1965-67* (2nd edition), Frankfurt, 1969, pp. 187-216; v. Groeling, 'Widerstand', op. cit., pp. 140-4; Jürgen Domes, *Kulturrevolution und Armee: Die Rolle der Streitkräfte in der chinesischen 'Kulturrevolution'*, Bonn, 1967, pp. 34-8 and 87 ff.; and *Internal Politics*, op. cit., p. 166; and Juliana Pennington Heaslett, 'The Red Guards: Instruments of Destruction in the Cultural Revolution', in *AS*, Vol. XII, No. 12, December 1972, pp. 1032-47.

11. Compare, in this context, a report some of the details of which are disputed, but which in its most important aspects has since been confirmed by Red Guard sources. This report was attributed to the then Tanyug correspondent in Peking, Branko Bogunovic (Chinese translation in *Mingpao* (Light), Hong Kong, 1 and 2 January 1967); Franz Michael, 'The Struggle for Power' in: *Problems of Communism*, Washington DC, May-June 1967, p. 19; v. Groeling, 'Widerstand', op. cit., pp. 136-9; and Domes, *Internal Politics*, op. cit., pp. 160 ff. Sources on the 11th Plenum: 'Decision of the Central Committee of the CCP on the Great Proletarian Cultural Revolution', 8 August 1966, in *URI Documents*, op. cit., pp. 33-54; and 'Communiqué of the 11th Plenum of the 8th Central Committee of the CCP', 12 August 1966, ibid., pp. 55-70.

12. The first of these mass rallies was held on 18 August 1966 (*JMJP* 19 August, 1966) and further rallies were on 31 August, 15 September, 1 October, 18 October, 3 November, 10 November and 26 November 1966. A first-hand account of the mass rally on 25 November can be found in Ken Ling, op. cit., pp. 173-81.

13. See *inter alia* ibid., pp. 9-24. Foreign Minister Marshal Ch'en Yi told Red Guards in Peking (during his 'self-criticism' on 24 January 1967) that in the late Summer and Autumn of 1966 alone more than 400,000 cadres had been physically liquidated. 'Ch'en's Self-criticism' (English in *Facts and Features*, T'aipei, No. 11, 20 March 1968, p. 28).

14. An incomplete list compiled by the author includes, for Peking, Canton, Shanghai, Kuangsi, Hunan and Hupei alone, 1,417 Red Guard organizations which were largely in conflict with one another. See also, Domes, *Internal Politics*, op. cit., pp. 167 ff.

15. Compare, ibid., pp. 157 ff; and Philip Bridgham, 'Mao's Cultural Revolution in 1967: The Struggle to Seize Power' in *CQ*, No. 34, April-June 1968, pp. 6-37.

16. *Wên-hui pao*, Shanghai (*WHP*), 9, 10 and 12 January 1967;

Chieh-fang jih-pao, Shanghai, 9 and 23 January 1967; *JMJP*, 9, 12, 20, 24, 25 and 30 January 1967; *New China News Agency (NCNA)*, Peking, 14 January 1967; *NCNA* T'aiyüan, 25 January 1967; *Heilungkiang jih-pao*, Harbin, 23 January 1967.

Also: Radio Canton, 16 January 1967; Wuhan Radio, 23 January 1967; Ch'engchou Radio, 23 January 1967; Fuchou Radio, 24 January and 8 February 1967; Nanch'ang Radio, 20, 22, 23 and 25 January 1967; Anhui Radio, 14 February 1967. Erik v. Groeling put together 139 reports in the Chinese media on strikes and interruptions in transportation ('Widerstand', op. cit., pp. 160 ff and note 123 to Chapter 2) as well as eighty-six reports on peasant unrest (ibid., pp. 168-73 and note 177 to Chapter 1). Compare with *China News Analysis*, Hong Kong *(CNA)*, No. 643, 644, 647, 648, 649 and 651, of 13 and 20 January, 10, 17 and 24 February, as well as 10 March 1967; *Current Scene*, Hong Kong *(CS)*, Vol. 5, No. 2, of 31 January 1967; and *Current Background*, Hong Kong *(CB)*, No. 852, 6 May 1968.

17. *Tung-fang-hung* (The East is Red), Peking, 28 January 1967; 'Decision of the CC of the CCP, the State Council, the Military Committee of the CC, and the Cultural Revolution Group on the PLA's decisive support for the Revolutionary Masses of the Left', 23 January 1967, in *URI Documents*, op. cit., pp. 193-97; and *Chieh-fang-chün pao (CFCP)*—the PLA's paper—25 January 1967.

18. See Jürgen Domes, 'The Role of the Military in the Formation of Revolutionary Committees, 1967-1968', in *CQ* No. 44, October-December 1970, pp. 120 ff; Domes, 'The Cultural Revolution and the Army', in *AS*, No. 5, May 1968, p. 356; and Domes, *Internal Politics*, op. cit., pp. 180 ff.

19. See: Gordon Bennet, 'Hsieh Fu-chih, China's Trouble-Shooter', in *Far East Economic Review*, Hong Kong *(FEER)*, Vol. 9, No. 5, 1968, p. 184; and Jürgen Domes, 'Generals and Red Guards: the Role of Huang Yung-sheng and the Canton Military Area Command in the Kuangtung Cultural Revolution', Part 2, in *Asia Quarterly*, Brussels *(AQ)*, No. 2, 1971, pp. 125 ff.

20. See: 'Wuhan Kang-erh-ssu' (Wuhan No. 2 Steel Works Headquarters), No. 38, 22 August 1967, in *SCMP*, 11 August 1967; *Union Research Service* Hong Kong *(URS)*, Vol. 48, No. 10, pp. 139-49, and No. 23, pp. 320-34; *CQ*, No. 32, October-December 1967, pp. 185-90; and v. Groeling, 'Widerstand', op. cit., pp. 191-4.

21. The only source for this conference is Lin Piao, 'What we really fear is the mistakes of the comrades in the Military Regions' (Speech to the Military Committee of the CC, 9 August 1967), in *Chu-ying tung-fang-hung* (Pearl River Studio The East is Red), Canton, 13 September 1967.

22. See Domes, *Internal Politics*, op. cit., pp. 191 ff.

23. Ibid., pp. 193 ff.

24. *URI Documents*, op. cit., pp. 565-67.

25. For example, Radio Peking, 14 October 1967; Radio T'ienchin, 17 and 19 October and 8 December 1967; and Radio Shantung, 4 November 1967.

26. v. Groeling, 'Widerstand', op. cit., pp. 197-9, 210-15 and 219.

27. *Hunan jih-pao*, 16 September 1967; Radio Kiangsi, 2 March 1968;

Radio Honan, 19 May 1968; *Honan jih-pao*, 19 May 1968 and Radio Anhui, 25 December 1968.

28. Domes, 'Generals', loc. cit., pp. 140 ff.

29. (1) 'Our Programme', 21 December 1967, in *Kuang-yin hung-ch'i* (Red Flag of the Canton Printing House), Canton, No. 5, March 1968; excerpts also in *Tung-fang chan-pao* (Eastern Battle Bulletin), Canton, No. 19, 29 February 1968.

(2) 'Whither China?', 12 January 1968, in *Kuang-yin hung-ch'i*, ibid.

30. *Pa-wu* (8-5), Canton, February 1968; *Wên-kê t'unghsün* (Bulletin of the Cultural Revolution), Canton, No. 12, February 1968 and particularly, *I-yüeh fêng-pu* (January Storm), Canton, No. 23/24, March 1968.

31. *JMJP*, 8 August, 15 August, and 31 October 1968.

32. See Domes, 'Generals', loc. cit., pp. 148-51.

33. Victor C. Falkenheim, 'The Cultural Revolution in Kuangsi, Yünnan and Fukien' in *AS*, Vol. IX, No. 8, August 1968, pp. 585-7.

34. *Ssu-erh-erh t'ung-hsün* (22nd April Bulletin), Liuchou, No. 6, 29 May 1968; *Hsi-chiang nu-t'ao* (Raging Torrent on the West River), Wuchou, No. 1, June 1968; *Wuchou lien-chih* (Wuchou Alliance), No. 4, 8 June 1968 and *Ta-chün pao* (Paper of the Great Army), Canton, July 1970.

35. Radio Ch'angch'un, 21 July 1968; Radio Honan, 8 August 1968; Radio Ssuch'uan, 24 October 1968; Radio Sinkiang, 21 November 1968. See *Summary of World Broadcasts*, London (*SWB*), No. 2912, 30 October and No. 2934, 25 November 1968.

36. Among others: Radio Canton, 4 October 1968; *Hsing-tao jih-pao*, Hong Kong (*HTJP*), 14 January 1969 and reports of young refugees in interviews given to the author in Hong Kong, June and July 1970, August 1972, as well as December 1973.

37. Radio Canton, 26 October 1968; Radio Shantung, 4 November 1968 and Radio Kiangsu, 7 December 1968.

38. See Dieter Heinzig, *Die Krise der Kommunistischen Partei Chinas in der Kulturrevolution*, Mitteilungen des Instituts für Asienkunde, Hamburg, No. 7, 1969, pp. 41 ff.

39. 'Wên-kê t'ung-hsün', 11 December 1967, English translation in *SCMP*, 11 January 1968; see also v. Groeling, 'Widerstand', op. cit., pp. 234 f.

40. *Chung-fa* Document (67), No. 358 in: *URI Documents*, op. cit., pp. 609-21.

41. For example, Radio Anhui, 10 February 1969; also *KMJP*, 24 February 1969.

42. Radio Hupei, 13 January 1969. Compare with *CNA*, No. 751, 4 April 1969.

43. 'Communiqué of the 12th Enlarged Plenum of the 8th Central Committee of the CCP', 31 October 1968, in *JMJP*, 2 November 1968.

44. *Hung-ch'i t'ung-hsün* (Red Flag Bulletin), Canton, No. 10, 25 January 1968; 'Wên-kê t'ung-hsün', No. 12, February 1968 and Radio Inner Mongolia, 20 November 1968. The Nationalist Chinese News Agency first released the draft of the new Party Constitution in *Fei-ch'ing yen-chiu: Studies on Chinese Communism (FCYC)*, Vol. 3, No. 1, January

1969, pp. 150-2. This text corresponds, apart from minor deviations, to the document which the 9th Party Congress released.

45. Chekiang, Kueichou, Hunan, Hupei, Honan, Kuangtung, Ssuch'uan and Yünnan. See *CNA*, No. 746, 28 February 1969.

46. Hunan, ibid.

47. *JMJP*, 2 April 1969; English translation in *Peking Review*, Peking (*PR*), No. 14, 4 April 1969.

48. This is the result of an analysis of a film made by the CCP about the Party Congress.

49. *JMJP*, 2 April 1969.

50. Mao Tse-tung's speech at opening of the 9th Party Congress, English in *Issues and Studies*, T'aipei, Vol. V, No. 8.

51. See, among others: v. Groeling, *Widerstand*, op. cit., pp. 229-34 and Jürgen Domes, 'China's spätmaoistische Führungsgruppe: Die soziopolitische Struktur des IX. Zentralkommitees der kommunistischen Partei Chinas', in *Politische Vierteljahresschrift*, Köln-Opladen, No. 2/3, September 1969, p. 191.

52. *JMJP*, 15 April 1969; English translation in *PR*, No. 16, 18 April 1969.

53. *JMJP*, 25 April 1969; English translation in *PR*, No. 18, 30 April 1969.

54. *JMJP*, 27 April 1969.

55. Chou En-lai, 'Report to the 10th Party Congress of the CCP', 24 August 1973, in *NCNA*, Peking, 31 August 1973.

56. English text in Supplement to *PR*, 28 April 1969.

57. English text of the Party Constitution can be found in *NCNA* London, No. 4102, 29 April 1969. See Heinzig, *Krise*, op. cit., pp. 45-8 and Erik v. Groeling, *Innenpolitik und Organization im kommunistischen China*, Hannover 1971, pp. 85-126.

58. Liu Shao-ch'i, Teng Hsiao-p'ing, P'eng Chen, P'eng Tê-huai, Ho Lung, Li Ching-ch'üan and T'an Chen-lin.

59. Ulanfu, Chang Wên-t'ien, Lu Ting-i and Po I-po.

60. Ch'en Yün, Ch'en Yi and Li Fu-ch'un.

61. Teng Hsiao-p'ing, P'eng Chen, Wang Chia-hsiang, T'an Chen-lin, Lu Ting-i and Lo Jui-ch'ing.

62. Liu Shao-ch'i, Teng Hsiao-p'ing, Lu Ting-i, Lo Jui-ch'ing, P'eng Tê-huai, Liao Ch'eng-chih, Lin Fêng, P'eng Chen, Ulanfu, Huang K'ê-ch'eng. T'an Cheng, Ho Lung, Yang Shang-k'un, Sung Jen-ch'iung, Liu Hsiao, Li Wei-han, Wang Chia-hsiang, Liu Lan-t'ao, Liu Ning-i, Po I-po, Hu Ch'iao-mu, Yang Hsiu-feng, Shu T'ung, Chang Chi-ch'un, Ch'eng Tzu-hua, Wu Hsiu-ch'üan, Hsiao K'ê, Mme. Ch'ien Ying, Wang Ts'ung-wu, Ma Ming-fang, Chang Wên-t'ien, T'an Chen-lin, Mme. Ch'en Shao-min, Li Pao-hua, Hsü Kuang-ta, Lin T'ieh, Cheng Wei-san, Hsiao Hua, Hu Yao-pang, Ouyang Ch'in, Hsi Chung-hsün, An Tzu-wên, Chia T'o-fu, Li Li-san, Li Ching-ch'üan, Wu Chih-p'u, Lü Cheng-ts'ao, T'ao Chu, Ch'en Shao-yü, Yang Hsien-chen, Lo Kuei-p'o, Chang Ching-wu and Yeh Fei.

Of these, the following had been rehabilitated by the end of January 1974: Teng Hsiao-p'ing, Liao Ch'eng-chih, Ulanfu, Wang Chia-hsiang (since died), Hsiao K'ê, T'an Chen-lin, Li Pao-hua, Li Ching-ch'üan, Lü Cheng-ts'ao and Yeh Fei.

63. *HC*, No. 7, 1970, and *WHP*, Hong Kong, 24 July 1970.

64. See pp. 178 ff.

2. The New Leadership—a Brittle Coalition

The final curtain was rung down on the Cultural Revolution at the 9th Party Congress on 15 April with the start of elections for the 9th Central Committee of the CCP, and the formation of a new leadership in the PRC. The election took about eleven or twelve days. The length of time which the election of the new leadership took suggests that there were considerable differences of opinion at the Congress about the composition of the new Party leadership which had to be settled through compromise. This also became apparent in the enlargement of the number of Central Committee members. In the middle of April, South Chinese provincial radio stations had already announced that Central Committee membership was to be reduced from ninety-seven to fifty-one and the number of alternate members from ninety-three to seventy-four, 'in order to guarantee a more effective and unified central leadership to our great Party'.[1] In fact, however, the number of full members rose to 170 and the number of alternate members to 109, increasing the total membership of the new Central Committee by 64% over that elected in September 1956.

A comparison of the socio-political composition of the 9th with the 8th Central Committee leads one to the conclusion that the new leadership was very similar to that of the pre-Cultural Revolution period. Even so, there were some remarkable differences. Only thirty-four of the ninety-two members of the 8th Central Committee, who by April 1969 had not been reported dead, succeeded in being re-elected. Three previous members were re-elected as alternate members, but 136 of the Party leadership were completely new entrants to the Central Committee.

There are no official biographies on the members of the 9th Central Committee. Furthermore the biographical content of the available information is frequently contradictory. The following investigation, therefore, has to rely on a plethora of individual sources.[2] It has to be confined to the full members of the Central Committee as there is not enough information on alternate members to make quantitative statements of any importance.

In studying the *age structure* of the members of the 9th Central Committee there is reliable data available on 118 or 69·4% of the 170 people in question:

By 31 December 1968 the average age of the ninety-two Members of the 8th Central Committee was 65·8 years. In contrast, the average age of the newly-elected members of the 9th Central Committee was 61·4 years (at the end of 1969). At its election in

Table 2/1

AGE STRUCTURE OF THE 9th CENTRAL COMMITTEE OF THE CCP

Age-group	Number	Percentage of 118 members	Percentage of 8th Central Committee
Under 40	—	—	—
40-49	4	3·4	—
50-59	44	37·3	9·8
60-69	50	42·4	56·7
70-79	16	13·5	27·1
Over 80	4	3·4	6·4

September 1956 the 8th Central Committee had had an average age of 56·4 years. Additional data on the fifty-two members of the 9th Central Committee, for whom no details are so far available, could slightly alter the average age. However, as a majority of them were older workers, peasants and soldiers who had taken part in the Civil War, it is doubtful whether their influence on the statistics would bring the average age down below sixty. The demands of the Cultural Revolutionary Left for a lasting rejuvenation of the leadership had certainly not been met.

The *regional origins* of members were, however, much more widely distributed than in the 8th Central Committee. While in 1956 only seventeen of the twenty-nine administrative units in China had been represented on the Central Committee, this number had now risen to twenty-one. However, the Central Committee remained dominated by a majority of South Chinese. Even though South China's share of the total population is only about 54%, almost 73% of the members of the 9th Central Committee for whom there is information had been born in South China. Furthermore, the proportion of members from inland provinces only changed very marginally. While in the 8th Central Committee it was 76·3% it had fallen to 68·9% on the 9th Central Committee.

Particularly remarkable is the fact that almost 20% of the members of the 9th Central Committee came from Mao Tse-tung's home province of Hunan, which only has about 6% of the country's total population. The same was true for Hupei, the home province of Lin Piao, which had less than 5% of the total population but had more than 17% of the membership of the Central Committee. A remarkable change, however, occurred in the ratio between these two provinces. While Hunan's share decreased by almost a third of what it was on the 8th Central

Committee, Hupei's share increased by about 60%. The decline in the representation from Hunan can be explained primarily by the fall of Liu Shao-ch'i, who like Mao came from Hunan. Many of his closest colleagues had been purged at the same time as Lin Piao had apparently been advancing his supporters, who had mostly been recruited from his home province. Table 2/2 shows the regional origin of 151 or 88·8% of the members of the 9th Central Committee for whom there is data available.

Apart from the change in the ratio between Hunan and Hupei the 9th Central Committee is similar to its predecessor in terms of the provincial origins of its members. There were, however, considerable changes in terms of the *educational background* of the members of the Central Committee. There is data available for 126, or 74·1%, of the 170 full members, as shown in Table 2/3.

More than three-quarters of the 126 members of the 9th Central Committee for whom there is relevant data available had been educated in institutes of higher education. This represented an increase over the 8th Central Committee. However, the proportion of university graduates dropped from 44·3% on the 8th Central Committee to 23·8% on the 9th. On the other hand the proportion of graduates of military academies rose from 15·5% to 35·7%—that is, it more than doubled. At this point the trend towards the militarization of the leadership, which had started towards the end of the Cultural Revolution, becomes apparent.

These figures indicate a marked difference between the leadership of the PRC and those of other developing countries, including those which are Communist. For in general over the last two decades university graduates have come to play an increasing role in the leadership of developing countries.

The extent of *foreign experience* of the members of the 9th Central Committee was a further important change in the leadership structure. In Table 2/4, the absolute figures for the individual countries in which members of the Central Committee have resided for any considerable length of time, particularly in order to study, add up to more than the total sum because some members were educated in more than one country.

The proportion of members with considerable foreign experience decreased dramatically. This was as true for the USSR as it was for the Western countries and Japan, although the ratio between these two groups changed only marginally. Nonetheless, it was of considerable importance to the composition of the 9th CC that only one in eight members—and possibly even fewer if data on all members were available—had gained experience abroad. It has to be acknowledged that the diminishing influence of Party leaders with experience abroad is a long-term trend within the Chinese leadership.

Table 2/2

REGIONAL BACKGROUND OF MEMBERS OF
THE 9th CENTRAL COMMITTEE OF THE CCP

Province	Percentage of China's population	Number	Percentage of 151 members	Percentage on 8th CC
Hunan	5·6	30	19·9	29·3
Hupei	4·8	26	17·2	10·9
Kiangsi	3·3	12	7·9	7·6
Ssuch'uan	10·5	11	7·3	10·9
Kuangtung	6·0	9	6·0	6·5
Hopei	6·5	9	6·0	4·3
Shantung	8·6	8	5·3	3·3
Fukien	2·1	7	4·6	5·4
Shansi	2·7	7	4·6	5·4
Kiangsu	7·8	7	4·6	4·3
Honan	7·5	6	4·0	3·3
Liaoning	3·6	4	2·6	1·1
Chekiang	4·7	3	2·0	1·1
Shensi	2·7	3	2·0	6·5
Kuangsi	3·5	2	1·3	—
Inner Mongolia	2·0	2	1·3	1·1
Heilungkiang	3·1	1	0·65	1·1
Anhui	4·5	1	0·65	2·2
Kansu	2·0	1	0·65	—
Kirin	2·6	1	0·65	—
Sinkiang	1·2	1	0·65	—
Coastal Provinces	42·6	47	31·1	26·1
Inland Provinces	57·4	104	68·9	73·9
North China[3]	46·3	41	27·2	29·4
South China[3]	53·7	110	72·8	70·6

Considerable changes occurred regarding the *length of party membership* of members of the Central Committee. However, these changes were mainly limited to the ratios between those generations of members who had joined the party in the autumn of 1935 before the end of the Long March. Although, on the other hand, the leadership remained dominated by the whole block of 'Old Guard' revolutionnaries. Information on the date of joining the Party is available for 143 or 84·1% of the 170 members of the Central Committee, as shown in Table 2/5.

Among the members of the 9th CC, 80·4% still came from that generation which had joined the Party before the end of the 'long March'.

Table 2/3

EDUCATIONAL BACKGROUND OF MEMBERS
OF THE 9th CENTRAL COMMITTEE OF THE CCP

Last attended educational institution	Number	Percentage of members	Percentage on 8th CC
University	30	23·8	44·3
Teacher training institute	21	16·7	13·4
Military Academy	45	35·7	15·5
Total Higher Education	96	76·2	73·2
Secondary School	13	10·3	7·3
Primary School	15	11·9	6·2
No formal education	2	1·6	4·1
Miscellaneous	30	23·8	17·6

Table 2/4

FOREIGN EXPERIENCE OF MEMBERS
OF THE 9th CENTRAL COMMITTEE OF THE CCP

Country	Number	Percentage of 126 members	Percentage on 8th CC
USSR	35	27·8	39·2
France	8	6·3	13·4
Japan	6	4·8	4·1
Germany	3	2·4	3·1
Great Britain	1	0·8	1·1
Turkey	1	0·8	—
USA	—	—	2·1
Total	41	32·5	46·4

The changes that occurred among the group of members who had joined the Party between 1928 and 1935 resulted mainly from the rise of leading military men, who, in the early civil war period between Communists and Nationalists had joined the Communist partisan forces. Not even a tenth of the members of the 9th CC had joined the Party after the Communist take-over. Among them were some elder politicians who had previously been affiliated to no particular party, or to some non-Communist United Front party. The leadership of the People's Republic of China therefore remained in the hands of the Civil War generation. The success of the discipline imposed on the young rebels became apparent when the new leadership was formed, for not even one of the full

Table 2/5

LENGTH OF PARTY MEMBERSHIP FOR
MEMBERS OF THE 9th CENTRAL COMMITTEE OF THE CCP

Date of joining CCP	Number	Percentage of 143 members	Percentage on 8th CC
1921–7	57	39·8	87·6
1928–31	41	28·7	7·3
1932–5	17	11·9	4·1
Total who joined before end of Long March	115	80·4	99
1936–7	6	4·2	—
1938–45	4	2·8	1·0
1946–9	7	4·9	—
Total who joined before establishment of PRC	132	92·3	100
Entry since 1949	11	7·7	—

members of the CC came from the ranks of the Red Guards, and even among the 109 Alternate Members only four had had any connection with Red Guard units.[4]

When in March 1967 the Maoist faction had called for the establishment of 'provisional organs of power' in the form of Revolutionary Committees, these were to be formed on the basis of a 'revolutionary trinity' of Maoist mass organizations, the People's Liberation Army and 'Revolutionary Cadres'.[5] The original intention was that the Shansi Provincial Revolutionary Committee was to be the model for the future composition of new 'leadership organs'. In the Shansi model, representatives of Maoist units contributed half, and the PLA and cadres each a quarter, of the total membership.[6] It therefore seems appropriate to examine the institutional origins of the members of the 9th CC. Particularly drastic changes are evident. As there is data on the institutional origins of 168 of the 170 members, each individual can be seen as a proportion of the total number of members (Table 2/6).

The PLA now accounted for exactly half the total membership of the CC, whereas the proportion of civilian cadres had declined by half. Members of mass organizations appeared for the first time in the leadership, their share, however, remained below the one-fifth mark. Furthermore, the majority of the thirty representatives of mass organizations had gained esteem, not only in the Cultural Revolution, but had already distinguished themselves in the mid-1950s as 'Model Workers' or 'Model Peasants'. They therefore have to be regarded as members of the pre-Cultural Revolution

Table 2/6

THE INSTITUTIONAL ORIGIN OF MEMBERS
OF THE 9th CENTRAL COMMITTEE OF THE CCP

Group	Number	Percentage on 9th CC	Percentage on 8th CC
Commander	60	35·3	26·4
Political Commissar	25	14·7	11·5
Total PLA	85	50·0	37·9
Party and State Cadres	48	28·2	59·0
Academics	5	2·9	3·1
Total 'Revolutionary Cadres'	53	31·1	62·1
Mass Organizations	30	17·7	—
Unknown	2	1·2	—

élite. However, their admission to the CC can be taken to be one of the results of the 'Cultural Revolution'.

Finally, another important change occurred in the *occupational background* of the members of the new leadership group. As it is generally the rule in the PRC that party leaders hold various positions in a number of *apparats*, Table 2/7 only lists the major occupations of members. Data is available for 162, or 95·3%, of the 170 members.

While the election of the 8th Central Committee in September 1956 clearly indicated the concentration of leadership personnel at the Centre, this development was now reversed: the proportion of CC members working in the Centre declined, approximately, from 70% to 40%. The proportion of regional cadres at the same time grew to include about three-fifths of the total Central Committee. In the same way there was a change in the ratio between military and civilian cadres; the proportion of civilian cadres declined from having constituted about three-quarters of the CC to just over half. It is thus apparent that the Cultural Revolution resulted in a process of *militarization and regionalization* of the leadership. This process becomes even more obvious in the following comparison: while the proportion of those from Central civilian organs declined from 46% to approximately 20%, the proportion of those from regional military units increased from just over 2% to almost 27%.

The Cultural Revolution brought about no significant changes in the age structure and regional origin of the leadership. There was also no real generational change in the new CC. The most significant developments in the creation of the new leadership were

Table 2/7

AREA OF ACTIVITY OF MEMBERS OF
THE 9th CENTRAL COMMITTEE OF THE CCP

Occupation	Number	Percentage of 162 members	Percentage on 8th CC
Central Civilian	33	20·4	46·1
Central Military	34	21·0	23·1
Regional Civilian	52	32·0	28·6
Regional Military	43	26·6	2·2
Total at Centre	67	41·4	69·2
Total in Regions	95	58·6	30·8
Total Civilian	85	52·5	74·7
Total Military	77	47·5	25·3

the decline in the proportion of university graduates and the increase in that of graduates from military academies; the decline in the proportion of members with experiences abroad; the increasing influence of top regional cadres and particularly the fact that about half the Central Committee now comprised delegates from the PLA. The vacuum that had been created in the Party by the purges of the Cultural Revolution was not filled by representatives of the Maoist avant-garde but by the PLA. The seizure of power (To-ch'üan), which the PRC media announced in Spring 1967, was therefore clearly carried out not by rebellious youth but by the military.

This development, which was clearly shown in the elections to the 9th Central Committee, had already become apparent in the formation of provincial, municipal and autonomous Regional Revolutionary Committees between 31 January 1967 and 25 September 1968, as well as in the changes in the composition of these bodies from after their formation until Spring 1969. Of the 439 Chairmen, Vice-Chairmen and members of the Standing Committees of these Revolutionary Committees, at the time of the Party Congress 224 or 51% were from the PLA, 113 or 25·8% were representatives of the Maoist mass organizations, and 102 or 23·2% were civilian cadres of the Party and State.[7] The strong representation of the armed forces was in fact only one example of the military's de facto seizure of power in the majority of China's provinces.

An analysis of the leadership which had taken over at the end of the Cultural Revolution should not, however, be confined to the official top positions. Although membership of the CC does bring prestige it does not in every case bring power, and political decision-making in Communist China since the early 1960s had increasingly taken place in more informal gatherings than the Central Committee. For this reason at this stage, apart from expanding on the mobility, age-structure and institutional background of leadership personnel, we will also have to describe those groups that are independent of the State and party constitutions. In this way it is possible to arrive at a differentiated analysis, with the help of which one can come closer to an understanding of the realities of Chinese politics.

It is possible to view the structure of leadership in the PRC in terms of a pyramid, which consists of five levels of political leadership:

(1) The *leadership strata* which includes all those who are politically active and whom, because of their positions and occasional appearances, one would assume to have a decisive role in the decision-making process both at the Centre and in the provinces. This would include all those members and alternate members of the CC who were active at the point of investigation; the heads of offices and departments of the CC; members of the Standing Committee of the National People's Congress; Ministers and heads of commissions of the State Council; the Chairman and Deputy Chairman of the National Defence Council; the President of the Supreme People's Court, as well as the leading People's lawyers; heads of state and Party organs at the provincial level; the Chief of the General Staff of the PLA and his deputies; the Director and Deputy Directors of the General Political as well as of the General Logistical Departments of the PLA; and finally the Commanders, Deputy Commanders, and Political Commissars of the PLA's Service Arms, Military Regions, Military Districts and Garrison Commands. As a sign of their continued activity we have chosen, for the purposes of this study, the fact of a name having been mentioned at least once in the media during the last two years before the date of investigation.

(2) The *leadership force* composed of leading personalities, whose individual leadership is apparent in the Party and state *apparats* at provincial level, and in the Military Regions and Districts, as well as in the political, administrative and military organs at the Centre. This group includes only the incumbents of top positions in the leading organs of the Party, state and armed forces.

(3) *The decision-making body*, a liaison group, comprising those leading personalities who, one can assume, directly serve exchange and adjustment functions between the Regions and the Centre as well as between the opinion groups within the leadership strata, and who therefore participate in the allocative process.

When trying to identify the members of this group one runs into peculiar difficulties. On the basis of intermittent documents which were published during the Cultural Revolution, one includes in this circle for the period before the Cultural Revolution all active members and alternate members of the Politburo, all the First Secretaries of the six Regional Party Bureaux, those Vice-Premiers of the State Council who are not members of the Politburo, the Chief of the General Staff and the Director of the General Political Department of the PLA. In this way thirty-two people can be included in this group. Taking as a second point in time for investigation the end of 1970 (that is at the beginning of the Lin Piao crisis) this group again includes all active members and alternate members of the Politburo, the Vice-Premiers of the State Council who were not members of the Politburo, those Commanders of Military Regions who at the same time held positions at the top of the State and Party *apparats* in the core province of their Military Region, as well as some leading personalities who, because they are persistently mentioned within the circle of the top power-holders, seem to be directly involved in the political decision-making process. Once again this group numbers thirty-two people.

(4) The *leadership core*, which implements the decisions of the decision-making body at the Centre and through its interpretive mechanism exerts a decisive influence. This leadership nucleus comprises the members of the Standing Committee of the Politburo. This had seven members in 1965 and five in 1970.

(5) Finally there is the *Legitimator* who gives his consent to decisions and thereby makes them executable, probably at times with various slogans, and also stimulates decisions—this is Mao Tse-tung.

In the quantitative analysis of the leadership personnel which we shall embark upon, one cannot include the Legitimator or the leadership core because this group is too small to produce statistically meaningful results. As the dates for investigation we have chosen the period immediately before the Cultural Revolution (1965) and the date of the beginning of the dispute, which led to the fall of Lin Piao,[8] that is the autumn of 1970. In this way one can isolate those changes in the leadership structure that resulted from the Cultural Revolution. The number of members of the 'leadership strata' and the 'leadership forces' was higher before the Cultural revolution than in 1970. This is because in 1970 the reconstruction of the State *apparat* had not been completed, and because after 1968-9 leading provincial cadres throughout the country came to hold the top positions of both Party and administrative hierarchies simultaneously. This latter had by no means been so to the same extent before the Cultural Revolution.

An investigation of *mobility* within the leading personnel points to the following conclusion. The *leadership strata* included 581 people in 1965. In 1970, 260 or 44·8% of them were still active. Of the leading strata 246 or 48·6% were newcomers to the new group of 506 people. A similar picture emerges when analysing the *leadership force*. Here only sixty or 30·8% of the 195 members from 1965 remained in 1970; seventy or 53·9% of the group of 130 people in 1970 were new entrants.

Only seventeen members of the *decision-making body* of 1965 remained by 1970, and there were fifteen new entrants.

An investigation of the *age-structure* of the leadership personnel puts this initial impression of substantial mobility into perspective. It is quite clear that even the Cultural Revolution did not basically produce any revolutionary changes as Table 2/8 shows.

The Cultural Revolution did not check the ageing tendency of the leadership. This becomes even clearer when one considers the proportion of the over-50s and over-60s in these three groupings of the leadership personnel (see Table 2/9).

Except for the decision-making body the proportion of the over-60s in the leadership rose even after the Cultural Revolution. This also affected the average age of each of the three groups. For the 'leadership strata' it rose from 58·8 to 59·1 years of age in 1970, although for the decision-making body it rose only marginally from 63·4 in 1965 to 64·1 in 1970. However, for the 'leadership forces' it rose quite significantly from 56·8 in 1965 to 60·1 in 1970.

Though the Cultural Revolution hardly brought about a change in the age structure of the leadership, there were significant changes in the institutional background of the groups under investigation, similar to the changes in the composition of the Central Committt (Table 2/10).

It appears that the Cultural Revolution brought about a significant advancement of the military at the expense of civilians in the three groups of the leadership. More than three-quarters of the 'leadership force' in 1970 were in the armed forces. However, one has to take into account that, given the positions included in the definition of 'leadership force', this figure is statistically biased. Representatives of mass organizations appeared for the first time at the leadership level in the course of the Cultural Revolution. However, they were not able to gain entry to the 'leadership force' and to the decision-making body. This fact strengthens the impression that most of them had only a decorative function.

Such an analysis of the leadership personnel leads one to the conclusion that despite the crises of the Cultural Revolution, a fundamental change of élites had not taken place. In all the three groups of the leadership personnel the old revolutionary generations were still dominant. Even before the Cultural Revolution the leadership had been ageing, and this had been particularly

Table 2/8

AGE GROUPS IN THE CHINESE LEADERSHIP

Age group	'Leadership strata' (%)		'Leadership force' (%)		'Decision-making body' (%)	
	1965	1970	1965	1970	1965	1970
Number of people	354 = 60·9	321 = 64·0	154 = 79·0	103 = 79·2	32 = 100	30 = 93·8
Under 30	—	0·9	—	—	—	—
30–39	—	2·5	—	—	—	—
40–49	7·1	4·4	2·6	1·9	—	3·4
50–59	56·8	47·3	56·5	52·4	21·9	23·3
60–69	27·4	36·1	27·3	33·0	65·6	46·7
70–79	6·5	6·3	9·7	8·7	12·5	23·3
Over 80	2·2	2·5	1·3	3·9	—	3·3

Table 2/9

PROPORTION OF AGE-GROUPS OVER 50 IN THE CHINESE LEADERSHIP

Age group	'Leadership strata' (%)		'Leadership force' (%)		'Decision-making body' (%)	
	1965	1970	1965	1970	1965	1970
Over 50	92·0	92·2	94·8	98·0	100·0	96·7
Over 60	36·1	44·9	38·3	45·6	78·1	73·3

apparent with respect to the 'leadership force' and the 'decision-making body'. This tendency has continued despite the Cultural Revolution. A situation emerged that justified the description of the Chinese political system as a 'gerontocracy'. The only changes that are apparent are the tendencies towards the militarization and regionalization of the leadership, as indicated in the analysis of the 9th Central Committee.

The composition of the Politburo, selected at the 1st Plenum of the 9th Central Committee on 28 April 1969, confirmed the increasing influence of the military on political decision making. It included twenty-one members and four alternate members:[9]

(1) Mao Tse-tung (76). Chairman of the CC and member of the Politburo since 1935.

(2) Marshal Lin Piao (62). Vice-Chairman of the CC, Acting

Table 2/10

INSTITUTIONAL BACKGROUND OF LEADERSHIP PERSONNEL

Group	Civilian cadre (%)	Mass organiza- zation (%)	Total civilian (%)	PLA commanders (%)	PLA political commissars (%)	Total military (%)
'Leadership Strata'						
1965	61·6	—	61·6	26·7	11·5	38·2
1970	18·4	13·2	41·6	40·1	18·2	58·3
'Leadership Force'						
1965	54·9	—	54·9	32·3	12·8	45·1
1970	22·3	—	22·3	46·1	31·6	77·7
Decision-making Body						
1965	62·5	—	62·5	34·4	3·1	37·5
1970	43·8	—	43·8	46·9	9·3	56·2

Chairman of the Military Committee of the CC, Vice-Premier and Minister of Defence, member of the Politburo since 1955.

(3) Chou En-lai (71). Prime Minister, member of the Standing Committee of the Politburo, member of the Politburo since 1927.

(4) Ch'en Po-ta (65). Chairman of the 'Cultural Revolution Group', member of the Standing Committee of the Politburo, alternate member of the Politburo 1956, member of the Politburo since 1966.

(5) K'ang Shêng (70). Adviser to the 'Cultural Revolution Group', member of the Standing Committee of the Politburo, member of the Politburo 1945–56 and again since 1966, alternate member 1956–66.

(6) Chang Ch'un-ch'iao (59). Member of the 'Cultural Revolution Group', Chairman of the Shanghai Revolutionary Committee, newly elected.

(7) General Ch'en Hsi-lien (55). Commander of the Shenyang Military Region, Chairman of the Liaoning Revolutionary Committee, newly elected.

(8) Mme. Chiang Ch'ing (55). Vice-Chairman of the Cultural Revolution Group, wife of Mao Tse-tung, newly elected.

(9) General Ch'iu Hui-tso (61). Director of the General Logistical Department of the People's Liberation Army, newly elected.

(10) Marshal Chu Tê (83). Chairman of the Standing Committee of the NPC, member of the Politburo since 1935.

(11) General Hsieh Fu-chih (71). Vice-Premier, Minister for Public Security, Chairman of Peking Revolutionary Committee, newly elected.

(12) General Hsü Shih-yu (63). Commander of the Nanking

Military Region, Deputy Defence Minister, Chairman of Kiangsu Revolutionary Committee, newly elected.

(13) General Huang Yung-sheng (61). Chief of General Staff of the People's Liberation Army, newly elected.

(14) Li Hsien-nien (64). Vice-Premier and Minister of Finance, member of the Politburo since 1956.

(15) Admiral Li Tso-p'eng (55). First Political Commissar of the Navy, newly elected.

(16) Marshal Liu Po-ch'eng (77). Vice-Chairman of the Standing Committee of the NPC and of the Military Committee of the CC, member of the Politburo since 1956.

(17) Tung Pi-wu (83). Vice-Chairman of the PRC, Member of the Politburo since 1945.

(18) General Wu Fa-hsien (55). Commander of the Air Force, newly elected.

(19) Yao Wên-yüan (46). Member of the 'Cultural Revolution Group', Vice-Chairman of Shanghai Revolutionary Committee, newly elected.

(20) Marshal Yeh Chien-ying (71). Vice-Chairman of the Military Committee of the CC, Director of the Training Section of the People's liberation Army, member of the Politburo since 1966.

(21) Mme. Yeh Ch'ün (53). Wife of Lin Piao and Director of his personal office, newly elected.

Alternate members of the Politburo:

(1) Chi Teng-k'uei (?). Vice-Chairman of Honan Revolutionary Committee, newly elected.

(2) Li Hsüeh-fêng (62). Chairman of the Hopei Revolutionary Committee, newly elected (removed from membership in winter 1969–70).

(3) General Li Tê-sheng (54). Director of the General Political Department of the People's Liberation Army, Chairman of Anhui Revolutionary Committee, newly elected.

(4) General Wang Tung-hsing (?). Commander of the Peking Guards, Director of the General Office of the CC, newly elected.

The average age of the twenty-three full and alternate members of the Politburo for whom a birth date is known, was sixty-four. Of the twenty-one members and alternate members for whom there is data available, nineteen had joined the CCP before the end of the 'Long March'. Only Chiang Ch'ing and Yao Wên-yüan—according to some as yet unverified reports, Mao's son-in-law—had joined the Party after 1937. If one counts Lin Piao's wife, Yeh Ch'ün with the PLA, which is acceptable considering her position in the PLA's headquarters, fourteen of the twenty-five (twelve members and two alternate members) belonged to the Armed

Forces, while eleven (nine members and two Alternate members) could be seen to be civilians.

Nine members and one alternate member were active in Central civilian organs, eight members came from Central Military units, and two from the Regional Military. Finally one alternate member held positions in the Central Military as well as in the Regional Civilian and Military *apparats.*

An analysis of organizational affiliations and what was made known during the Cultural Revolution about the attitude of these members and alternate members reveals that there are five politically distinct groups:

(1) *The Cultural Revolutionary Left* which was represented by the 'Cultural Revolution Group' until the end of 1969 in the CC by Mao, Ch'en Po-ta, K'ang Shêng, Chiang Ch'ing, Chang Ch'un-ch'iao, Yao Wên-yüan, Hsieh Fu-chih, as well as by alternate members Chi Teng-k'uei and Wang Tung-hsing.

(2) *The Cadres of the Administrative Apparat* with Chou En-lai, Tung Pi-wu and Li Hsien-nien.

(3) *The Central Military Group* with Lin Piao, Huang Yung-sheng, Ch'iu Hui-tso. Li Tso-p'eng, Wu Fa-hsien, Yeh Chien-ying, Mme. Yeh Ch'ün and the alternate member, Li Tê-sheng.

(4) The *Regional Commanders* with Hsü Shih-yu and Ch'en Hsi-lien which initially also included Huang Yung-sheng because of his associations with the Canton Military Region before 1969 and Li Tê-sheng because of his continuous involvement in Anhui Province.

(5) A group of *Party veterans* whose public appearances had become increasingly rare and who probably only occasionally took part in the decision-making process. This included the old Marshals Chu Tê and Liu Po-ch'eng.

The nomination of Lin Piao as the Chairman's designated successor emphasized the PLA's gain of power in the Cultural Revolution. It would, however, be a mistake to view the PLA, which had now become a decisive factor in Chinese internal politics, as a monolithic bloc. Even the functional contrast between the interests of the Central Military *apparat* and the Regional Commanders indicates a future difference of opinion within the Armed Forces. Furthermore, within the PLA, five *loyalty groups*[10] had emerged from the five larger historical battle units that had existed in the last phase of the Civil War (1947-9) and their antecedents. The significance of these *loyalty groups* has to be taken into account in any analysis of political events in China generally, and in particular in any evaluation of the role of the armed forces in Chinese politics. These groups are as follows:

(1) The 1st Field Army which included in particular those troops commanded by Marshal Ho Lung and which in 1949-50

had been under the command of Marshal P'eng Tê-huai, who as Minister of Defence in 1959 had been brought down for opposing Mao.

(2) The 2nd Field Army under the command of Marshal Liu Po-ch'eng which was represented on the Politburo by Ch'en Hsi-lien and Li Tê-sheng.

(3) The 3rd Field Army under the leadership of Marshal Ch'en Yi (later Foreign Minister), represented on the Politburo after Ch'en Yi's relegation during the Cultural Revolution by Hsü Shih-yu.

(4) Lin Piao's 4th Field Army, which had Huang Yung-sheng, Ch'iu Hui-tso, Li Tso-p'eng, Wu Fa-hsien and Mme. Yeh Ch'ün on the Politburo.

(5) Finally the North China Field Army sometimes also called the 5th Field Army, led by the current Vice-Premier Marshal Nieh Jung-chen, member of the CC.

It would most certainly be wrong to attribute factionalism and conflict within the PLA solely to the existence of these 'loyalty groups'. That they should increase in significance during times of crisis, is apparent from the changes in the proportions of their military command positions during the Cultural revolution. These changes resulted in a remarkable increase in the number of command positions held by people associated with the 4th Field Army and a considerable decrease in those held by the 1st Field Army of the two purged Marshals, P'eng Tê-huai and Ho Lung (Table 2/11).

The ability of the Mao-made post-Cultural Revolution leadership coalition to work together rested in 1969 basically on the fact that the different expectations of four groups have been met by way of compromise and the distribution of political spoils:
— the Cultural Revolutionary Left gained control over the cultural and propaganda systems and was now in the position to experiment in some of the provinces with their ideas for an 'educational revolution' (*Chiao-yü kê-ming*).
— the room for political manoeuvre of Lin Piao's 4th Field Army loyalty group which had a decisive influence within the *Central Military*, was greatly widened.
— the *Regional Military Commanders* gained control over the Party and State *apparats* in the provinces.
— the *State Administration* was now free of intensive supervision by civilian party cadres, as had generally been the case before 1965.

However, individual elements in this compromise were mutually exclusive. The autonomy of the Regional Commanders, who mainly took a pragmatic developmental approach, and the normalizing interests of the State *apparat* had to go against the

Table 2/11

DISTRIBUTION OF POSTS OF MILITARY
LEADERSHIP AMONG THE FIELD ARMIES,,

Date	1 FA (%)	2 FA (%)	3 FA (%)	4 FA (%)	North China (%)	Unknown (%)
1965	17·2	20·2	19·5	25·2	9·2	8·4
1970	9·3	13·2	21·2	34·0	7·8	14·5

grain of the innovatory enthusiasm of at least the leading group of the Cultural Revolutionary Left, which had endured despite all setbacks. A common commitment to return to the Maoist ideas of 1958 was shared by both Lin Piao's Central Military and the Left, but the Left stood to lose even its last following unless it resisted Lin's demands for a thorough discipline via a militarized society. Finally the Regional Commanders carefully guarded their newly acquired autonomy, which was endangered by the increasing demands for power from the Central Military. The way was already paved for future conflicts within the leadership. They were to erupt when Lin attempted to combine the reconstruction of the party system in provincial China with a return to the ideas of 1958 for development through mobilization. This time such a programme would be implemented through the PLA and the extensive militarization of society—that is via a Bonapartist state.

REFERENCES

1. Radio Kuangsi, 15 April 1969, *inter alia.*
2. The following sociological examination of the leadership is based on biographical data taken in the main from the following sources:
URI, *Who's Who in Communist China,* Vol. I and II, Hong Kong, 1969 and 1970; Ministry of Defence, Republic of China, *Fei-tang cheng-kan-pu jen-shih tzu-liao hui-pien* (Collection of Biographical material on the Rebel Party's Political Cadres), T'aipei, 1966; Ministry of Defence, Republic of China, *Fei-chün kan-pu jen-shih tzu-liao hui-pien* (Collection of Biographical Material on the Rebel Army's Cadres), T'aipei. 1967; Kuo Hua-lun (ed.), *Chung-kung jen-ming lu* (Data on Chinese Communist Personalities), T'aipei, 1968; Institute for the Study of Chinese Communist Problems, *I-chui-ch'i-ling chung-kung nien-pao/*1970 Yearbook on Chinese Communism, T'aipei, 1970; Institute for the Study of Chinese Communist problems, *I-chui-ch'i-erh chung-kung nien-pao/1972 Yearbook on Chinese Communism,* T'aipei, 1972; Ho Yü-wên and Li Chê, *Chung-kung shih-chieh chung-yang wei-yüan-hui jen-shih tzu-liao hui-pien* (Collection of materials of the Personalities of the 10th Central Committee of the CCP), T'aipei, 1973; Howard L. Boorman and Richard C. Howard (ed.), *Biographic Dictionary of Republican China,* 4 Vols., New York-London,

1967-71; Donald W. Klein and Anne B. Clark, *Biographic Dictionary of Chinese Communism*, 1921-65, Cambridge, Mass., 1971; Huang Chen-hsia, *Chung-kung chün-jen chih/* Mao's Generals, Hong Kong, 1968; *K'an yu-lan, Chung-kung jen-wu su-miao* (Chinese Communist Personnel), Hong Kong, 1954; *Chao kuan-yi and Wei Tan-po, Mao Tse-tung chih chu-t'uan* (Mao Tse-tung's leadership group), Hong Kong, 1951; Whitson, *succession*, op. cit., Appendix B: 1956-8, 1966, 1969 and 1971 Military Lists with Biographical Analysis; the 'Biographical Service' of the URI, Hong Kong, from June 1967; and data collected from various newspapers and journals emanating from the PRC, Hong Kong, T'aiwan, the USSR and other western countries.

For sources on Elite studies of the PRC see Donald W. Klein, 'Sources for Elite Studies and Biographical Materials on China' in Scalapino, op. cit., pp. 609-56.

At present the best studies of the membership of the CCP's Central Committee, can be found in: Robert C. North and Ithiel de Sola Pool, *Kuomintang and Chinese Communist Elites*, Stanford, 1952; Frank W. Houn, 'The Eighth Central Committee of the Chinese Communist Party: a Study of an Elite', in *The American Political Science Review*, June 1957, pp. 392-404; Domes, 'China's spätmaoistische Führungsgruppe', loc. cit., passim; Domes, 'The 9th CCP Central Committee in Statistical Perspective in: *CS*, Vol. IX, No. 2, 7 February 1971, pp. 5-14, Donald W. Klein and Lois B. Hager, 'The Ninth Central Committee', in *CQ*, No. 45, January-March 1971, pp. 37-56; v. Groeling, *Innenpolitik*, op. cit., pp. 91-114; Derek J. Waller, 'The Evolution of the Chinese Communist Political Elite', in Scalapino, op. cit., pp. 41-66; Robert A. Scalapino, 'The Transition of Chinese Party Leadership: A Comparison of the 8th and 9th Central Committees', ibid., pp. 67-148.

3. Here the generally accepted practice has been followed of referring to everything north of the Yangtze as 'Northern' (Pei-fang) and everywhere south of this river as 'Southern' (Nan-fang).

4. Mme. Nieh Yüan-tzu, Ch'en Kan-fêng, Ta Luo, and Lung Kuang-ch'ien.

5. See Domes, *Internal Politics*, op. cit., p. 180.

6. Radio Shanghai, 23 March 1967, *inter alia*.

7. Calculated in Domes, *Role of the Military*, loc. cit., pp. 143 f.

8. See pp. 91-137.

9. As the media in China present the namelist of members of the Politburo in order of the number of strokes in the ideograph of their family-name, except for the members of the Standing Committee, they are presented here in alphabetical order from position six onwards. Age has been calculated as on 31 December 1969.

10. See William W. Whitson, 'The Field Army in Chinese Communist Military Politics', in *CQ*, No. 37, January-March 1969, pp. 1-30; Whitson, *High Command*, op. cit., pp. 498-517; Jürgen Domes, 'The Cultural Revolution and the Army', in *AS*, Vol. VIII, No. 5, may 1968, p. 390.

11. Interpolated from Whitson, *Succession*, loc. cit., Appendix B; as well as the author's still unpublished studies.

3. The Reconstruction of the Party and the Position of the PLA

When in January 1967 the Maoist Revolutionary Rebel organizations started their attack on Party leaders in the provinces and in a large number of municipalities, the civilian Party system quickly broke down. Where Maoist organizations were not able to overthrow the Provincial Party leadership, these latter were removed from Office during February and March 1967 by the regional military, who now took responsibility for the management of Party, State and economic affairs in the country's administration.[1] In many of these towns and in a number of villages, particularly those within easy reach of towns, party cadres left their offices, were arrested by Maoist organizations and exposed to the harshest forms of personal criticism—or they took refuge by hiding with friends or relatives.[2] As a result, Party work in most places came to a halt. Membership fees were no longer collected; Party meetings no longer took place; no new members were admitted and certain administrative duties which the Party had assumed, particularly in areas of social welfare, were no longer carried out. A similar situation emerged within the organs of the State *apparat*. The armed forces system generally remained intact, however, so that at the end of the Cultural Revolution it was the only one of the three pillars supporting the political system—Party, State and Army—which still functioned. Under the circumstances the PLA was inevitably placed in a decisive role in the reconstruction of the Party *apparat*.[3]

This reconstruction had begun with the creation of new central leadership organs at the 9th Party Congress in April 1969. Several weeks after the Congress, the leadership started its attempt to reconstruct the civilian Party organization: in May 1969 'the movement to rectify and reconstruct the Party' (*Cheng-tang chien-tang yün-tung*) was given the go ahead. The course of this movement clearly leads to the conclusion that the Party leadership had originally intended to start with reconstruction at basic-unit level, that is, with Party branches in the villages, the rural People's Communes, townships and industrial enterprises, and only later to form Party organs at the county and county town levels, before finally establishing the new Provincial Party Leadership.

However, the movement for the reconstruction of the Party ran into considerable difficulties at the basic-unit level and progress was consequently very slow.[4] On the one hand, the former Party cadres, whose cooperation was being sought once again, hesitated to accept renewed responsibilities, as they were still affected by the memory of attacks by Red Guards and Revolutionary Rebels during the Cultural Revolution. On the other hand, members of Maoist mass organizations now demanded a considerable share in the new Party, which neither the PLA nor the remaining civilian Party cadres were willing to allow them. In this situation the Centre had to rely mainly on the armed forces in its attempt to reconstruct the Party.

However, even the PLA had difficulties in solving the problems that emerged at basic-unit level. There were still rivalries left over from the Cultural Revolution amongst the Mass organizations and the military forced them to unite only with great difficulty.[5] For example, as late as May 1969 the radio station of the North Chinese province of Shensi was still calling for 'the final consolidation of the Great Alliance' of all the Rebel organizations, which had originally been formed in the Spring of 1968.[6] In Chekiang during the same month, a Maoist organization which was marked by its radicalism had to be disciplined with the aid of Army reserves.[7] In the South China Province of Kuangtung it was reported in June of 1969 that the unification of two factions which had been locked in combat since the spring of 1967 had finally been achieved. However at the same time the Provincial leadership had to admit that factional fighting continued.[8] Similar difficulties were reported in June 1969 from an oil refinery in Shanghai, from engineering works in Shensi province, Anyang (Honan) and K'unming (Yunnan), as well as from a tobacco plant in Shihchiachuang (Hopei), where Army units had to be employed to bring the workers back 'under control'.[9] Other reports mentioned that factory workers were often under the impression that the Revolution had 'come to an end',[10] and that young workers in particular spent their time in working the black market and gambling instead of in productive labour.[11] The PLA's intervention does not seem to have been welcomed everywhere. In the province of Anhui there was a general appeal for 'the masses and the PLA not to become estranged', for 'extensive anarchy' could only be fought if everyone 'obeyed orders'.[13] In Hunan, where in the later stages of the Cultural Revolution 'underground bookstores' in which 'feudal and bourgeois books' were sold had spring up, and where frequently 'bad plays were produced in the provincial theatre', 'commandos' were put into action against such 'monsters'.[14]

In Chekiang the propaganda media warned against a 'reactionary trend against the Army'.[15] In the face of these manifestations of resistance the PLA felt obliged to recruit 'Red Sentinels', mainly from the industrial workforce who were to be used as an armed worker's defence.[16]

The Peking leadership, after having faced such difficulties at the basic-unit level, seemed to have come to the decision in the autumn of 1969 to abandon the principle of reconstructing the Party from the base upwards and to concentrate on the county level, even though the Party had not yet been re-established at the basic level. On 18 November 1969 the first County (*hsien*) Party Committee was formed in Ch'angtê (Hunan).[17] But even at the County level progress did not match the Centre's expectations. In the course of the eleven months, i.e. until mid-October 1970, only forty-five of the 2,185 counties in China established new Party Committees.

The slow progress which the movement made at basic-unit and County level before Autumn 1970, led the Party leadership to change its emphasis once again. Although there is no reliable documentation for this decision, developments after Autumn 1970 point to the conclusion that the Centre had decided sometime in September or October of that year (perhaps as early as the 2nd Plenum of the 9th CC at the end of August) to start the reconstruction of new Provincial Party Committees without waiting for the end of the movement at lower levels. There is no information at all as to whether the Provincial Party Congresses, which now took place in relatively quick succession, were actually elected by Party members. Most probably the delegates had been appointed by the Revolutionary Committees of China's twenty-nine major administrative units.

In Hunan, the home province of Mao Tse-tung, the first post-Cultural Revolution Provincial Party Congress met on 21 November 1970. On 4 December it appointed the first new Provincial Party Committee with the civilian Party official Hua Kuo-fêng as First Secretary.[18] In December 1970 Provincial Party Committees were formed in Kiangsi, Kiangsu and Kuangtung.[19] In January 1971 Provincial Party leaderships were established in Shanghai, Liaoning, Anhui and Chekiang.[20] In February Kuangsi and Kansu followed;[21] in March Shensi, Honan, Ch'inghai, Peking, Kirin and Hupei;[22] in April Fukien, Shantung and Shansi;[23] and in May Sinkiang, Kueichou, Hopei and T'ienchin.[24] In June Yünnan also established a new Party Committee.[25] The leadership was clearly keen to finish off this process of establishing Party Committees in the Provinces, Autonomous Regions and Municipalities before the fiftieth anniversary of the founding of the CCP on 1 July 1971. However, they did not manage this, no doubt because in the summer of 1971 the conflicts at the Centre, which ended in the fall of Lin Piao, had worsened. Nonetheless, in August it was possible finally to establish new provincial Party leaderships in Tibet, Ssuch'uan, Ninghsia and Heilungkiang.[26]

While the process of reconstructing the Party at provincial level was taking place, the establishment of new Party leadership organs at county level was also proceeding more rapidly than in 1969–70. By 19 August 1971 county Party Committees had eventually been established in 401 local authorities, with 356 of them having been established since October 1970.[27]

The reconstruction of the Party in China's provinces had four distinct characteristics:[28]

(1) From a quantitative viewpoint, the proportion of the military in the Secretariats of the new Provincial Committees was initially even larger than in the Revolutionary Committees and in the Central leadership groups of the Party. Of a total 158 members and alternate members of the secretariats, ninety-eight or 62% came from the PLA, and ninety-three or 58·9% kept their position in the armed forces even after being elected to these secretariats. Fifty-eight or 32·9% of the members of the new Provincial Party leaderships were civilian cadres and only eight or 5·1% could be said to be representatives of Maoist mass organizations. Three of these were nominated in Shanghai alone, and the leadership in this city thereby made a clear distinction between itself and the rest of the provinces. In Shanghai the Cultural Revolutionary Left succeeded in maintaining the influence it had lost in most of the other regions.

(2) Nearly all the Regional Military Commanders took on leading positions in the new Provincial Party leaderships. Of the ten Commanders of Military Regions (the Commander of Peking Military Region had not yet been nominated), six became First Secretaries of the Party Committees in the economically and strategically most important province of their Region.[29] The remaining four joined the Provincial Party Committees as secretaries.[30] In five cases Commanders of Provincial Military Districts were appointed First Secretary.[31] In ten provinces political commissars with past military careers gained the top position in Party Committees.[32] As a result, altogether twenty-one of China's twenty-nine major administrative units had Military personnel in the position of First Secretary of the Party Committee. Furthermore, twenty-two Military District Commanders were Secretaries in the new Provincial Party Leaderships. If one includes in these calculations those Deputy Commanders of both Military Regions and Districts and regional political commissars, who had been appointed to the new Provincial Party Committees, then it becomes apparent that the Regional military had so much influence in the new Provincial Party leadership that in most of the provinces the leadership of the Army and of the Party were identical. The same was also true for control of the administration, because in twenty-eight of the twenty-nine Provinces the positions of First Party Secretary and Chairman of the Revolutionary

Committee were held by the same individual.[33] This made the share of the PLA in the regional leadership even larger than it had been in the period immediately after the Civil War. At that time only 30·1% of all members of regional leading groups were from the Army, which corresponded to 36·4% of all Communists in such positions. Now, in 1971, it was more than half. In this way the consolidation of the power structure after the Cultural Revolution had become a consolidation of the leading position of the military in the Provinces. At least at this level, it was a confirmation of Ralph Powell's remark that 'the Party still controls the gun, only because the generals control the Party.'[34]

(3) Some of the group of civilian Party cadres who now joined the Secretariats at the Provincial Committees, had been strongly criticized and purged during the Cultural Revolution and they now reappeared in lower positions (if only initially) than they had held in 1965 and not always in their old province. For example, the former First Secretary of the Shantung Provincial Party Committee, T'an Ch'i-lung, became a Secretary in Fukien; the former Party leader in Hunan, Chang P'ing-hua, appeared as a Secretary in Shansi; and the former First Secretary in Kuangtung, Chao Tzu-yang, found a new role in Inner Mongolia. The same was true of some of the Vice-Ministers who were transferred from Peking to the provinces to become Party secretaries. Of further particular significance, the former Governor of Shantung, Pai Ju-ping, who had been turned out of office by the Left in the Spring of 1967, was readmitted into the Secretariat of his former Province, and Chia T'ing-San, one of the closest colleagues of P'eng Chen on the former Peking City Committee, was nominated as an alternate member of the Provincial Secretariat in Kueichou. The reconstruction of the Party *apparat* went hand in hand with the beginning of a trend of rehabilitation for former Party officials who had been purged during the Cultural Revolution. This trend was to become even more pronounced after the fall of Lin Piao in the autumn of 1971.

(4) The establishment of new leadership groups in the Provinces confirmed the continuation of the decline of the Cultural Revolutionary Left. By the summer of 1971, four of the six Chairmen of those Revolutionary Committees, which had been established with strong Maoist participation in the period between January and April 1967, had disappeared. All four were replaced by generals. Two of Ssuch'uan's most important leaders of the Left, Liu Ch'ieh-t'ing and his wife, were missing from that province's list of the new Party leadership. In Peking the Red Guard leader and editor of 'China's first Marxist–Leninist wall-poster', Nieh Yüan-tzu, did not even become an alternate member of the full new Party Committee on which there were more than 100

members. This development points to the conclusion that the organizational base of the left in the Provinces had been dismantled during 1970 and 1971.

Of these four aspects of the reconstruction of the Party leadership in the Provinces, the most important seems undoubtedly to be the barely disguised assumption of power by representatives of the PLA. However, it was not only at Provincial level that the new Party organs were led by the military. Even though there is not enough data for an extensive statistical statement, in most cases where the names of Party leaders in the counties and large towns were made public, they were those of officers or political commissars of the PLA.[35] Even in industrial enterprises, shipyards, shipping companies, department stores and in a number of schools, it was soldiers or reservists who took on the duties of Party secretary.

As a result, the presence of the military became, purely in quantitative terms, a decisive factor in the political system during the initial period after the Cultural Revolution. But this tendency was not limited to quantitative and formal aspects. More important, the PLA played a decisive role also in a qualitative sense at the grassroots, as well as in the Provinces, in the reconstruction of the Party. The armed forces relied mainly on three organizational devices:

(1) The *'Three Support and Two Military'* units (*San-shih-liang-chün pu-tui*; referred to as 3-2 Units). These units were formed initially in the spring of 1967 as an essential organizational force for the intervention of the military in the Cultural Revolution. At that time their definition of intent was of 'threefold support' to the workers (*Chih kung*), peasants (*Chih nung*) and the Left (*Chih tso*), as well as the military management of the administration (*Chün-kuan*) and the military education of the people (*Chün-hsün*). After the summer of 1969, 'Support the workers' (*Kung-jen*) was redefined as 'Support industry' (*Kung-yeh*), and 'Support the peasants' (*Nung-min*) as 'Support agriculture' (*Nung-yeh*). The '3-2 Units' were of greatly varying size: often only a platoon or a company, but at times the size of a division and, in at least one instance, even an Army corps.[36] In the later stages of the Cultural Revolution, the divisions and Army corps that were on duty and the '3-2 Units' were put under the direct command of Central military units, and smaller units under the command of their military region or district. After the autumn of 1970 most of these units were smaller than divisions and were generally under the command of the Military Regions.[37]

(2) The *'Military Representatives'* (*Chün-tai-piao*). To control the re-establishment of law and order after the crisis of the Cultural Revolution, officers or political commissars of the PLA

were sent into almost all the sectors of state and society, where they took on leadership roles as 'military representatives'. Mostly they were under the supervision of the regional military command. They were put into action in universities and industrial plants, schools, agricultural production brigades, rural people's communes, local authorities, newspapers, radio stations and all cultural establishments. A great number of reports of the establishment of new Party organs in these units point to the fact that the military played a decisive role in this movement. Often it was they who had taken the initiative to form the new Party Committees.

(3) The *'CCP Core Groups' (Kung-ch'an-tang hê-hsin hsiao-tsu)* referred to Party members in the Revolutionary Committees at all levels of the administration including the Provinces, the Autonomous Regions and the Municipalities. In most cases the 'core groups' prepared for the establishment of new Party organs and before they were formed they were the sole representtives of the Party in their particular area. As all the military in the Revolutionary Committees were members of the Party, the share of the armed forces in the 'core groups' was generally higher than in the whole of the Revolutionary Committee, which also had members who were affiliated to no party and representatives from the mass organizations. In the provinces these groups were generally identical to those groups which later comprised the secretariats of the Provincial Party Committees.

The PLA had a decisive influence on the reconstruction of the Party machine via these three organizational devices. Often it was the '3-2 Units' or the 'military representatives' who called for meetings and congresses, on the basis of which the new Party organs were to be established. They recruited former Party officials to work in the new Party organization, and they decided which members of Maoist mass organizations were to be admitted to the Party. Often local military leaders themselves took on the leadership of Party departments.[38] Where this was not so, they at least safeguarded their right to approve the list of the new Party Committee before it was publicized. In some cases, as for example in a cement factory in the Tibetan capital, Lhasa, this list was referred three times to the Party members by the military authorities until the composition of the Committee proved acceptable to the armed forces' leadership.[39] In the face of this situation it is understandable that the civilian cadres 'were inclined to fear responsibility and to leave the problems to the comrades of the PLA', as was reported by a shipping company in Ch'ungking (Ssuch'uan) in August 1971.[40]

This apart, the '3-2 Units' were responsible for the ideological education of new Party members and, in many cases, even for that of the entire population. They organized study groups, sent agitators down to basic-unit level and distributed their own educational literature.[41]

In the Soviet Union and the Communist-ruled countries of Europe, following Lenin's definition, mass organizations serve as 'the transmission belts' between the rulling Cadre-Party and the masses. Facing no competition in their particular orbit, they are in the position to transmit to the people the will of the political leadership. The relationship between the Party and the mass organizations in these countries can be defined according to four criteria:

(1) Party members form a majority within the leading organs of the mass organizations.

(2) Party cells have the final say on questions of membership in mass organizations.

(3) The Party selects the cadres for the mass organizations and has control over their training.

(4) The Party directs the greater part of the political education in the mass organizations.

If one uses these criteria to measure the relationship between the Army and the Party *apparats* in China during the period from the 9th Party Congress to the autumn of 1971 when Lin Piao had reached the height of his power, one comes to the conclusion that, at least at that time, the Party was about to become a mass organization of the PLA, particularly at basic-unit, county and provincial levels.

However, this remark does not answer the queries that remain regarding the political meaning of the Army's unmistakable leadership role. Is there any justification in speaking of the Lin Piao period as a period when military rule was established, or (as Joachim Glaubitz put it in the spring of 1971[42]) of when 'Proletarian Military Dictatorship' existed in Communist China? Or is this a false concept, since the character of the PLA is so markedly different from that of other military establishments that a comparison is almost impossible?

There can be little doubt that the Chinese Communist armed forces differ from those of other countries, particularly from those in other developing countries, in three important respects:

(1) As to its origins: during the entire Civil War period in China, there was an exceptionally strong relationship between the Party and the Army. During two periods—from 1928 until the winter of 1931-2 and during the 'Long March' of 1934-5—the Party was almost identical to the Red Army, and the Red Army was a party in arms. This is why in some, if not all cases it is difficult to ascertain whether members of the Chinese leadership had a predominantly military or civilian career before 1949. Furthermore, during the First Civil War (1927-37) and during most of the

Anti-Japanese War it was a political act to join the Red Army. As a result, the Chinese Communist armed forces developed a higher degree of political consciousness than is usual in a regular army. Even so, at that time Mao Tse-tung regularly and repeatedly lamented the lack of just this political consciousness in the ranks of the Red Army.

(2) In the first months of the Partisan War (the summer and autumn of 1927) the newly-emerged Red Army had taken over the system of Party representatives and political commissars from the 'National Revolutionary Army' of the Kuomintang, which had in turn originally copied it from the Soviet Union. Within the CCP's guerrilla army this system developed into a tightly-knit organizational network. Nearly all the members of the CC before 1949 followed Mao Tse-tung's example, and served as political commissars in the fighting forces in addition to their other roles. After 1949 a slow process of differentiation in this sector asserted itself. While civilian Party officials continued to serve as political commissars in the territorial branches of the PLA, particularly in the period from 1958 until 1965, a specific career structure was developed for political commissars of fighting units. They were given military rank in 1955, and frequently changed between command positions in the political *apparat* and the immediate military system.

(3) In the Civil and even more so during the Anti-Japanese War in Northern China, the Chinese Communist armed forces had taken on duties that transcended any narrow definition of their purpose. Often they lived off food they had planted themselves, produced a large part of their own equipment, and participated to a very large extent in the reclamation of land. When Lin Piao took on the leadership of the Ministry of Defence in the autumn of 1959, he began to re-institute this system. The involvement of the military in industry, agriculture, trade and administration after the Cultural Revolution was therefore also rationalized ideologically by reference to the extra-military activities of the Red Army during the Anti-Japanese War. However, there is an essential difference between the situation in 1969 and that of the Yenan Period in the CCP's history. While military involvement in production and society before 1949 was seen primarily as an auxiliary aid, in the later phases of the Cultural Revolution and in the years after the 9th Party Congress, the PLA took on leadership positions in politics and administration. The same was also true to some extent of the leadership of the Regional administration during 1949-52. However, at that time the proportion of representatives of the armed forces in the regional leadership was only half of what it was to become after the Cultural Revolution.

Furthermore, one has to question whether these particular

aspects of the role of the PLA are truly unique. An extraordinarily strong similarity could be found between the Army and the 'Socialist Programme Party' of Burma. The system of political commissars was copied from the Soviet example, even though today it may differ considerably from its Soviet counterpart. In terms of its societal involvement the PLA has gone much further than the military in other developing countries. However, in some of these countries one can find tendencies towards a deeper involvement by the armed forces in administration, education and production, as is true in Thailand, Burma, Iran, Brazil and Peru.

When describing the particular character of the Chinese armed forces, one also has to mention those factors that they have in common with other military establishments. There are three factors in particular:

(1) In spite of its extra-military activities the professional military standard of the PLA rose in the early 1950s and has remained at a high standard ever since. In studying the internal documents of the PLA *Work Bulletin* of 1960-1 (i.e. those that reached the West[43]), one finds that the vigorous attempts to professionalise the Chinese armed forces in the period 1955-65 had led to a remarkable expansion of military technology.[44] Moreover, one must emphasize that since 1954 the close relationship between the civilian party *apparat* and the PLA had eased somewhat and that, as a consequence, contrary to the situation before 1949, two parallel and clearly distinguishable sub-systems had developed. That PLA which intervened in the 'Cultural Revolution' showed much clearer traditional military traits than would have been acknowledged by observers who still thought of the guerrilla army of the 1930s and 1940s.

(2) The majority of the leading personalities in the PLA who after 1967 took on political leadership duties had a traditional military career. Careful study of their biographies shows that as a rule they were promoted on grounds of military rather than political merit.[45] Their behaviour in the crisis of the 'Cultural Revolution' also points to the emphasis of an orthodox military value system. This accounts for their hesitation to give their full support to the Maoist mass organizations and for their ambivalent response to Mao's call to cooperate with the Cultural Revolutionary Left early in 1967, as well as their interest in discipline, law and order, which they have since openly demonstrated. A number of public speeches by leading Regional military commanders after the beginning of 1968 made this point even clearer. Whenever they spoke, whether at student meetings or cadre conferences, they clearly showed that they were accustomed to giving orders and demanding obedience, and that they expected the same degree of

obedience in their new positions in the Party and State administration.[46]

(3) Quite apart from its peculiarities, there is an essential similarity between the PLA and the armies of other developing countries: it acts as an *élite for national integration* which, with a moral code that cuts across traditional boundaries, seeks to implement political decisions based on pragmatic criteria for modernization. This is particularly true of the members of the Regional military. During the crisis of the Cultural Revolution, this élite did, at least temporarily, take on this function which it had already been carrying out for some time in other developing countries.

After the autumn of 1970 there were a number of declarations in the Chinese media that lead one to the conclusion that efforts were being made to justify ideologically the Army's new role as the main agent of social development. The activities of the '3-2 Units', which had originally sprung from pragmatic efforts at consolidation, were now made out to be a 'fundamental development in Chairman Mao's administrative principles',[47] and it was pointed out that their work was a 'fundamental duty of our Army during the total historical period of Socialism'.[48]

This was only a few steps away from the idea contained in a commemorative article published by the central media for the centenary of the Paris Commune, which declared that 'according to the Marxist doctrine of the State, the Army contributes the main part of State power'.[49] Such declarations suggested the conclusion that in future the transition to a Communist social order in China had to come about in the context of military principles of organization and on the basis of norms of political and social behaviour which were set by the armed forces. The military seemed to want to take over the roles of the proletariat as a model for the whole country, and as a determining factor in the development of a Socialist and a Communist society.

However, a rift developed within the PLA after the autumn of 1969. While the majority of the Regional military commanders saw the role of the armed forces as being particularly one of safeguarding law and order, and of furthering pragmatic growth- and consumption-oriented development concepts, the central military *apparat* around Lin Piao wanted if possible to force the Chinese people to return to Mao's ideas of 1958 and development through mobilization.

REFERENCES

1. See p. 11.

2. See, *inter alia*, Ken Ling, *The Revenge of Heaven: Journal of a Young Chinese*, New York, 1972, pp. 82–95 and 128–46.

3. See, *inter alia*: Dieter Heinzig, 'Der Wiederaufbau der Kommunistischen Partei Chinas', in *Aussenpolitik*, Stuttgart, XIX, November 1969, pp. 580-90; Harry Harding Jr., 'China: The Fragmentation of Power', in *AS*, Vol. XII, No. 1, January 1972, pp. 1–15; Hai Fêng, 'China's Domestic Politics in 1971', in *Tsu-Kuo/China Monthly*, Hong Kong, No. 96, March 1972, pp. 2-11; Hai Fêng, 'The Chinese Communist's Party Problems in 1971', ibid., No. 100, July 1972, pp. 2-11; Hai Fêng, 'The Cultural Revolution and the Reconstruction of the Chinese Communist Party', in *AQ*, No. 4, 1972, pp. 303-20 and Jürgen Domes, 'Transition Towards a New Political System in China: the Role of the Party and the Army', in Ian Wilson (ed.), *China and the World Community*, Sydney, 1973, pp. 8–21.

4. See *CNA*, Nos. 755, 764, 768, 769 and 771, of 2 May, 11 July, 8 August, 15 August and 29 August 1969.

5. Radio Honan, 9 May and 3 June 1969; Radio Chekiang, 30 May 1969 and *JMJP*, 27 June 1969.

6. Radio Shensi, 26 May 1969.

7. Radio Chekiang, 27 May 1969.

8. *Nan-fang jih-pao* (South Chinese Daily) Canton, 18 June 1969.

9. *JMJP*, 10 June 1969; Radio Shensi, 11 June 1969; Radio Honan, 17 June 1969; *JMJP*, 24 June 1969. See also *CNA*, No. 769, 15 August 1969.

10. Radio Kiangsu, 8 July 1969.

11. Radio Kiangsu, 22 June 1969.

12. *Hsin Anhui jih-pao* (New Anhui Daily), hofei and Radio Anhui, 13 June 1969.

13. *Hsin Anhui jih-pao*, 23 July 1969 and Radio Anhui, 24 July 1969.

14. Radio Hunan, 18 July and 1 August 1969.

15. '*Chekiang jih-pao*', Hangchou and Radio Wênchou, 30 July 1969.

16. Radio Kiangsi, 5 July 1969 and *JMJP*, 7 July 1969.

17. Radio Hunan, 2 December 1969.

18. *NCNA*, Peking, 13 December 1970.

19. *NCNA*, Peking, 31 December 1970.

20. *NCNA*, Peking, 14, 16, 21 and 30 January 1971.

21. *NCNA*, Peking, 20 and 21 February 1971.

22. *NCNA*, Sian, 8 March 1971; *NCNA*, Peking, 11 and 13 March 1971; Radio Peking, German Service, 21 March 1971 and Central Broadcasting Station Peking, home service, 30 March 1971.

23. *NCNA*, Peking, 6 April 1971; *NCNA*, Chinan, 8 April 1971; *NCNA*, T'aiyüan, 16 April 1971.

24. Central Radio, Peking Home Service, 17 May 1969; *NCNA*, Peking, 24 and 30 May 1971.

25. *NCNA*, Peking, 9 June 1971.

26. *NCNA*, Peking, 21 August 1971.

27. See Domes, *Internal Politics*, op. cit., p. 216.

28. Cf. this extract: Erik v. Groeling, *Die Volksrepublik China nach dem IX. Parteitag: Einheit oder Dissens*, Berichte des Bundesinstituts für ostwissenschaftliche und internationale Studien, No. 60, 1970, Köln, 1970,

passim and v. Groeling, *China's Generale und ihre Politik*, Teil II: *Die Provinzkongresse der CCP*, ibid., No. 50, 1971, passim.

29. Ch'en Hsi-lien (Shênyang) in Liaoning, Yang Tê-chih (Chinan) in Shantung, Hsü Shih-yu (Nanking) in Kiangsu, Tseng Ssu-yü (Wuhan) in Hupei, Han Hsien-ch'u (Foochou) in Fukien and Lung Shu-chin in Sinkiang.

30. Ting Shêng (Canton) in Kuangtung, P.i Ting-chün (Lanchou) in Kansu, Wang Pi-ch'eng (K'unming) in Yünnan and Liang Hsing-ch'u (Ch'engtu) in Ssuch'uan.

31. Liu Hsien-ch'üan (Ch'inghai), Wang Chia-tao (Heilungkiang), Yu T'ai-chung (Inner Mongolia) Lan I-nung (Kueichou), and Li Tê-sheng (Anhui).

32. Hsien Hêng-han (Kansu), Wang Huai-hsiang (Kirin), Nan P.ing (Chekiang), Wei Kuo-ch'ing (Kuangsi), K'ang Chien-min (Ninghsia), Hsieh Chen-hua (Shansi), Chang Kuo-hua (Ssuch'uan), Ch'eng Shih-ch'ing (Kiangsi), Jên Jung (Tibet) and Liu Hsing-yüan (Kuangtung).

33. See the orgograms in v. Groeling, *Die Volksrepublik China ...*, *op. cit.*, *p. 6 a/b.*

34. Ralph Powell, 'The Party, the Government and the Gun', in *AS*, Vol. X, No. 6, June 1970, p. 471.

35. See, *CNA*, No. 856, 1 October 1970.

36. The 38th Army Corps was put into action in Peking during the Summer of 1968.

37. This information was passed to the author in interviews with refugees from different Chinese provinces in June and July 1970, as well as in August 1971.

38. E.g. Radio Canton, 17 April 1971.

39. Radio Lhasa, 25 September 1970.

40. Radio Ssuch'uan, 20 August 1971.

Radio Hainan, 28 April 1971 and Radio Canton, 17 April 1971, *inter alia*.

42. In a lecture at a China conference on political science held by the German Society for Asian Studies, Hamburg, on 14 February 1971.

43. Translation of the *Kuang-tso t'ung-hsün* (Work Bulletin) in J. Chester Cheng (ed.), *The Politics of the Chinese Red Army*, Stanford, 1966.

44. See, Hartmut Fackler, *Aussen- und innenpolitische Aspekte der Strategiediskussion in der Volksrepublik China von 1949 bis 1969*, Berlin, 1972, pp. 42-94 and James D. Jordan, 'Political Orientation of the PLA', in *CS*, Vol. XI, No. 11, November 1973, pp. 3-5.

45. This is certainly true, for example, of the Chief of the General Staff appointed in 1968, General Huang Yung-sheng, and for three Commanders of Military Regions newly appointed in 1969-70, General P.i Ting-chün (Lanchou), General Wang Pi-ch'eng (Kunming) and General Cheng Wei-shan (acting, Peking). See, *inter alia*, Huang Chen-hsia, op. cit., pp. 13 ff., 60 ff., 493 ff. and 589 ff.

46. Compare Hsû Shih-yu's speech to students from the University and Technical High School in Nanking, 11 June 1968; Translation in *Selections from China Mainland Magazines*, Hong Kong (*SCMM*), No. 623 (1968), pp. 11-14; and that by General Yen Chung-ch'uan to the

Standing Committee of the Kuangtung Provincial Revolutionary Committee, in Canton, 9 July 1968; translation in *SCMP*, No. 4234, 8 August 1968, pp. 1-5.

47. Radio Shantung, 24 December 1970; and Radio Fukien, 25 December 1970.

48. Ibid. and Radio Honan, 10 February 1971.

49. *JMJP* and *Chieh-fang-chün pao* (Liberation Army Daily), Peking (*CFCP*), 18 March 1971.

4. Back to the 'Great Leap'

Lin Piao personally set the theme for the policies which the Central Military now wanted implemented. In his speech on China's National Day (1 October) 1969, he referred to the theme of 'More, Faster, Better, and More Economical' (*To-k'uai-hao-sheng*), which had been put forward in 1958 as one of the most essential slogans in the programme of the 'Three Red Banners'.[1] A few weeks later he once again started to talk about a 'Leap', which this time was to be 'new and flying' (*Hsin fei-yüeh*): 'We will advance in flying leaps, and at a speed which will turn one day into twenty years.'[2]

In this way Mao's deputy and appointed successor made it clear that he seriously wanted to attempt to reverse the revisionist interpretation of Mao's concept of development, and to reintroduce essential elements of this concept into China. Among these there were the following:

(1) an emphasis on the simultaneous and equal development of industry and agriculture;

(2) the simultaneous promotion of modern and traditional methods of production in industry and agriculture;

(3) the decentralization of planning and administration in agriculture and local industry to the level of People's Communes with, at the same time, the centralization of the 'modern sectors' of industry;

(4) the strengthening of the position of the People's Communes with repect to that of their subordinate smaller agricultural production units;

(5) the replacement of shortage in investment capital by the mass mobilization of the work force—i.e. a renewed transition to labour intensive instead of capital intensive methods of development;

(6) the rejection of attempts to elicit positive mass response towards the leadership through material incentives. Instead this was to be achieved through a change of consciousness during mass campaigns;

(7) a contempt for profit as a standard of industrial development;

(8) a demand for intellectuals to arrive at a uniform style of 'revolutionary romanticism' in literature and the arts;

(9) an emphasis on the personal initiative of the Party Leader as opposed to that of the 'collective leadership'—i.e. an emphasis on individual charisma as opposed to rule by an organization.

Once again the Maoist concept of 'politics in command' was to be the basic principle for China's development; existence was to be determined by consciousness, and the country's underdevelopment was to be overcome by the revolutionary enthusiasm of the masses.[3]

By 1969 it was obvious to Lin Piao and his colleagues in the Central military that the attempt to reintroduce the Maoist concept of development during the Cultural Revolution had failed. The mobilization of youthful dynamism and the trust placed in the spontaneity of the revolutionary masses had both been proved wrong. Discipline and military organization were therefore to be the basis for a new start. This is shown in particular by the choice of *methods for mobilization*, which were now employed by the Central Army leadership. Of these, three achieved supreme importance during the period from the summer of 1969 to the spring of 1971:

(1) *The 'four-good, five-good movement'* (*Ssu-hao wu-hao yün-tung*).

The terms 'Four-Good' and 'Five-Good' had been introduced into the PLA's political work by Lin Piao in 1960 when he began his efforts to remould the Army as an instrument of the Maoist counter-offensive against the attempts, launched by the majority of the Party leadership, to correct Mao's 1958 concept of development. At an enlarged Plenum of the Military Committee of the CC of the CCP in October 1960, Lin had put through a resolution which had led to the introduction of a 'Five-Good-Soldier-Movement' in the armed forces. This movement served the efforts of the leadership to explain to the soldiers that they had to be good in five ways: in their political thinking, in their military training, in the so-called 'Three-Eight work-style', at the completion of tasks, and at physical exercise.[4] (The term 'Three-Eight work-style' referred to 'Three Phrases' and 'Eight Characters' in Chinese. The 'Three Phrases' demanded a correct political orientation, hard work and a frugal life, as well as tactical flexibility; the 'Eight Characters' represented the Chinese terms for unity, sincerity, energy and liveliness.) The first four of these virtues were offered shortly afterwards in the summer of 1961 as a challenge to the units of the PLA and so led to the 'Four-Good Company Movement'. Within the framework of this campaign, competitions were organized among the companies, and each year the military leadership designated particular units as 'Four-Good Companies' (*Ssu-hao lien-tui*). Officers and troops thus honoured generally earned financial benefits and an increase in their food ration.[5] In Spring 1969 the,leadership of the CCP decided to expand the 'Four-Good' campaign in some of the provinces so that it included the civilian sectors of society as well as the armed forces. Soon there were to be 'Four-Good Companies' and 'Five-Good-Soldiers' not only within the PLA but also general 'Four-Good Units' (*Ssu-hao tan-wei*) and 'Five-Good Cadres' (*Wu-hao kan-pu*). The standards and rules of behaviour which had been developed in the PLA before the Cultural Revolution were to apply to these people. In this way political loyalty and positive ethical norms (in the interests of the leadership) along military lines could be organized even outside the Army. In the winter of 1969-70 vigorous attempts were made to extend the campaign to the whole country. In Hunan the provincial leadership observed that such attempts, once started, could expect a positive response in all parts of society.[6] In Kiangsu it was emphasized that the movement would be the 'solution to the problem of political orientation'.[7] In June 1970, the Commander of the provincial Military District, General Huang Chao-t'ien, stated that the expansion of the 'Four-Good Movement' to the civilian sectors of society meant 'making uninterrupted revolution'.[8] The provincial leadership in Fukien was of the opinion that 'the true dictatorship of the proletariat' would be established if all the factories, People's Communes, administrative units and commercial enterprises 'were to become like the PLA'.[9] Finally, in some of the Provinces, particularly in Hupei, people went so far as to remark that the 'Four-Good-Movement' was an excellent way 'to bring the Revolution to an end and finally realise Communism'.[10] The idea was clearly expressed that it was for the Army to lay down the basic laws of the historical process through which the country would pass. Clearly defined hierarchical relationships, the supremacy of political thought over professional skills, and strict discipline were to create that dynamism in Chinese society which the leadership had not been able to engender for any length of time during either the period of the 'Three Red Banners' or the Cultural Revolution.

(2) The *'Activists' Congresses'*

During that period when the first steps were taken to reconstruct the civilian Party *apparat*, there were still no organizational mechanisms for the recruitment of new 'mobilizatory' cadres in many parts of the country. Even before the 9th Party Congress, some provincial leaderships had attempted, with strong PLA participation, to re-institute those indoctrinational functions which, before the Cultural Revolution, the Party had attended to in seminars of the 'living study and application of the Thought of Mao Tse-tung' (*Huo-hsüeh huo-yung Mao Tse-tung Ssu-hsiang*). These seminars were usually under the supervision of '3-2 Units'.[11] Their name stemmed from the challenge which Lin Piao had personally thrown down at the beginning of the Cultural Revolution.

The representatives of the armed forces in these seminars then selected those participants, distinguished by their outstanding ideological discipline and purity, to become 'activists in the living study and application of the Thought of Mao Tse-tung' (*Huo-hsüeh huo-yung Mao Tse-tung ssu-hsiang chi-chi-fên-tzu).* As early as January 1968 the Ch'inghai Revolutionary Committee became the first regional leadership group to call a provincial congress of these activists. Kiangsi followed suit in May of that year, as did Kuangsi Autonomous Region in December. The year 1969 saw the movement for the convocation of these congresses in many parts of the country. By the turn of the year (1969–70) thirteen provinces had already held one or more of these 'Activists' Congresses'.[12] Six other provinces had held such Congresses by February 1971.[13] In January 1969, a new type of recruitment-congress emerged alongside the already existing 'Activists' Congresses'. This was the so-called 'Congress of Activists in the living study and application of the Thought of Mao Tse-tung and in Four-Good Units'. This type of congress emphasized not only ideological education and the study of the 'Thought of Mao Tse-tung', but was also very much oriented towards the military rules of conduct, introduced into the Army by Lin and intended by him for society at large. They clearly helped to recruit new cadres who were prepared to serve fully the transformation of China through the militarization of society. In eight of the twenty-nine major administrative units in the country this new type of congress was used after March 1970 to mobilize new cadres.[14] The contrast between the pure 'Activist Congresses' and the combined congresses of activists and representatives of the 'Four-Good Units' indicates the conflicts that were going to emerge in the course of 1970 within the Chinese leadership. A number of provinces obviously opposed the attempt of Lin's and the Central Military leadership to create a parallel élite in competition with the Party *apparat*, which was still in the process of reconstruction.[15]

(3) *The 'Down to the Countryside' Movement (Hsia-fang)*

In the dispute between the Armed Forces and members of Red Guard units, which had developed in 1968 from the efforts of the PLA to discipline the Maoist mass organizations, the Army soon fell back on a technique already used during the period of the 'Great Leap Forward' (1958–9) in dealing with cadre and student opposition. Combined storm-troops of soldiers and worker-militia, who had been sent into the universities to put an end to Red Guard activities, found there—as reported from Nank'ai University in T'ienchin[16]—'Three Kinds of Feeling' (*San-ch'i*): bitterness (*Nu-chi*), despair (*Sang-ch'i*) and insubordination (*Pu-fu-ch'i*). In order to meet such resistance effectively, the PLA decided to deport members of the Red Guards and other rebel organizations in large numbers to the villages, where they were to learn the discipline of hard work from the poor and lower-middle peasants. Mao-Tse-tung personally legitimized this policy in one of his general 'instructions', which had been the basic method for promoting new political measures since the end of the Cultural Revolution. On 23 December 1968 he declared: 'The young rebels must go to the villages and accept re-education by the poor and lower middle peasants. This is a necessity.'[17]

Even before this directive by the Chairman, the movement to deport the young rebels of the Cultural Revolution to the country had begun on a large scale in some of the provinces. In September 1968 alone, 1,800 students from Nanking were sent down to the villages to settle there for the rest of their lives.[18] Between September 1968 and September 1969 the new Anhui leadership deported 600,000 youngsters to the countryside,[19] and in Fukien 160,000 young people were similarly treated during the same period.[20] The purpose of these measures was publicized in Hupei, where students were sent to military training camps for re-education, 'so that they could rid themselves of their anarchist tendencies'.[21] However, it was not until the end of 1969 that rustication developed into an extensive system which was implemented throughout the whole of the country. Depending on the level of their activity during the Cultural Revolution, four different methods of deportation were applied to these young people:

— Leading members of Red Guard units were taken to military camps and farms run by the PLA, where they came under the particularly strict supervision of soldiers.[22] This was already true by 1968 for 60–70,000 university graduates.[23]

— Active Red Guards who had not occupied leading positions in the Maoist organizations, were sent to do irrigation and forestry work in the desert areas of Northern China. In this way a number of female students of Ch'inghua University (in Peking) were sent to the edge of the Gobi Desert to work on the construction of canals.[24]

— Many members of the rebel organizations were resettled for life in small groups in villages away from their home provinces.

— Students and pupils who had only been active in a very limited way during the Cultural Revolution were sent for an indeterminate period to villages in their home province, whence they could occasionally (during holidays) return to their home towns.[25]

The leadership pursued a threefold aim with these measures: first, the concentrations of rival leftist youngsters in the cities was to be broken up, and in this way the consolidation policy of the new leadership was to be supported. Secondly, they were hopeful that the youngsters would learn discipline from the peasants while working in the field. Finally, the Centre expected a mobilizatory effect from this campaign which would result in the gradual reduction of the differences between town and country and between mental and manual labour.

During the course of 1970 this campaign of rustication to the countryside took on a new dimension, which until then had hardly been heard of in China. In the town of Wuhan alone, almost 200,000 youths were deported within a short period: 51,000 had to leave the town of I-chang (Hupei); 130,000 left the province of Kuangsi. In the villages of Heilungkiang province in August 1970 there were 135,000 former Red Guards from other parts of the country. In the area around Yenan (Shensi) there were 20,000 Red Guards, and in Yünnan Province there were as many as 200,000 youths from Peking alone.[20] In view of these and similar figures one is bound to come to the conclusion that, even at a conservative estimate, after the summer of 1968—and particularly after the beginning of 1970—hardly less than 15 million young people throughout China were affected by the deportations. Even though the Chinese media tried to give the impression that students and pupils followed the appeal to settle in the villages enthusiastically, there were growing signs of considerable and widespread resistance to the campaign. Frequently they left the villages and stayed illegally in their home towns.[27] Moreover, after the Autumn of 1968 there was a dramatic rise in the number of young refugees entering Hong Kong. This trend continued until well into 1972, so that by August 1972, without considering the highest possible figure, there were over 35,000 former Red Guards resident in Hong Kong.[28]

Corresponding to the deportation of former Red Guards there was a movement for the creation of so-called 'May 7th Cadre Schools' (Wu-ch'i kan-hsiao) for the cadres of the civilian Party apparat who had been criticized during the Cultural Revolution. These institutions were named after Mao's directive of 7 May 1966, in which he called for the division of labour to be overcome through an extensive training of all cadres, soldiers and young people in a great variety of disciplines.[29] After the 9th Party Congress these schools were quickly set up in most of the provinces. They served mainly to re-educate members of the civilian Party and administration who were to be returned to duty after differing periods of indoctrination.[30] There are very differing interpretations of the character of these schools. While the central media made much of the fact that the 'May 7th Cadre Schools' were now 'remand homes',[31] the provinces emphasized repeatedly that the cadres were sent to these institutions for the purposes of 'reform'.[32] There can essentially be no question about the fact that rustication and the cadres schools were to play a major part in the attempt to re-educate particular groups in Chinese society, so that they became instruments for the creation, through organizational strength and strict discipline, of the new society and the 'new man' as envisioned by both Mao and Lin Piao.

The effort to instil in the population the highest ethical norms established the major *mobilizatory content* of this attempt once again to enforce China's development towards a Socialist and later Communist society, initially not by changing material conditions but revolutionizing consciousness.[33] The leadership expected everyone to have the utmost personal commitment to 'serve the people' (*Wei jen-min fu-wu*)—to quote Mao in turn quoting from a citation in 1912 by the President of the First Chinese Republic, General Yüan Shih-k'ai.[34] Part of this was a requirement to do without personal comfort and without the quick acquisition of wealth. The ideal type of the Chinese citizen was now someone who, without regard for comfort and health, gave his whole life in the service of the goals set by the leadership. This person is to work for the whole, is to limit his leisure time to a minimum and is to live even without material compensation, with only his most basic needs being met. His clothing is plain and chosen only with a view to practicality; his diet is simple; his home modest. He does without amusements and receives his sole pleasure from his involvement in the community. The relationship between man and woman is for the biological preservation of the Chinese nation within the quantitative limits set by the leadership in the interest of particular policies; it is for the sharing of work experiences and the mutual revolutionary experiences of the partners; never is it to be solely for the individual's happiness. To whatever position the individual may be assigned, as a member of the 'New Society', he must complete his workload quickly and efficiently, and consider his real wage to be his personal contribution to the development of the nation. The picture of the collective being that emerges is of a person with a passionate desire to construct, with modest personal demands, and with the readiness to make large sacrifices for the good of a social utopia.

Although during the period of the 'Great Leap Forward' (1958–9) the ideal type for the 'new man' had been predominantly the civilian Party cadre, this position was now filled by the soldier. He was to become, with the extension of military norms and rules of conduct throughout society, the model of the conscious proletarian, whose behaviour exemplified the characteristics of a wholly transformed member of the 'new society'. In this way a code of behaviour which had originated in the Armed Forces was added to the ethics of the ideal type representative of the historical development towards a Communist society. The real intention of Lin Piao and his followers in the Central Military was to arrive at a militarization of Chinese society by means of the 'Four-good/ Five-good' movement, the recruitment techniques which developed within this movement, and the 'Down to the Countryside' movement.

This *practice of mobilization* was not oriented only along lines suggested by the PLA's leadership; it was also decisively determined by the leading representatives of the Cultural Revolutionary Left which, although it may have lost important parts of its organizational base through the disciplinary measures inflicted on the Red Guards, still had a great influence on the content of Lin Piao's new Maoist offensive, at least in the areas of education and cultural policy.

During the Cultural Revolution in some parts of China the primary schools were closed for several months in the winter of 1966-7; in almost the whole country the secondary schools were closed until 1968; and all the universities and colleges remained closed for more than four years. The reconstruction of the educational system was now to be combined with a fundamental revolution in this system, the principles of which were defined partly by Mao personally, and partly by the leaders of the Cultural Revolutionary Left:

— A drastic shortening of the period for formal education and training;

— The abolition of entrance examinations to secondary schools and colleges, as well as open entry for industrial workers, peasants and soldiers in particular.

— A reduction of teaching materials in fewer subjects, with an emphasis on ideological indoctrination and pre-military training;

— Priority of practical training over theoretical knowledge in each subject; and

— A combination of manual labour with specialized professional training.

The reopening of colleges and universities was delayed even after the end of the Cultural Revolution, particularly because the function of the third sector in the educational system which the leadership had envisioned could not be clearly defined. On 21 July 1968, at a time when storm-troops of soldiers and worker-militia turned the Red Guards out of the major universities in order to restore law and order, Mao had still emphasized the necessity for a number of highly qualified Institutes of National Science.[35]

On the other hand, the storm-troops who had taken over the provincial Medical School in Kirin, for example, had declared that the usual five-year term of study that had existed before the Cultural Revolution was far too long, that theoretical studies were unnecessary and that pure research had to come to an end.[36] At the same time, however, the Dean of the Faculty of Mathematics and Vice-Chairman of the Revolutionary Committee of Ch'inghua University in Peking, Professor Hua Lo-kêng, expressed the opinion that even though one ought to build small factories in the universities, where students could participate in production, pure research ought to continue.[37]

There were also difficulties with the employment of qualified staff in the colleges. While some Regional Military commanders emphasized that they only intended 'to distinguish between good and bad people among the teachers' and to give the 'good' ones the opportunity to teach as soon as possible,[38] there were still many lecturers who hesitated to offer their services again. During the Cultural Revolution they had been the victims of harsh criticism and extreme violence by the Red Guards, and it was therefore not surprising that they should now regard teaching as a 'dangerous task'[39] or even as the 'worst type of work imaginable'.[40] The Cultural Revolutionary Left therefore concentrated its efforts in places like Shanghai, where it still had a strong position. In particular, they concentrated on the establishment of new-type 'universities', which had the character of Institutes of Further Education for industrial workers. The Shanghai '21 July Workers' University' was praised in July 1969 as a model for such institutions, and it was there that in the course of half a year fifty-two unskilled workers were given full-time training to become skilled workers, and where in evening classes 252 electricians were trained.[41] Its success, however, is seen in its correct perspective when one considers that, in the same city in 1965, factory-attached training schools provided further education for 12,000 workers of whom eleven became chief engineers, 1,300 engineers and 2,800 foremen.[42] The efforts towards a fundamental reform of the content of higher education was seemingly limited at first to some isolated experiments. Students were only re-admitted to the universities in large numbers in September 1971, but a year later only one-third of all the colleges were again in action, at only half the previous working time·and with only a fifth of the 1965 student intake.

In the primary and secondary school sectors, a general attempt was made to shorten the period of studies from six to four or five years and to put these schools under the control of committees of the 'poor and lower-middle peasants'.[43] Peasants were encouraged to write the teaching materials themselves or at least to supplement them with their own work.[44] Occasionally, astounding reports of successes emerged. A People's Commune of 1,600 households in Hupei province reported having collated and produced 3,000 new school books.[45] However, it was necessary in some areas to rely on oral transmission, because even in 1969 there were still illiterates on the school committees in the Communes,[46] despite Mao's prediction as early as 1956 that illiteracy would be overcome in China by 1967.[47]

In 1969 the provincial leadership of Kirin provided a description of the new model school system which was to be developed in China's villages. According to this, the primary schools were to be put under the control of the Agricultural Production Brigades and the secondary schools under the command of the People's Communes. Instruction in the primary schools was limited to politics, arithmetic, 'revolutionary literature', military training and manual labour. In the secondary schools teaching was to include the 'Thought of Mao Tse-tung' (including modern Chinese history), agricultural knowledge (including arithmetic, physics and chemistry), 'revolutionary literature', and military training combined with manual labour.[48]

Admission to higher levels of education was sometimes made independent of academic achievement. In August 1969 Kuangtung began to admit all children of industrial workers and of 'poor and lower middle peasants' to middle schools on application.[49] During 1970 it became the established practice in many Provinces for agricultural production teams and firms to nominate young people to middle schools and colleges on the basis of their political attitudes.

The multitude of educational experiments undoubtedly made it possible for basic education to be spread to a limited extent in a country with a relatively low level of education. The strong orientation towards practical work as against classroom teaching, and the emphasis on experience rather than on book knowledge, brought a new and fruitful stimulus to the traditional Chinese educational methods of rote-learning. On the other hand, political indoctrination and military training starting with six-year-olds took up valuable teaching time. Most of all, the principle of decentralized experimentation led to divisions in the educational system which would be hard to overcome. In 1971 teaching content and the prescribed length of study differed from one province to another and in some cases from one town to another. In practice, therefore, the 'educational revolution' counteracted the policy of mobilization of which its initiators intended it to be a part—a development which the cadres of the Central administration viewed with increasing anxiety. They viewed with growing scepticism these experiments which had taken their cue from the Cultural Revolutionary Left and which were approved and sponsored by the Central Military.

The Left even set the keynote in cultural policy. At the centre of their efforts to create a new image of Chinese society were the 'Revolutionary Model Operas' (*Kê-ming yang-pan chü*),[50] propagated largely by Mao Tse-tung's wife. The term 'Revolutionary Model Opera' was used for stage plays which combined themes of contemporary (generally political) relevance, using modern costume and scenery, with musical pantomime and artistic elements of the classical Chinese opera. During the years from 1958 to 1964 a number of such musicals had already been produced in China, generally by collective effort. Since the early 1960s Chiang Ch'ing had personally publicized these plays, but after the summer of 1964 she encountered resistance from the anti-Maoist opposition.[51] The fall of her adversaries—headed by P'eng Chen, the First Secretary of the Peking Municipal Party Committee until 1966—gave her the opportunity to implement her ideas for a fundamental reform of the hitherto remarkably popular classical opera. Before the Cultural Revolution only two of a large number of productions of this new type of opera had gained relatively wide acceptance, namely *The White-haired Girl (Pai-mao-nü)* and *Liu Hu-lan.*[52] In November 1967, however, Chiang Ch'ing managed to move the Peking leadership to suggest the production of 'Revolutionary Operas' all over the country.[53] Five of these plays were then selected, and since the end of the Cultural Revolution they have been much propagated in all China's regions. This included the operas *Assault on White Tiger Regiment (Ch'i-hsi pai-hu-t'uan)*, a presentation of an event in the Korean War; *In the Docks (Hai-kang)*, a report on the successes of ideologically motivated dock labourers; *Taking Tiger Mountain by Strategy (Chih-ch'ü wei-hu-shan)*, a scene from the Civil War against the troops of the Kuomintang and two stories from the Anti-Japanese War, *The Red Lantern (Hung teng-chi)* and *Shachiapang.*[54] All these five operas were intended to make the masses familiar with the virtues of the 'new man' as he was seen by the leadership. Here again, military rules of conduct prevailed; in three of the five plays the heroes were soldiers, and four of the plays were set in wartime. Particular significance was given to the third of the five Model Operas, *Taking Tiger Mountain by Strategy.* Written in 1958, it was revised by Chiang Ch'ing personally for the first time in 1963-4; a second particularly significant revision of it was done with her cooperation in the autumn of 1969. Soon after the appearance of this third version, the opera received tremendous praise in the Central media.[55] At the heart of the second revision was a change in the character of the opera's hero, an officer of the PLA named Yang Tzu-jung. While in the 1964 version he had an ambivalent image, his courage and wisdom being then seen only as the result of studying the 'Thought of Mao Tse-tung', he now seemed a hero in his own right; his character was faultless and he maintained a correct ideological stance at all times. This 'proletarian hero'[56] did not believe in bourgeois democracy, freedom and equality. He was the unquestionable personification of the 'Thought of Mao Tse-tung' and he yearned for a world revolution, for which he was always ready to give his life. He acted according to the principle which became the main slogan in China during the summer of 1969: 'First, do not fear bitterness; Secondly do not fear death!' (*I, pu p'a k'ui; êrh, pu p'a ssu*).

There can now be no doubt that the second revison of this opera was an important watershed in China's internal political development after the Cultural Revolution. It marked the limit of success in Lin Piao's attempt to achieve the militarization of Chinese society in order to bring back the policy of mass mobilization. There is much evidence for believing that the hero Yang Tzu-jung represented nobody but Mao's designated successor himself.

At the same time as Lin Piao began to speak of a 'Leap Forward', and when the revised version of *Tiger Mountain* pointed to the development of a personality cult centred on the Defence Minister, tendencies seemed to emerge which clearly indicated a return to the 'Great Leap Forward'. In November 1969 the Southern Chinese Province of Kiangsi, whose leaders were closely aligned to Lin Piao, had its first mass work mobilization in a long time. Of the 800,000 residents of the provincial capital of Nanch'ang 500,000 were given a number of days off in order to do water-conservation work.[57] Payment for this work was not even mentioned, and the service of the mobilized masses was apparently for 'the glory of the great leader, Chairman Mao, and for the glory of the Socialist fatherland'.[58] One of the determining factors in Lin Piao's social policy offensive thereby became apparent. However, the Kiangsi experiment did not initially spark off similar actions in the rest of China. Only in the winter of 1970-1 did the provincial leaderships in Kansu, Hunan, Shansi and Kiangsu proceed (and then at times hesitantly) to implement the decision to reintroduce a 1958-style mass mobilization of labour.[59]

There seemed to be some promising signs of success in the attempts made to recreate the mobilizatory desire of the 'Great Leap Forward' in factories and rural People's Communes. In November 1969 the leadership of the Peking Iron and Steel Works made exemplary demands for a tighter management of work in industrial plants. 'Anarchy and Factionalism' were to be done away with, all machinery was to be used efficiently, raw materials were to be handled economically, and the managers were to be involved regularly in manual labour.[60] After the summer of 1970 these efforts were interspersed with attempts at the parallel development of small, medium and large-scale enterprises using both modern and traditional methods of production.[61] This too was a return to the ideas of 1958-9.

In the agricultural sector there was a movement during the winter of 1969-70 to reverse the concessions granted to peasants' private enterprise in the early 1960s.[62] Again it was the Provincial leadership in Kiangsi who piloted this movement. Here the demand was first made for the collectivization of pig-breeding, which had been part of the peasantry's private enterprise ever since 1961.[63] Soon afterwards, attacks on part-time private production in the rural communes followed, and in some of the regions the allotment of small private holdings to individual peasants was criticized.

It seems that by the autumn of 1970 the basic elements of the mobilization campaign to be introduced by Lin Piao and his closest collaborators in the Central military had clearly taken shape. The goal of Mao's concept of development through mobilization, which been sacrificed during the economic crisis of 1960-2, was now finally to be realized through the extension of military principles of organization and behavioural norms to the civilian sector of society. For this reason the leadership had to make increased demands on the masses. They were all to become like soldiers,[64] for the PLA was an example for the whole nation. All good citizens in enterprises, factories, schools and agricultural production units were expected to live according to the rinciples of the 'Four-good Movement' in order to become 'Four-good Units'.[65] As early as June 1969, a unit closely associated with Lin Piao, the 4635 unit of the PLA Air Force in Kiangsu, had defined the aim in this way: a strong state with a totally collective economy where '700 million people, 700 million soldiers, and 10,000 million miles of rivers and mountains were to become a single military camp'.[66] Thus the image of a new nation and a 'new man' following Mao's ideas of 1958 re-emerged. One of the most knowledgeable and most experienced observers of Chinese politics described this image as that of a people under an iron hand, led by an Army and motivated by a pugnacious Marxist spirit.[67]

The Army, it seems, was to be *Carnotist*:[68] utterly convinced of its ideological duty, and thus actively committed to the militarization of society in order thereby to realize the concept of a thoroughly indoctrinated and egalitariàn Army-State. However, in the course of 1970 this concept was to be met by a counter-concept. The majority of regional military commanders were in practice oriented towards notions of a *Wallenstein-type* army, namely a loose coalition of professional soldiers, each with his own power base. For them internal stability as a basis for external security had priority over economic experiments. They therefore favoured a reduction of the leadership's demands on the masses in order to arouse its sympathies and cooperation.

The contradictions which therefore developed in China were bound to result in conflict. This conflict so weakened Lin Piao's position that the fall of Mao's designated successor was almost inevitable. The country entered another internal crisis, with effects comparable to those of the Cultural Revolution, even if the form of those effects was fundamentally different.

REFERENCES

1. *JMJP*, 2 October 1969.

2. 'Hunan jih-pao', Ch'angsha, and Radio Hunan, 27 November 1969.

3. Compare Domes, *The Internal Politics of China*, op. cit., pp. 128 ff.

4. 'Resolution of an Enlarged Meeting of the Military Committee of the Central Committee of the CCP', 20 October 1960, in *Kung-tso t'ung-hsün*, No. 3, 7 January 1961, translation in Cheng, op. cit., pp. 65-94. See also CFCP, 16 September 1961.

5. CFCP, 13 October 1961.

6. Radio Hunan, 30 November 1969.

7. Radio Kiangsu, 29 July 1970.

8. Radio Kiangsu, 18 June 1970.

9. Radio Fukien, 3 December 1969.

10. Radio Hupei, 6 November 1970.

11. See p. 52. See in this context Erik v. Groeling, *China's Generale und ihre Politik*—Teil I: *Zur allgemeinen politischen Entwicklung nach dem IX. Parteitag*, Berichte des Bundesinstituts für ostwissenschaftliche und internationale Studien, No. 49/1971, Köln, 1971, pp. 10-14.

12. Ch'inghai, Kiangsi, Kuangsi, Anhui, Shensi, Chekiang, Yünnan, Kansu, Ninghsia, Heilungkiang, Inner Mongolia, Kuangtung and Liaoning. See *CNA*, Nos. 796 and 797, 3 and 10 April 1970.

13. Hupei, Honan, Shansi, Shantung and in 1971, Sinkiang, and Kiangsu (which was the last province in February 1971).

14. Hunan (where there was no pure Congress of Activists), Kiangsi, Kuangsi, Anhui, Hupei, Kansu, Heilungkiang, and Fukien.

15. See *CNA*, ibid.

16. *JMJP*, 2 February 1969. See *CNA*, No. 772, 5 September 1969.

17. *KMJP*, 23 December 1968.

18. Radio Kiangsu, 11 September 1968.

19. Radio Anhui, 30 September 1969.

20. Radio Fukien, 9 October 1969.

21. Radio Hupei, 19 August 1969.

22. *JMJP*, 7 May 1969.

23. *JMJP*, 11 February 1969.

24. *JMJP*, 7 JUly 1969.

25. This schema arises out of the author's interviews with young refugees in Hong Kong during June and July 1970, August 1971 and September and October 1972.

26. Radio Hupei, 31 May and 22 June 1970; Radio Kuangsi, 23 December 1970; Radio Heilungkiang, 16 August 1970; *JMJP*, 8 May and 25 December 1970. See CNA, No. 835, 19 March 1971.

27. As reported by young refugees to the author in the interviews mentioned in footnote 25.

28. The total number of registered refugees from the PRC in Hong Kong was according to the British police 11,396 during 1967, 14,289 in 1968, 8,041 in 1969, 9,669 in 1970, 11,300 in 1971, 24,100 in 1972; quoted in *Chung-yang jih-pao* (Central Daily), T'aipei, 12 September 1973.

29. Mao Tse-tung, 'Letter to Lin Piao', 7 May 1966, in *I-chiu-ch'i-ling chung-kung nien-pao/1970 Yearbook on Chinese Communism*, T'aipei, 1970, Vol. II, Chapter 7, p. 46. The crucial sentences of this directive were

originally quoted in a joint editorial of *JMJP* and *CFCP* of 1 August 1966. The directive itself was first officially quoted in *JMJP*, 7 May 1967.

30. See *CNA*, No. 779, 24 October 1969.

31. *JMJP*, 22 August 1969.

32. E.g. *Shensi jih-pao*, Sian, 5 October 1969.

33. Cf. Jürgen Domes, 'Moral in der Vorstellungswelt und Praxis Mao Tse-tungs' in: Rolf Italiaander (ed.), *Moral—wozu?*, München, 1972, pp. 186-90.

34. In a declaration made by the members of the first Chinese parliament on 14 April 1913 in Peking.

35. *CNA*, No. 772, 5 September 1969.

36. *KMJP*, 28 June 1969 and *JMJP*, 8 July 1969.

37. *JMJP*, 8 June 1969.

38. E.g. the then Commander of Kuangtung Military District and Chairman of Canton Municipal Revolutionary Committee, General Huang Jung-hai, to High School Teachers in Canton—Radio Kuangtung, 1 Programme, 17 August 1969.

39. Radio Kuangtung, 2 Programme, 15 July 1969.

40. E.g. *JMJP*, 28 July 1969 and Radio Honan, 6 December 1969.

41. *JMJP*, 21 and 24 July 1969.

42. *CNA*, ibid.

43. *JMJP*, 28 October 1969.

44. *KMJP*, 12 December 1969; *JMJP*, 11 January 1970.

45. Radio Hupei, 10 December 1969.

46. Radio Anhui, 17 December 1969.

47. Mao Tse-tung, *Chung-kuo nung-ts'un-te shê-hui chu-yi kao-ch'ao* (The Socialist High Tide in China's countryside), Peking, 1956, p. 362. Compare, on the other hand, *JMJP*, 28 October 1969.

48. *JMJP*, 12 May 1969. See *CNA*, No. 792, 20 February 1970.

49. Radio Kuangtung, 1 Programme, 24 August 1969.

50. See Douwe W. Fokkema, 'The Maoist Myth and its Exemplification in the New Peking Opera', in Daniel Ellegiers (ed.), *China After the Cultural Revolution*, Brussels, 1972, pp. 207-13.

51. Ibid., pp. 213 ff. See also Byung-joon Ahn, 'The Politics of Peking Opera, 1962-1965', in *AS*, Vol. XII, No. 12, December 1972, pp. 1060-81.

52. (1) First publication in English: Ho Ching-shih and Ting Yi, *The White-Haired Girl: an Opera in Five Acts*, Peking, 1954. Revised Chinese edition as collective work: *Pai-mao nü*, Peking, 1960.

(2) Yang Wei and Kuo Chien, Liu Hu-lan, Peking. Translated in *Chinese Literature*, Peking (*CL*), No. 6, 1965, pp. 107-12.

53. *JMJP*, 12 November 1967.

54. Texts of these operas:

(1) Shantung Provincial Peking-Opera Troupe, *Ch'i-hsi pai-hu-t'uan* (White Tiger Regiment Incident) Peking, 1967; English in *CL*, No. 10, 1967, pp. 13-59.

(2) Shanghai Peking-Opera Theatre, *Hai-kang: Ching-chü* (In the Docks: Peking-Opera); English in *CL*, No. 1, 1969, pp. 3-54.

(3) Shanghai Peking-Opera Troupe, *Chih-ch'ü wei-hu-shan* (Taking Tiger Mountain by Strategy) in *HC*, No. 11, 1969, pp. 32-62; English in *CL*, No. 1, 1970, pp. 3-58.

(4) National Peking-Opera Troupe, *Hung-teng chi* (The Red Lantern) in *HC*, No. 5, 1970, pp. 23–47; English in *CL*, No. 8, 1970, pp. 8–53.

(5) Peking Municipal Peking-Opera Troupe, *Shachiapang*, in *HC*, No. 6, 1970, pp. 8–40; English in *CL*, No. 11, 1970, pp. 3–63.

55. *JMJP*, 7, 25 and 30 October and 7 November 1969; *CFCP*, 24 October 1969. See *CNA*, No. 787, 9 January 1970.

56. *JMJP*, 30 September 1969.

57. *JMJP*, 18 August 1969.

58. Radio Kiangsi, 6 and 25 November 1969.

59. Radio Kansu, 16 November 1970; Radio Hunan, 5 January and 16 March 1971; Radio Shansi, 13 January 1971; Radio Kiangsu, 21 January 1971; *JMJP*, 12 and 25 January 1971. See *CNA*, No. 837, 9 April 1971.

60. *JMJP*, 11 September 1969; *CNA*, No. 781, 14 November 1969.

61. E.g. *JMJP*, 24 August 1970.

62. See pp. 143 ff. See also Colina MacDougall, 'The Cultural Revolution in the Communes: Back to 1958?' in *CS*, Vol. VII, No. 9, 11 April 1969, pp. 1–11.

63. Radio Kiangsi, 23 January 1970. See also *CNA*, No. 778, 17 October 1969.

64. Radio Anhui, 22 November 1969.

65. Radio Yünnan, 5 November 1969; Radio Hunan, 30 November 1969; *Fukien jih-pao*, Foochow, 30 November 1969.

66. Radio Kiangsu, 16 June 1969.

67. Dr. Ladislao La Dany in *CNA*, No. 826, 1 January 1971.

68. This term refers to Lazare Carnot, who was responsible for military questions in the Welfare Committee of the First French Republic. Cf. Domes, 'Orbis', loc. cit., p. 877.

PART TWO

THE FALL OF LIN PIAO: A CRISIS WITHOUT THE MASSES

5. The Campaign Against the Left, 1970-1

The concerted attack of the Central military leadership, the regional commanders, and the remains of the State administration led by Chou En-lai on those organizational bastions which had remained in the hands of the Cultural Revolutionary Left, even after the PLA's disciplinary campaign of 1967-8,[1] was at the centre of the new disputes which erupted in China after the Spring of 1970. Although these three functional groups combined in their attack on the Left, they were motivated by very different considerations. On the one hand, whereas Lin Piao and his followers in the Central PLA had adopted essential aspects of the Left's doctrine,[2] they nonetheless saw their tactics as a threat to their own efforts to create military discipline through the new 'Leap Forward'. On the other hand, the vast majority of regional commanders and civilian administrative cadres wanted to put an end to the Maoists' power in order to revise fundamentally the programme of the Cultural Revolutionaries.

Already in 1967-8 the Left had itself lost a large part of its organizational base and was therefore no longer in the position to push through political decisions it had taken independently. However in a number of provinces, particularly in Heilungkiang, Shantung, Shansi and Kueichou, as well as in Shanghai, its leaders were still influential in the top positions of the Revolutionary Committees, and in other provinces like Kiangsu, Kuangsi, Honan, Hunan, Chekiang, Ssuch'uan, Yünnan and Tibet it still controlled a number of units, while in Anhui a regional commander, General Li Tê-sheng (alternate member of the Politburo), continued to work sporadically with a group of 'rebel organizations'. At the Centre itself, the Left, with Ch'en Po-ta, Chiang Ch'ing and the Shanghai Party leaders Chang Ch'un-ch'iao and Yao Wên-yüan, continued to rule the propaganda machine. The close personal relationship between this group and the Chairman secured its position even after the end of the Cultural Revolution. Through K'ang Shêng (member of the Standing Committee of the Politburo), Wang Tung-hsing and Chi Teng-k'uei (alternate members of the Politburo) it even had close connections with the secret police and the intelligence service.

The campaign which the new rulers waged against the Cultural Revolutionary Left therefore started with the attempt to cut off the 'rebel organizations' at the grassroots and their leaders in the Provinces from the Left group in the Politburo.

The new wave of liquidation of Maoist organizations was made out to be the continuation of disciplinary measures started in the final stages of the Cultural Revolution, and the 'revolutionary rebels' actually supported the version of events provided by the military and veteran cadres by making the movement for the reconstruction of the Party organization at the basic-unit level and in rural and urban districts extremely difficult.[3] Where their organizations had already been dissolved, they even resorted to active resistance: thus in the vicinity of Canton during the winter of 1969-70 a group of former Red Guards created a 'World Freedom Party' (*Shih-chieh tzu-yu tang*), which became known for its bombings and attacks on police stations. As a result, the provincial authorities in Kuangtung felt induced to announce heavy retribution against any sabotage activity by 'class traitors'. Several hundred former Red Guards were arrested, and a leader of the group was publicly executed.[4] From Kuangtung the campaign spread to many other provinces. In the name of 'the one struggle, three anti-movement' (*I-ta san-fan yün-tung*)—the struggle against counter-revolutionaries and measures against corruption and theft, speculation, luxury and extravagance—the attempt was made to break the resistance of the Maoist organizations with waves of arrests and a large number of executions of former Red Guards, who were branded as 'anarchists' and 'bad elements'.[5]

These measures brought quick results. By March 1970 articles had appeared even in Central publications under the influence of the Left, strongly criticizing the 'anarchist trend'.[6] The extent to which the 'rebel organizations' were already restricted by March of that year is revealed by reports from twenty-eight of China's major administrative units concerning the mass meetings held in support of Mao's proclamation on 20 May 1970 against American intervention in Cambodia.[7] In thirteen of these—Chekiang, Ch'inghai, Fukien, Inner Mongolia, Kansu, Kuangsi, Kueichou, Liaoning, Ninghsia, Shansi, Sinkiang, Ssuch'uan and Tibet—the Red Guards were no longer mentioned. In five provinces—Anhui, Honan, Hunan, Kuangtung and Shensi—they were ranked after the PLA and the civilian cadres. In nine provinces—Hopei, Hupei, Kiangsi, Kirin, Shanghai, Shantung, T'ienchin and Yünnan—they were ranked higher than the cadres but lower than the Army. In only one of the provinces did they precede the PLA on the list of participants: in Heilungkiang, which at that time was still led by the Left civilian cadre P'an Fu-sheng. Shanghai and Anhui differed from the other provinces in that the Red Guards were mentioned in the headlines of the reports which as a rule only mentioned the 'Army and the People' (*Chün, min*).

Closely linked with the efforts to reconstruct the Party, the campaign against the Left became systematized in the summer of 1970. Under the slogan 'Revolutionize the Thinking of Leadership Groups' (*Ling-tao pan-tzu ssu-hsiang kê-ming-hua*), more and more representatives of Cultural Revolutionary 'Rebel organizations' were being excluded from the Revolutionary Committees at basic-unit and county level.[8] Their place was taken by military men, veteran cadres or 'worker heroes' and 'model peasants' who had already achieved a certain degree of local prominence before the Cultural Revolution and against whom the Maoist organizations had struggled in 1966-7. The rulers in the provinces criticized the 'bourgeois spirit of factionalism' and 'sectarianism', which hindered the work of the Revolutionary Committees.[9] They warned of the possible effects of 'fights over orientation' within local leadership groups,[10] and of the possibility of Revolutionary Committee members getting lost and 'deviating to the Left or the Right'.[11] As a result, for the first time since the Cultural Revolution, 'left deviations' were taken to be mistaken behaviour. At the same time the leadership of Shensi province made it clear that membership of Revolutionary Committees offered no protection against purges: the belief that the new leadership groups were 'sufficiently revolutionized' and therefore unimpeachable was said to be 'false and very dangerous'.[12] Honan seconded this with the remark that 'enemy agents' had in many cases infiltrated the Revolutionary Committees.[13] The attempts of the Left to gain control in the People's Communes and so prejudice the reconstruction of the Party were now seen as particularly objectionable.[14] Representatives of the mass organizations were reprimanded for 'not accepting the Party's leadership' due to their 'bourgeois factionalist spirit'.[15]

It was not only the regional leadership groups that turned against the remaining mass organizations which had sprung up during the Cultural Revolution outside Party control; the latter were soon under fire from the Centre in Peking as well. In August they were reproached in the *JMJP* for 'not accepting leadership through the Party' and for 'wanting to substitute it with the mass organization'. The central organ of the CCP warned of 'factionalist tendencies' and explained quite clearly—'It is dangerous to succumb to the principle: "If it is the will of the masses it will be put into action".'[16]

* * * * * *

Neither the Army-State dreamed of by Lin Piao and his collaborators, nor the policies of normalization and consolidation of development-oriented leadership structures promoted by the majority of regional commanders and the administrative cadres, had room for the spontaneity of the Cultural Revolutionary *avant-garde*.

For this reason the members of the Left were purged in those provinces where in 1967 they had reached the top of the new leadership organs.[17] The Chairman of Shantung Revolutionary Committee, Wang Hsiao-yü, whose continuous arguments with the Commander of the Tsinan Military Region, General Yang Tê-chih, had been described by Mao himself in April 1969 as a 'contradiction within the people',[18] appeared for the last time in public on 1 October 1969; in April 1970 his opponent was given the title 'Leader of the CCP's Core-group in the Revolutionary Committee',[19] and soon afterwards Yang also officially assumed the Chairmanship of the Revolutionary Committee. In Shansi, the two mutually opposed Leftist officials—Liu Kê-p'ing and Chang Jih-ch'ing, Chairman and First Vice-Chairman of the Revolutionary Committee—'disappeared' in the winter of 1969-70. Their places were taken initially by an 'important and responsible person of tne Revolutionary Committee', who was later confirmed as the Committee's new Chairman: the Commander of the Provincial Military District, General Hsieh Chen-hua.

The name of the Chairman of the Kueichou Revolutionary Committee, Li Tsai-han, who in the spring of 1967 had worked closely with the Red Guards, also disappeared from the media at the beginning of 1970. His place was at first taken by a 'responsible person of the Revolutionary Committee'—General Lan I-nung, until then Ch'ungking (Ssuch'uan) Garrison Commander, and a long-time follower of the Chief of the General Staff, Huang Yung-sheng.[21] The Commander of the 47th Army Corps, General Li Yüan, who owed his position as Chairman of the Hunan Revolutionary Committee to the understanding he had shown as late as August 1967 towards Left-wing Red Guards, was transferred soon after 1 April 1970,[22] together with his unit, to North-West China. He was succeeded in the Hunan leadership by the former Party cadre, Hua Kuo-fêng. In Tibet the Political Commissar of the Military Region, General Jên Jung, took the place of the Commander, General Tseng Yung-ya, at the head of the Revolutionary Committee.[23] Tseng had paid close attention to Red Guard representatives when in September 1968 the new leadership group in Lhasa was formed. Finally even P'an Fu-sheng in Heilungkiang, who had managed to keep his place until May 1970, was sacrificed in the purges. For over a year the media did not release the names of the leaders of this strategically important

Province bordering on the USSR, until in August 1971 the Commander of the Provincial Military District, General Wang Chia-tao, took over the Leadership of the Revolutionary Committee and the position of First Secretary of the new provincial Party Committee.[24]

The Cultural Revolutionary Left could probably still count on the sympathetic ear of the Commander of the Military Region and Chairman of the Revolutionary Committee in Anhui, General Li Tê-sheng. But only one major administrative area remained under their control: the city of Shanghai, whose Maoist leaders, because of their close alliance with Mao and his wife, remained unimpeachable even in 1970.

However, similarly close relationships which had developed over the years were not sufficient to protect the most important leader of the Cultural Revolutionary Left and member of the Standing Committee of the Politburo, Ch'en Po-ta. His fall in August 1970 was the first dramatic climax in the campaign of the rulers against the Left, and gave it at the same time a new quality.[25] This was not only because Ch'en was the fourth-ranking member of the inner-leadership core in the PRC after Mao, Lin Piao and Chou En-lai, but also because he was one of the oldest, and probably for many years the closest, of Mao's colleagues.

Born in 1904 in the southern Chinese coastal province of Fukien, son of a civil servant and landowner, Ch'en had joined the CCP at the age of nineteen or twenty and studied in Moscow from 1927 to 1931. On his return to China he became actively involved in the Communist underground movement in Peking and at the same time made his name as a Party theoretician. In the 1930s he was for a while a prisoner of the Kuomintang, but at the start of the Anti-Japanese War in 1937 he was freed and left for Yenan, where in the autumn of that year he took up the position of personal secretary to Mao Tse-tung. Only from this time onwards did Mao make fundamental theoretical statements. In fact it was Ch'en who drafted the essays *On Contradiction, On Practice* and *On New Democracy*. He was also responsible for collating the teaching materials used in the CCP's first big indoctrination campaign, the 'Cheng-fêng Movement' of 1942–4. In 1945 he joined the 7th Central Committee as an alternate member and in 1946 he gained full membership. In the summer of 1949, in addition to being the Director of Mao's personal secretariat, he became Deputy Director of the Propaganda Department of the CC, Vice-Chairman of the Central Party School and in the autumn of 1949 Vice-President of the Chinese Academy of Sciences. At the 1st Plenum of the 8th Central Committee in September 1956 he was appointed an alternate member of the Politburo. After that he became known as the most intelligent and enthusiastic spokesmen for the policy of mobilization developed by Mao and implemented despite resistance in the Party leadership—the policy of 'The Three Red Banners'—which he had played a large part in formulating. As the chief editor of the theoretical journal of the CC, *Red Flag* (first published in May 1958), Ch'en, in an article published in this journal on 1 July 1958, coined the term 'Commune' to describe the then developing agricultural collectives, and provided an essential contribution to the design of their basic structure.[26] In the early stages of the Cultural Revolution he was associated with the leadership of the Maoist faction. As the uncompromising propagator of the Maoist concept of development, he took on the Chairmanship of the Cultural Revolution Group of the CC in May 1966, and in August he joined the Standing Committee of the Politburo. Even before the first mass meeting of Red Guards, on 16 August 1966 he called upon 10,000 representatives of the Maoist mass organizations to 'release a ruthless revolutionary storm'.[27] Together with Mao's wife he was the moving force behind the offensive of 'Rebel Organizations' against the leaders of the Party in the provinces during the spring of 1967. The first draft of the new Party constitution approved by the 9th Party Congress originated with him; and it was this Congress which also confirmed his position as fourth of the five members of the Politburo's Standing Committee.[28]

The actual grounds for, and circumstances surrounding, the purge of Ch'en Po-ta and the extent of his involvement with Lin Piao have still not been sufficiently clarified. According to the Peking leadership's official version,[29] Ch'en—together with Lin Piao, Huang Yung-sheng, Wu Fa-hsien, Li Tso-p'eng, Ch'iu Hui-tso, Mme. Yeh Ch'ün, Li Hsüeh-feng and the acting Commander of the Peking Military Region, General Cheng Wei-shan—prepared a 'surprise attack on Chairman Mao' shortly before the 2nd Plenum of the 9th Central Committee, held from 23 August to 6 September 1970 in Lushan. On the eve of this meeting, which was attended by 155 of the 169 members and 100 of the 109 alternate members of the CC,[30] Lin, apparently surrounded by his followers, was to have given an 'anti-Party speech'. According to the documents of the present Chinese leadership, Ch'en and the group surrounding him had attempted, from 23-25 August, to alter the agenda for the Plenum. Instead of tackling the problems of the National People's Congress, whose convention had been overdue since the beginning of 1969, passing the National Economic Plan for 1970 and discussing a report by the CC's Military Committee on preparations for a defensive war, they were said to have intended passing a resolution on the significance of 'Genius' (*T'ien-ts'ai*) in the processs of historical development, and nominating Lin as Chairman of the People's Republic of China—that is as

Head of State. This move had apparently not been previously discussed either with Mao or with the other members of the Standing Committee of the Politburo. The attempt failed after two and a half days of resistance from the majority in the CC, who then stripped Ch'en of his offices and put him 'under surveillance'.

However, this account raises some doubts as it appeared only after the fall of Lin Piao in order to clarify these events for cadres in the CCP. Ch'en's life history does not induce a belief that he would have turned against the Chairman. If he had really been so closely allied to Lin against the majority of the leadership, then the 2nd Plenum would also certainly have meant the end to the political career of Mao's appointed successor. The *ex-post-facto* explanation given by the Peking leadership is not, therefore, fully satisfactory. In the light of internal political developments since the autumn of 1969, it seems more likely that Ch'en had decided to support Lin's attempt to return to the development concepts of 1958 (in the drafting of which he had been Mao's closest collaborator), in spite of his dislike of the movement, also backed by Lin, to discipline the Maoist organizations. The suggestion that Lin should be made the Head of State in Mao's lifetime was put forward in order to ensure his succession as Party leader, even against the growing resistance of the majority of regional commanders and Chou En-lai's civilian administration. However, it seems that with this suggestion Lin and Ch'en aroused Mao's suspicion. The majority of the CC, which was opposed to Lin's direction, was able to use this point to persuade Mao to drop his long-time private secretary. Lin Piao and his followers in the Central Military behaved towards Ch'en similarly to the way that Liu Shao-ch'i and the majority of the then Politburo had acted towards Marshal P'eng Tê-huai, Lin's predecessor in the post of Defence minister, at the 8th Plenum of the 8th Central Committee in the summer of 1959.[31] In the same way that P'eng, who had openly criticized the Chairman, had at that time been sacrificed by Liu in order to safeguard the policy of 'Readjustment', it was now Ch'en who was being sacrificed to the aim of saving, after he had been purged, the policy of a return to the 'Great Leap Forward'. The only clearly identifiable point of dispute between Lin and Mao—the question of filling the post of Head of State—was settled by a compromise that was much to Mao's advantage. The Plenum passed the draft of a new constitution for China in which Mao was named for life as the 'Head of State of the proletarian dictatorship in our country and Commander-in-Chief of the whole country and the Armed Forces'. Lin was mentioned by name as Mao's successor and, as such, as 'Deputy Commander-in-Chief of the whole country and the Armed Forces'.[32] Shortly after this 2nd Plenum, Mao wrote an open letter to all Party members which was made public to the organs of the CCP only after Lin's fall, on 14 September 1971. In this letter he strongly reproached Ch'en, demanded the opening of a criticism campaign against him, and at the same time stated that 'Comrade Lin Piao was fundamentally of the same opinion'.[33]

Even so the role of the Chairman in the purge of Ch'en Po-ta remains obscure. No one since the mid-1950s had promoted Mao's ideas so consistently or with such devotion as Ch'en. His fall therefore had to be understood by the nation as the Party's renunciation of the fundamental ideas of its Chairman. Only when all the documents on the Lushan conference of August 1970 become available for historical analysis will one be able to clarify whether Mao had consented, as Lin Piao certainly had, to the purge of Ch'en, so that through the sacrifice of a scapegoat for the excesses of the Cultural Revolution his policy could be saved despite the opposition of the majority of the CC, or whether he was in no position to prevent the decision from being taken by the 2nd Plenum because his influence had been so greatly reduced.

One can however be certain that the dispute between the group around Lin Piao, on the one hand, and the majority of regional commanders and the members of the diplomatic and administrative *apparats*, on the other, developed fully after the 2nd Plenum. This conflict was to determine the development of China's politics over the following twelve months.[34]

At first the Chinese masses learned nothing of the fall of the fourth man in the Party leadership. They could only find out through the media that Ch'en had last been seen in public on 1 August 1970. Now he was no longer mentioned. At the beginning of 1971 attacks began to appear on a 'Pseudo-Marxist swindler like Liu Shao-ch'i' (*Liu Shao-ch'i i-lei chia ma-k'ê-ssu-chu-yi cheng-chih p'ien-tzu*), who was held responsible for the 'deviation to the Left'.[35] In March 1971 *Red Flag* first indicated the identity of this 'swindler': he was said to have 'created a truce between the two lines in literature' in 1936, and in 1943 'waffled on' about the 'character of the Party'. Ch'en was thus identified by the mention of two pieces of writing which he had published in those years under his own name.[36]

However, it was not until the 10th Party Congress of the CCP in August 1973 that Ch'en was formally damned: '... expel Ch'en Po-ta, principal member of the Lin Piao anti-Party clique, anti-Communist Kuomintang element, Trotskyite renegade, enemy agent and revisionist, once and for all from the Party!'[37]

Mao's long-time confidant was now made out to be simultaneously a follower of the Kuomintang, anti-Communist, a Trotskyite, and a friend of the 'revisionist' Soviet Union—a surprising combination which cast considerable doubt on the

Chairman's knowledge of human nature and on his personnel policy.

The fall of Ch'en Po-ta signalled a great change in the content of the campaign against the left in China's provinces. While the emphasis had hitherto been on the enforcement of discipline and obedience to the new leadership organs, the regional rulers now began to add attacks on Cultural Revolutionary doctrine to their critique of the Cultural Revolutionary groups. In 1967 the Maoist mass organizations in many firms demanded equal pay for all workers irrespective of individual productivity. At the beginning of October 1970 in the province of Kansu this behaviour was branded as 'egalitarianism' (*P'ing-chün chu-yi*), a 'typical petit-bourgeois and putschist deviation'. The Kuangsi Autonomous Region took up the attacks on the 'egalitarianism' of the Left in November,[38] and soon most of the other provinces joined in.

At the end of November 1970 the offensive against the 'Left deviation' began to flourish. Those considerations, which since the 2nd Plenum had dampened the attacks on the Cultural Revolutionary *avant-garde*, were dropped altogether. Their attitudes were now seen to be 'Left in form, but Right in content'.[39] The leadership of Anhui province took up this theme and remarked that there are 'Leftists, who in reality support a Right-wing opportunism'.[40] In Canton on 3 December, a leader in the newspaper *Nang-fang jih-pao* stated it even more clearly:

Reject all counter-revolutionary black products which may seem Left but which in reality are Right-wing. Discredit them totally and wash that poison away![41]

Soon the provinces departed from the custom of branding deviations from the party line in the following order—'Right and Left'. Now when doctrines considered incorrect were criticized, the 'Left' deviation was put before the 'Right'.[42] While Mao, at the height of Red Guard excesses in August 1966, declared that 'Chaos' (*Luan*) was 'a good thing', in December 1970 the rulers in the Provinces turned against the 'bad elements, who want to create 'Chaos' [*Luan*] in order to stir up muddy waters'.[43]

In the basic-level units, particularly in the rural areas, this fundamental change of direction by the leadrship led to much confusion. It was the attitude of many local cadres that 'deviations to the Right' were 'a matter of political line', i.e. of fundamental importance; whereas 'Leftist deviations' were only 'a question of method'. This, it was felt, was why, if occasionally one had to deviate from the Party line, 'it was better to deviate to the left than to the Right' (*Ning tso wu yu*).[44] It was this very attitude that was now criticized for being 'wrong and counter-revolutionary behaviour'.[45] The use of the term 'counter-revolutionary' in the critique of the Left was now used to clarify the fact that in the resolution of conflict with the earliest Maoists of the Cultural Revolution it was no longer a question of a 'contradiction within the people' but an antagonistic 'conflict between the enemy and ourselves', which could only be resolved by physical force.

When in January 1971 the campaign against Ch'en Po-ta (still unnamed) began in the media, the catchword 'pseudo-Marxism' provided the leadership groups in the provinces with a new weapon in the war against the Left. In January 1971 *Red Flag*, which was still influenced by the rump of the 'Cultural Revolution Group of the CC' in the Politburo, had emphasized that even new leaders should continuously reform and that veteran cadres entering the new Party *apparat* should give their political attitudes a critical check-up.[46] On the other hand, the Revolutionary Committee in the provincial capital of Chekiang, Hangchou, declared that the veteran cadres had in the past been exposed to so much criticism that they 'could under no circumstances still be mistaken in their political line'.[47] The Commander of the Hunan Military District, General Yang Ta-i, averted all attacks on the top positions in the new leadership organs:

The high-ranking cadres exercise power on behalf of the proletariat. They follow the Party's political line closely. This is why they are able to recognize pseudo-Marxism. Everyone else should be equally wary![48]

The Cultural Revolutionary idea that the masses could, according to the Chairman's policy, oppose the provincial rulers was now termed 'Left opportunism'[49] (*Tso-ch'ing chi-hui chu-yi*). The fact that the leadership made a point of putting the term 'Left' in inverted commas, hardly changes the substance of the attacks on the Left. Strictest discipline and the recognition of re-established command structures were now to be the revolutionary virtues; 'rebellion' was no longer heard of.

The Paris Commune had served in January and February 1967 as the model of a new State administrative structure for the earliest Maoist leadership groups;[50] the centenary of the Commune allowed the group around Chiang Ch'ing and the Shanghai Left to remember their services during the Cultural Revolution in a commemorative article in the *JMJP* on 18 March 1971. At the same time they tried to safeguard themselves by including friendly remarks about the role of the Army in the State.[51] However, this apparently did not satisfy the generals. Only in Peking and Shanghai were there mass meetings to commemorate the Paris Commune. On 16 March the PLA announced the launching of the second Chinese satellite;[52] in Tibet, Kuangsi, Hunan, Yünnan, Hupei, Kuangtung, Shensi and on the island of Hainan public meetings were called on 18 March to celebrate the occasion. In no instance was the Paris Commune so much as mentioned.[53] The memory of the drive to 'rebel' in 1966-7 seemed to fade away slowly, but not, however, the memory of the PLA's first attack against the Cultural Revolutionary Left in August 1967. At that time some of the closest collaborators of Chiang Ch'ing in the 'Cultural Revolution Group' of the CC were arrested as 'agents of the Kuomintang'. They were accused of building up a counter-revolutionary organization under the cover of '16 May Corps' (*Wu-i-liu ping-t'uan*). The former Chinese chargé d'affaires in Jakarta, Yao Teng-shan, who together with some Red Guard groups had occupied the Ministry of Foreign Affairs in Peking for a few days at that time, was regarded as one of the leading figures of this organization. It was only now, on 6 June 1971, that he had to face a mass trial in a stadium in Peking, at which he was sentenced to twelve years in jail.[54] This signalled new attacks on the Left in the Provinces, which were presented as attacks on the 'May 16 Corps'.[55]

The attack on the 'May 16 Corps' provided the cue for the last phase of the campaign against the Left. As early as April and May, the media in Tibet had called for an attack on the 'extreme-Left trend' (*Chi-tso ssu-ch'ao*).[56] This term was to be used after July 1971 for all 'Leftist deviations' in the Provinces. The organizational and social doctrines of the Cultural Revolution could thereby be disqualified as anti-Party heresies, and its followers in the basic-level units and counties could be removed from leading positions in the Party.[57] In this way the Cultural Revolutionary Left, with the exception of the group closest to the Party Leader and in Shanghai, lost all the influence which it had retained until the summer of 1971.

Considering that by 1970-1 the campaign against all Cultural Revolutionary traits and Maoist 'Rebel Organizations' had spread all over the country, it necessarily followed that all the regular mass organizations, which had crumbled under the attack of Maoist groups during the Cultural Revolution, now re-emerged. The Young Communist League, which in 1966 was said to have been replaced by the Red Guards, was mentioned again in Hunan in April 1970. In September that year *Red Flag* announced its reconstruction, which meant that even the Centre had given its approval.[58] In February 1971 the 'All-China Federation of Trade Unions' was again mentioned in the media for the first time since December 1966.[59] What is even more significant is that a little later the *JMJP* published an article on the re-establishment of a Youth League Branch in Cotton Plant No. 17, Shanghai.[60] This is surprising because the security police unit supplying the security service to this plant had at one time included Wang Hung-wên, the third-ranking leadership cadre in Shanghai and a member of the

CC very closely associated with the group surrounding Chiang Ch'ing. His involvement in the reconstruction of the Youth League had to be interpreted as a change of course for the remaining Cultural Revolutionary Left that would bring them into line with the majority of the regional commanders and the members of the civilian *apparats*.

The group around Chiang Ch'ing and the Shanghai local leadership was faced with the decision either to disregard all prospects of success and to continue to represent the doctrines of the Cultural Revolution and thereby—as became clear in 1970—simultaneously to support Lin Piao's course of a return to the 'Great Leap Forward', or to give higher priority to the preservation of positions of power at the Centre. They had decided in favour of political survival, and were therefore ready to join that coalition which was now in the process of being formed in opposition to Lin Piao. This decision was made easy for the remaining leaders of the Cultural Revolution Group of the CC, as the power of the anti-Lin coalition had been demonstrated to them in the purge of Ch'en Po-ta. Apart from this, it must not be forgotten that Lin and his collaborators in the Central military had participated in the campaign against the Cultural Revolutionary Left, even at a time when the campaign was confined to disciplinary measures. The conflict with the majority of regional commanders and civilian cadres, now gathered round Prime Minister Chou En-lai, had only arisen when this group began to press for a fundamental revision of the Cultural Revolutionary doctrines. Lin Piao, however, was not ready to consent to such a revision. His policy included the removal of leftist organizations in favour of the PLA, but not the abandonment of the principles of mobilization, which he needed in order to establish his idea of an ideologically motivated Army-State against the opposition of generals and cadres.

REFERENCES

1. See p. 11-15.
2. See p. 61.
3. See pp. 47ff.
4. Radio Canton, 1 April and 15 August 1970.
5. *Inter alia*, Radio Shansi, 17 February 1970 and Radio Fukien, 8 February 1970.
6. *JMJP*, 16 March 1970, in a report on clashes in Chekiang Province.
7. *JMJP*, 22 and 23 May 1970.
8. Reports from young refugees in interviews with British officers in Hong kong, July and August 1970.
9. Radio Honan, 19 August 1970.

10. Radio Hunan, 22 August 1970.

11. Radio Kuangsi, 26 August 1970.

12. Radio Shansi, 26 August 1970.

13. Radio Honan, ibid.

14. Source as in footnote 8.

15, Radio Kiangsu, 11 August 1970.

16. *JMJP*, 21 August 1970.

17. See pp. 50 f.

18. Mao Tse-tung's speech to the 1st Plenum of the 9th Central Committee of the CCP, 24 April 1969, loc. cit.

19. Radio Shantung, 26 April 1970.

20. *JMJP*, 23 May 1970.

21. Ibid.

22. Data of his last public appearance in Ch'angsha (Radio Hunan, 1 April 1970).

23. *JMJP*, 23 May 1970.

24. *NCNA*, Peking, 24 August 1971.

25. Compare with this section: CNA, No. 851, 13 August 1971; Hsüan Mou, 'The Mystery of Ch'en Po-ta's disappearance: Have the early secret capitulation records and anti-Communist vows been unveiled?', in *CKYC*, Vol. 5, No. 3, March 1971, pp. 28-48; and Fang Chün-kuei, 'The purge of Ch'en Po-ta confirmed', ibid., No. 7, July 1971, pp. 4-7.

26. *HC*, No. 4, 1 July 1958.

27. *HC*, No. 11, 1966.

28. The particulars of Ch'en Po-ta's life follow, in particular: URI, *Who's Who*, op. cit., Vol. I, pp. 94 f.

28. The description of the events at the 2nd Plenum of the 9th Central Committee of the CCP by the leadership group can be found particularly in two circulars of the CC under the heading of *Chung-fa* (a short-form of *Chung-kung chung-yang fa-pu*—i.e. Publication of the Central Committee of the CCP).

(1) 'Report of Chairman Mao's discussions with responsible comrades during his Inspection tour in areas outside the capital (mid-August to 12 September 1971)', Draft of *Chung-fa* No. 12 (1972), 17 March 1972; published as 'Ts'an-k'ao tzu-liao' (information material) from the News Bureau of the Ministry of Defence, Republic of China, T'aipei, 16 August 1972; also in Yüan Yüeh, op. cit., pp. 122-30, particularly pp. 125 ff.

(2) 'Report on the examination of the counter-revolutionary crimes of Lin Piao's anti-Party clique' (10 July 1973)—*Chung-fa*, No. 34 (1973), 8 September 1973; translation in *Background on China*, New York, No. B 74-2, 14 February 1974. See also Chou En-lai, 'Report', loc. cit., p. C/2.

30. Communiqué of the 2nd Plenum of the 9th Central Committee of the CCP, in *NCNA*, Peking, 9 September 1970.

31. See, Domes, *Internal Politics*, op. cit., pp. 110-13.

32. 'Draft of a revision of the Constitution of the PRC', *Chung-fa*, No. 56 (1970), 12 September 1970, in Yüan Yüeh, op. cit., pp. 7-20.

33. *Chung-fa* Document, No. 57 (1971), 14 September 1971 in Yüan Yüeh, op. cit., pp. 113 ff.

34. See pp. 104-37.

90   *China After The Cultural Revolution*

35. E.g. *JMJP*, 30 January, 6 and 28 February 1971, and *HC*, No. 2, 1971.

36. *JMJP*, 1 May 1971; *HC*, No. 5, 1971. See Fang Chün-kuei, loc. cit., passim.

37. Communiqué of the 10th Party Congress of the CCP, *NCNA* English, 29 August 1973, in *SWB*, No. FE 4384, 30 August 1973, p. C/3.

38. Radio Kansu, 6 October 1970, and Radio Kuangsi, 22 November 1970.

39. Radio Kuangsi and Radio Shansi, 24 November 1970.

40. Radio Anhui, 1 December 1970.

41. *Nan-fang jih-pao* and Radio Kuangtung, 2 Programme, 3 December 1970.

42. For the first time, Radio Honan, 12 December 1970.

43. Radio Canton, 22 December 1970.

44. Radio Haik'ou, 6 January 1971 and Radio Hunan, 10 February 1971.

45. Radio Hunan, 12 August 1971.

46. *HC*, No. 1, 1971, 9 January 1971.

47. *NCNA*, Hangchou; 4 January 1971.

48. Radio Hunan, 8 January 1971.

49. *JMJP*, 30 January 1971.

50. See Domes, *Internal Politics*, op. cit., p. 180.

51. *JMJP*, 18 March 1971.

52. *NCNA*, English, 16 March 1971.

53. Radio Lhasa, Haik'ou, Kuangsi, Hunan, Yünnan, Hupei, Kuangtung, 1. Programme, and Shensi—all 19 March 1971.

54. *CNS*, No. 347, 24 June 1971.

55. Radio Kueichou, 16 June 1971; Radio Kuangsi, 21 June 1971; Radio Ssuch'uan, 10, 25 and 27 August 1971.

56. Radio Lhasa, 22 April, 28 and 30 May 1971.

57. E.g. Radio Kuangsi, 8 July 1971; Radio Fukien, 8 July, 29 and 30 August 1971; Radio Shensi, 11 and 14 September 1971.

58. Radio Hunan, 2 and 4 April 1970; *HC*, No. 9, 1970.

59. *NCNA*, Peking, 2 Fenrurary 1971.

60. *JMJP*, 19 February 1971.

60. *JMJP*, 19 February 1971.

6. Power Struggles in the Provinces and at the Centre

Although the actual behaviour of Lin Piao and the leading representatives of the Central Military at the 2nd Plenum of the 9th Central Committee in August 1970 remains uncertain, this meeting was nonetheless clearly seen by all the groups in the Party leadership as the first climax in a conflict which now demanded urgent resolution.[1] There can be little doubt that after the autumn of 1969 Mao's appointed successor—occasionally in cooperation with the Cultural Revolutionary Left—had decided to press energetically for a return to Mao's 1958 concept of development in agricultural policy, the reconstruction of the Party and cultural policy. This policy necessarily aroused opposition from those forces who were governed by the idea that after the unrest of the Cultural Revolution there ought to be a lengthy phase of consolidation and that this could only arrive through a reduction of the leadership's demands on the population. In the months before the 2nd Plenum in the summer of 1970, the position of Lin's critics was not quite clear. However, it became apparent that in the provinces there were differences in the evaluation of his personality. A number of conferences called by the regional leaderships at the time of the 2nd Plenum indicated significant differences. For example, a meeting of Kiangsu Revolutionary Committee between 7 and 10 August 1970 emphasized the priority of party reconstruction and the discipline it made necessary. At the same time, however, it set a high priority on the re-establishment of the Youth League in clear opposition to the Cultural Revolutionary mass organizations.

Lin Piao was only mentioned once in the resolution of this meeting, right at the end in conjunction with Mao and a slogan.[2] In a resolution of a meeting of Shansi Revolutionary Committee, which heavily criticized 'bad elements', Lin's name was not mentioned at all.[3] On the other hand, he was mentioned twice on a similar occasion in Sinkiang, and much was made of his contribution to the Communists' triumph in China.[4] A Plenum of Hunan Revolutionary Committee backed him even more clearly. This Plenum took place at the same time as the 2nd Plenum of the Central Committee, and in the absence of the new leader of this province, Hua Kuo-fêng, was strongly influenced by General Pu Chan-ya, a close associate of Lin Piao. In Hunan's resolution of 1 September 1970, Lin was celebrated as the perfect example of a good party leader:

The essential substance of efforts concerned with the supremacy of politics and the creation of political power is that Vice-Chairman Lin is to be regarded as a shining example.... We must always learn from Vice-Chairman Lin, circle closely around the Red Sun and follow Chairman Mao at every step.[5]

Since the beginning of the Cultural Revolution, Mao Tse-tung had been called 'Red Sun' and often even 'the brightest, brightest red sun' (*Tsui-hung tsui-hung-te hung-sê t'ai-yang*). However, there was a significant variation in some of the provinces after the summer of 1970: in addition to the Party leader himself, even the 'Thought of Mao Tse-tung' was now given the title 'Red Sun'.[6] This seemingly was to suggest that even after Mao's death the Party would posses the power to lead through his doctrine. Consequently, Lin Piao as a correct and true advocate of the 'Thought of Mao Tse-tung', could demand a leadership role which was similar only to Mao's role itself.

Of a different character again was the talk given by the Chairman of T'ienchin Revolutionary Committee, Hsieh Hsüeh-kung, at a conference for activists on 21–25 September. He strongly criticized the 'blind use of political measures, born out of wishful thinking and therefore reflecting a non-proletarian idealism and metaphysics'. Hsieh did not mention Lin Piao at all. Instead he made some remarks about a combination of 'quotations made out of context, which could in no way substitute for the in-depth study of the Works of Chairman Mao'.[7] This remark quite obviously referred to the 'Quotations from Chairman Mao' (*Mao chu-hsi yü-lu*), the well-known 'Little Red Book'. This collection of quotations was put together under Lin's direction and with his introduction. Originally, in the early 1960s, it was intended for circulation inside the PLA, and only later during the Cultural Revolution was it widely distributed throughout China. Not least because of this, the T'ienchin Party leader's criticisms could be interpreted as an attack on Mao's deputy.

In an atmosphere of emerging fundamental differences over the future development of the Party and the nation, the establishment of the new Provincial committees of the CCP from December 1970 to August 1971 became in effect a power struggle between the group around Lin Piao and its enemies.[8] Considering that the representatives of the armed forces were almost always dominant in the top positions of the provincial committees (the secretariats), the distribution of regional positions of power among the members of loyalty groups, which dated back to the Field Armies of the Communist Civil War, achieved a particular political significance.

In the Hunan provincial Party secretariat the First Secretary Hua Kuo-fêng, a civilian cadre personally associated with Mao, encountered two generals who were both from Lin Piao's former 4th Field Army.[9] Hua, however, was seldom in the province, so that Lin Piao's confidant, General Pu Chan-ya, practically took over the provincial leadership. Without a doubt the Kiangsi Party was also controlled by Lin's followers. The same was also true for the Kuangtung Party leadership even though in this case the new leaders were drawn from a special group of the 4th Field Army whose immediate allegiance was to the Chief of the General Staff, Huang Yung-sheng. In the autumn of 1971 the Kuangtung provincial leadership was to change allegiance and thereby contribute considerably to Lin Piao's isolation.[10] On the secretariat in Kiangsu which like those in Kiangsi and Kuangtung was formed on 26 December 1970, there was only one of Lin Piao's followers to stand up to the Commander of Nanking Military Region, General Hsü Shih-yu, and two other generals from the loyalty group of the 3rd Field Army.[11] During the Cultural Revolution, Hsü had shown particular reserve towards the intentions of the Mao-Lin faction, and now again he was opposed to Lin's policies.

As was expected from the course of events during 1970, the leaders of the Cultural Revolutionary Left—Chang Ch'un-ch'iao, Yao Wên-yuan and Wang Hung-wên—retained the top positions when the Shanghai Municipal Party Committee was formed.[12] In Liaoning on 13 January 1971 the Commander of Shenyang Military Region, General Ch'en Hsi-lien of the 2nd Field Army loyalty group, took over the leadership of the new Party organization, in which none of Lin's followers managed to gain an influential position. However, the Left was represented in the new leadership by an alternate member of the Secretariat, Mao's nephew, Mao Yüan-hsin.[13] Associations with the Left could also be discerned in the Anhui Provincial Secretariat, which had been established on 21 January under the leadership of Li Tê-sheng, a member of the 2nd Field Army group and an alternate member of the Politburo.[14] In spite of having carried out harsh disciplinary measures against Red Guard organizations at the end of the Cultural Revolution, Li had maintained a close relationship with Chiang Ch'ing. The fact that he agreed to the appointment of the former Deputy Political Commissar of Kiangsu Military District, Liang Chi-ch'ing (who had been dismissed by Hsü Shih-yu because of his close relationships with the rebel organizations) as an alternate member of the Anhui secretariat pointed to a strengthening of the influence of the Left in this Province.[15] In Chekiang Province, which like Anhui is part of Nanking Military Region, General Nan P'ing, an undoubted follower of Lin Piao, became the head of the new Party organization, in which members of the Air Force, who were extremely loyal to Lin, exercised considerable influence.[16] Chekiang's close links with Lin were underlined by a leading article in the provincial newspaper on 31 January 1971. In it the new Party leaders emphasized that there was to be no opposition to the Central leadership in Peking. In particular, Lin's role within this leadership was pointed out:

There can only be this one Centre of leadership—the Party Centre led by Chairman Mao with Vice-Chairman Lin as the deputy leader. We will permit no other Centre of leadership![17]

This declaration was an obvious criticism of Hsü, who at that time tried to implement independent policies which ran counter to Lin's ideas in the Nanking Military Region.

In the Kuangsi Autonomous Region on 12 February, the Political Commissar, Wei Kuo-ch'ing, who had led the Party before the Cultural Revolution and who belonged to the loyalty group of the 3rd Field Army, was appointed First Secretary of the Provincial Committee.[18] All the other members of the Secretariat were also military and Party personnel who had served in the region for a long time. Lin Piao's group was also unsuccessful in exerting its influence on the establishment of the new leadership group in Shensi on 5 March 1971. Here the civilian Party cadre Li Jui-shan, who in 1967 had been ousted by the Red Guards from his position as Party leader in Ch'angsha, Hunan, was now confirmed as the leader of the Province. In addition, a long-established official, two generals from the original 1st and 3rd Field Armies and a representative of a mass organization, which had been considered 'conservative' during the Cultural Revolution, all joined the Provincial Secretariat.[19] In Honan the leadership consisted of two well-established cadres, a general from each of the 1st and 2nd Field Army groups and an official from the secret police *apparat*, also an alternate member of the Politburo, Chi Teng-k'uei.[20]

The Ch'inghai Secretariat, formed by the Provincial Party Congress on 11 March, appeared to have a closer relationship with Lin. Liu Hsien-ch'üan, a general from the 4th Field Army group, became the First Secretary of this province, even though he simultaneously had official positions at the Centre in Peking. Apart from him, two other members of the 4th Field Army, a member of the 1st Field Army and a veteran cadre all joined the new Secretariat, as well as the only one of the four original alternate Red Guard members of the Central Committee who was still active at the beginning of 1971.[21]

The establishment of the new Peking Municipal Committee on 15 March demands particular attention. In April 1967 the last of the six Revolutionary Committees which were strongly influenced by the Maoist organizations had been formed in the capital. The Chairman of the Revolutionary Committee was the Minister of Public Security, General Hsieh Fu-chih (a member of the Politburo), who had not been seen in public since March 1970. He was now appointed as First Secretary, but did not personally attend the Party Congress. Already, apparently, he was suffering from a serious cancer condition to which he was to succumb the next year. As Second Secretary, the Party official Wu Tê (who during the Cultural Revolution had proved himself a particularly loyal follower of Mao) took on *de facto* the top position in the new city leadership. Apart from him, two generals from the 2nd Field Army Group, two from the North-China Field Army and a former ambassador were appointed as Secretaries. This seems to indicate that an anti-Lin coalition had emerged successfully in the capital.[22] The First Secretary of the Party Committee appointed on 24 March in Kirin, General Wang Huai-hsiang, originated from the 4th Field Army but had not had any close contacts with the Lin Piao group for a long time. Apart from Wang there were two generals from the 2nd and one from the North-China Field Armies, plus two Party cadres, who before the Cultural Revolution had been members of the Provincial leadership and were now nominated to the new Secretariat.[23]

The Lin Piao faction managed to exert a strong influence over the establishment (on 28 March) of the Provincial Secretariat in Hupei. The First Secretary and Commander of the Wuhan Military Region, General Tseng Ssu-yü, may have served in the 2nd and in the North-China Field Armies. However, the Second Secretary, General Liu Fêng (First Political Commissar of the Wuhan Military Region), was a loyal follower of Lin's from the 4th Field Army, and there were three other officers in the Secretariat who shared this characteristic. Apart from these five military men, two civilian cadres, who had been part of the Provincial Secretariat in Hupei before 1967, appeared in the new Provincial leadership.[24]

The formation of the new Party Committee in Fukien appeared to be equally beneficial to Lin. Under the leadership of the Commander of Fuchou Military Region, General Han Hsien-ch'u, a previous Corps Commander in the 4th Field Army, two civilian cadres equally closely linked to the loyalty group, and three Generals of the 3rd Field Army plus a former official of the Central administration all joined the Secretariat.[25] In Shantung, on the other hand, the Commander of the Tsinan Military Region, General Yang Tê-chih, a leading member of the North-China Field Army group, became the leader of the Provincial Secretariat of the CCP. Nominated as Secretaries were two other military men from this group and two cadres of the former pre-Cultural Revolution provincial Party Committee.[26] However, one ought to mention that the Second Secretary, General Yüan Sheng-p'ing, had only come to prominence in the Cultural Revolution with Lin Piao's decisive support.

It was a coalition of military personnel and cadres that made up the Secretariat in Shansi, appointed on 11 April 1971. It was led by the Commander of the Provincial Military District, General Hsieh Chen-hua from the 3rd Field Army group. The other Secretaries that were appointed were a general from the North-China Field Army, the Secretary of the Party Committee in the model agricultural production brigade of Tachai, Ch'en Yung-kuei,[27] and the former First Secretary of the Hunan provincial Committee Chang P'ing-hua.[28] In the Sinkiang Autonomous Region on 11 May the Chairman of the Revolutionary Committee and previous Commander of the 43rd Army Corps, 4th Field Army, General Lung Shu-chin, became First Secretary. The other Secretaries, however, had not previously had close connections with Lin Piao. The Second Secretary was to be someone who had served in the region since 1948: the Uighur, Saifudin. The other Secretaries were to be a general from the 2nd Field Army and two former Deputy Ministers in the Peking Central administration.[29] The new leadership in the province of Kueichou, on the other hand, was strongly influenced by Lin's followers. Its First Secretary, General Lan I-nung, and one other military member of the Secretariat originated in the 4th Field Army. In addition, a general from the 2nd Field Army, the former Provincial Governor, and a civilian official who had been transferred from Peking to Kueichou, were appointed as Secretaries.[30] In Inner Mongolia a general from the 3rd Field Army, Yu T'ai-chung, was appointed First Secretary. The remaining posts in the Secretariat were filled by two military men from the North-China Field Army, one former Deputy Minister, and the former First Secretary in Kuangtung, Chao Tzu-yang, who had been purged and denounced as 'a Party enemy' in the spring of 1967.[31]

It was a serious setback for Lin Piao's group when the new leadership in the province of Hopei was announced on 20 May 1971.[32] The civilian Party cadre Li Hsüeh-fêng (an alternate member of the Politburo since 1969) and the acting Commander of the Peking Military Region General Cheng Wei-shan had taken on the leadership of the Revolutionary Committee here in 1968. Li worked closely with the 'Cultural Revolution Group' of the CC and Ch'en Po-ta; while Cheng belonged to the inner circle around Lin Piao. These two officials were the first to be sacrificed in the purges after the fall of Ch'en: in December 1970 the Party leadership called a North-China Conference at which not only was Ch'en strongly criticized, but also Li and Cheng were severely attacked. Again it seemed that Lin Piao dropped his followers: in January 1971 the Conference decided to remove Li and Cheng from their positions.[33] Shortly afterwards Lin's position in Peking and in the surrounding province of Hopei became even weaker. In the summer of 1966 the Defence Minister had secured Mao's control over Peking by transferring the 38th Army Corps from Manchuria to Peking and the surrounding area. Now, however, the Military Committee of the CC decided, under the pretext of a Soviet threat, to transfer the 38th Army Corps back to the province of Heilungkiang. The garrison in the capital was taken over by the 2nd Army Corps, a unit of the 3rd Field Army, which was transferred there from Nanking. The new leadership group in Hopei was therefore now a coalition of civilian cadres and PLA representatives from the groups of the 3rd and the North-China Field Armies. At its head as First Secretary was Liu Tzu-hou, the former Provincial Governor, who had close personal relations with Chou En-lai.

The change-over of high-ranking personnel in Hopei also had its effects on the nomination of the T'ienchin Municipal Party Committee on 26 May. Here, under the leadership of the civilian official Hsieh Hsüeh-kung, five officers from the North-China Field Army group and only one Political Commissar with 4th Field Army associations joined the Secretariat.[34] A change of leadership was brought about by the formation of the Party Committee in Yünnan on 3 June 1971. In this Province, bordering Vietnam and Burma, there had been serious confrontations during the winter of 1970-1, in the course of which the Chairman of the Revolutionary Committee, General T'an Fu-jen, was probably murdered. At least the Chinese media reported his death without mentioning, as usually happens, that he died from a serious illness. In June 1971 the Chinese Nationalist press reported that on 9 March of that year twenty-six persons had been charged by a 'mass tribunal' in K'unming with the murder of T'an and been sentenced and put to death.[35] The former Deputy Minister of Public Security and confidant of Chou En-lai, Chou Hsing, was appointed as First Secretary. The new Commander of the K'unming Military Region, General Wang Pi-ch'eng, became Second Secretary, and the remaining Secretaries were two generals from the 2nd Field Army.[36]

Between 12 and 19 August 1971, after a break of about six weeks, the top Party positions in the remaining four major administrative units were also finally filled.[37] In the Tibet Autonomous Region, a member of the 4th Field Army loyalty group, General Jên Jung, a Political Commissar of the Military Region became First Secretary, but with him as Secretaries were four military men from the 2nd Field Army, one former official and a woman representative of a mass organization.

When the Party Secretariat was formed in the huge Southern Chinese province of Ssuch'uan, there was—probably as a consequence of long negotiations—a compromise between members of the 2nd and 4th Field Armies and civilian cadres. General Chang Kuo-hua of the 2nd Field Army, the Political Commissar of Ch'engtu Military Region, was appointed First Secretary. The Commander of the same Military Region, General Liang Hsing-ch'u of the 4th Field Army, became the Second Secretary, and the third-ranking cadre was the former Provincial Governor Li Ta-chang. Two generals of the 4th and one of the 2nd Field Armies, and two former Vice-Ministers from the Centre in Peking, made up the leadership group. The Ninghsia Autonomous Region remained under the leadership of the Commander of that Military Region, General K'ang Chien-min of the 1st Field Army, and of the Commander of the 31st Army Corps (which had been part of the 3rd Field Army), General Kao Jui. Finally, in Heilungkiang, under the leadership of General Wang Chia-tao of the 3rd Field Army, an officer of the 3rd and one of the 4th Field Armies, as well as two long-serving Party officials, joined the Secretariat.

The establishment of new provincial Party leaderships led to a curtailment of the sphere of influence of the group around Lin Piao. This event, of paramount importance for future developments, confirmed the strength of the coalition, between members of the diplomatic and administrative *apparats* and the majority of regional commanders, which had been based on military personnel in the loyalty groups from the 2nd, 3rd and North-China Field Armies. Certainly the Lin Piao crisis soon demonstrated that these loyalties would not always hold, but it gives important clues to the distribution of power in the country. From the point of view of the representation of opinion and functional groups, the Provincial Committees of the CCP can be divided into five sectors:

(1) In five of the provinces Lin Piao's loyalty group based on the 4th Field Army was clearly dominant. These were Chekiang, Tsinghai, Hunan, Kiangsi and Kueichou.

(2) In two of the provinces Lin Piao's group had a strong position, but for various reasons could not be counted upon as totally safe for the Defence Minister—Fukien and Kuangtung.

(3) Lin Piao's followers were involved in six of the new provincial leaderships, Heilungkiang, Hupei, Kirin, Sinkiang, Ssuch'uan and Tibet—without, however, having a dominant position.

(4) Coalitions of members of the remaining loyalty groups of the PLA and civilian cadres were in control of fourteen of the Provinces—Honan, Hopei, Inner Mongolia, Kansu, Kiangsu, Kuangsi, Liaoning, Ninghsia, Peking, Shantung, Shansi, Shensi, T'ienchin and Yünnan.

(5) Two administrative units remained to differing degrees under the influence of the Cultural Revolutionary Left—in Shanghai they were undoubtedly dominant, and in Anhui the leadership was at least favourably inclined towards them. The cooperation between

Shanghai and Anhui was confirmed in January 1971 when at their Party Congresses, in contrast to all the other major administrative units, they both demanded that the country's economic sectors should be inter-connected 'like a large chess-board'.[38] This formula, which is taken from particular rules in Chinese chess, was used in the spring of 1958 (when Mao implemented the policy of the 'Three Red Banners') as a slogan for the Party leaders' supporters. It was meant to indicate the necessity of combining the decentralization of agriculture and small-scale industries with the tight centralization of the modern industrial sector.

The appointment of the new Provincial leaderships and the movements of military units became increasingly important in the power struggle between Lin Piao's group and its enemies. Transfers of military units were made after the Sino-Soviet border incidents in the spring of 1969, particularly during 1970. The Peking Government moved eight Army brigades from the South Chinese Military Regions into border areas with the Soviet Union and the Mongolian People's Republic. These troop movements had undoubtedly become necessary in the interests of foreign and security policy. However, the choice of relocated units confirms that they were intended particularly to break up the concentrations of the former 4th Field Army units in the Canton Military Region, and at the same time to ensure their neutralization in their new positions in North China by units of the former 3rd Field Army.[39]

Along with the loyalty group of the 2nd Field Army, that of the 3rd Field Army thereby gained in importance for future political decision-making. After the summer of 1970 almost without exception members of these two groups were appointed to leading military positions. Thus General Li Tê-sheng, while retaining his position in Anhui, also took on the influential post of Director of the General Political Department of the PLA, which thereby came under the control of the 2nd Field Army. In the autumn of 1970 the new Deputy Chief of the General Staff was Ch'en Chi-tê, who had also originated in this group, but he later apparently joined the group around Lin Piao.[40] In the spring of 1971 the 3rd Field Army group also obtained a position in the Central military organs for one of their number as a new Deputy Chief of the General Staff, Chang Ts'ai-ch'ien;[41] the newly-appointed Commanders of the K'unming and Lanchou Military Regions, Generals Wang Pi-ch'eng and P'i Ting-chün, belonged to this same group. Furthermore, its position was strengthened by the fact that generals from this group became leaders of the Heilungkiang, Inner Mongolian and Shansi Military Districts.

The struggle for positions of organizational control did not, however, remain confined to the regional leadership groups. Ever since the summer of 1970, a power struggle had developed within the Centre, mainly as a result of the attempt to re-establish the organs of the Central administration. In fact the extreme slowness of this process indicated conflicts of opinion and interest on matters of personnel policy.

In order to strengthen his position against the Central military, Prime Minister Chou En-lai used his powers in the Spring of 1970 more than ever before to ensure the rehabilitation of the former state officials who had been attacked by Red Guards during the Cultural Revolution and removed from office. This rehabilitation began rather unobtrusively with the reappearance of second-ranking cadres, among whom were, in particular, Vice-Ministers from the Ministries and Offices under the State Council (the Cabinet). Thus even before the 2nd Plenum of the 9th Central Committee, the Vice-Ministers of the 3rd Ministry of Machine-Building and of the Textile Industry, Generals Hsüeh Shao-ch'ing and Wang Yü-lo; the Deputy Secretary-General of the State Council, Fêng Hsüan; as well as the Vice-Minister of Geology, Li Hsüan; the ambassador to Tanzania, Ho Ying; and another Vice-Minister of the Textile Industry, Ch'en Wei-chi, were all recalled to office.[44] From the 2nd Plenum to the end of 1970 there followed the rehabilitation of the Vice-Chairmen of the State Capital Construction Commission, Sung Yang-ch'u and Hsieh Pei-i, as well as that of the Vice-Ministers of the 1st Ministry of Machine-Building, Yang Tien-k'uei and Wang Li.[45] In the first six months of 1971 a number of leading cadres of the same or similar rank appeared in public for the first time since 1966.

With the reappearance of the former Chairman of the Commission for Overseas Chinese, Liao Ch'eng-chih, rehabilitation took a step forward. Liao had been a member of the 8th CC but after extremely serious attacks by the Red Guards during the Cultural Revolution was not re-elected to the 9th CC in April 1969. His rehabilitation on 22 August 1971[46] indicated that even top officials of the old Party leadership could count on re-acceptance. Chou En-lai was obviously eager to strengthen his own following with civilian Party leaders from among the former followers of Liu Shao-ch'i. Such a strengthening certainly appeared necessary because, after the autumn of 1970, the reconstruction of the organs of the State Council had begun in earnest. Such a measure had to be taken because, although only twenty-eight of the fifty-six Members of the Cabinet had been singled out as 'Party enemies' in the spring of 1969, a mere four of them had taken up their jobs again since the beginning of 1970—namely Prime Minister Chou En-lai, Vice-Premier and Defence Minister Lin Piao, Vice-Premier Li Hsien-nien and the Minister of Construction Lai Chi-fa. There were indications that Vice-Premiers Marshal Nieh Jung-chen and

Li Fu-ch'un had remained in office; however, the latter was not in his former post of Chairman of the State Planning Commission.

The reconstruction of the top of the State administration was carried through with the idea of reducing the number of ministries and offices and amalgamating suitable posts. Thus in the autumn of 1970 the Ministries of Agriculture, Forestry, and the 8th Ministry of Machine-Building (responsible for the construction of agricultural equipment) were amalgamated into a Ministry of Agriculture and Forestry,[47] just as the Ministries of Roads and Railways were shortly afterwards brought together in a Ministry of Communications.[48]

Eventually the first naming of a new Minister was announced on 28 November 1970: the former Commander of the Armoured Forces Academy, General Sha Fêng from the 4th Field Army loyalty group, was appointed head of the Ministry of Agriculture and Forestry.[49] On 22 December 1970 the media published the appointment of General Pai Hsiang-kuo as Minister of Foreign Trade.[50] Pai was also from the 4th Field Army. As Deputy Political Commissar of the Canton Military Region he had been responsible for disciplinary measures against the Red Guards in and around Swatow (Shant'ou), in the province of Kuangtung. Because of the thoroughness with which he had carried these out he had become known as 'the Butcher of Swatow'. In 1969 he had joined the Ministry of Foreign Trade as a 'military representative'.

Immediately after Pai's appointment was publicized, the former Chairman of the Commission for Economic Relations with Foreign Countries, the veteran cadre Fang Yi, became the leader of a new Ministry for Economic Relations with Foreign Countries.[51] The amalgamation of the Ministries of Fuel and the Chemical Industry followed in January 1971,[52] and in February the former Deputy Commander of the Armoured Corps, General Yang Chieh from the North-China Field Army loyalty group, was named as Minister of Communications.[53] In March the leadership nominated the previous Commander of the 67th Army Corps and Chairman of the Ch'ingtao Municipal Revolutionary Committee, General Li Shui-ch'ing of the North-China Field Army, to be the leader of the 1st Ministry of Machine-Building.[54] The newly-appointed (during the summer of 1971) Chairman of the Commission for Physical Culture and Sport, General Wang Mêng, the former Political Commissar of the Peking Military Region, came from the same loyalty group.[55] Moreover, in the first half of 1971, the Vice-Ministers who had hitherto only been provisionally authorized to lead the Ministries of Foreign Affairs and Light Industry, the career diplomat Ch'i P'eng-fei, and the civilian Party official Ch'ien Chih-kuang were officially confirmed as Ministers.

Thus the State Council, at the time of Lin Piao's fall, was

composed of at least twelve, if not fourteen, members of Ministerial rank, of whom seven were civilian cadres and seven were military. However, among the eight who were newly appointed there were five military men and only three civilians. The PLA had apparently gained a foothold even in Chou En-lai's domain. The weakening of the group around Lin Piao, which had started in January 1971 with the reorganizations of the Hopei provincial leadership and the command of Peking Military Region, became evident here as well: the three military men who joined the State Council after the end of January 1971 could no longer be counted as followers of the Minister of Defence.

Around the turn of the year 1970-1, the nucleus of the Anti-Lin coalition had clearly emerged: officials of the diplomatic and administrative *apparats* were now cooperating with the majority of regional commanders (comprising members of the 2nd, 3rd and North-China Field Armies) against the group around the Minister of Defence. However, the consolidation of these functional and opinion groups into factions necessitated the formulation of alternative political ideas. This first became apparent in a field of activity which is of concern to the lives of four-fifth of the Chinese population–rural social policy.

REFERENCES

1. See p. 83.
2. Radio Kiangsu, 14 August 1970.
3. Radio Shansi, 27 August 1970.
4. Radio Sinkiang, 16 August 1970.
5. Radio Hunan, 7 September 1970.
6. Radio Anhui, 16 July 1970; Radio Hupei, 17 July 1970.
7. *NCNA*, Peking, 10 October 1970.
8. See pp. 49-52.
9. *NCNA*, Peking, 13 December 1970.
10. See p. 130.
11. *NCNA*, Peking, 31 December 1970.
12. Ibid., 14 January 1971.
13. *NCNA*, Shenyang, 16 January 1971.
14. *NCNA*, Peking, 21 January 1971.
15. In Autumn 1970 Liang was appointed to an unspecified leadership position in the Anhui Military District (Radio Anhui, 3 October 1970). After his nomination as a Deputy Secretary of the Anhui Provincial Party Committee, he was appointed Political Commissar in the Nanking Military Region (*CNA*, No. 859, 22 October 1971).
16. *NCNA*, Peking, 30 January 1971.
17. *Chekiang jih-pao* and Radio Chekiang, 31 January 1971.
18. *NCNA*, Peking, 20 February 1971.
19. *NCNA*, Sian, 8 March 1971.

20. *NCNA*, Peking, 11 March 1971.
21. Ibid., 13 March 1971.
22. Ibid., 19 March 1971.
23. Central Radio, Peking Home Service, 30 March 1971.
24. Ibid., 1 April 1971.
25. *NCNA*, Peking, 6 April 1971.
26. *NCNA*, Chinan, 8 April 1971.
27. See pp. 109 ff.
28. *NCNA*, T'aiyüan, 16 April 1971.
29. Central Radio, Peking, 17 May 1971.
30. Ibid.
31. *NCNA*, Peking, 22 May 1971.
32. Ibid., 25 May 1971.
33. Chung-fa Document No. 12 (1972), 17 March 1972, in, Yüan Yüeh, op. cit., p. 127. See also Domes, *Orbis*, loc. cit., p. 867.
34. *NCNA*, Peking, 30 May 1971.
35. A report from the *CNA*, T'aipei, 15 June 1971, quoted in v. Groeling, *Chinas Generale*, II, op. cit., p. 3.
36. *NCNA*, Peking, 9 June 1971.
37. Ibid., 21 August 1971.
38. Ibid., 12 and 23 January 1971.
39. The details in this section are confirmed by Huang Chen-hsia, 'Strength and Deployment of the Chinese Communist Army', Hong Kong, 1971 (photocopy), p. 4.
40. *NCNA*, Peking, 2 October 1970.
41. Ibid., 1 May 1971.
42. See Jürgen Domes, 'New Course in Chinese Domestic Politics: The Anatomy of Readjustment', in *AS*, Vol. XIII, No. 7, July 1973, pp. 638 ff.
43. *NCNA*, Peking, 21 May 1971.
44. Ibid., 21 and 22 June, 5 and 7 July and 6 August 1970.
45. Ibid., 2 October, 28 November and 22 December 1970.
46. Ibid., 22 August 1971.
47. *CNS*, No. 342, 22 October 1970.
48. *NCNA*, Peking, 22 October 1970.
49. Ibid., 28 November 1970.
50. Ibid., 22 December 1970.
51. Ibid., 23 December 1970.
52. Ibid., 7 January 1971.
53. Ibid., 11 February 1971.
54. Ibid., 22 March 1971.
55. Ibid., 24 September 1971.

7. The Rural Debate

Many observers of the Chinese political scene believe that the controversies which reached their climax in September 1971 with the fall of Lin Piao were, more than anything, the result of personal rivalries within the Peking leadership group.[1] It was thus a question of gaining and exercising political power. Fundamental differences of opinion had, if anything, been of only secondary importance. It is quite certain that the content of conflicts cannot be separated from the personalities of the opposing parties. Consequently there can be no doubt that the question of the succession to Mao Tse-tung was of considerable importance in the development of the Lin Piao crisis. However, if one believed that this crisis was only concerned with finding a solution to the succession question, one would completely overlook the debates on fundamental concepts which were at the centre of Chinese politics and which involved the CCP's leadership. I have already mentioned that the question of the extent and intensity of the revision of Cultural Revolutionary methods and ideas played a significant role in this context.[2] In addition, the available information suggests that there have been diferences of opinion over the middle-term strategy and tactics of Chinese foreign policy, as well as over whether there should be re-centralization or continued decentralization in planning and economic management.[3] However, the controversy over agricultural policy—or rather over social policy in China's villages—was of even greater significance. This in fact came down to a conflict over the nature of Chinese society in which there was no room for compromise. This was not the first time that fundamental political decisions within Communist regimes had centred on questions of agricultural policy. The Stalinist purges in the USSR were connected with the collectivization of agriculture. Controversies over agricultural policies caused the fall of Imre Nagy, the Hungarian Prime Minister, in 1955, and it was such controversies that led to the fall of Edward Ochabs and the assumption of leadership in Poland by Wladyslaw Gomulka. In the PRC they were at the centre of the intra-Party controversies of 1955-6 and again those of 1958-65. Lin's attempt after the autumn of 1969 to enforce a return to the mobilizatory concepts and practices of the policy of the 'Three Red Banners' led China once again into a socio-political conflict over the circumstances of agricultural production.

In 1955 Mao Tse-tung had managed, despite considerable resistance within the Party leadership, to accelerate the collectivization of Chinese agriculture.[4] It came about with such force that by the spring of 1957 93·3% of the Chinese rural population had been collectivized into 'Higher Stage Collectives' (HSCs). Members of these HSCs retained only their houses and surrounding gardens, while all arable land, instruments and machinery became collective property and the members of the collectives were paid exclusively according to their productivity. In the autumn of 1957 the Party leader—once again despite the resistance of part of the leadership—began to advocate the merging of large numbers of the HSCs into larger agricultural collectives. As a result the concept of the People's Commune (*Jen-min kung-shê*)[5] developed, and its influence has been felt throughout China ever since Spring 1958. Originally conceived in 1958 as a prescribed model for the rural population, the Communes were then characterized as 'large' (*Ta*) and 'communal' (*Kung*). 'Large' meant that in the communes all the occupational groups and local economic enterprises—farming, small-scale industry, fishing and forestry—came under the control of a unified leadership.

The term 'communal' referred to united leadership over both the commune and state administration; the inclusion of houses, domestic utensils, animals and gardens into the communal property; as well as a far-ranging regulation of the private lives of the peasants in the Commune by the collective. During the summer and autumn of 1958 the working day in most communes was at least twelve hours a day, and during the harvest could have been anything between sixteen and eighteen hours a day. Meals, except for breakfast, were taken in communal mess-halls, children and babies were sent to kindergartens and nurseries for the whole of the working week, and the old were put in old people's homes. The communes were divided into Production Brigades (*Shêng-ch'an ta-tui*). They conformed to the former HSCs, usually with 120 to 150 households, and they received their instructions from the commune management. They enjoyed a certain independence in running the mess-halls and organizing cultivation. The brigades were further divided into production teams (*Shêng-ch'an hsiao-tui*) containing ten to fifteen families.

Of particular significance for the structure of the Commune was the system of 'production guarantees' through which the relationships between the large rural collectives and the State organization for grain procurement were regulated. According to this, the Commune guaranteed before every harvest to produce an expected target. If output was in fact less than expected, the communes had to reduce the supplies to their own members in order to ensure the guaranteed delivery target. This system automatically made the Commune management responsible for the planning of agricultural production. Mao and his collaborators considered that the People's

Communes were the basic units for the 'Transition to Communism'. For this reason these collectives experimented with systems of remunerative distribution 'to each according to his need', whereby roughly 70% of wages were paid in kind and 30% in cash 'according to productivity'.[6]

At first, the movement to establish People's Communes met with considerable success. By the middle of November 1958 the Party leadership were able to announce the merging of 99% of the rural population into 26,578 People's Communes, each with an average of 4,637 households.[7] However, after September 1958 imperfect planning on a large scale, an over-estimation of the rural workforce, and the widespread passive resistance of peasants caused considerable problems. The movement threatened to collapse.[8] This fact led the Party leadership to its first retreat at the 6th Plenum of the 8th CC held in Wuhan during December 1958. A 'Resolution on some problems of the People's Communes'[9] guaranteed 'for all time' that the peasants could own houses, gardens and domestic animals as private property. Work in the Commune should be limited to eight hours a day, and political education should not exceed two hours a day—the resolution of the CC even spoke of a 'guarantee' of eight hours' sleep and four free hours. Most wage payments were now to be paid in cash once again; the use of kindergartens, nurseries and mess-halls was to be optional for the peasants of the commune; and it was prohibited for cadres to destroy stoves and kitchen utensils in order to force peasants into the collective. With these warnings the Party leadership started the policies of 're-adjustment' which were to fundamentally alter Mao's summer 1958 concept during the following three years.

The 7th Plenum of the 8th Central Committee in April 1959 confirmed a resolution which was to be of decisive importance for the future of Chinese agricultural policy. It was a resolution originally agreed at the beginning of the year by an enlarged meeting of the Politburo, according to which the property of the People's Communes—i.e. the arable land, local industries, equipment, cattle and crops—was to be distributed at three different levels: commune, production brigade and production team. However, the arable land, factories, and crops were initially to remain with the communes. Apart from that, the profit-sharing bonuses for the members of the collective, which had been discontinued in the summer of 1958, were now reintroduced. Additionally, the guarantee given in December 1958 about privately-owned houses and gardens was clarified.[10] The resolutions of the 8th Plenum of the 8th CC, held in August 1959 at Lushan, went even further than this.[11] The military-type organization of the workforce, which had been established during the summer of 1958, was now discontinued. The authority of the communes was limited to include only the administration of schools, factories, transport, equipment and crops. In future they were only to supervise the production brigades' cultivation, although they retained the right to involve the members of these brigades, to a limited extent, in public works. The emphasis was now shifting to the brigade, i.e. to the level of the former Higher Stage Collectives, to whom all landed property was transferred, and whose rights of ownership over agricultural equipment and cattle were also now confirmed. Furthermore, the brigades were given the right to handle their own accounts, and therewith the right over the distribution of profits. Reforming resolutions made by a meeting of the Politburo in November 1960 and at the 9th Plenum of the 8th CC in January 1961—certainly without the Chairman's participation and even perhaps despite his resistance—finally led to such measures, which remoulded the system of the People's Commune so thoroughly, that it ended up far from resembling the concept of 1958. Arable land, cattle, equipment, engineering plants, workshops and crops were now to become the property of the smallest units, the production teams. The brigades retained the authority over primary schools, nurseries and local industry. They initially also handed over the 'production guarantee' and retained temporarily the responsibility for production plans and for the payments of salaries and distribution of profits. The People's Communes only retained control over public works, security services and secondary schools, as well as the somewhat ambiguously-worded authority to see to the 'coordination of the brigades'.[12] Already by the autumn of 1960 the mess-halls were only serving one meal a day, and in February 1961 their services were required by no more than one-third of commune members.[13] During 1961 many communes closed their old people's homes and the number of kindergartens and nurseries was reduced dramatically. The principle of compensation generally attributed to Communist societies of 'each according to his need!' now disappeared entirely, and the time devoted to political education was reduced from two hours a day to three to four hours a week. Of particular importance was a change in the system (only made public by the Chinese media in 1964) involving a permanent reduction in the size of the ural production units, and in particular of the People's Communes and production teams. As a result, the number of communes rose from 24,000 in 1959 to 74,000 at the beginning of 1962, that of production brigades from 500,000 to more than 700,000, and that of production teams from 3 to 7 million.[14] These communes (in 1962) had very little in common with the original type. The nature of property and production corresponded once again to the situation in the Higher Stage Collectives of 1957. The People's Commune movement was thereby *de facto* liquidated.

However, the revision of the Maoist measures of 1958 went even further. In the spring of 1961 the Party had begun in some places to concede the cultivation of small pieces of private land to the Commune peasants, their size fluctuating between 20 and 50 square metres per working family member.[15] In the summer of 1962 these measures spread all over the country. There was an 'upsurge of individual production'. Even though the share of private land in the total of arable land only amounted to approximately 5-7%, the peasants nonetheless managed to cultivate more than 30% of all grain production on these private holdings in 1962.[16] At the same time, commune members were encouraged to pursue private livestock raising, in particular of pigs. In the 'free markets' the produce of private holdings and of private livestock raising could be sold at prices that depended on supply and demand. Equally important was the transfer of production guarantees in the spring of 1962 from the brigades to the production teams, units of at most fifteen families to whom the responsibility for the planning and implementation of agricultural production was now given.

The opponents of the Maoist concept around Liu Shao-ch'i and Teng Hsiao-p'ing were not satisfied with these correctives. They prepared a resolution for the 10th Plenum of the 8th Central Committee in September 1962 under the slogan of 'Three Freedoms, one Guarantee' (*San-tzu i-pao*). This aimed at the enlargement of the private plots for the peasants, an increase in private livestock holdings, open market operations and, in particular, the transfer of production guarantees to the individual peasant household. This would have meant not only the liquidation of the policy of the 'Three Red Banners'—which had in fact already taken place—but also the death sentence for the rural collective economy as practised since 1955. However, at the 10th Plenum Mao managed to obtain a majority in the leadership against these proposals of Liu and Teng.[17] With the introduction of the 'Socialist Education Movement'[18] he attempted to reverse these trends. He failed in this attempt, however, due to the passive resistance of the civilian Party *apparat*, whose leaders turned the new movement into a campaign in the course of which the policy of readjustment was not reversed. Instead, those cadres who had been active in the establishment of the People's Communes in 1958 became the target of purges in this new campaign.

Without a doubt it was the strengthening of the position of the collective against the individual peasant (the effective limitation of private land holdings, private livestock raising and private part-time earnings by the peasants) and the transfer of property and authority rights from the production teams to the brigades and from them to the communes that made up the programme of the Cultural Revolutionary Left and started off their counter-attack against the anti-Maoist majority in the Cultural Revolution. However, the crisis from 1966 to 1969, and in particular the collapse of the civilian party *apparat* in 1967, had precisely the opposite effect. Wherever the State grain procurement agencies and the administration of the communes was no longer functioning (in effect due to the conflicts between rival factions), the peasants resorted to individual production and to the free trading of their production. As a result, the system of production suggested by Liu and Teng for implementation from above after September 1962 became permanent in many villages. However, the consolidation of the distribution of power during 1968-9 finally gave Lin Piao and his collaborators the opportunity to initiate a return to the ideas of 1958 in agricultural social policy.

An important vehicle for this attempt was the movement, 'In Agriculture, learn from Tachai' (*Nung-yeh hsüeh Tachai*),[19] introduced in the spring of 1970. Tachai is a village and at the same time an agricultural production brigade in the mountainous county of Hsiyang in the North China province of Shansi.[20] Under the leadership of the Party secretary of the brigade, Ch'en Yung-kuei,[21] in the early 1960s its members had endeavoured to direct the reconstruction of their village strictly according to the Maoist development concept of 1958. At its centre was the idea of independence both from investment by State organs and of help from the administratively superior People's Commune. In fact the Tachai Brigade seems to have achieved some remarkable successes with this developmental strategy, because it very quickly aroused the interest of the leadership organs of the Party. As early as February 1960 the then First Secretary of the Shansi CCP Provincial Committee, T'ao Lu-chia, pointed out the experiences of the Tachai Brigade, and in March 1963 a conference of representatives of People's Communes and production brigades in Shansi studied the achievements of this brigade for several days. When in August 1963 a large part of Tachai was destroyed by a flood, the brigade offically waived all ofers of material help from the State and carried out its reconstruction 'through its own efforts', as it became known in the media.[22] This event was mentioned by T'ao Lu-chia in November 1965 in an article in *Red Flag*, and the brigade was thereby promoted as an example for the country as a whole.[23] As a result, even at this time, a movement started in which the villages of China were called upon to 'Learn from Tachai'. However, this campaign came to nothing and was in fact interrupted when at the turn of 1966-7 the troubles of the Cultural Revolution had enveloped even the Chinese rural communities. In the early 1960s, some doubts had developed within the Party as to the reliability of the reports about its successes which the brigade had published. Thus the Party Secretary in Hsiyang county where Tachai is located pointed out that in 1961 the brigade had provided false figures when giving an account of its grain output: it had in fact achieved a production of 115 kg. *per capita* in that year and not, as had been reported, 280 kg.[24] The leadership of the civilian Party *apparat* frequently questioned the claim made by Tachai that its members had achieved their success without any help from the State. There was in fact some evidence that a model had been deliberately constructed in Tachai with outside help before the Cultural Revolution. Nonetheless, this model had already become extremely significant, not least because it involved Tachai which was a production brigade and not a People's Commune. From this one can conclude that even that faction in the Party leadership which, during the years before the Cultural Revolution, advocated the Maoist development concept of 1958, had come meanwhile to see the production brigade as the most important agricultural unit, while the People's Commune was only of secondary importance.

In 1970 Lin Piao and his followers re-started the movement to 'Learn from Tachai'. Only some parts of this campaign had anything in common with that of the early 1960s. General Lung Shu-chin, the Commander of Sinkiang Military Region, launched this campaign in a speech to representatives of activist groups on 1 February 1970, when he called upon them to learn from the 'Tachai System' whereby the distribution of wages and bonuses was clearly to follow criteria of political loyalty.[25] Four ideas in particular were emphasized during the course of this campaign. First, Tachai was now to be the model for the principle, developed by Lin Piao, that politics was to take supremacy over all other considerations and areas of operations. Secondly, the important role of a correct ideological standpoint for the individual and the collective was particularly emphasized. Only in third place was the idea which in the early 1960s had determined Tachai's model character—the independence of the production unit from sources of State investment, and its development from its own resources. Finally, in fourth place, was the point that the masses were to be constantly reminded during the campaign that the nation had to develop through 'bitter struggle' (*K'u-chan*), and that in the interests of a better life for future generations they had to make heavy personal sacrifices.[26]

During the implementation of the Tachai-movement in 1970, the distribution of wages and bonuses according to estimates of the peasants' political behaviour became increasingly predominant. To give only one example among many, in Tungkuan district (Kuangtung) this was the first criterion of remuneration, followed by the individual's ability to work and his productivity.[27] In this way the essential content of the campaign was determined—it aimed, above all else, at the mobilization of the rural population for ideologically and politically correct behaviour.

However, the direction of the new socio-political offensive initiated in the Chinese villages by the group around Lin Piao was not only visible in the Tachai movement. Associated with these efforts were others which aimed at obstructing the peasants' feelings of private ownership towards the plots of land which had been given to them for private cultivation. Under the slogan of 'Equal distribution first, exchange second' (*I-p'ing êrh-tiao*), an attempt was made, first, to distribute the land among the peasants equally according to size and quality, and then to change it around between the households annually, regardless of the output of the land in question.[28] At least as important as this was the trend to place the emphasis in agricultural ownership on higher-level units than the production teams. At the end of January 1970 an article in *Red Flag* indicated that the production teams would soon lose their independence in decision-making once again:

The system of collective property in the People's Communes must progress from the lower to the higher levels, and we even more urgently need to develop from collective property to that of the whole nation.[29]

Finally it was strongly emphasized in a number of provinces that the peasants had delivered a greatly increased quantity of grain to the State procurement agencies. In particular the spring harvest of 1970 yielded a higher output in many parts of the country than in the previous twelve years. At this the peasants in the production teams seemed to think that they could retain more for their use since the delivery target would remain the same. On the other hand, the State Procurement Agencies—particularly those with the support of provincial leaderships who were on good terms with Lin Piao—wanted to acquire the production surpluses and not allow them to be used for increases in the rations which the peasants retained. In Kuangtung this ration was reduced by 20% and the purchase price of 2 cwt. of rice fell from 19·60 Yüan JMP to 17·60 Yüan JMP.

The peasants responded in many villages by 'going slow' during the harvest.[30] In Shensi the authorities reproached the peasants 'for being infected by the theory that "one only cultivates the land in order to have enough to eat" '.[31] The good harvest of 1970 also caused 'bourgeois tendencies' in the province of Hunan. Here the authorities were extremely critical that 'collective resources' had been used 'to celebrate a harvest festival' and that the peasants had even gone so far as 'to think about new houses and furniture, weddings and birthday parties'.[32]

It was not only in their efforts to extract higher procurement targets from the peasants that the leadership met resistance. In the autumn and winter of 1970-1 there were increasing reports that the Tachai movement had run up against scepticism and indifference in many villages. Hainan Island broadcasting station praised Tachai as a model for the whole country, but added: 'We must vigorously confront the right-wing mentality of people who say: we are poor. It will take time to learn from Tachai. One just cannot expect people to leap straight into the sky.'[33]

In the Canton area there was a warning of the 'mentality of stagnation, of pessimism and of the attitude that one cannot achieve anything of significance', but also of a 'false pride and self-satisfaction' which could 'prevent people really learning from the Tachai example'.[34] Similar behaviour was reported from Shensi, Hupei, Kuangsi, Anhui, Yünnan and Chekiang.[35]

At the end of the summer of 1971 the media of Hunan and Fukien provinces even reported open and active resistance by the peasantry to the attempts of the local Party organs to implement principles of the Tachai movement in the villages.[36]

The obviously widespread opposition to Lin Piao's offensive in the villages was a clarion call in August 1970 for those regional commanders who regarded the attempt to return to Mao's social policy of 1958 as a threat to the policy of consolidation which had been introduced after the Cultural Revolution. The experiences of the economic crisis of 1960-2 taught them that to implement the mobilizatory concept of development in agriculture could result in defective planning and resistance from the peasants. On the contrary, they regarded the stability of the social and economic basis as much more important for the success of their policy of security, in the interest of which they were prepared to work towards a reduction of leadership demands on the population. The first evidence that the situation was being looked at differently from the view of Lin Piao, and that consequently people in the provinces were coming to conclusions which ran counter to the policy of the Central military, came from the province of Kuangtung. In the middle of August 1970 a telephone conference of local Revolutionary Committees emphasized Lin's line that 'leadership in the villages should be strengthened during the Autumn Harvest'; however, a rider was added clearly differentiating between it and Lin's policy:

We must regulate the relationship between the State, the collective and the individual correctly. This is why we have to establish the principle of 'each according to his labour', so that the peasants are in the position to increase their income from surplus production in normal harvest years.[37]

A few days later the provincial leadership in Kuangtung gave a warning:

If we merely consider the interests of the State and the collective and attach too little weight to the interests of the individual, then we will hinder the efforts to bring the socialist activity of the masses to a new climax.[38]

However, other provinces still supported Lin Piao's policy. In stark contrast to the points of view expressed in Kuangtung, the leadership of Honan province declared that 'in spite of the opposite point of view of some comrades', there could be no doubt that 'individual interests and partial interests had to be subordinate to the general interest'.[39] However, by as early as the end of September 1970 even Shensi had joined the criticism from Kuangtung. The opposition had begun to take shape.[40]

A few weeks later it was to find its spokesmen from within the circle of the Politburo. The Commander of Nanking Military Region and Chairman of Kiangsu Revolutionary Committee, General Hsü Shih-yu, threw down the gauntlet to Mao's appointed successor when, at a working conference of leading Party members in Nanking, he gave a speech which was twice broadcast verbatim from Kiangsu, where he said:

We must combine revolutionary enthusiasm with a practical and scientific attitude. We have to avoid blind passion and under all circumstances be considerate of the suffering of the masses.[41]

Hsü's intervention encouraged the leadership in the Kuangsi Autonomous Region to turn with equal frankness against the policy of Lin and his followers at the Centre. The Chairman of the Kuangsi Revolutionary Committee, General Wei Kuo-ch'ing—who, like Hsü, had come from the 3rd Field Army—made use of a decision of his Revolutionary Committee to introduce the Tachai movement in order to stress his rejection of political criteria for the remuneration of commune members. In this resolution it was pointed out that agricultural policy had to be protected against 'influences of the Right *and the Left*'. Payments to the peasants should depend only on their labour: any other policy of remuneration would betray 'an egalitarian deviation'. The procurement agencies should not be allowed to hold too much in reserve in good harvest years, and to leave too little for the peasants' own consumption. The cultivation of private landholdings and the individual part-time earnings of the rural population had to be safeguarded. The whole country may have to 'learn from Tachai'; however, it was essential that production teams were allowed to remain flexible to accord with local circumstances. The production teams were under no circumstances to be called upon by the brigades or communes 'to carry out public works without payment'.[42] In December 1970 the provincial leadership in Fukien also decided to confirm peasants' private holdings of land and to encourage part-time earnings for individual consumption.[43]

The battle-lines in the confrontation had become clearly defined. Lin Piao's efforts had aroused the resistance of some provincial leaders, who now turned openly against the policies of the Central military. It seems that opposition from some of the regional commanders had been encouraged by the purges of Li Hsüeh-fêng and General Cheng Wei-shan and by the weakening of Lin's position of power through the removal of the 38th Army Corps from Peking.[44] In February 1971, for the first time, they received some support at the Centre. An editorial in the *JMJP*, contrary to all Lin Piao's efforts during the previous year, officially sanctioned the system of 'property at three levels, with the production team as the foundation' (*San-chi so-yu, tui wei chi-ch'u*); it pointed out that wages and bonuses were to be distributed according to labour.[45] This turn of events prompted Hsü Shih-yu to disregard all his previous considerations and proceed to a direct attack on Lin and on the Maoist concept of development that he represented. In a speech to activists, which was broadcast by the Kiangsu provincial broadcasting station on 27 February, he stated:

It is not necessary to make the rich and the poor equal in order to make a revolution ... There are people who condemn private holdings and part-time earnings [of individual peasants] as hangovers of capitalism, although such practices are expressedly accepted by Party policy. This type of thinking may be Leftist in appearance, but its content is Right-wing. Such people are of the opinion that the more Leftist they are, the better. They are not aware of the fact that they are becoming detached from reality. In their activities, they can be taken advantage of by class traitors ... Under no circumstances in future should there be the desire to accumulate the resources of the collective too quickly and, hence, to the detriment of living standards. Furthermore, we have to make it perfectly clear that the peasants have the right to raise chickens and ducks for their own consumption![46]

Hsü seems to have felt empowered to use such harsh language by the fact that at approximately the same time a decision of fundamental importance had been taken at the Centre which signalled the end of the socio-political offensive in the Chinese villages. The details of this decision are still unknown to this day; outside China there are no Party documents which would reveal its content in any great detail. However, as there had not been a Plenum of the Central Committee and the next publicly-known large conference of the leadership only took place in April 1971,[47] we have to assume that in the last days of February or March a session of the Politburo made the decisions concerning agricultural policy which, in the following weeks, were publicized in the media of the People's Republic of China. After the middle of March, a new 'rural economic policy' (*Nung-ts'un ching-chi cheng-ts'ê*) was mentioned in the course of which many of the limitations that had been set in 1969 and 1970 on the individual peasants' initiative were lifted.

On 21 March 1971 the *JMJP* published a report of a district Party Committee in the province of Anhui, which thoroughly explained the new policy. This article followed the technique normally used in China to explain a change in the leadership's ideas and the new purpose of a continuing campaign which was started earlier with completely different aims. Thus it was initially said that the 'rural economic policy' was based on the movement to 'Learn from Tachai'. Apart from this remark, the article stressed to a considerable extent the agricultural concepts of the 'Readjustment'-phase of the early 1960s, which had been represented in particular by Hsü Shih-yu since the autumn of 1970. The importance of private land and part-time work for the peasants was emphasized, and it was unequivocally stated that the brigades and communes could not draw workforces from the production teams without the approval of 'higher-ranking officials'—which presumably referred to the county administration. Basically it was stated that 'one should not behave in an extreme manner' and in any case 'not declare the ideology to be absolute'. The article stressed the duty of Party cadres to resist all plans for a change in the property structure of agriculture which would work to the disadvantage of the production teams:

There are leading cadres who do not take a definite standpoint when people come asking for a change in the system of property relationships. They know exactly that these proposals are not in line with the [Party] policy. This policy says that property must be divided between three levels with the production team as the foundation. But these men are paralysed from fear. They neither nod nor shake their heads in a clear Yes or No.[48]

The change in the Party's line on social policy in China's villages was further clarified at the end of March 1971, when the *JMJP* printed over a period of five days an extensive report of events from a model production brigade in Chinghsien Commune, Chiangshan county, Chekiang province. This report emphasized the role of the production teams. While it stressed the importance of the collective economy, it put a high value at the same time on the private plots of land, private livestock raising and part-time working of the peasants as an essential supplement to the production of the collectives. Particularly remarkable was the determination with which this report stated that the situation in the production brigades varied greatly from place to place, and that consequently the experience of Tachai could only be adopted 'according to local conditions'.[49]

From now on more and more provinces followed the change sanctioned by the Centre, which basically resulted in a considerable reduction of the leadership's demands on the masses. Already at the beginning of April, Fukien province had changed its attitude with the publication of an editorial in the provincial paper, which differed little in its biting criticism of the attempt to implement the policies of 1958 from Hsü Shih-yu's point of view.[50] But this was not enough! In the course of the spring and summer of 1971, the tendency for some People's Communes to spread exaggerated reports of success came under attack.[51] Thus the *JMJP* demanded in April 'honesty and realism' in reports on the development of small-scale industry in the communes,[52] after the central organ of the CCP had two days earlier praised 'the new High Tide of industrial production'.[53] In July, Fukien province stressed the theme of sobriety and honesty in such reports, and a little later it demanded that all exaggeration should be completely avoided.[54] During August most of the provinces followed this example. Even the Hunan Party leadership, which on 27 July was still of the opinion that China was in 'a Great Flying Leap',[55] turned a few days later towards a demand for a realistic view of production management and a similarly realistic reporting of production.[56]

Ever since the beginning of July 1971 the proponents of the pragmatic and development-oriented course in agricultural policy had begun to reach beyond their criticism of the attitudes represented by Lin Piao, and to go as far as to question the Maoist concept of 1958 itself. Here the campaign against Ch'en Po-ta, who had played a decisive role in the formulation of Mao's ideas in the spring and summer of 1958, served a useful purpose. In the beginning the attacks were carefully formulated, and straightforward denunciation of the policy of the 'Three Red Banners' was carefully avoided.[57] However, on 15 August 1971 the *JMJP* chose to use more direct language. By holding Ch'en alone responsible for the 'mistakes' made in the enforcement of the People's Commune movement, the paper (that is the majority of the Central Party leadership) turned against Mao himself:

In the summer of 1958 the Pseudo-Marxist political swindler like Liu Shao-ch'i deceived the Chairman and madly excited the villages in a Pseudo-Marxist boom ... As a result, a tyranny developed which brought much suffering to the masses.[58]

This attack had to be understood in China as a criticism of the Chairman. It showed, more clearly than on any previous occasion, that Lin Piao's attempt to return—in terms of social policy in the villages—to the Maoist concept of development had failed, due to the resistance of the majority of regional commanders and of the civilian administration. In the course of the conflict which had resulted from this attempt, the nucleus of the anti-Lin coalition had solidified. The decision over the direction of the rural economic policy anticipated that over Lin's own personal fate. After this the fall of Mao's appointed successor became unavoidable.

REFERENCES

1. In particular, the majority of Nationalist Chinese observers of Chinese politics.

2. See pp. 84 ff.

3. See pp. 133 f.

4. See, *inter alia*, Schurmann, op. cit., pp. 442-64; Tang/Maloney, op. cit., pp. 341-53; Yang Mo-wen, 'Socialist Transformation of Agriculture in Communist China', in URI, *Communist China 1949-1959*, Hong Kong, 1961, Vol. I, pp. 152-76; Werner Klatt (ed.), *The Chinese Model*, Hong Kong, 1965, pp. 99 ff.; Kenneth R. Walker, 'Collectivization in Retrospect: the "Socialist High Tide" of Autumn 1955-Spring 1956', in *CQ*, No. 26, April-June 1966, pp. 1-43; Thomas P. Bernstein, 'Leadership and Mass Mobilization in the Chinese and Soviet Collectivization Campaigns of 1929-30 and 1955-56: a Comparison', in *CQ*, 31, July-September 1967, pp. 1-47; *CNA*, No. 7, 9 October 1953 and *CNA*, No. 23, 12 February 1954.

5. See footnote 1, Chapter 1.

6. *Nung-ts'un kung-tso t'ung-hsün* (Agricultural Work Bulletin), Peking, No. 12, 1958; *Ching-chi yen-chiu* (Economic Studies), Peking, No. 12, 1958; *JMJP*, 30 August and 7 October 1958.

7. *JMJP*, 15 November 1958.

8. See Domes, *Internal Politics*, op. cit., pp. 101 ff.

9. *JMJP*, 18 and 29 December 1958. Compare *CNA*, No. 258, 2 January 1959.

10. *JMJP*, 8 April, 28 and 29 August 1959. See Schurmann, op. cit., p. 484, who has wrongly dated the introduction of the distribution of property at three levels at the end of August 1959.

11. *JMJP*, 26 August 1959.

12. *JMJP*, 20 and 25 November 1960 and 24 January 1961; *Jen-min shou-ts'ê 1961* (People's Handbook 1961), Peking, 1961, p. 11. See Cheng, op. cit., p. 137; Schurmann, op. cit., pp. 491 ff.; Domes, *Internal Politics*, op. cit., p. 118.

13. *WHP*, Shanghai, 17 February 1961.

14. *TKP*, 17 and 24 September 1964.

15. *TKP*, 10 April 1961.

16. *Inter alia*, Wang Hung-shih (Secretary of the Lienchiang CCP District Committee, Fukien), 'Carry out the resolutions of the 10th Plenum of the 8th CC of the CCP on the consolidation of Rural People's Communes and the development of agricultural production!' Text of a

speech in *Fan-kung yu-chi-tui t'u-chi Lienchiang lu-huo fei-fang wên-chien hui-pien* (Collected Documents of the Rebels, obtained by an anti-Communist Commando exercise in Lienchiang), 42 Documents ed. by the Republic of China's Defence Ministry, T'aipei, 1964.

17. *Jen-min shou-ts'ê 1963* (People's Handbook 1963), Peking, 1963, p. 1.

18. See p. 9.

19. Compare *CNA*, No. 827, 8 January 1971.

20. A detailed report of a visit to Tachai together with the official Chinese version is in Klaus Mehnert, *China nach dem Sturm*, Stuttgart, 1971, pp. 47–65.

21. On Ch'en Yung-kuei, see *CNA*, No. 957, 19 April 1974.

22. *CNA*, No. 827, loc. cit.

23. *HC*, No. 11, 1965.

24. *JMJP*, 6 August 1967.

25. Radio Sinkiang, 1 February 1970.

26. *JMJP*, 25 August and 23 September 1970.

27. Radio Canton, 29 December 1970.

28. Radio Amoy, 5 November 1970.

29. *HC*, No. 2, 1970.

30. See footnote 4 to Chapter 5.

31. Radio Shensi, 26 July 1970.

32. Radio Hunan, 5 August 1970.

33. Radio Haik'ou, 23 November 1970.

34. Radio Canton, 14 January 1971.

35. Radio Shensi, 22 September 1970; Radio Hupei, 12 October 1970; Radio Kuangsi, 16 November 1970; Radio Anhui, 17 November 1970; Radio Yünnan, 26 November 1970; Radio Chekiang, 19 December 1970.

36. Radio Hunan, 12 August and 4 September 1971 and Radio Fukien, 4 September 1971.

37. Radio Kuangtung, 1 Programme, 15 August 1970.

38. Ibid., 19 August 1970.

39. Radio Hunan, 19 August 1970.

40. Radio Shensi, 28 September 1970.

41. Radio Kiangsu, 28 October and 5 November 1970.

42. Radio Kuangsi, 22 November 1970.

43. Radio Fukien, 10 December 1970.

44. See p. 97.

45. *JMJP*, 18 February 1971.

46. Radio Kiangsu, 27 February 1971.

47. See pp. 129 ff.

48. *JMJP*, 21 March 1971. See also *CNA*, No. 839, 23 April 1971.

49. *JMJP*, 25 to 29 March 1971. See *CNA*, No. 847, 9 July 1971.

50. Radio Fukien, 2 April 1971.

51. See *CNA*, No. 853, 3 September 1971.

52. *JMJP*, 22 April 1971.

53. *JMJP*, 20 April 1971.

54. Radio Fukien, 24 July and 17 August 1971.

55. Radio Hunan, 27 July 1971.

56. Ibid., 31 July and 17 August 1971.

57. *Inter alia: JMJP*, 6 July 1971 and Radio Yünnan, 21 July 1971.
58. *JMJP*, 15 August 1971.

8. The End of the Successor

The first chapter of the Party Constitution of the CCP, passed by the 9th Party Congress on 14 April 1969, stated:

Comrade Lin Piao has consistently held high the great red banner of Mao Tse-tung's Thought and he has most loyally and resolutely carried out and defended Comrade Mao Tse-tung's proletarian revolutionary line. Comrade Lin Piao is Comrade Mao Tse-tung's closest comrade-in-arms and successor.[1]

Not quite four-and-a-half years later, on 29 August 1973, the communiqué of the 10th Party Congress of the CCP reported:

The congress indignantly denounced the Lin Piao anti-Party clique for its crimes. All the delegates firmly supported this resolution of the Central Committee of the Communist Party of China: Expel Lin Piao, the bourgeois careerist, conspirator, counter-revolutionary double-dealer, renegade and traitor from the Party once and for all![2]

The reputation of the second man in the PRC's leadership can indeed be ephemeral. However, the transformation of Lin in the Party's judgement did not take as long as four-and-a-half years. Instead it was condensed into a period of little more than two months during the autumn of 1971.

As late as 12 September 1971, the day of Lin Piao's fall—also perhaps the day of his death, the *People's Daily* wrote:

Comrade Lin Piao has at all times held high the great red banner of Mao Tse-tung Thought. He has at all times defended Chairman Mao's proletarian revolutionary lines and put it into practice, and he has always been a shining example to the whole Party, to the Army, and to the people of the whole country![3]

Before seven weeks had passed, this 'shining example'—who was not mentioned again by name in the Chinese media until his denunciation by the 10th Party Congress—had become, like Ch'en Po-ta, a 'Pseudo-Marxist political swindler like Liu Shao-ch'i', an 'Army-splitter like Chang Kuo-t'ao' and a 'conspirator, opportunist, renegade and traitor'.[4] One week later he was even referred to as 'dog-shit, indigestible to human society'.[5]

On 18 November 1971 the Garrison Commander of Hangchou, in Chekiang, made the following statement about Lin and his collaborators:

They pretended to have mastered Marxism-Leninism and the Thought of Mao Tse-tung, but at the same time they had a superior attitude towards the masses. This took the form of *Left-extremism*, which in fact established a system of slavery.... They pretended to be prophets and geniuses. This was nothing but reactionary voluntarism, and it greatly exaggerated the subjective power of the individual. They denied ... that thoughts are determined by the material environment, and for them thoughts took the place of the material environment. At work, they replaced labour by politics and production by revolution. They were empty-headed politicians, who denied the unity of politics and economics, and of politics and technology.... They substituted emotions for politics.[6]

These quotations give an impression of how great an impact Lin's fall must have made on the political scene in China generally, and on the political system of the country in particular. Indeed the Lin Piao crisis came as a total surprise to the mass of the population. The decisions which led to the fall of the Lin Piao group were taken behind closed doors—contrary to the fundamental Maoist principle that political development is determined by the masses, and doubtless contrary also to the romantic ideas held by some Western observers about mass participation in the political decision-making process in China.[7] The oft-berated masses knew nothing of these decisions for more than a month. After the political crisis of the Cultural Revolution, which had been marked by street demonstrations and unrest, the crisis that followed had much more in common with an old-fashioned palace revolution.

Even so, both the people of China and foreign observers of Chinese politics became aware of some astonishing events during and after the summer of 1971. Lin Piao appeared in public for the last time on the occasion of the visit of the Romanian Head of Party and State, Nicolai Ceausescu, on 3 June 1971.[8] Many observers were surprised that the fiftieth Anniversary celebration of the Foundation of the CCP on 1 July 1971 was marked only by a joint leading article in the People's Daily, the Liberation Army Daily and Red Flag and without any mass rallies or mass demonstrations. On 2 September in Hong Kong an illuminated sign bearing the slogan (Which had first been used by Lin Piao) 'Long live the invincible Thought of Mao Tse-tung!' was removed from the Bank of China's building, and replaced by the words 'Long Live Chairman Mao'.[9]

After 10 September the Chief of the General Staff of the PLA, Huang Yung-sheng; the Commander of the PLA Air Force, Wu Fa-hsien; and the Political Commissar of the PLA Navy, Li Tso-p'eng, no longer appeared in public. The Director of the General Logistics Department, Ch'iu Hui-tso, was seen for the last time on 24 September.[10] Street papers in Hong Kong, which are noted for their unreliability, reported on 13 September that the Air Force had been grounded throughout China.[11] On 23 September it was reported from Tokyo that all leave had been cancelled for the PLA.[12]

Speculation about a crisis in China increased when, on 30 September, the news agency of the Mongolian People's Republic reported that on the night of 12–13 September a Chinese Trident had penetrated Mongolian airspace and crashed near the village of Undur Khan. All the people on board were reported to have been killed in the crash.[13]

Shortly before this the Ministry of Foreign Affairs in Peking had informed the foreign embassies that, for the first time since the foundation of the PRC in 1949, there would be no mass rally in front of the T'ien-an-mên (Gate of Heaven) on National Day (1 October).[14] In place of the traditional eve-of-holiday banquet there was only to be a reception this year. Hong Kong China-watchers reported that since the middle of September stereotyped references which had been made ever since 1968 to the 'Thought of Mao Tse-tung' were no longer given first place, and in some cases had stopped altogether, in the news reports of meetings and conferences broadcast by the provincial radio stations.

In spite of this evidence, it was not at all easy to conclude that the only Vice-Chairman of the Central Committee of CCP and Mao Tse-tung's appointed successor had in fact actually fallen. On 12 September *JMJP* reported the delayed publication of an album commemorating the fiftieth anniversary of the CCP's foundation with fifty pictures of Mao, eight of which showed him side by side with Lin Piao.[15] On 30 September, the Fukien provincial broadcasting station also mentioned this album.[16] The newspaper of the PLA (on 13 September)[17] and the Kiangsi broadcasting station (on 16 September)[18] both still quoted Lin Piao's directives. The broadcasting station of Sinkiang Autonomous Region reported on 18 September that a combined July–August edition of *Jen-min hua-pao* (China Pictorial) and the *Chieh-fang-chün hua-pao* (Liberation Army Pictorial) had been received in Urumchi, in which it was stated that 'Vice-Chairman Lin was a shining example for the whole of the Army, the Party, and the people of the country'. The report did not fail to refer to both Mao's and Lin Piao's 'outstanding good health'.[19] The term 'shining example' was again applied to Lin by the Hupei broadcasting station on 3 October,[20] and the Tibet broadcasting station mentioned his name in a positive fashion for the last time on 8 October.[21] Nonetheless, at the end of October the English-language version of the Chinese illustrated magazine *China Pictorial* published thirteen pictures of Lin in a series of photographs of the full and alternate members of the Politburo, which omitted only Ch'en Po-ta's and Li Hsüeh-fêng's pictures. During the last week of October this magazine was still being sold in Hong Kong's Communist bookshop, and only after 7 November was it no longer available although, as we now know, the Central Postal Administration had on 30 October ordered that no more copies were to be released.[22]

However, after the middle of September signs that Lin Piao's position might be somewhat precarious increased in Chinese publications. On 13 September Kiangsi province referred to a new campaign, in which the text of *The Internationale* and a song praising the '3-8 work style' composed by Mao were to be learned by the PLA and the people. Kuangsi and Chekiang followed shortly after, and the Central media took up this theme after 30 September.[23] Both songs replaced the Cultural Revolutionary *The East is Red!* and the one written by Lin Piao, *Sailing the seas depends on the helmsman*, which would have been 'Top of the Pops' over the last five years if China had a 'hit-parade'. In a leading article about the achievements of the armed forces during 1971 (published on 30 September) and a review of night fighting (published on 9 October) in the PLA newspaper—both of which would normally have been associated with the name of the Defence Minister—Lin Piao was not mentioned.[24] His words 'the living study and application of Mao Tse-tung Thought', as well as 'Four-good, five-good', disapeared from the newspapers and radio broadcasts.[25]

It was more than a month after 12 September 1971 that the media began to launch veiled attacks on Lin. Since 1969 Mao Tse-tung's Kut'ien Resolution of 1929, dealing with political work in the army, had always been mentioned in tandem with the 1960 resolution of the Military Committee of the Central Committee of the CCP which had been drafted by Lin Piao. For the first time, on 16 October the leadership of Kuangsi Autonomous Region mentioned the Kut'ien Resolution without at the same time referring to the 1960 document, and this practice was soon followed by Yünnan and Ssuch'uan Provinces.[27] On 30 October Hunan and Ssuch'uan spoke of 'intriguers, opportunists, political swindlers, renegades and traitors' who had 'seized power'. At the same time they emphasized that the PLA was not only 'led' *(ling-tao)*, but also 'directed' *(Chih-chieh chih-hui)* by Mao—a term which had previously been reserved for Lin Piao.[28] Chekiang province took up this theme on 2 November.[29]

At the beginning of November, observers positively identified Lin Piao as the target of a massive denunciation campaign, which had started in China's press and broadcasts. On the 19 August the *JMJP* had quoted a remark of Lin's in which he had described Mao as a 'genius'[30]—a term previously used by Ch'en Po-ta in a discussion preceding the 2nd Plenum of the 9th Central Committee in August 1971.[31] Tibet's and Chekiang's broadcasting stations both now vigorously opposed the 'Theory of Genius' *(T'ien-ts'ai-lun)*. On 9 November Anhui was even plainer:

The small clique of class enemies considered themselves and others to be 'geniuses' and great personalities. They won't escape their own self-destruction![33]

The identification of Lin Piao as the new 'political swindler like Liu Shao-ch'i' was furthered by a broadcast from Sinkiang on 10 November which said: 'Anyone who talks politics yet neglects military affairs and technology is an empty-headed politician.'[34] This was a clear reference to Lin's frequently repeated demand in 1959 that politics must have priority over everything.

First indications of Lin Piao's possible end were provided in an extraordinarily severe commentary on a 'Clique of Party Enemies', broadcast from Haik'ou (on Hainan Island) on 22 November:

They are finished; their bodies and bones were scattered; they died without a trace.... These men whose crimes will stink forever.... Everyone who dares to oppose Chairman Mao's revolutionary line will be struck down; his body and bones will be scattered without ever finding a grave.[35]

After these reports observers began to connect the reports of the plane crash in the Mongolian People's Republic with Lin Piao's fall. Peking had obviously intended this because the official account of the Lin Piao crisis used this accident as evidence for the attempt by Mao's deputy to escape to the USSR.

It is noticeable that among the provinces which in the middle of October had been particularly active at the start of the campaign against Lin, there were three whose leaders had previously stood on his side during the incidents which culminated on 12 September 1971—Chekiang, Hunan and Sinkiang. At present we still do not know whether the leaders of these provinces tried to escape the purge in this way, or whether they had already been removed by the middle of October, and their successors used the campaign to establish themselves quicker in their new leadership posts.

Until the end of November the Central media allowed the provinces to lead the criticism of Lin Piao. Peking spoke *ex-cathedral* for the first time on 1 December 1971. A joint leading article in the *JMJP*, *CFCP* and *Red Flag* stressed that the Party stood at the top of all society's activities. It, and only it, leads 'Industry, Agriculture, Trade, Schools, the Army and Politics'. However, the 'political swindler' had apparently opposed the leading position of the Party and openly struggled against 'Chairman Mao's Revolutionary line'. These people were, as the article continued,

Opportunists, intriguers, and elements with leanings towards foreign countries, who must eventually lose their lives, ruin their reputations and try to destroy themselves.[36]

This article signalled the promotion of the campaign throughout the whole country. For ten months 'The Movement to Criticize Revisionism and Correct the Work-style' (P'i-hsiu cheng-fêng yün-tung) dominated the media. However, it took two-and-a-half months after Lin's fall before the Chinese people were generally engaged in the criticism against him. Only in the summer of 1972 did Chinese diplomats in foreign capitals begin in conversation to confirm Lin's purge and death. At the 10th Party Congress in August 1973 his name was at last for the first time openly associated with those epithets which till then had been used to condemn him.

While the masses of the Chinese population and the world outside still puzzled their heads over the events of 12 September in Peking, the victors of this severe internal Party conflict had already begun in September to inform the leading cadres of the Party, Army and State administration about their version of events. For this reason Central internal Party circulars were used and published in quick succession after 12 September. On 14 September the Centre in this way publicized the contents of an open letter from Mao Tse-tung to Party members in which Ch'en Po-ta was described as a 'Pseudo-Marxist-Leninist'. In this letter, said to have been written before 12 September, Mao pointed out that Lin—here still called 'comrade'—'had fundamentally agreed' with him.[37] In spite of this, the document indicated for those in the know that Lin had lost his influence because somewhat later the Party Centre stated that he had opposed criticism of Ch'en by name.[38]

The first official explanation of the events of 12 September 1971 was given to leading cadres in a report dated 18 September. In this the Centre stated that on 12 September Lin Piao had tried to have the special train carrying Mao from Shanghai to Peking bombed by a plane somewhere in the vicinity of Shanghai. It was said that on the same afternoon after his plot had been discovered, he had taken a great number of secret documents and a large amount of foreign currency, injured his long-time bodyguard who had tried to block his way and finally boarded a PLA Air Force Trident. He had apparently been accompanied by his wife Yeh Ch'ün (a member of the Politburo and Director of the General Office at the PLA Headquarters) and his son Lin Li-kuo (an officer in the Political Department of the PLA Air Force). The three of them and their pilot had died when the plane crashed somewhere near Undur Khan in Mongolia. Lin's accomplices—the Deputy Commander of the Air Force, Yü Hsin-yeh; the Deputy Director of the office of the Party Committee in the Air Force, Chou Yü-ch'ih; and the Political Commissar of the 4th Air Corps, Ch'en Li-yün (Secretary of the CCP Provincial Committee in Chekiang)—were said to have boarded two other military planes in order to escape. However, just short of the border these two planes appeared to have been forced to turn back by some Air Force units from the Peking Military Region. Yü and Chou had then murdered their pilot and had themselves committed suicide. The second plane was apparently forced to land, and Ch'en Li-yün, who had been badly injured, was arrested. It had apparently proved possible to save all the documents that had been carried by these two planes. Lin Piao's daughter, Lin Tou-tou, is said to have told Prime Minister Chou En-lai about the escape route and to have 'been of great service to the Party and the State by helping the Party Centre break up a dangerous counter-revolutionary coup'.[39]

A second document put out by the Party leadership and circulated among leading cadres after 20 September, claimed that the group, now seen as the 'Anti-Party clique of Lin and Ch'en' *(Lin-Ch'en fan-tang chi-t'uan)*, had not taken shape suddenly. As early as the Land Reform Movement (i.e. the period of the Kiangsi Soviet from 1931 to 1934), during the Anti-Japanese War of 1937-45 and in the Civil War of 1945-9, Lin Piao had apparently attacked the Party on several occasions, and behind the backs of the Centre he had eventually established an 'Independent King-dom' in Manchuria. However, after he had taken on the director-ship of routine work in the Military Committee of the CC in 1959, his performance had become satisfactory—to the extent that the Party was in the position to 'educate' and 'help' him patiently over a long period of time. However, he had not accepted this help but had, on the contrary, begun to work with Ch'en Po-ta after the 9th Party Congress in forming a faction. Ch'en had apparently laun-ched his attack on the Centre at the 2nd Plenum of the 9th CC with Lin's support and protection. The 'core group' *(ku-kan)* of the 'Anti-Party Clique'—Huang Yung-sheng, Wu Fa-hsien, Yeh Ch'ün, Li Tso-p'eng and Ch'iu Hui-tso (in other words containing, with Lin and Ch'en, as much as one-third of the total Politburo membership)—had supported Ch'en in this by attempting to draw other CC members to their side. After the 2nd Plenum, Lin had apparently refused to join in the criticism of Ch'en, even though Mao had tried very hard to convince him. Finally, Lin was said to have avoided making a decision on this by 'playing sick' for a long time and failing to observe his duties. After the North-China Conference in December 1970 and January 1971,[40] protected by his 'illness', he is said to have plotted to prepare a putsch, together with his wife and the four leaders of the Central Military *apparat*. His son Lin Li-kuo was to have travelled under his command to Shanghai, Nanking, Hangchou and Canton, where he performed liaison duties for the rebel group and established 'three fascist spy organizations' in Canton.[41] However, no connection between Lin and the USSR was mentioned in this document.

At the end of September 1971, the Party Centre informed the leading cadres in a further circular that the leadership had set up a 'Special Investigation Group of the CC of the CCP' *(Chung-kung chung-yang chuan-an shên-ch'a-tsu)* in order to 'inquire into the Lin-Ch'en Anti-Party Clique'. The members of this Special Investigation Group were Marshal Yeh Chien-ying, Chang Ch'un-ch'iao, General Li Tê-sheng, Chi Teng-k'uei, General Wang Tung-hsing and General Ch'en Hsi-lien. Ch'en Po-ta was removed from all the posts he had occupied in the Party and the State, was arrested and handed over to the Investigation Group. Huang Yung-sheng, Wu Fa-hsien, Li Tso-p'eng and Ch'iu Hui-tso were removed from office by the Party leadership and commanded to perform extensive 'self-criticism' before the Investigation Group. Marshal Yeh took over the routine work of the Military Committee. At the same time the Centre ordered that all the information on the circumstances surrounding the Lin Piao crisis should be discussed by Party and Revolutionary Committees at all levels. However, 'landlords, rich peasants, counter-revolutionaries, bad elements and right-wing deviants' were, like foreigners and 'Overseas Chinese' from Hong Kong, Macao and elsewhere, not to hear of all this, which is why the documents were not to be 'copied, reprinted or duplicated'.[42]

In the middle of November the Party leadership proceeded with the difficult task of eliminating all traces of Lin Piao. The order was given that, as from 1 January 1972, the 'Four Good, Five Good Movement', 'Congresses of Activists in the living study and application of the Thought of Mao Tse-tung' and the 'Conferences for the exchange of experiences in the study of the Thought of Mao Tse-tung' were all to be discontinued. The text of the CCP Constitution, the documents of the 9th Party Congress, Lin's paper 'Long Live the Victory of People's War!' and other publications and pictures of Lin Piao were to be confiscated.[43]

However, it was only during 1972 that the leadership group in Peking fully reported its version of the Lin Piao crisis to the cadres. On 13 January, they publicized a document which was supposed to represent Lin Piao's plan for a *coup d'état* under the guise of 'Engineering project No. 571' *(Wu-ch'i-i kung-ch'eng chi-yao;* 'the 571 Document'), and a written confession by the Deputy Secretary of the Political Department of the 4th Air Corps, Li Wei-hsin.[44] On 17 March, there followed a summary of Mao's remarks, made on an inspection tour from the middle of August until 12 September 1971,[45] and finally on 2 July 1972 a synopsis was produced of all the incriminating material the 'Special Investigation Group' could compile.[46]

These documents fell into the hands of the Secret Service in T'aiwan and were published in T'aipei. Data that reaches foreign observers via such sources generally has to be regarded with scepticism. However, the authenticity of these documents has since been fully confirmed not only by the reports of Chinese refugees in Hong Kong, but also by comparison with reports from the official Chinese media, and finally by the 'Political Report' given by Chou En-lai at the 10th Party Congress of the CCP in August 1973.[47] Their contents, however, leave considerable room for doubt, since the circulars only relate one side of the confrontation—the point of view which the victors want to reveal.

According to these sources, Lin Piao and his wife Yeh Ch'ün had appreciated their weakening position as a result of both the purges of Li Hsüeh-fêng and Cheng Wei-shan at the North-China Conference and the removal of the 38th Army Corps from Peking. During February 1971, in Suchou (Kiangsu), they had begun to discuss plans for a coup with their son Lin Li-kuo, who had then apparently travelled to Shanghai and Hangchou in order to discover on whom the conspirators could rely. On 18 March he travelled with Yü Hsin-yeh to Shanghai, where the two of them met Li Wei-hsin, and on 20 March Chou Yü-chih from Peking joined the conspirators. Lin Li-kuo informed the other three that he had told Lin Piao that a *coup d'état* had to be prepared and that Lin had answered that the first thing to do was to draw up a plan. Between 22 and 24 March the four young Air Force commanders drafted the 571 Document.[48]

This document [49] was based on the assumption that Lin Piao's position had been greatly weakened and his chances of succeeding Mao reduced. Mao, whom the conspirators expressively termed 'B-52'—flying far above the clouds but attacking suddenly—was described as a tyrant as cruel as the Emperor Ch'in Shih-huang[50] and as a 'feudal lord in the guise of socialism'. In order to ensure his downfall the conspirators were to capture him dead or alive. At the same time a raiding party from the conspiratorial group was to arrest Chang Ch'un-ch'iao in Shanghai,[51] and Li Wei-hsin's confessions also named Yao Wên-yüan and General Hsü Shih-yu as dangerous opponents.[52] After securing a base in the Shanghai-Nanking area, the conspirators were to launch an attack on Peking and take over the command of the Central Party organs and radio and television stations. In these operations the conspirators intended to rely above all on the 4th and 5th Air Corps, under the Generals Wang Wei-kuo, Ch'en Li-yün and Chiang T'eng-chiao, on the 9th, 18th and 34th Infantry Divisions, on the 21st Tank Regiment (units stationed in Chekiang, Kiangsu and Shanghai) and on the Chinese Air Transport Company. In addition they hoped to receive active support from the 20th Army Corps stationed in Nanking, and the 38th Army Corps in Manchuria, from Huang Yung-sheng, from the Defence-Sciences Commission—responsible for the establishment of Chinese nuclear and rocket power—as well as from the Military Regions of Canton, Ch'engtu, Wuhan, Tsinan, Fuchou, Sinkiang, the Kiangsu Military District and the Garrison Commander of Sian (Shensi). According to the 571 Document, there were to have been secret talks with the USSR in order to elicit their support.[53]

At about the same time as the conspirators were planning their coup, an enlarged session of the Military Committee of the CC met in Peking and, apparently under Lin's influence, could not be persuaded to condemn Ch'en Po-ta, as the majority of the Party leadership expected it to do. This majority consequently called a conference of ninety-nine Members of the Central Committee in the capital during April 1971, which included all regional commanders and leading personalities of the Central military and administration. At this conference Chou En-lai delivered the report of an investigation which finally confirmed the purges of Ch'en Po-ta, Li Hsüeh-fêng and Cheng Wei-shan. A document of the North China Group of the CC drafted by Lin Piao's followers, which criticized Ch'en only very mildly, was rejected by the majority at the meeting. Of even greater significance was the fact that for the first time severe criticisms were directed at Yeh Ch'ün, Huang Yung-sheng, Wu Fa-hsien, Li Tso-p'eng and Chiu Hui-tso. The conference called upon these Politburo members to carry out self-criticism.[54]

There is a great deal of evidence that the anti-Lin coalition gained the upper hand over Lin Piao and his followers in March and April 1971. With the publication of a new 'Rural Economic Policy' the leadership group supported Hsü Shih-yu's and the majority of the regional commander's concept of social policy in the villages against that of Lin Piao's.[55] In addition, there are indications that at about this time the decision was taken to emphasize middle-range ballistic missiles (IRBMS and MRBMS) rather than long-range inter-continental missiles (ICBMs) in the development of China's guided weapons system—a decision contrary to Lin's armaments policy.[56] Finally, this was the time when an American table-tenis team visited the PRC,[57] and when the Chinese leadership decided to accept the USA's proposals for détente. Both decisions reflected a fundamental change of attitude in the Sino-Soviet conflict. Since 1968 this conflict had, with increasing clarity, assumed the characteristics of a confrontation between states with different political and social systems. As a result, the Chinese attitude towards the USSR was now determined predominantly by considerations of national security and no longer by the attempt to create a pro-Chinese faction *inside* the world communist movement. By contrast Lin Piao and his followers held fast to Mao's policy of conflict with both super-powers at the same time, formulated in the early 1960s with the Defence Minister's strong support.

The Party documents so far available do not give any information about developments between the beginning of May and the middle of August 1971. By August, the Anti-Lin Coalition seemed to have succeeded in bringing the leadership of Canton Military region (controlled by the loyalty group of the 4th Field Army) over to its side, so that Lin and his followers in the Central Military were completely isolated. This explains why on 20 August Mao explicitly approved the records of a conference of '3-2 units' in this Military Region.[58] All the Central Party circulars distributed since 18 September 1971 confirm that on 12 September Lin gave orders to implement the principles of the 571 Document and to murder Mao, that this plan failed, and that the group when trying to escape to the USSR was either accidentally killed or forced to return.

The final report of the 'Special Investigation Group of the CC'—drafted on 10 July 1973, approved by the Party Centre shortly before the 10th Party Congress on 23 August and distributed to all levels of the Party after the Congress on 8 September[59]—changed the date of Lin Piao's alleged call for a coup from 12 to 8 September 1971. Furthermore, Lin's 'crimes' were described in a detailed biography, and he was accused of having tried in 1967 to 'sabotage the Great Proletarian Cultural Revolution' by identifying Teng Hsiao-p'ing as Liu Shao-ch'i's closest accomplice and demanding a purge of the PLA.[60] The report not only recommended the expulsion of Lin, Ch'en Po-ta and Yeh Ch'ün from all their positions and from the Party in perpetuity, but demanded the same treatment for Huang Yung-sheng, Wu Fa-hsien, Li Tso-p'eng, Ch'iu Hui-tso and Li Hsüeh-fêng.[61] From the documents of the 10th Party Congress already made available, it is not clear whether the Central Committee followed this recommendation.

A critical examination of this official version of the Lin Piao crisis reveals some remarkable contradictions. The earlier documents from September 1971 say nothing about secret contacts with the USSR, and they are only mentioned briefly in passing in 1972. Before summer 1973 the Centre's circulars maintained that these events had been concentrated on 12 September, and it was only afterwards that they started to mention Lin's call for a *coup d'état* on 8 September and his letter to Huang Yung-sheng on 10 September in which he referred to the plan for the *coup* having been wrecked.[62] Had the original version with events concentrated on 12 September, met with Party cadres' scepticism so that corrections were needed? In September 1971 the Party leadership had attested to Lin's positive achievements during his time as

Defence Minister and Director of the Military Committee of the CC's day-to-day work.[63] On the other hand, the final report of July 1973 stated that 'when he (Lin) directed the work of the Military Committee of the CC, he promoted his protégés, dealt blows to the revolutionary cadres, persecuted them and did his best to implement a bourgeois military line.'[64]

Such contradictions strengthen the doubts about Peking's presentation of the events leading to Lin's fall. Three questions need to be asked if we want to discover what actually happened in 1971:

(1) Is there enough evidence for the allegation that Lin planned a *coup d'état* against Mao?

(2) Did he really die in the plane that came down over the Mongolian People's Republic on the night of 12–13 September 1971? and

(3) How was it possible that the Anti-Lin coalition became strong enough to overthrow him?

In answering the first question it is an important piece of evidence that the 571 Document was only circulated *after* Lin's fall and then by those members of the leadership who were the victors. As a result there must be doubts about the authenticity of this source. In any case it is hard to imagine that veteran revolutionaries like Lin and his close colleagues in the Central military, who had been through four decades of intra-Party conflicts, civil wars and struggles for power, could have been so stupid as to write down their plans for a *coup* with no subterfuge whatever. One ought also to ask why Chang Ch'un-ch'iao was the only Party leader to be mentioned by name in this document. Apart from him only Mao, under the alias 'B-52', had been attacked, and Li Wei-hsin's written confession further mentions Yao Wen-yüan as well as Hsü Shih-yu. Why were the names of Mao's wife and Chou En-lai missing, since they too must certainly have been overthrown in such a coup? Did this happen in order to raise the prestige of the two Shanghai leaders and of the Commander of Nanking Military Region? If this were so, then it would seem most likely that the document was forged in Shanghai or Nanking, either after 12 September, or before Lin Piao's fall in order to win the Party leader over to the anti-Lin coalition. The only fact that counts against this interpretation is that the document contains sharply formulated slogans against Mao. However, they could just as well have been used to create the impression of authenticity.

Another possible interpretation results from the suggestion that the authorship of the 571 Document can be ascribed to Lin Piao's son Lin Li-kuo and other young Air Force officers. The statement that in March 1971 they had proposed plans for a *coup* to the Defence Minister and that he had told them first to outline their plans in writing demonstrates that the author of the Party documents concerning the Lin Piao crisis distinguished clearly between Lin and a group of 'young Turks' in the Air Force. Taking all this into consideration, the supposition that Lin himself had planned a *coup* does not seem very likely.

Two other explanations seem more probable. One is that on 12 September there was not a *coup* led by Lin, but an uprising of Lin's opponents against him. Another is that the 'young Turks' in the group around Lin's son had decided to attempt a putsch, realizing that Lin and his group had lost their political influence and become isolated. The later interpretation is also suggested by the fact that in the two weeks immediately after 12 September there was an extremely confused reaction from the Chinese leadership. In this case the 571 Document as we know it could easily have been based on notes taken by the group around Lin Li-kuo, and have been supplemented at a later date.

On the second question, it can be pointed out that most observers of Chinese politics take the reports of Lin's death in a plane crash on the night of 12–13 September to be true, although there are many who doubt the authenticity of the 571 Document. However, even here there is room for scepticism. If Lin did in fact die in a plane crash, why then was he mentioned positively after 8 October in some Provinces? If he and the group of his followers from the 'young Turk' clique in the Air Force had really been dead by then, why was the Air Force grounded for almost three weeks after 12 September? Finally, why did the Chinese Party document of 18 September report the death of only four people, and the news report from the Mongolian People's Republic on 30 September mention the deaths of nine people of whom, according to Soviet reports, none was over the age of fifty?[65]

The official Chinese version of the end of Lin Piao seeks to give the impression that he was a traitor and an instrument of the Soviet Union, who wanted to bring China back under Soviet control. This, however, seems highly unlikely, as in the whole decade before 1971 his behaviour had not given the slightest hint of a pro-Soviet attitude. Consequently, blaming him for treacherous contacts with Moscow is of the same quality as Stalin's allegation in the 1930s that Trotsky was an agent simultaneously of the Gestapo and of the Western allies. Such reproaches are made because it is in the interest of Communist one-Party systems to explain political deviance in terms of the bad character of the deviant. Doubts remain here too, but they cannot be solved with the material currently available. One can only be certain that Lin Piao and probably his wife Yeh Ch'ün died during this crisis. This need not, however, necessarily have happened on 12 September 1971.

We are on safer ground when answering the third question. Mao's deputy and appointed successor lost his role and his life in conflict with that coalition, which in 1970 and 1971 had formed in opposition to him. It seems today that this coalition was brought together by Chou En-lai. It was made possible by the fact that the PLA under Lin Piao's leadership was not a monolithic entity. This is why it would also be incorrect to interpret the Lin Piao crisis simply as a conflict between the Party and the Army, as some observers have done.[66] Certainly, the crisis strengthened the position of the civilian *apparat vis-à-vis* that of the PLA in the Chinese political system. However, this is more the result of a split in the Army than a victory of the civilians over the generals.

Nonetheless, in the course of the Lin Piao crisis we can see particularly clearly the characteristics of the allocative process through which the Party leader *constructed* a majority as opposed to merely finding one. Mao had probably already begun to distrust his appointed successor shortly before the 9th Party Congress in April 1969. In this, he was probably aware that it is by no means rare in political systems for an important leader to see his influence wane from the moment when he appoints a successor. However, the actual formation of factions within the leadership—a necessary pre-condition for the emergence of a political crisis—only occurred when four simultaneous conflicts made possible a coalition of the institutional and opinion groups of the State administration and the majority of regional commanders:

(1) The argument over the future of Chinese foreign policy, in which Chou En-lai's concept of détente with one of the super-powers contrasted with Lin Piao's concept of a continuing conflict with both the USSR and the United States.

(2) A conflict over economic planning and administration. Here the majority of regional commanders stood for a continuation of the policy of decentralization, which was introduced in the early 1960s and which they had fully implemented during the crisis of the Cultural Revolution, whereas Lin Piao and the Central Military advocated a policy of recentralization.

(3) A confrontation over whether one should regard the 'liquidation' of the Cultural Revolution as having ended with the disciplining of the Maoist organizations—which was Lin Piao's view—or whether one should go as far as to suggest a further fundamental revision of Cultural Revolutionary doctrine, as Chou and the majority of regional commanders envisaged.

(4) A fundamental conflict over social policy in the agricultural sector, which during the winter of 1970-1 had developed into a critical confrontation. Behind this conflict there were, as we have seen, fundamentally opposed ideas on the role of the armed forces in the State, and mutually exclusive views on the ranking of

priorities in development policy. Here the civilian administration around Chou En-lai supported the view of the majority of regional commanders.

From the start there appears to have been a consensus in two of these four areas of conflict between the civilian administration at the Centre and the majority of regional commanders. The clear institutional contrast between the Central and Regional military was intensified by the rivalry between the loyalty groups of the 4th Field Army and that of the 2nd, 3rd and North-China Field Armies, who were united in their majority against Lin Piao's following.

Chou En-lai, as skilled as he was, took the chance that presented itself. He arranged a coalition between the regional commanders and the Central civilian *apparat*, by obtaining the support of the most influential regional leaders for his foreign policy of détente with the West and of closer relations with the USA, and through his own acceptance of a continued policy of economic decentralization.

In this way the nucleus of the anti-Lin coalition arrived at agreement in all four conflict areas. The strength of this new alliance was demonstrated at the beginning of March 1971 when a fundamental change in agricultural policy was carried through, and also a month later at the conference of ninety-nine leading cadres in Peking.[67] In view of these initial successes, even the remainder of the Cultural Revolutionary Left, who could now only count on the city of Shanghai as their own area of support, joined the coalition. There is much evidence to suggest that Chou and other representatives of the anti-Lin coalition succeeded sometime during the summer of 1971 in bringing the Party leader, who was already predisposed to distrust his appointed successor, over to their side. In August, Mao managed to separate the strongest base of the 4th Field Army loyalty group, the Canton Military Regional Command, from Lin, and succeeded in bringing it into the coalition. In this way Lin's isolation and that of his followers in the Central military was successfully achieved.

Internal political developments shortly after the Lin Piao crisis have demonstrated that the position of the civilian administration had been further strengthened. The regional commanders were in the position to expand the boundaries of their economic and politico-administrative autonomy even further, and the members of the 4th Field Army in the Canton Military Region—in contrast to other areas of this loyalty group—were largely spared the purges which followed the fall of Lin Piao. The Cultural Revolutionary Left finally secured its influence on cultural policy and in the Party's propaganda *apparat*.

The full long-term effects of the Lin Piao crisis on the Chinese political system still can not be fully appreciated. The man whom Mao had described as his 'closest comrade-in-arms' and had accepted as his only deputy in the Party leadership had fallen and had lost his life. Before him Ch'en Po-ta, the Party leader's long-serving and closest colleague, had been purged. It is hardly imaginable that these events had no effect on the cadres' trust in the reliability of cooperation with the Chairman. Although it was only two-and-a-half years since the end of the Cultural Revolution, once again a third of the members of the inner leadership circle were being described as 'Party enemies'. The consolidation of the leadership structure had been interrupted and the effectiveness of the Chinese armed forces had suffered at least temporarily.

However, the crisis was a turning-point in the development of Chinese politics. Until 1973 pragmatic and development-oriented concepts were given priority—a phase of a return to the policy of 'readjustment' in a 'New Course' which could now fully develop.

REFERENCES

1. *NCNA*, Peking, 15 April 1969.
2. *NCNA*, Peking, 29 August 1973.
3. *JMJP*, 12 September 1971.
4. Radio Hunan and Radio Ssuch'uan, 30 October 1971. Chang Kuo-t'ao was a founder-member of the CCP in 1921, a member of the CC after 1924, a one-time member of the Politburo. After the 'Long March' he took over the office of Vice-Chairman of the government in Yenan (North-Shensi). Here he came into conflict with Mao and in 1938 he went over to the Kuomintang, being elected to the latter's Central Executive Committee in 1945. He went to Hong Kong in 1949, where he lived for almost twenty years. He now lives in Canada.
5. Radio Chekiang, 7 November 1971.
6. Ibid., 18 November 1971.
7. E.g. Richard M. Pfeffer, 'Serving the People and Continuing Revolution', in *CQ*, 52, October–December 1972, pp. 620–53.
8. *JMJP*, 4 June 1971.
9. The author's own observation in Hong Kong.
10. *NCNA*, Peking, 24 September 1971.
11. *Hsing-pao* (The Star), Hong Kong, 13 September 1971. This report was confirmed by the US Air Force on 16 September 1971.
12. *UPI*, Tokyo, 23 September 1971.
13. Mongolian News Agency, Ulan Bator, 30 September 1971.
14. Details from, *inter alia, CNA*, No. 857, 8 October 1971.
15. *JMJP*, 12 September 1971.
16. Radio Fukien, 30 September 1971.
17. *CFCP*, 13 September 1971.
18. Radio Kuangsi, 16 September 1971.
19. Radio Sinkiang, 18 September 1971.

20. Radio Hupei, 3 October 1971.

21. Radio Lhasa, 8 October 1971.

22. Hsüan Mo, 'A provisional answer to the question as to why Mao Tse-tung purged Lin Piao', in *CKYC*, Vol. 6, No. 4, April 1972, p. 54. See also Li T'ien-min, 'Chung-kung chün-chung tui Lin Piao-te p'i-p'an hê tou-cheng' (Criticism and Struggle against Lin Piao in the Chinese Communist Army), report to the 3rd Sino-American Conference on Mainland China, T'aipei, December 1973, p. 3.

23. Radio Kiangsi, 13 September 1971; Radio Kuangsi, 16 September 1971; Radio Chekiang, 17 September 1971; *JMJP*, 30 September and 28 October 1971.

24. *CFCP*, 30 September and 9 October 1971.

25. *CNA*, No. 862, 19 November 1971.

26. Radio Kuangsi, 16 October 1971.

27. Radio Haik'ou, 25 October 1971; Radio Yünnan, 31 October 1971; Radio Ssuch'uan, 3 November 1971.

28. Radio Hunan and Radio Ssuch'uan, 30 October 1971.

29. Radio Chekiang, 2 November 1971.

30. *JMJP*, 19 August 1971.

31. See pp. 82 ff.

32. Radio Lhasa, 4 and 5 November 1971 and Radio Checkiang, 7 November 1971.

33. Radio Anhui, 9 November 1971.

34. Radio Sinkiang, 10 November 1971.

35. Radio Haik'ou, 22 November 1971.

36. *JMJP*, 1 December 1971.

37. *Chung-fa* Document No. 57 (1971), 14 September 1971, in: Yüan Yüeh, op. cit., pp. 21 ff. This document—like some others which will be mentioned—is not available abroad in its original form, but only as a text transmitted by letter.

38. 'Communiqué on Lin and Ch'en's Anti-Party Clique', *Chung-fa* Document No. 61 (1971), end of September 1971, ibid., p. 26.

39. 'Communiqué on Lin Piao's treason of 12 September', *Chung-fa* Document No. 60 (1971), 18 September 1971, ibid., pp. 23 ff.

40. See pp. 96 ff.

41. *Chung-fa* Document No. 61 (1971), ibid., pp. 25-7. In the reported text the generally used term in the PRC 'after the Liberation' *(Chieh-fang hou)* is not applied to the period after 1949, but instead the term originating in the Kuomintang terminology 'after the construction of the country [or of the Republic]' *(Chien-kuo hou)*. This fact raises considerable doubts as to the authenticity of the Document. Even so it is used here as a source because its content had been completely confirmed as the Peking Government's attitude in the public criticism of Lin Piao. The weakness in terminology is due probably to a mistake in the process of transmission.

42. 'On the Handling of Lin and Ch'en's Anti-Party Clique', *Chung-fa* Document No. 62 (1971), September 1971, ibid., pp. 29 ff.

43. 'Circular on the abolition of "4 Good-5 Good Movement" and the withdrawal from circulation of Lin Piao's pictures and writings', *Chung-fa* Document No. 64 (1971), Mid-November 1971, ibid., p. 31.

44. 'The Struggle to put down the counter-revolutionary *coup d'état* of the anti-Party Lin-Ch'en clique (Material No. 2), *Chung-fa* No. 4 (1972), 13 January 1972, ibid., pp. 83-100.

The term '5-7-1' for the plan of the *coup d'état* can in Chinese *(Wu-ch'i-i,* or *yi)* also, when used with a different intonation, refer either to the Revolution of 1911 in Wuch'ang *(Wuch'ang ch'i-yi)* or the term 'armed uprising' *(Wu-chuang ch'i-yi).*

45. *Chung-fa* Document No. 12 (1972), 17 March 1972, ibid., pp. 121-30.

46. 'The Struggle to put down the counter-revolutionary *coup d'état* of the anti-Party Chen-Lin clique (Material No. 3)', *Chung-fa* Document No. 24 (1972), 2 July 1972, ibid., pp. 131-40.

47. See p. 185.

48. *Chung-fa* No. 4 (1972); ibid., pp. 85 and 96.

49. Ibid., pp. 86-95.

50. Ch'in Shih-huang (221-207) BC) was the first Emperor of the Ch'in dynasty, who created in China (with considerable determination and cruelty) a tightly centralized administration. In spite of his achievements he is traditionally thought of negatively in China, because of the burning of books at his instructions and the persecution of Confucian scholars, also because of the tough system of enforced labour he introduced.

51. Ibid., p. 68.

52. Ibid., pp. 70 ff.

53. Ibid., pp. 66 ff.

54. *Chung-fa* No. 12 (1972), ibid., p. 127.

55. See p. 114.

56. See Whitson, *High Command,* op. cit., pp. 542 ff.

57. See p. 230.

58. *Chung-fa* No. 12 (1972), loc. cit., p. 128.

59. *Chung-fa* Document No. 34 (1973), 8 September 1973; English in *Background on China,* loc. cit.

60. Ibid., p. 3.

61. Ibid., p. 4.

62. Ibid., p. 2.

63. *Chung-fa* Document No. 61 (1971), in Yüan Yüeh, op. cit., p. 25.

64. *Chung-fa* No. 34 (1973), loc. cit., p. 3.

65. Communications by Soviet China specialists at international conferences to the author and other Western scholars.

66. See particularly Parris H. Chang, 'The Changing Patterns of Military Participation in Chinese Politics' in *Orbis,* Vol. XVI, No. 3, Autumn 1972, pp. 797 ff.; Richard E. Thornton, *The Bear and the Dragon: Sino-Soviet Relations and the Political Evolution of the Chinese People's Republic, 1949-1971,* New York, 1972, pp. 65 ff.

67. See pp. 129 ff.

PART THREE

THE NEW COURSE: TOWARDS A DIRECTORY?

9. Purges, Rehabilitations and the Continued Reconstruction of the State Structure

Specific battle-lines had been drawn in the course of the conflict within the Chinese leadership that culminated in Lin Piao's fall on 12 September 1971, and these were now to determine the policies of the victorious coalition. So this 12 September did not signify an entirely new start for Chinese domestic policy, but rather the implementation of a political line of which the basic principles had been apparent in the programme of the anti-Lin coalition ever since the middle of 1970.

The changes which occurred during the following eighteen months throughout the whole country were particularly noticeable in three areas of domestic policy. The decisions about personnel which were made from the autumn of 1971 to the summer of 1973 led to the downfall of a number of Lin's followers in the Central military and in the regional Party leaderships. New appointments favoured long-serving officials, and military men from the PLA loyalty groups that had opposed Lin. In order to widen its political base, the new leadership intensified the movement to rehabilitate those cadres who had been the targets of attack for the Maoist organizations during the Cultural Revolution, and who had been described as 'Party enemies'.

In the areas of economic and social policy the New Course, which the Party leadership was now pursuing at full speed, had its major impact with changes in the planning system and economic management, salary structures and the treatment of peasants. Finally, there was evidence to justify the belief that yet another revision of Cultural Revolutionary doctrines was emerging in cultural and educational policies, as well as in the methods of Maoist indoctrination which had been in use since the mid-1960s.

After the experiences of the Cultural Revolution, observers of Chinese politics could expect that further purges in the Central Committee and in the regional Party leaderships would follow the purge of one-third of the members of the Politburo. The victory of Lin's opponents in the September 1971 crisis did in fact bring about significant changes in personnel, particularly within the armed forces. Although there may seem to be similarities with the Tukatchevsky crisis of 1937, these purges in no way reached the same proportions as Stalin's struggle with the leaders of the Red Army.

According to the currently available information there were altogether sixty leading military men who were dismissed from office in the course of the purges following the fall of Lin Piao.[1] The Central military organization was particularly badly hit by these purges since, after his nomination as Minister of Defence in 1959 and especially after the Cultural Revolution, Lin had appointed his followers to these positions.

The thirty-four leading soldiers to be purged were:

(1) Huang Yung-sheng, Chief of the General Staff and member of the Politburo.

(2) Li Tso-p'eng, Deputy Chief of the General Staff, First Political Commissar of the PLA Navy, and member of the Politburo.

(3) Wu Fa-hsien, Deputy Chief of the General Staff, Commander of the PLA Air Force and member of the Politburo.

(4) Ch'iu Hui-tso, Director of the General Logistics Department PLA and member of the Politburo.

(5) Yen Chung-ch'uan, Deputy Chief of the General Staff and alternate member of the CC.

(6) Ch'en Chi-tê, Deputy Chief of the General Staff.[2]

(7) Huang Chih-yung, Deputy Director of the General Political Department, PLA, and Alternate member of the CC.

(8) Chang T'ien-Yün, Deputy Director of the General Logistics Department PLA and member of the CC.

(9) Chang Ming-yüan, Deputy Director of the General Logistics Department PLA.

(10) Wang Hsi-kê, Deputy Director of the General Logistics Department PLA.

(11) Yen Ch'ün, Deputy Director of the General Logistics Department PLA.

(12) Ch'en Hung, Deputy Director of the General Logistics Department PLA.

(13) Wu Jui-lin, Deputy Commander of the PLA Navy and member of the CC.

(14) Chao Ch'i-min, Deputy Commander of the PLA Navy.

(15) Chang Ching-yi, Deputy Commander of the PLA Navy.

(16) Chang Hsiu-ch'uan, Deputy Political Commissar and Director of the Political Department of the PLA Navy, and alternate member of the CC.

(17) Wang Ping-chang, Deputy Commander of the PLA Air Force and member of the CC.

(18) Tseng Kuo-hua, Deputy Commander of the PLA Air Force and member of the CC.

(19) K'uang Jên-nung, Deputy Commander of the PLA Air Force, Director of the Office for Civilian Air Transport, and member of the CC.[3]

(20) T'an Chia-shu, Deputy Commander of the PLA Air Force.

(21) Lo Yüan-fa, Deputy Commander of the PLA Air Force, Commander of Air Force units in the Peking Military Region, and alternate member of the CC.

(22) Ho Chen-ya, Deputy Commander of the PLA Air Force.

(23) Wang Hui-ch'iu, Political Commissar of the PLA Air Force and member of the CC.

(24) Liu Ch'iu-p'ing, Deputy Political Commissar of the PLA Air Force.

(25) Yü Wên, Deputy Political Commissar of the PLA Air Force.

(26) Yang Chin, Deputy Political Commissar of the PLA Air Force.

(27) Lu Min, Deputy Chief of Staff of the PLA Air Force.

(28) Wang Fei, Deputy Chief of Staff of the PLA Air Force.

(29) Hu P'ing, Deputy Chief of Staff of the PLA Air Force.

(30) Lin Li-kuo, Deputy Director of the Combat Department of the PLA Air Force.

(31) K'uang Yü-min, Deputy Commander of the Artillery.

(32) Yü Ch'ing-shan, Deputy Political Commissar of the Missiles Force.

(33) Ch'iu Chuang-ch'eng, Minister of the 5th Ministry of Machine Building, in an unknown capacity at PLA Headquarters since 1969, member of the CC.

(34) Mme. Yeh Ch'ün, Director of the General Office of the Defence Ministry and member of the Politburo.

However, the regional military organizations were less affected by the purge. Apart from the Commander of Peking Military Region, General Cheng Wei-shan,[4] who had already been overthrown in January 1971, only two of the eleven commanders of Military Regions were dismissed from office: General Liang Hsing-ch'u in Ch'engtu and General Lung Shu-chin in Sinkinag. Both were members of the Central Committee. In addition, the First Political Commissars of the Wuhan, Foochow and Chinan Military Regions, Liu Fêng, Chou Ch'ih-p'ing and Yüan Sheng-p'ing[5]—all three members of the Central Committee—three of the twenty-six Commanders of Provincial Military Districts[6] and thirteen leading officers of the regional units of the PLA Air Force were affected by the purge.

The supposition that the regional leaderships were less affected by the purge than were the Central military is confirmed by the changes in the Secretariats of the provincial Party committees which occurred between September 1971 and June 1973. In Sinkiang, Lung Shu-chin, the First Secretary fell and his place was taken by the former Second Secretary and veteran official, who was also a Uighur—Saifudin. Extensive changes occurred in three other Provinces, which in 1970-1 had strongly supported Lin Piao. In Chekiang, the First Secretary, Nan P'ing, and two secretaries, Ch'en Li-yün and Hsiung Ying-t'ang, were purged. In Kiangsi, the First Secretary, Ch'eng Shih-ch'ing, and a secretary, Yang Tung-liang; and in Kueichou, the First Secretary, Lan I-nung, as well as the secretaries Chang Jung-sen and Li Li were all dismissed.

The position of the former First Secretary of Kuangtung Provincial committee and Political Commissar of Canton Military Region, Liu Hsing-yüan, remained obscure for some time. He was mentioned for the last time in Canton on 8 March 1972.[7] On 7 April 1972 the Commander of Canton Military Region, Ting Sheng, took over Liu's position.[8] However, in November 1972, Liu re-appeared in Ssuch'uan,[9] and in February 1973 it was announced that he had succeeded General Chang Kuo-hua (who had died on 21 February 1972)[10] as First Secretary of the Ssuch'uan Provincial Committee and First Political Commissar of Ch'engtu Military region. In March, 1976, Liu was appointed Commander of the Ch'engtu Military Area; but he lost his civilian Party position in October 1975.

Of those who were the most convinced supporters of Lin Piao, the one who held on to office the longest was the Secretary of the Hunan Provincial Party Committee, General Pu Chan-ya. In the autumn of 1971 he had already been reduced in rank from First to Second Political Commissar of the Hunan Military District.[11] However, he remained active in this province during the whole of 1972 and was mentioned for the last time only on 19 November.[12] The long absence of General Wang Chia-tao, First Secretary of Heilungkiang, indicates that he too had temporary difficulties. He appeared in public for the last time (as it seemed) on 29 December 1971 and was not mentioned again in his position until May 1973.[13] His election as an Alternate Member of the CC at the 10th Party Congress in August 1973, however, indicates that he succeeded in escaping the purge.

The Party leadership in Kiangsi and Kueichou Provinces was taken respectively over by Generals Shê Chi-tê and Lu Jui-lin, which meant that apart from Sinkiang, Chekiang was the only Province where a civilian Party cadre took the place of an army officer as head of the provincial Party committee: T'an Ch'i-lung, who had lost his position as First Secretary of Shantung during the Cultural Revolution but who had maintained close contacts with the 3rd Field Army loyalist group.[14]

As a result, the number of provinces in which the Party and

administration were led by generals fell from twenty-one to nineteen. Nonetheless, the PLA maintained its strong influence within the regional leadership groups. On 1 July 1973, of 174 active members of the provincial Party secretariats, eighty-eight or 50·6% came from the Army, (as compared to 62% in August 1971); seventy-six or 43·7% (against 32·9%) were civilian Party cadres and ten or 5·7% (compared to 5·1%) were representatives of the mass organizations. These numbers show that after Lin's fall there was a definite trend to bring veteran Party cadres back into positions of responsibility. On the other hand the Army still remained in control of its regional positions. As a result, the Centre's appeal—which was strongly emphasized after Lin's fall—to the PLA to subordinate itself to the 'leadership of the regional and local *(Ti-fang)* Party committees'[15] amounted in reality to nothing more than a demand for the obedience of Army officers to their regional commanders in their roles as Party leaders.

A review of the purge in the PLA reveals that it mainly affected two areas which in the past had maintained particularly close relations with Lin Piao. Of the sixty overthrown military leaders twenty-eight or 46·7% belonged to the Air Force and thirty-nine or 65% to the 4th Field Army loyalty group. This re-confirms the importance which should be attached to the loyalty groups within the Army when analysing the political process in the PRC, and in particular during crisis periods.

In spite of Lin Piao's purge and that of his group in the Central military, it took some time before the new leading coalition gained control in all Provinces. Thus, while at the beginning of January 1972 the broadcasting stations of Hupei, Kuangsi, the island of Hainan, Shansi, Ssuch'uan, Yünnan, Kueichou, Shensi and Tibet sharply attacked Lin, who throughout was called a 'Pseudo-Marxist political swindler' as well as an 'opportunist, conspirator and traitor', and not mentioned by name,[16] nonetheless, some provinces, as for example Hunan, were still using terms at the turn of the year (December 1971/January 1972) which had originally been formulated by Lin Piao.[17] It was not until Pu Chan-ya's removal in autumn 1972 that this Province was brought fully into the camp of the Peking coalition.

After the beginning of December 1971, the victors in the Lin Piao crisis took great pains to strengthen their position in the Provinces and at the Centre by the rehabilitation of an increasing number of veteran officials. After December 1971 the media were increasingly favourable towards those Party cadres who had been exposed to criticism and persecution during the Cultural Revolution. Now it was said that these confrontations had only been 'contradictions among the people' and that 95% of the cadres were 'fundamentally good'.[18] At the beginning of March 1972, the efforts being made towards the veteran cadres were intensified,[19] and on 28 April the Party leadership published an editorial in *JMJP* which could only be understood as a recommendation to re-employ at all levels many of the officials who had been over-thrown during the Cultural Revolution. The cadres were said to be 'loyal in the majority'. They had 'considerable organizational skills' and were 'relatively rich in experience' and must therefore be considered as 'the Party's valuable property'.[20]

These declarations rationalized the wave of rehabilitation which had started after Lin's fall. It had begun with the reappearance of Liao Ch'eng-chih before the September crisis at a new and higher rung.[21] In January 1972 old Marshal Chu Tê, who had remained a member of the Politburo even after the 9th Party Congress but who could not be identified in an official position for over six years, was once again mentioned as Chairman of the Standing Committee of the National People's Congress.[22] In April of this same year, some important leading cadres of both Party and State, who had been particularly severely attacked by the Maoist organizations during 1967–8, re-appeared in public in Peking. Among these were the former Minister of Petroleum, General Yü Ch'iu-li, the former Minister for Internal Affairs Tsêng Shan, and the former First Secretary of the Communist Youth League, Hu Yao-pang, who until 1965 had worked closely with Liu Shao-ch'i.[23] In October the former Mayor of Canton, Ch'iao Lin-yi,[24] followed, and at the end of January 1973 he returned to the top admin-istrative post in that city.[25] In December 1972 the wave of rehabilitation affected, among others, the former Chairman of the Commission for Capital Investment, Ku Mu, the Ministers for the Construction Industry and for Health, Li Jen-chün and Ch'ien Hsin-chung (respectively), as well as the pre-1967 Secretary of the Kuangsi Provincial Committee, Yang Shang-k'uei, and the former Governor of Liaoning, Huang Ou-tung.[26] The former Minister of Education, Ho Wei, who had been paraded through Peking in 1966 by the Red Guards, wearing a dunce's cap, was only rehabilitated posthumously with a ceremonial funeral in March 1973. Hardly four weeks later, the surge of rehabilitation reached a new peak which drew everyone's attention: Teng Hsiao-p'ing, referred to as the 'second capitalist power-holder in the Party' since 1967 and who had even been attacked by name by the broadcasting station of his home province, Ssuch'uan, re-appeared in Peking in his former role as Vice-Premier of the State Council.[28] (Almost exactly three years later, on 7 April 1976, Teng was again dismissed from all his position 'inside and outside the Party' and was branded a 'power-holder in the Party who chose the capitalist way, and who is unable to reform himself'. Such are the risks of holding high positions in the PRC.) The rehabilitation of Teng, who had in fact been the second leader of the Anti-Maoist opposition after Liu Shao-ch'i, had become possible because the leadership in Peking could no longer do without his outstanding administrative ability. Furthermore, they intended to give a clear signal to veteran Party cadres all over the country that their time had come again. However, his reappearance had also been made possible because he had the support of the leading officers of the 2nd Field Army, whose First Political Commissar Teng had been for a long time. Teng's reappearance opened up the way for the further extensive rehabilitation of Liu Shao-ch'i's followers. Thus on 1 May 1973 a former member of the Secretariat of the Central Committee, Wang Chia-hsiang, reappeared in public.[29] At the end of July, the former First Secretary of Chekiang, Chiang Hua, was rehabilitated.[30] The election of the new Central Committee of the CCP at the 10th Party Congress (28 August 1973) gave evidence of the return of former Politburo members, Li Ching-ch'uan, T'an Chen-lin and Ulanfu, the former Ministers of the 4th Ministry of Machine-Building and of Internal Trade, Wang Cheng and Yao Yi-lin, as well as the former First Secretaries of Anhui, Shansi, Kiangsu, Ssuch'uan, Ch'inghai and Fukien: Li Pao-hua, T'ao Lu-chia, Chiang Wei-ch'ing, Liao Chih-kao, Wang Chien and Yeh Fei, who all returned as members or alternate members in the Party leadership.[31]

In many cases, however, rehabilitation by no means implied that the veteran officials were returning to their former field of work. Where this did happen, there was generally a time-lag between first public re-appearance and nomination to a leading position. Two former Provincial leaders, whose rehabilitation had taken place at the same time as the foundation of the new Provincial Party committees in 1970-1, led the way back into their former areas of power, ahead of other provinces. Thus the First Secretary of the Kuangtung Provincial Party Committee appeared first as a Deputy Secretary in Inner Mongolia. In April 1972 he returned to Kuangtung as a member of the Provincial Secretariat.[32] However, little more than half a year after the 10th Party Congress, in April 1974, he became First Secretary and Chairman of the Provincial revolutionary committee.[33] The former First Secretary of Hunan, Chang P'ing-hua, after two years of activity in Shansi, returned in the middle of April 1973 to his former region as a Secretary of the Provincial committee,[34] where today he exercises decisive influence, since the First Secretary of Hunan, Hua Kuo-fêng, concurrently holds an important position in the Centre. Chang's return to Hunan is of fundamental interest since Chiang Ch'ing herself had in 1967 attacked him personally and severely:

Chang P'ing-hua has severely opposed Comrade Lin Piao. When working in the North East he always opposed Comrade Lin Piao. Later he became Liu [Shao-ch'i]'s, Teng [Hsiao-p'ing]'s, T'ao [Chu]'s and Wang [Jên-chung]'s closest follower. Chang P'ing-hua cannot be reformed until death. I hate him whenever I think of him. I never thought that he could be so bad; but he is very bad indeed. What he did showed what sort of man he is. According to our experience a person like Chang P'ing-hua cannot be without stains and problems, which have developed over a long period. I have to settle an old account with him: I shall always remember that![35]

It is difficult to believe that Chang's return to office was accepted by Mao's wife. If, however, this was not the case, then we have to assume that by the spring of 1973 she had lost at least some of her previous influence.

In the armed forces Lin's fall also cleared the stage for the re-emergence of a number of generals who had been demoted and struggled against during the Cultural Revolution. Rehabilitations extended initially only to the former subordinates of the purged Marshals P'eng Tê-huai and Ho Lung from the 1st Field Army. The former Deputy Chief of the General Staff, Chang Tsung-hsün, reappeared in June 1972 as the Deputy Commander of Tsinan Military Region,[36] and in the autumn of that year he took on the office of Director of the General Logistics Department of the PLA.[37] By March 1972 the former Vice-Minister of Land Reclamation, General Hsiao K'ê, and the former First Political Commissar of the PLA Navy, Admiral Su Chen-hua,[38] had both reappeared. Su now became the Deputy Commander of the PLA Navy. On 1 May 1973 the Deputy Political Commissar of the PLA Navy, Admiral Tu Yi-tê, and the former Deputy Director of the General Political Department of the PLA, General Liang Pi-yeh, joined the group of those rehabilitated.[39]

In November 1972 Li Ta, the General from the 2nd Field Army, then seventy-seven years old, was appointed Deputy Chief of the General Staff,[40] and on 1 May 1973 the former Commander of K'unming Military Region, General Ch'in Chi-wei, also reappeared.[41] Ch'in was to become in August 1973 the Commander of Ch'engtu Military Region and Secretary of the Ssuch'uan Provincial Party Committee.[42] In late 1975, Ch'in was recalled to Peking, and in April 1976 he could be identified as the Second Political Commissar of the Peking Military Area.

The reappearance of the former Commander of Peking Military Region, General Yang Yung, is also remarkable. He had been dismissed from office in the summer of 1966 because he had refused to support Mao and Lin Piao at the Party Centre with military action. On 1 August 1972 he reappeared for the first time in Peking, and in October the same year he became Deputy Commander of Shênyang Military Region,[43] and finally, in July

1973 he became Commander of the Sinkiang Military Region and Second Secretary of the regional Committee of the CCP.[44]

It is particularly significant that on the eve of Army Day (31 July) 1972, the two leaders of the Wuhan Mutiny of July 1967, Generals Ch'en Tsai-tao and Chung Han-hua, should have reappeared in public.[45] They were the only leading military men who had openly opposed Mao and Lin Piao during the Cultural Revolution. A few months later Chung reappeared as one of the leading officers in the Canton Military Region,[46] and in January 1973 Ch'en was indentified in Foochou, probably as the Deputy Commander of the Foochou Military Region.[47]

The fall of Lin Piao made it possible for Prime Minister Chou En-lai to push forward with the reconstruction of the Central State administration, which had only advanced slowly during 1970-1. However, it still remained general practice that members of the PLA took over the majority of the new leadership positions even in this sector. In October 1971 the former Political Commissar of the Shênyang Military Region, General Ch'en Shao-k'un, was appointed Minister of the Metal Industry. The leadership of the new Cultural Group under the State Council was taken by the civilian Party cadre, Wu Tê, who also succeeded the late Hsieh Fu-chih as First Secretary of the Party Committee and Chairman of the Revolutionary Committee in Peking.[49] On 5 October 1972 General Li Chen of the 2nd Field Army loyalty group was appointed as the new Minister of Public Security.[50] A short while later, General Chang Wên-pi of the 2nd Field Army became Minister for Water Conservation and Electricity, and the former Minister of Petroleum, General Yü Ch'iu-li of the 1st Field Army, became Chairman of the State Planning Commission.[51] In 1975 Chang Wên-pi was transferred back to the military as commander of the Chekiang Provincial Military District. The appointment of General Fan Tzu-yü of the 2nd Field Army as Minister for Internal Trade soon followed. In June 1973 Hsieh Fu-chih's widow, Mme. Liu Hsiang-p'ing became Minister of Public Health, and Ku Mu returned to the Directorship of the Commission for Capital Investment.[52] By the summer of 1972 the civilian Party cadre, Liu Hsi-yao, had followed the late Professor Li Ssu-kuang as leader of the Science and Education Group under the State Council.[53] Before the 10th Party Congress of the CCP in August 1973 the reconstruction of the Central Administration continued with the nomination of a technician, Chung Fu-hsiang, as Minister of Posts and Telecommunications, and the replacement of General Pai Hsiang-kuo (who was to become Deputy Director of the General Logistics Department of the PLA) by the civilian administrative cadre, Li Ch'iang, as leader of the Ministry of Foreign Trade.

As a result of these changes the Cabinet now consisted of

twenty-four members. Of these fourteen were civilian cadres,[54] and ten were military men.[55] However, even among these eleven top officials in the State Council who had been appointed since Lin Piao's fall, there were still five generals, so that any reduction in the predominance of the Armed Forces was becoming apparent only very slowly, if at all.

We have seen that the purges which followed the fall of Lin Piao affected the 4th Field Army most among the PLA's loyalty groups. This had the result of greatly increasing the influence of the 2nd and 3rd Field Army loyalty groups. After September 1971 they occupied these following posts;

— from within the group of the 2nd Field Army: the Ministries of the Metal Industry, Public Security and Internal Trade, as well as two Deputy Chiefs of the General Staff, and the Commander of the Ch'engtu Military Region.[56]

— from within the group of the 3rd Field Army: the Minister for Water Conservation and Electricity, the First Political Commissar of Wuhan Military Region, and the Commanders of the Canton and Foochow Military Regions, a Political Commissar of Ch'engtu Military Region and a Deputy Political Commissar of Tsinan Military Region.[57]

Finally, the importance of the 3rd Field Army loyalty group was emphasized by the fact that Mao personally appeared at the funeral of the late Foreign Minister, Marshal Ch'en Yi, who died on 6 January 1972, and who had previously been the leader of this group.[58] Ch'en's funeral received a degree of publicity which had not been the custom since 1966.

The group of the North-China Field Army could also register a success with the nomination of Yang Yung as Commander in Sinkiang. From September 1971 till August 1973 little happened with regard to members of the 4th Field Army group apart from the transfer of General Liu Hsing-yüan from Kuangtung to Ssuch'uan. The fact that the loyalty groups within the PLA were still of considerable importance to Chinese personnel policies was reinforced by changes in the CC of the CCP brought about by the 10th Party Congress of August 1973.

Of the thirty-six members of the 9th Central Committees who did not reappear either as members or alternate members of the 10th Central Committee, eight were either purged even before the Lin Piao crisis, or they were not re-elected for some reasons which are not clear.[59] Five of these did not reappear on the new Central Committee, but nonetheless appeared again in public.[60] Twenty-three members of the 9th Central Committee who disappeared altogether from the Chinese political scene can be directly associated with the Lin Piao crisis, and this included Ch'en Po-ta, Li Hsüeh-fêng, and Cheng Wei-shan.[61] Twenty-four of the thirty-six members of the Central Committee who were not re-elected were military men. Of these seventeen or 71% were from the 4th Field Army loyalty group,[62] three from the 3rd,[63] and a total of four altogether from the 1st, 2nd and North-China Field Armies.[64]

The struggle of the post-Cultural Revolutionary leadership against the Left[65] and the consequences of the fall of Lin Piao brought about long-term changes in the Provincial revolutionary committees. These bodies, whose functions were limited after the establishment of Provincial Party Committees in all the twenty-nine major administrative units from December 1970 to August 1971 to the running of the civilian administration in the provinces, underwent at the same time a significant change in personnel. Of their twenty-nine Chairmen in September 1968, twenty-one were members of the PLA and eight cadres. During the period between the 9th Party Congress in April 1969 and 1 July 1973 nine Chairmen of the provincial revolutionary committees were purged,[66] three were transferred away from their posts,[67] and three died.[68] Of these fifteen leaders of provincial administrations ten were military men and five civilian cadres. Their places were taken by nine officers[69] and six civilian officials.[70]

During the same period, ninety-six or 50·3% of the 121 Vice-Chairmen of the provincial revolutionary committees who were dismissed from office, eight were transferred and one had died. Of the 113 newly-appointed Vice-Chairmen of the revolutionary committees, sixty-one (or 54%) were veteran party officials. Forty-one or 42·7% of the purged had been representatives of Maoist mass organizations. Where new representatives of mass organizations entered the provincial leadership groups, they were no longer former members of Rebel Organizations from the Cultural Revolution but cadres who had already been active in the ordinary mass organizations before 1965–6. There was therefore a clear change of emphasis away from the Cultural Revolutionary groups to representatives of such organizations, which the Red Guards and rebels had attacked during the Cultural Revolution. However, the PLA's sphere of influence was only marginally reduced. In July 1973 generals still headed the administration of nineteen out of the twenty-nine Provinces, Autonomous Regions and Municipalities in China.

According to this study, the fall of Lin Piao and his followers in the PLA was only of real benefit to the cadres of the civilian administrative *apparat* of all the groups who had come together in the Anti-Lin coalition. The dominant position of the Army in the Chinese Provinces remained until the 10th Party Congress. The military still also had considerable influence in the Central State *apparat*. The Cultural Revolutionary Left, on the other hand, had gained little from the division of the spoils before the summer of

1973. However, this was to change when the Left was able to strengthen its position in the course of the reconstruction of the regular mass organizations, and to make close contacts with the secret police and security forces.[71] Until then, however, the Left was not in a position to hinder the full development of the New Course in policies, which had come with the fall of Lin Piao.

REFERENCES

1. The dates for the following section are taken, *inter alia*, from *CKYC*, Vol. 6, No. 9, September 1972, pp. 6 ff.; and Whitson, *Succession*, Appendix B, loc. cit., passim.
2. Ch'en appeared for the last time on 29 March 1972 publicly as Deputy Chief of the General Staff (*NCNA*, Peking, 29 March 1972) and was in May 1973 mentioned in a lower position as a Political Commissar in Hupei Military District (Radio Hupei, 19 May 1973).
3. K'uang's purge became known only when in July 1973 he was replaced in his position as Director of the Office for Civil Aviation, and was not re-elected to the Central Committee (*NCNA*, Peking, 13 July 1973).
4. See pp. 96 ff.
5. Yüan still appeared in public on 8 June 1973 (*NCNA*, Chinan, 8 June 1973) but was not re-elected to the CC, and has not been mentioned since.
6. Hsiung Ying-t'ang (Chekiang), Yang Tung-liang (Kiangsi) and Lung Ping-ch'u (Kansu).
7. Radio Kuangtung, 2 Programme, 8 March 1972.
8. *NCNA*, Canton, 7 April 1972.
9. Radio Ssuch'uan, 22 November 1972 and 2 February 1973.
10. *NCNA*, Peking, 25 February 1972.
11. Radio Hunan, 4 December 1971.
12. Ibid., 19 November 1972.
13. Radio Heilungkiang, 29 December 1971 and 4 May 1973.
14. Radio Chekiang, 16 May 1973.
15. E.g. *HC*, No. 1, 1972; *JMJP*, 1 and 5 December 1971.
16. Radio Hupei, Kuangsi, Haik'ou, and Shansi, all 2 January 1972; Radio Ssuch'uan, 3 January 1972; Radio Yünnan and Kuangsi, 4 January 1972; Radio Kueichou, 5 and 6 January 1972; Radio Shensi and Lhasa, 6 January 1972.
17. Radio Hunan, 26 December 1971 and 2 January 1972.
18. E.g. Radio Kansu, 2 December 1971; Radio Ch'inghai, 31 December 1971; Radio Shensi, 25 and 27 January 1972; Radio Shansi, 30 January 1972.
19. Radio Hunan, Kuangsi, and Ssuch'uan, all 3 March 1972; Radio Shansi and Yünnan, 4 March 1972.
20. *JMJP*, 28 April 1972.
21. See p. 100.
22. *NCNA*, Peking, 24 January 1972.
23. *NCNA*, Peking, 13 April 1972.

24. Radio Canton, 1 October 1972.

25. Ibid., 29 January 1973.

26. *NCNA*, Peking and Shênyang, 14 December 1972.

27. *NCNA*, Peking, 16 March 1973.

28. Ibid., 12 April 1973.

29. Ibid., 1 May 1973.

30. Ibid., 28 July 1973.

31. Ibid., 29 August 1973. See also p. 240.

32. Radio Canton, 7 April 1972.

33. *NCNA*, Canton, 15 April 1974.

34. Radio Hunan, 14 April 1973.

35. *Tzu-liao chuan-chi* (Collection of Materials), Canton, 3 May 1968. Names supplemented by the author.

36. *NCNA*, Chinan, 2 June 1972.

37. *CKYC*, Vol. 8, No. 4, April 1974, p. 50.

38. *NCNA*, Peking, 29 March 1972.

39. Ibid., 1 May 1972.

40. Ibid., 6 November 1972.

41. Ibid., 1 May 1973.

42. Radio Ssuch'uan, 13 August 1973.

43. *NCNA*, Peking, 1 August and 2 October 1972.

44. *NCNA*, Urumchi, 3 July 1973.

45. *NCNA*, Peking, 1 August 1972. See p.

46. *NCNA*, Canton, 1 October 1972.

47. Radio Fukien, 11 January 1973.

48. See pp. 100 ff.

49. *NCNA*, Peking, 1 May 1972.

50. Ibid., 5 October 1972.

51. Ibid., 17 and 18 October 1972.

52. Ibid., 18 and 20 June 1973.

53. Ibid., 1 July 1972.

54. Chou En-lai (Premier); Li Hsien-nien, Teng Hsiao-p'ing, Li Fu-ch'un (Vice-Premiers); Ch'i P'eng-fei (Foreign Secretary), Lai Chi-fa (Building Materials), Fang Yi (Economic Relations with Foreign Countries), Li Ch'iang (Foreign Trade), Ch'ien Chih-kuang (Light Industry), Mme. Liu Hsiang-p'ing (Public Health), Chung Fu-hsiang (Posts and Telecommunications), Ku Mu (State Capital Construction Commission), Wu Tê (Cultural Group), and Liu Hsi-yao (Educational and Scientific Group).

55. Marshal Nieh Jung-chen (Vice-Premier), as well as Generals Sha Fêng (Agriculture and Forestry), Yang Chieh (Communications), Li Chui-ch'ing (1st Machine-Building), Ch'en Shao-k'un (Metal Industry), Li Chen (Public Security), Chang Wên-pi (Water Construction and Electricity), Fan Tzu-yü (Commerce), Wang Mêng (Physical Education and Sports Commission) and Yü Ch'iu-li (State Planning Commission).

56. The Generals Ch'en Shao-k'un, Li Chen, Fan Tzu-yü, Hsiang Chung-hua, Li Ta, and Ch'in Chi-wei.

57. The Generals Chang Wên-pi, Wang Liu-sheng, T'an Chih-kêng, Wang Chien-an, Yen Cheng and Pao Hsien-chih.

58. *JMJP*, 10 January 1972.

59. Wên Yüch'eng, Hsü Hai-tung, P'an Fu-sheng, Liu Kê-p'ing, Wang Hsiao-yü, Liu Chieh-t'ing, Ma Fu-ch'üan and Wang Pai-tan.

60. Wang Hsin-t'ing, Lai Chi-fa, T'eng Hai-ch'ing, Kao Wei-sung and Ch'iu Kuo-Kuang.

61. Lin Piao, Ch'en Po-ta, Huang Yung-sheng, Wu Fa-hsien, Li Tso-p'eng, Ch'iu Hui-tso, Mme. Yeh Ch'ün, Chang T'ien-yün, Wu Jui-lin, Wang Hui-ch'iu, K'uang Jên-nung, Tseng Kuo-hua, Wang Ping-chang, Ch'iu Chuang-ch'eng, Liang Hsing-ch'u, Lung Shu-chin, Cheng Wei-shan, Nan P'ing, Chou Ch'ih-p'ing, Li Hsüeh-fêng, Liu Fêng, Ch'eng Shih-ch'ing and Yüan Sheng-p'ing.

62. Lin Piao, Huang Yung-sheng, Wu Fa-hsien, Li Tso-p'eng, Ch'iu Hui-tso, Mme. Yeh Ch'ün, Wên Yü-ch'eng, Wu Jui-lin, Chang Yün-t'ien, Ch'eng Shih-ch'ing, Ch'iu Chuang-ch'eng, Hsü Hai-tung, Liang Hsing-ch'u, Lung Shu-chin, Chou Ch'ih-p'ing, Ch'iu Kuo-kuang and Yüan Sheng-p'ing.

63. Nan P'ing, K'uang Jên-nung, and T'eng Hai-ch'ing.

64. Wang Hui-ch'iu and Liu Fêng (2nd), Kao Wei-sung (1st) and Cheng Wei-shan (North China).

65. See pp. 77-90.

66. P'an Fu-sheng (Heilungkiang), Wang Hsiao-yü (Shantung), Liu Kê-p'ing (Shansi), Li Tsai-han (Kueichou), Lung Shu-chin (Sinkiang), Li Hsüeh-fêng (Hopei), Nan P'ing (Chekiang), Tseng Yang-ya (Tibet) and Ch'eng Shih-ch'ing (Kiangsi).

67. Liu Hsing-yüan (Kuangtung), Li Yüan (Hunan) and T'eng Hai-ch'ing (Inner Mongolia).

68. Hsieh Fu-chih (Peking), Chang Kuo-hua (Ssuch'uan) and T'an Fu-jen (Yünnan).

69. Wang Chia-tao (Heilungkiang), Yu T'ai-chung (Inner Mongolia), Ting Shêng (Kuangtung), Hsieh Chen-hua (Shansi), Yang Tê-chih (Shantung), Liu Hsing-yüan (Ssuch'uan), Jên Jung (Tibet), Shê Chi-tê (Acting, Kiangsi) and Lu Jui-lin (Acting, Kueichou).

70. Liu Tzu-hou (Hopei), Hua Kuo-fêng (Hunan), Wu Tê (Peking), Chou Hsing (Yünnan), Saifudin (Sinkiang) and T'an Chi-lung (Chekiang).

71. See pp. 175 ff.

10. The Second 'Readjustment'

Lin's opponents, probably not without the agreement of the Party Leader, initiated social and economic measures which in practice resulted in a reduction of the leadership's demands on the masses—as opposed to Lin's previous attempt at a return to the 1958 concept of development through mobilization. After Lin's fall these measures were not only implemented throughout the whole country, but they also formed the basis of a programme which appeared with increasing clarity to be becoming a coherent alternative. During the two years between the late summer of 1971 and the autumn of 1973 the PRC thus experienced a second 'readjustment'. The use of this term to characterize the economic and social policies of the anti-Lin coalition refers to the first period of 'readjustment' initiated by Liu Shao-ch'i and the majority of the Party leadership after 1959.[1] In fact, the most important characteristics of the policies of the anti-Mao opposition in the early 1960s actually reappeared, at least temporarily, after 1971; and, with regard to agricultural policy, the readjustments made to Mao's concept of development were even greater during the second period of 'readjustment' than they had been during the first.

We have seen that after 1958 Liu Shao'ch'i's economic advisers—in contrast to the Maoist principle of the decentralization of agriculture and local small-scale industries to the level of the People's Communes, with a simultaneous strict centralization of the modern industrial sector—had realized, partly at least, the principle of the decentralization of all economic sectors to the provincial and regional levels.[2] When the central civil administration temporarily lost control during the chaos of the Cultural Revolution, the position of the regional leadership in the fields of planning and administration was, almost inevitably, strengthened. This trend continued even after the end of the Cultural Revolution. This is most clearly seen in the announcement of Provincial development plans which at this time provided for differing economic sectors and diverse planning periods.[3] Lin Piao's attempts and those of the Central military to counteract this development essentially failed. With Lin's fall, the autonomy of the regional leadership organs for planning and administration of the economy was clearly confirmed. In November 1971, a leading article in *Red Flag* indicated that the regions were already on the point of reaching self-sufficiency in food supplies.[4] A little later, in January 1972, it became known for the first time that the largest heavy industry complex in China, the Anshan-Penshi steel plant in

South Manchuria was no longer directly controlled by the Centre but by the provincial leadership of Liaoning. The large steel works in Wuhan were also, as was confirmed in August 1972, now subordinated to Hupei's leadership.[5] On the basis of the material at present available we cannot clearly distinguish the powers of the Centre in planning and administering the modern industrial sector. After the Cultural Revolution, Peking's ministries certainly did not supervise the large nationwide enterprises; they seemed rather to have restricted themselves to the coordination of problems. It was logical, therefore, that the journal *Red Flag* should in January 1972 clearly come down on the side of regional prerogatives of planning and administration in the balance between the regions and the Centre. In the theoretical journal of the Party it was said that ministries could in future only give orders to individual factories through, and with the agreement of, local Party committees. Any other procedure would be a 'vertical dictatorship' *(T'iao-t'iao chuan-cheng)* and 'leadership by command' *(Ch'ui-chih ling-tao)*; modes of behaviour which would now be considered as deviations from the Party's 'correct line'.[6]

During the spring of 1972 the regional leaderships clearly over-exploited the expansion of their autonomy. This stimulated the Centre into emphasizing—sometimes in contradiction to basic decisions made in 1971-2—that all economic organs had to 'consider the whole'.[7] Such references were to exert a balancing influence, but the principle which gave Provincial and regional leaderships considerable leeway in their own operations was hardly affected. Whether regional leaders can in future maintain the decentralization of economic planning and administration against the now reinforced Central power remains to be seen. Until now, however, the Chinese economic system has not returned to the centralized economic administration by which it was characterized at the end of the 1950s.

Alongside this strengthening of the role of regional leadership organs after the autumn of 1971 throughout China, there has been a revaluation of technical personnel and, associated with this, an expansion of management power in industry. Many plants during the Cultural Revolution had subordinated technical and business management to the strict control of workers' committees, and limited management's authority. These trends were now strongly opposed. Even though the Party leadership had refrained from publicly stating its point of view, so as not to make too obvious the break with the ideas of the Cultural Revolutionary Left, there were still reports from plants throughout the country clearly indicating the direction of this new trend. During January 1972 in Ssuch'uan strong criticism had already been made of 'persons who were misled by anarchist ideas and who were blindly attacking management, control and supervision in factories' and of 'the absurd theory that one could do without rational systems of direction and control'.[8] For the first time since 1965, the achievements of the technical intelligentsia in the factories was regarded as having positive value. Those who opposed the principle that 'experts must lead the factories', were no longer regarded as Revolutionary Rebels but as deviants from the Party Line.[9] In March 1972, even the *JMJP* promoted the new industrial management policy. In a series of articles about different kinds of industrial plants in many parts of the country, it reported how the 'strengthening of management' showed advantageous results in production.[10] These guidelines, emphasizing pragmatic development ideas, were not being voluntarily adhered to by all factory workers. In July there were reminders from the capital, Shansi, Yünnan and Kueichou pointing to the fact that attacks on industrial discipline from the 'extreme Left' had been repudiated, and that the system of factory management had to be further strengthened. This included efforts to reduce waste in production, to cut down on stores, and in particular to establish reliable systems for accounts and stocktaking. The Revolutionary Committees, which since the Cultural Revolution had not been sufficiently careful in this respect, were reminded to let the experts have a free hand since 'carelessness and inexperience' would lead to losses which the country could not afford.[11]

The basic outline of the New Course were shown even more clearly in the area of wage policy. In the early 1960s a clearly graded system of 'material incentives' had largely contributed to overcoming the economic crisis which had followed the policy of the 'Three Red Banners'. In many enterprises during the Cultural Revolution, the Maoist mass organizations enforced the establishment of a system of equal wages for all workers, regardless of their productivity. During the conflict of 1970–1, those provinces whose leaderships had close links with Lin Piao retained this system,[12] even though in other parts of the country it had already been condemned as 'egalitarianism'.[13] Barely four months after the fall of Lin, in January 1972, there were renewed attacks on 'egalitarianism' in some of the Central Chinese provinces, and soon this campaign spread all over the country.[14] The principle of equal wages for all workers was now seen as an expression of 'bourgeois idealism' and of 'extreme Left adventurism' which had to be overcome. The new official view was laid down in an article in the *JMJP* of 12 June 1972. The 'material incentives' of the early 1960s had been an instrument through which the 'renegade, traitor and blackleg' Liu Shao-ch'i had hoped to bring about the 'restoration of capitalism'. This attempt had failed because the workers had recognized the tricks of the class traitor. However, one had to distinguish between such 'material incentives' and 'a sensible wage structure' contributing to the 'socialist activism of the masses'.[15] What actually distinguished the 'sensible wage structure' from a system of 'material incentives' remained unexplained by the Party leadership. Nonetheless, after the summer of 1972, in all the Chinese factories for which there is information, workers were paid according to one initial and eight further productivity scales, where the amount of remuneration ranged from 18 to 109 JMP. Wages on the higher productivity scale were six times higher than those on the lowest. Classification into scales was according to criteria of qualification, seniority and actual productivity.[16] Apart from this, enterprise managements distributed bonuses when plan targets were over-fulfilled, according to the individual's work input.[17]

In the spring of 1972, for the first time since the mid-1960s, it was once again pointed out to commercial enterprises that they had to work for a rise in the general standard of living. The Peking leadership demanded a greater variety in the supply of 'foods, clothing and hairstyles'.[18] Such improvements only filtered through slowly and only marginally changed the scene in the streets of Chinese towns. Even so, some visitors to China reported that during the first months of 1973 the demand for a greater variety of goods was already noticeable in some of the larger cities. In April 1973 the First Secretary and Chairman of the Revolutionary Committee in Kuangtung, General Ting Shêng went so far as to declare before a meeting in Canton that he was not opposed to young girls occasionally wearing lipstick.[19]

However, the characteristics of the New Course in policy were most clearly demonstrated in rural social policy—precisely that area which had provided the decisive resolution of the conflict over the general direction of policy in Chinese politics during the winter and spring of 1970-1. The announcement of the 'rural economic policy' in March 1971 had shown that the anti-Lin coalition had succeeded in forestalling the attempt to return to the ideas of 1958.[20] After the fall of Lin and the purge of his followers, the victorious group in the Party leadership decided on an even more dramatic change of direction in rural economic policy. On 26 December 1971 it released a 'directive on the problem of distribution in the rural People's Communes'.[21] This internal Party document was distributed to cadres down to the county level. It began with the statement that 'the counter-revolutionary conspiracy of the opportunist, conspirator, renegade and traitor Lin Piao, and his followers has been put down' and that 'Lin's and Chen's counter-revolutionary political line has been shattered'. In this way a connection was forged between the implementation of the policies of the New Course and the Lin Piao crisis. In this document, Mao Tse-tung was quoted as saying: 'We have to pay an equal amount of attention to the interests of the state, the collective and the individual.' This, so the document continues, had not happened in the past, but an 'artificial egalitarianism had hampered the realization of Chairman Mao's revolutionary line'.[22]

Even though the 'general situation' in the villages was 'excellent', difficulties had emerged which had to be overcome. For this reason grain rations should in future go straight to the individual peasant households, where they should be independently administered.[23] The communes and production brigades were forbidden to take manpower from the production teams unless they had the latter's explicit permission to do so.[24] Of equal importance was the statement that the example of Tachai ought not to be 'adopted or copied indiscriminately'.[25]

With this decision the People's Communes were in practice limited once again to the administration and control of secondary schools and hospitals. The responsibility for local small-scale industries, primary schools, health clinics and, to a certain extent, public works remaining with the production brigades. The responsibility for agricultural production and distribution was again returned to the production teams. As a result, the division of powers in the rural areas reverted to the situation that had existed in the early 1960s.

The change of course in rural social policy after the publication of these new guidelines for the Communes was accompanied by a campaign, in most of China's provinces, which severely criticized basic-level cadres in the villages. During the Cultural Revolution and in the period of Lin Piao's 'mobilizatory' offensive many of these cadres had attempted to portray themselves as representatives of the Left by attacking the privileges conceded to the peasants during the first phase of 'readjustment'. They were now severely criticized for this very behaviour. Shortly after the announcement of these guidelines on 26 December, the media began to provide clear references to the new trends in agricultural policy. In Inner Mongolia a leader in the regional newspaper refuted Liu Shao-ch'i's social policy and then with particular vigour also criticized the ideas of the Cultural Revolutionary Left:

On the other side they [i.e. the Party Enemies] came from the Left. They tried 'to cut the pigtail of private property', and 'to bring about the transition to Communism', renounced the Law of Value ... and advocated Left-opportunist political measures.

According to the leadership of Inner Mongolia, the policy of the Party was based 'on the experiences gained in developing the People's Communes'. This included the principle of 'the distribution of property at three levels with the production team as the foundation', the payment of wages according to productivity, and the distribution of small private plots to the peasantry and the encouragement of private, part-time activities, although there was the reservation that 'the development of the People's Commune must be given priority'.[26]

In January 1972, some Provinces were even more explicit. In Hupei it was said that there had been sabotage attempts as a result of the cadres' radical policies in the countryside. It was therefore necessary to consider the peasants' welfare as much as the State's grain procurement.[27] The cadres were reproached because, 'under the influence of Left-extremist tendencies', they had 'criticized the peasants' authorized part-time activities as capitalism' and confiscated private plots, 'which the Party's policies on the peasantry definitely allowed'.[28] The leadership of Kuangsi expressed similar opinions.[29] In Kuangtung it was now stipulated that crop rations and peasant wages should 'be raised accordingly', when there was an increase in production.[30] A Plenum of Shansi provincial Party Committee vigorously opposed the widespread idea among cadres at the basic-unit level that deviations to the Left were better than those to the Right, and re-confirmed the 'four principles of agricultural policy's distribution of property at three levels', wages according to labour, the encouragement of part-time work and the distribution of private plots to the peasantry.[31] In Yünnan too the principles of the 26 December 1971 guideline were quickly taken up. Here an internal document from a district administration, which has become available in the West, explained the new policy even more thoroughly than the Centre. By allowing individual peasant households to account for their grain allocations, it came very close to Liu Shao-ch'i's and Teng Hsiao-p'ing's attempt, which had failed in 1962, to transfer production guarantees from the State procurement agencies to the individual households.[32]

The Centre soon involved itself in the campaign to implement the New Course in China's villages. In the late summer and autumn 1972, it criticized even more intensely the mistakes of the basic-unit level cadres during 1968–71, and by making its disapproval known it also clarified which policy it wanted implemented in the villages. Thus in the *JMJP* more than thirty articles and reports on the situation in the villages were published between 1 and 8 August 1972, thoroughly condemning the principles of Lin Piao's offensive.[33] The cadres were blamed for having confiscated the peasants' privately raised pigs, and prohibiting part-time activities in many villages.[34] Fruit trees in the private sector were seized,[35] and the peasants were not allowed to pick herbs for medicines, to catch snakes for the production of traditional Chinese drugs or to weave mats and straw hats.[36] In an extremely critical way the leadership blamed the production brigades for attempting both to replace the production teams as the agricultural accounting unit, and to put under their control the workshops of these units.[37] This had caused severe setbacks to agricultural production.[38]

However, the campaign to promote the New Course was not limited to criticism of the behaviour of the cadres during the Cultural Revolution and the influence of Lin Piao's suggestions. In some cases, the campaign considerably exceeded the criticism which demanded a return to the principles of the early 1960s. Thus in some provinces it was suggested that the production teams for the organization of labour were to be divided into even smaller units of 'work groups' *(Tso-yeh-tsu)* with three to five families at the most.[39] While during the first 'readjustment' period the peasants were allowed to own the fruit trees next to their houses now the fruit trees on private land were withdrawn from the collective sector altogether and were given to individual households too.[40] Special allowances were made for privately raised cattle which officially remained collective property after August 1972.[41] In the same month, reports from People's Communes in different provinces began to confirm that the encouragement of 'individual initiative' was part of 'Chairman Mao's correct revolutionary line'.[42]

The efforts of the Party leadership to reduce its demands on the rural population were without doubt stimulated by the fact that the 1972 harvest had suffered from particularly severe weather. In this situation it was necessary to stimulate the initiative of the individual peasants and of the small production teams in order to ensure food supplies. Thus the rights of the production teams were stressed even more than in the early 1960s. On 16 October 1972, an editorial in the *JMJP* urged all organs to unreservedly observe 'the production team's right to self-determination' *(Shêng-ch'an-tui-te tzu-chu-ch'üan)*. In the teams there should be more room for the self-determination of the peasants, and the system of payment according to labour should be generally followed.[43] From here it was only a small step to the suggestion that from now on the political behaviour of commune members should play absolutely no part any more in the distribution of work points.[44]

Consequently, one of the central principles of the Tachai model had clearly been abandoned. Nonetheless, the campaign to 'Learn from Tachai' had not been interrupted at any time, and in fact has continued right up to the present. In implementing the New Course, the content of this movement had changed. Until the autumn of 1971, as we have seen, the Tachai model stood for the overwhelming priority of political criteria and for the development policy of self-sufficiency in the production brigades. However, in April 1973, Tachai Party Secretary, Ch'en Yung-kuei, in a lecture to a conference of agricultural cadres in Ch'engtu declared that a study of the experiences of his brigade revealed five principles:

(1) The production of crops and the quotas of delivery to State procurement agencies must be raised along with the peasants' rations.

(2) Forestry, livestock raising, fishery and side-line activities had to be developed in 'a big way'.

(3) There should be a 'great leap' in water conservation and irrigation work.

(4) The mechanization of agriculture must be emphatically promoted.

(5) There should be 'great changes' in all villages.[45]

At this time, during the period of the 'second readjustment', the Tachai campaign stood for a movement which was clearly pragmatic. The improvement of agricultural techniques prevailed over demands for political reliability and integrity. In contrast to the original aims of the Tachai movement, it was also the case that since the beginning of 1973 in some provinces the necessity of directing State investment into agriculture had been emphasized. In addition, more funds for the development of production should be made available by reducing the construction of small-scale local industries in the communes, brigades, and the production teams.[46]

As in the economic crisis of 1960-2, which had been caused essentially by the failure of the policies of the 'Three Red Banners', so now once again the Chinese leadership emphasized pragmatic considerations in their development policy. The slogan of a 'great Leap Forward' was rarely heard. Instead the leadership talked about 'planned and balanced development' *(Yu chi-hua, an pi-li-te fa-chan)*[47]. Furthermore as in 1962, discussion centred around the slogan formulated by the centre, to promote development 'with agriculture as the foundation and industry as the leading factor' *(I nung-yeh wei chi-ch'u, i kung-yeh wei chu-tao)*. In Anhui during April 1972, the leadership explained the developmental policies of the New Course:

Agriculture is the foundation. Only when agriculture has been developed can light industry have more raw materials at its disposal and heavy industry be given greater latitude. The development of light industry satisfies the demands of the population, makes higher accumulation possible and promotes the development of heavy industry.[48]

The order of priorities now current in China is clearly demonstrated in this explanation, which can be taken as representative of many others with similar contents. There is, first, agriculture and implicitly agricultural support industries; secondly, light industry; and only thirdly, heavy industry. This ranking did not only apply to the first 'readjustment' period, but in fact has been a necessity resulting from the rather slow progress of China's agricultural production since the middle of the 1950s. Official and semi-official pronouncements from Peking concerning the size of grain production provided the information that in 1970 the grain harvest had been 240 million tons and in 1971 246 million tons. A figure of 236 million tons for 1972 is provided in such sources. These figures greatly exceed Western calculations, and one should remember that Chinese sources had reported a production of 375 million tons for 1958, which was later amended to 250 million tons. In 1971 China's index of foodgrain production was 148 (taking the average of 1952-6 as the base figure of 100). In comparison to the developing parts of the world, China was only one point ahead of Africa (147) and 17 behind Latin America, the Near East and the non-communist states of Asia (165). The following table shows the situation within Asia;

Table 10/1

INDICES OF FOOD GRAIN PRODUCTION IN
ASIAN COUNTRIES

(100 = average 1952-6)[49]

Country	1955	1971	Difference
Malaysia	105	246	141
Thailand	104	220	116
Taiwan	100	193	93
Philippines	100	193	93
South Korea	115	196	81
Ceylon	112	173	61
Pakistan	98	159	61
India	104	155	51
Japan	113	163	50
Burma	101	149	48
Indonesia	102	148	46
China	105	148	43

One has to doubt whether the aims which had been set by the twelve year Agricultural Development Plan of 1956 had in fact been achieved. By 1968 only two of the twenty-nine Provinces had reported achieving the targets originally set for 1967, and by 1970 these had been reached by three further Provinces. Seven Provinces reported that by 1970 they still had not achieved the targets of 1967, and fourteen Provinces gave no account at all of their achievements.[50] In 1972 only seventeen of the ninety-nine districts in Shensi Province had arrived at their 1970 targets.[51] In Anhui it was twenty-eight out of sixty-eight districts.[52]

It is seldom indeed that the Chinese media report the exact

figures of agricultural production. From the Cultural Revolution until the end of 1973, this in fact only happened in four Provinces for which there are comparative figures for 1956, or for 1957, and comparatively reliable population data in existence. If one uses this data, it can be seen that *per capita* grain and potato production in Honan had risen from 266·1 kg. in 1956 to 299·03 kg. in 1972, i.e. a total rise of 12·4% in sixteen years.[53] Shansi reported a *per capita* production of 273·05 kg. in 1956, and 290·25 kg. in 1971, an increase of 6·3% in fifteen years.[54] More favourable results were produced in the province of Hopei. Here *per capita* production in 1957 was 223·61 kg. and in 1972 333·27 kg., an increase of 49% in fifteen years.[55] In Anhui, on the other hand, a reduction in production is clearly observable. Here there was a *per capita* grain production of 369·48 kg. in 1957 and of 303·33 kg. in 1972, 17·9% less than it had been fifteen years earlier.[56]

These figures make apparent the extent of the developmental problems which the leadership of the CCP had to face. The New Course which had emerged since the Autumn of 1971 in the second period of 'readjustment', approached the problem of China's development with a concept that differed fundamentally from Mao's ideas of 1958.

The characteristics of these concepts are evident in an examination of the economic and social policies of the anti-Lin coalition during the period from autumn 1971 to the summer of 1973:

— The regional leaderships were granted a relatively high degree of autonomy in economic planning and administration. This is contrary to the Maoist concept of a highly centralized modern industrial sector with a simultaneous decentralization of agriculture and small-scale local industry to the level of the People's Communes.

— Technicians once again became important in the administration of industrial and commercial enterprises, and the powers of management were increased. In contrast, it had been the idea of the Cultural Revolutionary Left, and probably of Mao Tse-tung as well, that managers and technical experts had to comply with the directives of their workers' committees.

— A clearly differentiated salary structure with considerable differences of income at various levels was established, in contrast to the demand for equal wages for all, without regard to productivity, that had been suggested by the Maoist mass organizations during the Cultural Revolution and initially established in some firms.

— As an incentive for higher achievements in production, the New Course reintroduced—as 'sensible remuneration'—the system of material incentives which had been in force before the Cultural

Revolution. This is contrary to the strong emphasis placed on the non-material incentives of idealistic service to the revolution and the construction of a class-free society, as represented by Mao and the Cultural Revolutionary Left.

— In the Chinese villages there was a return to a distribution of work and property at three levels, with the most important duties left to the production teams. On the other hand, Mao's ideas of 1958 emphasized the People's Commune, while Lin Piao and his followers attempted to delegate powers to the production brigade.

— The ownership of some small private plots was once again guaranteed to the peasants, and in some cases the size of those plots was even marginally enlarged. Private livestock-raising and part-time work was again encouraged. By contrast, Mao in 1958 and Lin in 1969-71 had attempted to enforce tight restrictions on private side-line activities.

— Technical improvements and a wide variety in agricultural production were becoming an important part of the movement to 'Learn from Tachai'—a movement of which the original character had now been totally changed. Mao, Lin Piao and the Cultural Revolutionary Left had used this campaign to emphasize the absolute pre-eminence of political considerations and the self-sufficiency of production brigades.

— The remuneration of peasants and industrial workers was again organized according to criteria of productivity. The introduction of political criteria into the remuneration and distribution system was now totally rejected.

This contrast between the two social policies shows that the idea held by many Western observers of a Chinese concept of development, which in its major characteristics is designed by Mao and is the antithesis of that practised in the USSR, just cannot be upheld. The determining feature of Chinese development politics is essentially the dichotomy between Mao's and his followers' mobilizatory development concept of 1958 on the one hand, and the concept of 'readjustment' on the other. The latter concept was formed, both in 1959-62 and again after the autumn of 1970, from improvized, pragmatic and development-oriented measures.

These two concepts certainly cannot always be easily distinguished in practice, since they influence one another. Lin Piao's socio-political offensive of 1969-70, for example, lacked the theoretical clarity of the programme of the 'Three Red Banners'. On the other hand, the second period of 'readjustment' is presented in propaganda for the outside world in similar tones to the rhetoric of 1958, and within China it has its ideological justification by an invocation of 'Chairman Mao's correct revolutionary line'. Furthermore, Mao's ideas have had at least a marginal influence on the policies of the New Course which, in practice, differ fundamentally from the policies of 1958-9, 1967-8 and 1969-70.

The speed of material development in China had certainly been affected by this dichotomy. The growth of the net national product by 12% in 1958 and 9% in 1970 brought at least temporary success to the mobilizatory policies. But in the years that followed these periods of high achievement, these policies caused considerable setbacks, from which the country only recovered after a 'readjustment' policy had become fully effective. As a result of this confusion, the average growth rate of the net national product in the twenty years from 1952 to 1972 remained only 3·5%.[57] This is not a particularly encouraging result for a developing country.

However, one must remember that in the mind of the Chinese leadership material growth is less important than the attempt to create a change of consciousness in the population. The policies of the New Course meant that in this respect, as during the earlier phase of readjustment in the early 1960s, there was a change of priorities in favour of growth. It is not possible yet to say whether or not this new policy will last. However, one can say with some certainty that in a country like China with such a low level of development, material growth must be a precondition to any form of social advance. This is what the architects of the first and second 'readjustments' have made quite clear, as opposed to those dogmatists who still cling to the ideas of 1958 and will only make half-hearted compromises.

REFERENCES

1. For an evaluation of this period see Domes, *Internal Politics*, op. cit., pp. 117-19 and 126-30.

2. See p. 133.

3. *CNA*, No. 781, 14 November 1969; Radio Heilungkiang, 18 January 1970; Radio Hunan, 5 February 1971 and Radio Kiangsu, 21 February 1971.

4. *HC*, No. 11, 1971.

5. *JMJP*, 15 January 1972; Radio Hupei, 17 August 1972.

6. *HC*, No. 1, 1972. See also *CNA*, No. 873, 10 March 1972.

7. *HC*, No. 4, 1972, *inter alia*.

8. Radio Ssuch'uan, 13 and 14 January 1972.

9. Radio Shensi, 4 February 1972.

10. *JMJP*, 2, 4, 5, 15 and 17 March 1972.

11. *NCNA*, Peking, 5 July 1972; NCNA, T'aiyuan, 7 July 1972; Radio Yünnan, 13 July 1972; Radio Kueichou, 16 July 1972.

12. Radio Chekiang, 13 February 1972.

13. See p. 85.

14. Radio Anhui, 10 January 1972, *inter alia*.

15. *JMJP*, 12 June 1972.

16. Lucian W. Pye, *China Revisited*, Cambridge, Mass., pp. 40 and 55; see also A. Doak Barnett, *Uncertain Passage: China's Transition to the Post-Mao Era*, Washington 1974, pp. 132 ff.

17. Radio Shansi, 4 January 1972.

18. *JMJP*, 5 April 1972.

19. Radio Canton, 17 April 1973.

20. See p. 115..

21. Chung-fa No. 82 (1971), 26 December 1971, first published in facsimile in *Ts'an-k'ao tzu-liao*, T'aipei, 16 August 1972, loc. cit. The authenticity of this document was confirmed by quotes from the Chinese media which covered almost the whole text, and by refugees from China in interviews with the author and other observers in Hong Kong during autumn 1972.

22. Ibid., p. 2.

23. Ibid., p. 3.

24. Ibid., pp. 4 f.

25. Ibid., p. 4.

26. *Neimêngku jih-pao* and Radio Inner Mongolia, 29 December 1971.

27. Radio Hupei, 10 January 1972.

28. Ibid., 13 January 1972.

29. Radio Kuangsi, 27 January 1972.

30. Radio Kuangtung, 1 Programme, 4 January 1972.

31. Radio Shansi, 30 and 31 January 1972.

32. 'The attitude of the Ssumao district Party Committee to the implementation of the 'Directive of the CC of the CCP on problems on distribution in Rural People's Communes', *Ssumao tang-wei fa-pu (Ssu-tang-fa)* (1972), No. 22, 26 March 1972; translated in *Issues and Studies*, T'aipei, Vol. 9, No. 6, March 1973, pp. 91-7.

33. *JMJP*, 1-18 August 1972.

34. *JMJP*, 5 September and 3 August 1972.

35. Ibid., 4 August, 21 and 23 October 1972.

36. Ibid., 4 August, 23 October, 7 August, 12 August and 13 September 1972.

37. Ibid., 7, 9 and 18 August 1972.

38. Ibid., 16 October and 19 October 1972.

39. Radio Anhui, 26 January 1972, *inter alia*.

40. Radio Kiangsi and Radio Shansi, 2 March 1972.

41. *JMJP*, 4 August 1972.

42. Ibid. and ibid., 5 September 1972.

43. Ibid., 16 October 1972.

44. Ibid., 20 October 1972.

45. Radio Ssuch'uan, 11 April 1973.

46. *Inter alia*, ibid., 17 February 1973 and Radio Canton, 18 February 1973.

47. Radio Hupei, 24 April 1972; *JMJP*, 22 June 1972.

48. Radio Anhui, 21 April 1972.

49. Tables and further calculations after, Oskar Weggel, 'Wie löst China das Ernährungsproblem?' in *China aktuell*, Hamburg, No. 3, April 1974, pp. 188 ff.

50. According to official information given by the Provincial Radio Stations on the occasion of the Provincial Party Congress of the CCP, from December 1970 to June 1971.

51. *NCNA*. Peking, 11 April 1973.

52. *NCNA*, Hopei, 26 February 1972.

53. *JMJP*, 1 December 1957; *NCNA*, Peking, 17 April 1973.

54. Radio Shansi, 6 November 1958 and 10 March 1972.

55. *JMJP*, 4 November 1957 and *TKP*, 3 July 1973.

56. Radio Anhui, 4 November 1958 and 4 July 1973.

57. Calculation from Subramanian Swamy, 'China's Economic Growth (1966-72)' in *China Report*, Delhi, Vol. IX, No. 6, November-December 1973, pp. 17-29, particularly pp. 28 ff. This article gives a very thorough and well-balanced study of economic growth in the PRC, with extensive statistical data.

11. The Demolition of the Maoist Position and the Counter-Offensive of the Cultural Revolutionary Left

In a study of the basic features of Chinese politics between 1949 and 1969, the American China specialist Frederick C. Teiwes has argued that it is wrong to analyse political developments from the perspective of a war between 'the two lines', which assumes that within the top leadership there was a group in opposition to the Party leader which had deliberately drafted an alternative programme. On the contrary, he believes that in the period before the Cultural Revolution, the majority of the civilian Party *apparat* around Liu Shao-ch'i believed that the policy of 'readjustment' which it had introduced was in tune with Mao's ideas.[1]

The first part of this argument is certainly correct. Apart from the periods of acute factional struggle—1962-5 and 1970-1—the positions of the opinion groups within the Party leadership cannot be explained simply in terms of 'the two lines'. On the other hand, the observation that the anti-Maoist faction on the eve of the Cultural Revolution still referred to the Chairman does not justify the rash conclusion that they agreed with him. From the behaviour of Liu Shao-ch'i and his followers we can only conclude that Mao's role as the 'legitimator' was claimed by all the opinion groups, even by those opposed to his concept of mobilization. The same was true for the core of the anti-Lin coalition, i.e. the civilian administrators and the majority of the regional military commanders, who initiated and implemented the New Course in 1971-2. They used the Chairman's name and quotations from his rather mild comments during the pre-1958 period to justify their own political actions. In fact, however, the New Course meant a revision of the concept of development through mobilization as designed by Mao and his colleagues. On the other hand, one could argue that the ageing Chairman had in the previous forty years suggested many very different ideas about nation-building and economic development, and that the New Course could therefore very well be attributed to his instigation; that in fact the dichotomy existed within him. Against this hypothesis one could argue that since 1958 radical movements like the Great Leap Forward, the Cultural Revolution and the attempt during 1969-70 to return to the ideas of 1958 were so closely identified with Mao that it is difficult to accept him as the driving force behind the policies of the New Course. In fact, there are better reasons for believing that the New

Course bears the stamp of Chou En-lai's political and social beliefs. It was, after all, this well-educated bureaucrat who had created the carefully-balanced network of political compromises that were to determine the politics of the Chinese gerontocracy after the fall of Lin Piao.

The question of Chairman Mao's real role in the second 'Readjustment' period comes closer to being answered if one examines developments in the Cultural Revolutionary Left's sphere of activity after the autumn of 1971—i.e. in educational and cultural policy.

In contrast to economic and social policy, the Lin Piao crisis did not initially bring about a clearly declared departure from the ideas of Mao, Lin and the Cultural Revolutionary Left in education. The central media continued, although ever less often and less intensively, to propagate the fundamentals of Maoist educational policy: the connection between work and study, the shortening of the length of courses, the open admission of 'workers, peasants and soldiers' to secondary schools and colleges, and a reduction of standards in examinations.[2]

Even so, after the spring of 1972 a number of reports from China's Provinces (partly supported by publications from the Central media) revealed that below the surface of Cultural Revolutionary rhetoric a change of climate was taking place in the schools. This first became apparent in the increased number of colleges which were again admitting students. At the end of February and beginning of March 1972, the enrolment of students for the spring term had begun according to the principle of admitting primarily candidates from a 'worker, peasant or soldier' background without regard to their age or formal educational experience.[3] However the admission criteria were becoming more formalized. Ever since 1970 enrolment had depended on the personal application of the candidate, a reference from the masses—i.e. a vote by the applicant's colleagues in his or her factory, agricultural production team or army unit—and the approval of the relevant revolutionary committee. Now, however, there was to be a fourth stage in the enrolment procedure, namely an 'investigation by the responsible educational establishment'.[4] This meant that now, contrary to what had been customary before the autumn of 1971, the colleges could again participate in the selection of their students. The provincial leaderships soon felt obliged also to point out the need for strict discipline in primary schools.[5] Moreover, a new emphasis soon became evident when students were reminded to 'serve the people' and that to this end they should 'come to grips with cultural and scientific facts'.[6]

Teachers, who had been severely attacked during the Cultural Revolution for their high—and generally also inflexibly applied—demands of educational performance, were now reprimanded for being too easy on their pupils. The Central Party organ wrote on 24 April 1972 that

Some [teachers] go to the opposite extreme. They have previously given away examination questions, and allowed students to answer examination questions in the classroom and to copy them ... this is a totally wrong attitude.[7]

In the late summer and autumn of 1972 the attempts to correct the Cultural Revolutionary trends in education appeared to have entered a new phase. In some of the Southern Chinese universities and colleges, formal entrance examinations were certainly again being held,[8] and there is some evidence that this also happened in other parts of the country. The *JMJP* in a series of articles in August and September pointed out the importance of independent research for the development of Chinese scholarship.[9] On 6 October the Vice-President of the Academy of Sciences, Professor Chou P'ei-yüan, a physicist who had been educated in the United States, was in a position for the first time since 1966 openly to defend the importance of pure research.[10] A short while later, the media began to explain that not only applied mathematics and applied sciences were to be taught in secondary schools and colleges, but also that theoretical mathematics and sciences had a legitimate role in the classroom.[11] At the same time it was pointed out, in a reference to words of Mao's dating from the early 1950s, that students should regard their 'studies as their major responsibility' *(I hsüeh wei chu)*.[12] In some of the Provinces half-yearly examinations were re-established in the secondary schools, as had been usual before the Cultural Revolution. In these, the pupils were consulted before the examination questions were set, but in addition to open book examinations, closed examinations were also reintroduced. Oral examinations were also re-established in the examination system.[13]

All this indicates that in education policy too the Maoist point of view was beginning to lose its power. In view of the importance attached by the Chairman and significant members of the Cultural Revolutionary Left to the education system, it is hardly surprising to find that a few months later, in the summer of 1973, there was a determined attempt to reverse these policies of the New Course so that they agreed with the ideas of the Cultural Revolutionaries.[14]

The Cultural Revolutionary Left under the leadership of Chiang Ch'ing had, through its participation in Lin Piao's fall, further secured its control over the Party's propaganda *apparat*. As a result, the fewest indications of revision in the Maoist course appeared in the area of cultural policy. The promotion of 'revolutionary model operas' continued unabated, even if some were textually revised. The pre-eminence of the heroic style of 'revolutionary romanticism' remained essentially untouched.

However, even in the cultural sphere there were now indications that changes in the direction of greater variety and less control were no longer altogether out of the question. Only a week after the incident of 12 September the *JMJP*, for the first time in over six years, printed three poems by the President of the Chinese Academy, Kuo Mo-jo, which had been written in the classical style.[15] In December 1971 the journal of the Central Committee put in a friendly word for those veteran writers and artists who during the Cultural Revolution had been vehemently attacked by the Maoist mass organizations:

It is necessary to have a revolutionary and creative army [of writers and artists] in order to develop serious literature and art. Ideological and organizational work have to be strengthened in order to build up this army. In accordance with Party policy towards the intellectuals efforts have to be made to educate and to train workers, peasants and writers and *the army of veterans in literature and art must be re-establish*ed.[16]

This quotation demonstrates the extent to which there was a change in emphasis under the cover of Cultural Revolutionary rhetoric. This became even clearer when the paper indicated in the same article that in the production of films and theatrical plays 'elements of traditional and foreign literature' could 'be used after careful selection'.[16] It was of particular significance that in this article, which dealt exclusively with cultural matters, Chiang Ch'ing's name was not mentioned at all.

In February 1972, for the first time since the Cultural Revolution, a scientific periodical appeared in Peking, the *Archaeological Journal (K'ao-ku)*,[17] and there soon followed a number of other academic publications in which there were factual articles next to expositions of doctrine. In April travellers from China reported in Hong Kong that ever since February, at least in Canton, it had been possible to buy the classical Chinese novels *The Dream of the Red Chamber (Hung-lou-mêng)*, *Water Margin (Shui-hu-chuan)* and *Monkey (Hsi-yu chi)*.[18] A communist newspaper in Hong Kong reported in February 1973 that a large number of copies of *The Dream of the Red Chamber* were available in the library of the National Peking University.[19]

Finally, there were even indications of changes in Mao's wife's area of special interest. On 16 October 1972 the official Chinese news agency reported that in November and December of that year the classical Chinese opera *Ch'u Yüan* was to be performed in Japan by a Japanese troupe. This may have concerned only a performance abroad by foreign actors, but the leadership in Peking demonstrated its approval of the affair by giving permission to the

Director of the Chinese office in Tokyo, Hsiao Hsiang-ch'ien, to participate in the preparations for the play and in announcing the fact publicly.[20]

In addition to these first hints of intrusion by the policies of the New Course into the areas of education and cultural policy, there were also unmistakable signs after the fall of Lin Piao of a reduction in the personality cult of Mao Tse-tung that necessarily accompanied the reduction in influence of Maoist doctrines. This had already become evident in September 1971 when seven provinces[21] and the island of Hainan omitted to read a quotation from Mao Tse-tung before the news on the radio, as had been usual since the Cultural Revolution. In four of the provinces Mao's quotations were used only occasionally,[22] while eight provinces certainly continued with this custom until the end of 1971 and read out the Chairman's words.[23]

The fact that since the beginning of 1972 all over China attacks on so-called 'egalitarianism' and 'ultra-Left' deviations became increasingly severe must have affected the role of Maoist doctrines. In January, cadres had already been urged not to let themselves be led from the correct course by ideas of 'eaglitarianism', but to take 'measures to adapt to the changed circumstances'.[24] At the same time it was pointed out in Shensi Province that the widespread view among basic level cadres that 'Leftist behaviour is an insurance, and Right-wing behaviour means danger' *(Tso pao-hsien, yu wei-hsien)* was wrong:

There is no difference in the amount of damage that these two attitudes create. The only difference is that leftist behaviour is more deceptive and more seductive.[25]

A few days later, the Party leadership of the same province spoke of the 'poison of the extreme-Left tendency' which had to be 'fought relentlessly'.[26]

The attacks on the doctrines and heritage of the Cultural Revolution took even more concrete form when the Little Red Book—the *Quotations from Chairman Mao*—the talisman for Maoist revolutionaries in China and throughout the world, came under attack from the victors in the Lin Piao crisis. The criticism of this symbol of the Cultural Revolution had begun during January in the province of Kueichou with the covert remark that 'pseudo-Marxist swindlers like Liu Shao-ch'i' had put together 'some phrases' *(shên-mo yü-lu)* 'completely out of context' 'in order to falsify the Thought of Mao Tse-tung'. This had 'led the masses into mental laziness'.[27] In February *Red Flag* made some careful remarks of the same order,[28] and in June the provincial Party newspaper in Kuangtung demanded rather more clearly that it was

Mao's original works which should be read, and that one should not be content to read only 'sayings and quotations'.[29]

However, these were only the first symptoms of a campaign which started in earnest with a leader in the *JMJP* on 6 July 1972. The Party leadership now demanded that all members of the CCP and officials of mass organizations start to study Marxism thoroughly. This was not to be limited to a reading of extracts and quotations but rather of complete texts. The central Party journal provided required reading for these studies which included three writings by Marx (*The Communist Manifesto, The Civil War in France* and *The Critique of the Gotha Programme*) one by Engels (*Anti-Dühring*), two by Lenin *State and Revolution* and *Material-ism and Empirio-criticism*) as well as five works of Mao Tse-tung (*On Practice, On Contradiction, On the Correct Handling of Contradictions among the People, Speech at the National Propaganda Conference of the CCP,* and *Where do correct ideas come from?*).[30]

In many parts of the country the new movement was taken up sooner than other campaigns in 1972. Within eight weeks a number of provinces not only put it at the centre of their propaganda, but also used it to attack the 'Little Red Book'.[31]

By 7 September at the latest it had become apparent that such procedures could count on the Centre for support. On this day the *JMJP* published an unconcealed attack on the Party leader's quotations that had been collected together under Lin Piao's influence. It stated that 'pseudo-Marxist swindlers like Liu' had 'collected quotations randomly and with anti-Party intentions'. In this way 'Party members and young people in particular had been misled into petit-bourgeois adventures'.[32]

The cautious reappearance of those principles of educational policy which had been the most influential before 1965, was the first clue that a relaxation in cultural policy had begun alongside the reduction in the personality cult of Mao Tse-tung. Moreover, towards the end of 1972 it became obvious that the New Course would not in practice be limited to a return to the politics of 'Readjustment'. It now seemed as if the New Course contained the fundamentals of a far-reaching revision of the Party's General Line, which had originally been written by Mao himself. China appeared about to enter a period of 'de-Mao-ization' which could have similar dimensions to the process of 'de-Stalinization' in the USSR.

At the turn of the year 1972-3 this development unsurprisingly aroused the Cultural Revolutionary Left's opposition. The last time the group of Chiang Ch'ing, Chang Ch'un-ch'iao and Yao Wên-yüan had been clearly identified by the Central media was shortly after Lin Piao's fall. On 25 September 1971 the *JMJP* published a commemorative article on the ninetieth anniversary of the birth of Lu Hsün, the writer, which contained an extremely severe attack on the followers of the teaching of the classical Chinese philosopher Confucius (K'ung-tzu). His administration as Prime Minister of a Chinese feudal state had had obviously tyrannical characteristics. This can be seen in particular from the fact that 'right after his appointment as Premier' he had his critic Shao Cheng-mao murdered.[33] This remark could be understood as a disguised attack on Chou En-lai. In September 1954, with the enforcement of the constitution of the PRC, he had been nominated Premier of the State Council. A few months later in spring 1955, the Chinese media announced that the former Chairman of the State Planning Commission, and member of the Politburo, Kao Kang, had committed suicide.[34]

After the publication of this article the Left kept silent for a long time. There are many signs to indicate that, in spite of far-reaching attacks against 'ultra-Left deviations' during 1972, the Left was able to shore up its extremely weak position. Without doubt they had the support of the Party leader, and probably with his help succeeded in establishing close contacts with the secret police and the security forces. After the radical groups of the Red Guard movement and the Maoist 'rebel organizations' had been put out of action, there remained enough representatives of the more moderate mass organizations who could be recruited as new followers of the Left. The danger of a complete collapse of the Maoist position was not overlooked by the Left, and at the end of 1972 this spurred them into action again. Because they controlled the Party's propaganda system and had good relations with the PLA's Political Department led by General Li Tê-sheng, they had the organizational instrument at hand for their counter-offensive against the New Course.

In the late summer and autumn 1972, after an interval of almost a year the central media sporadically mentioned themes which should be understood as early symptoms of a change to a more positive appraisal of the Cultural Revolution. In August an article in *Red Flag* pointed out that 'at intervals of some years struggles within the Party' would repeatedly occur because one had to counter further attempts to create a 'restoration of capitalism'.[35] Two months later, for the first time after a much longer period, the *JMJP* took up the idea formulated by Mao and Lin Piao's faction in 1964, to train 'millions of revolutionary successors' from the younger generation.[36] The December issue of *Red Flag* spoke of the 'new-born things' in the Cultural Revolution *(Hsin-shêng shih-wei)*, which had 'to be supported and thoroughly developed'.[37]

The Left's first breakthrough came with the revaluation of the character of Lin Piao's 'deviation', promoted by the Party's propaganda system since 1972–3. After the middle of November 1971 most of the media accused 'pseudo-Marxist swindlers like Liu Shao-ch'i' of 'Left-opportunism' and of supporting an 'ultra-Left tendency'.[38] Only the broadcasting stations of Anhui and Hupei insisted on the judgement that Lin Piao and his followers had deviated 'sometimes to the Right, sometimes to the Left',[39] whereas in Ssuch'uan and on Hainan island both versions were used.[40]

In the spring of 1972 the judgement of Lin as a 'Left deviationist' prevailed all over the country. This served well as a justification for the far-reaching corrections of Mao's development concept as well as of the doctrines and methods of the Cultural Revolution, which the New Course of the anti-Lin coalition introduced. Thus on 25 November 1972 Sinkiang's Party leader, Saifudin, still spoke of Lin Piao's group as 'left-extremists' *(Chi-tso fên-tzu)*.[41] Meanwhile, *Red Flag* issued a new slogan. It accused Lin Piao and his followers of being guilty of 'ultra-*Right*' *(Chi-yu-te)* deviations.[42] The reaction of the regional leaderships towards this change in emphasis was at first both reluctant and diffuse. Some provinces helped themselves with the remark that the policies of the 'pseudo-Marxist swindlers' were 'Left in form, but Right in essence' *(Hsing tso shih yu)*.[43] Others, however, began quickly to fall into line with the new form of words. Thus the provincial leadership in Kirin declared on 9 January 1973 that the 'essence' of the behaviour of Lin Piao's faction had been 'ultra-Right'.[44] One week later, the organ of Kuangtung Provincial Party Committee spoke of the 'ultra-Right character of the anti-Party line of the pseudo-Marxist political swindler like Liu Shao-ch'i'.[45] At the end of January the Ssuch'uan party leaders went even further in emphasizing that it would be 'a mistake' *(Ts'o-wu)* to call Lin Piao and his followers 'Left-extremists'.[46]

These or similar formulas were adopted in the course of January and February 1973 by the provinces of Shantung, Chekiang, Kuangsi, Inner Mongolia, Ch'inghai, Hunan, Yünnan, Sinkiang and Tibet.[47] As a result, the form of words of the Central media was already well established by the end of February in twelve of the twenty-nine major administrative units in China. However, even here there was still occasionally the remarkable variation that 'even ultra-Leftist tendencies should be rejected'.[48] This only changed when the total unifying force of the criticism of Lin as a Right-wing extremist was clarified by the fact that *JMJP* took over, on 7 March, an article from *Red Flag*, which had warned unmistakably about describing the deviations of the 'pseudo-Marxist swindlers' as Leftists. It had served much more as a cover for ultra Right-wing tendencies. In reality it had been 'aligned with landlords, rich peasants, counter-revolutionaries, bad elements and with Right-deviationists, in order to attempt a restoration of capitalism'.[49] *Roma locuta, causa finita.* After the middle of March 1973, those provinces which until then had held back with their judgment of Lin, now also joined in condemning him as a 'Right-wing extremist'. At the end of February in Hupei, in line with the emerging tendency to re-emphasize the mobilizatory aspects of Chinese Communist doctrine, there was a reminder for the first time in a long time of the Model Soldier Lei Fêng, whose example had been promoted, if not designed, by the Lin Piao group in the early 1960s to portray ideologically correct behaviour in the PLA.[50]

Further indications of an attempt to bring about a change of direction towards the Left and thus of a renunciation of the New Course, were evident from an appeal published at the beginning of March 1973 in *Red Flag*, to 'defend and develop the fruits of the victory of the Great Proletarian Cultural Revolution, which had been 'both necessary and opportune'.[51] This wording was used on 11 March in Tibet,[52] on 24 March in Kuangsi, and also in Shansi and in the city of Canton. In addition, the Party leadership of Kuangsi Autonomous Region expressed its concern about the fact that there was 'a nasty smell of capitalism in the villages which was causing the sabotage of the movement to Learn from Tachai'.[53]

The return to the rhetoric of the Cultural Revolution which was now becoming apparent did not, however, correspond to political practice in the late summer of 1973. Both the Central administration and the regional leadership groups continued unperturbed with the policies of the second 'readjustment' period. Apparently the power of the Cultural Revolutionary Left was not great enough to enforce really effective corrections to the New Course. The Party's propaganda system was not sufficient as an organizational instrument to ensure a return to Mao's 1958 idea of development through mobilization. As a result, in the spring and summer of 1973 the Left concentrated on gaining control over the largest possible number of organs of the official mass organizations, the reconstruction of which was now being energetically pursued. The vanguard in this process was the Shanghai leadership. In addition to Chang Ch'un-ch'ao and Yao Wên-yüan, who were mainly occupied in the capital, there was a young Party official who had gained increasingly in importance since 1972; the approximately forty-year-old Wang Hung-wên.[54] Wang came from the security police system and had taken a leading role in the 'General Headquarters of the Revolutionary Rebel Workers' (*Kung-jen tsao-fan tsung-ssu-ling-pu*), under whose leadership the Maoist mass organizations overthrew the city leadership in January 1967. In February 1967 he had belonged to the leadership group of the 'Shanghai Commune' which, under the Centre's pressure, was transformed after only a few days into a Revolutionary Committee, within which Wang held the third position after Chang and Yao.

Appointed in June 1969 as a member of the 9th Central Committee, he became Secretary of the Shanghai Municipal Party Committee in January 1971, and in 1972 he became Political Commissar of the Shanghai garrison. After February 1973 he apparently also took on responsibilities at the Centre in Peking, as he now frequently appeared there in public.

In a leader in the *JMJP* on New Year's Day 1973, the leadership of the CCP had declared the reconstruction of the official mass organizations, which had collapsed in the Cultural Revolution, to be one of the major tasks for the new year.[55] The Left Shanghai leadership group was the first to respond to this appeal and began by establishing new leadership groups for the Communist Youth League and also for the Federation of Trade Unions.

On 21 February 1973, *NCNA* reported that the Shanghai Municipal Committee of the Youth League had been established by a congress at which Wang Hung-wên had given one of the major speeches.[56] In March, Liaoning Province was the second major administrative unit to follow suit. Here Mao Yüan-hsin, the nephew of the Chairman, played an important part as Secretary of the Provincial Committee of the CCP.[57] At the beginning of April, Peking and Kiangsu started to reconstruct the Party Youth organization,[58] and at the end of the month T'ienchin, Anhui and Shansi followed suit.[59] In May, Shensi, Kansu, Kueichou, Hopei,[60] Hupei, Kirin, Heilungkiang, Hunan, Yünnan, Honan and Shantung all followed.[61] On 1 June the establishment of Provincial committees of the Youth League in Chekiang, Fukien, Kuangsi and Inner Mongolia were reported.[62] On 29 June the *NCNA* reported the successful reconstruction of the same organization in Kuangtung, Ts'inghai, Ninghsia and Kiangsi.[63] After leadership groups for the Youth League had also been re-established in Tibet, Ssuch'uan and Sinkiang,[64] the reconstruction of this organization in all China's twenty-nine major administrative units could (by 18 July 1973) be said to be complete.

The re-organization of the Federation of Trade Unions began with the nomination of the General Council of this organization in Shanghai on 23 April 1973. Wang Hung-wên was appointed its Chairman. On the same day, the trade unions in Peking were also given a new leadership group headed by the 'Model Worker', Ni Chih-fu (a member of the CC).[65] The reconstruction of this mass organization apparently did not go as smoothly as that of the Youth League, because no progress was reported during the whole of May. It was not till 1 June that the *NCNA* reported the establishment of the trade union leadership in the city of T'ienchin.[66] During the next two weeks Kirin, Shansi, Anhui and Liaoning followed.[67] At the end of June new leadership groups for the trade unions in Kuangsi, Yünnan and Hupei emerged;[68] and at the beginning of July the establishment of the general councils of the trade union federations in Kuangtung, Hopei, Kansu, Shantung, Heilungkiang, Kiangsu, Shensi and also in Inner Mongolia were reported.[69] Another pause followed, so that by the 10th Party Congress of the CCP at the end of August 1973, the reconstruction of these mass organizations had been completed in only eighteen of the twenty-nine Provinces. Although the new leadership groups of the workers' organizations contained a large number of officials who had only emerged during the Cultural Revolution, nonetheless there were many who came from those mass organizations that had been opposed to the Leftist 'rebels'. These apart, there were many officials who had returned to positions of responsibility and who before 1966 had headed the trade union organs and been exposed to the criticism of the rebels during the Cultural Revolution.

The reconstruction of the Chinese Democratic Women's Association was not very different in character from that of the Youth League and the trade unions. Even though there were women officials in some of the provinces who, because of their contacts with Chiang Ch'ing during the Cultural Revolution, were seen as part of the Left, the majority of the leading positions in this organization were filled by old Party cadres, who before 1966 had already been active in the association. Shanghai did not take the lead in this particular movement. Its place was taken by the city of T'ienchin, which was controlled by the military and veteran cadres, and which formed a leadership group for the women's association on 2 July, 1973.[70] On 19 July Anhui, Hupei, Shansi, Kirin and Hopei followed suit,[71] and on 5 August Kuangsi, Kuangtung, Kansu, Heilungkiang; Fukien and Tibet all finally followed.[72] By the 10th Party Congress, the organization of the Women's Association had been completed in twelve of the twenty-nine major administrative units. Among these, however, were neither Shanghai nor Peking nor Liaoning, all of which had taken the lead in the reconstruction of the Youth League and the trade unions. This leads one to assume that there may have been some arguments over reconstruction within the leadership between members of the Left on the one hand, and members of the civilian administration and the regional military commanders on the other.

After the Left had established itself totally in the new provincial organs of the Youth League and at least partly in the trade unions, it started (in the summer of 1973) a new stage in its counter-offensive against the representatives of the policy of the New Course. Now it was a question no longer solely of judging Lin Piao and the Cultural Revolution but of a full frontal attack on both those corrections which had been made to Cultural Revolutionary education policy and on Prime Minister Chou En-lai, the leading personality at the centre of the anti-Lin coalition.

The first assault was launched by Liaoning Province's propaganda department (led by Mao Yüan-hsin), which criticized the system of entrance examinations to colleges that had been in use since 1972. On 19 July the provincial media published a letter from a candidate for examination called Chang T'ieh-sheng.[73] After the Cultural Revolution, Chang had been sent to work in the countryside in his home province, where he had given valuable service to production. His application for admission to the Liaoning Technical University had therefore been supported by the peasants of his production brigade and by its Revolutionary Committee. He had been asked to take the entrance examination while in the middle of harvesting, and had therefore had little time for preparation. As a result, in the maths examination paper he had to return empty pages, on which he had written the remarks that he considered work in the countryside and correct political thinking to be more important than achievements in these subjects, and that he therefore would not sit examinations on subjects which he had not been able to work at for some time. The media in Liaoning introduced Chang's letter with a remark strongly criticising 'old traditions, old customs, and the old examination policy'. For almost three weeks nothing was heard about the case of Chang T'ieh-sheng. However, it then gave rise to a wave of massive criticism of the attempts by the politicians of the New Course to limit the effects of the Cultural Revolution on educational policy.

On 9 August Chang's letter was read out by the broadcasting stations of the capital and in Heilungkiang,[74] and a day later *JMJP* printed the letter with the introduction it had been given by the media in Liaoning.[75] At the same time the media in Anhui, Hopei, Fukien, Honan and Inner Mongolia took up the letter and its introduction,[76] and on 11 August Shanghai, Chekiang and Yünnan followed.[77] The fact that *JMJP* on 10 August stipulated that in the 'proletarian revolution in the educational sector', 'good workmanship' and 'political criteria were to be given priority' marked the importance with which this incidence was invested by the propaganda system of the CCP. Here it was no longer a matter of a factual debate over educational matters but the beginning of a new and fundamental debate on the future internal political development of the People's Republic of China. This became even clearer on 18 August when *JMJP* published not only three commemorative articles on the seventh anniversary of the first mass meeting of Red Guards in Peking in 1966, which paid tribute to the *avant garde* of the Cultural Revolution, but also a speech given by Chang T'ieh-sheng in Shênyang. Finally the same edition of the Central Party organ also contained the text of a song in which a slogan of Lin Piao's social policy offensive—'700 Million

People are going to be 700 Million Soldiers'—was taken up once again.[78]

But this was not all! At the same time the Left also revived the attempt, which had proved unsuccessful in September 1971, to start a major attack on the person and policies of Chou En-lai, with the help of a campaign of criticism against the teachings and activities of Confucius 2,500 years ago. On 7 August 1973, *JMJP* had an article written by Yang Jung-kuo, Professor of Philosophy at Chungshan University in Canton, entitled 'Confucius, a thinker who stubbornly supported a system of slavery'. It began with the remark that Confucius 'came from the slave-owing nobility of a moribund clan aristocracy'. He had 'followed a reactionary line' over the question of the removal of the system of slavery, and his interest in an ethically based leadership and his concept of 'Charity' *(Jên)* had been limited to the 'slave-owing class'. As in the commemorative article on the ninetieth anniversary of Lu Hsün's birth in September 1971,[79] Yang also mentioned the supposed execution of the reformer Shao Cheng-mao at the order of Confucius in 479 B.C., thereby re-emphasizing the implied connection with Kao Kang's death in 1955. However, his article was even clearer:

In the Spring and Autumn periods 52 slave states were eliminated; the system of slavery began to disintegrate. At that time Confucius promoted the political slogan 'Restore the states which have been eliminated, rebuild families whose line of descent has been interrupted, call those back to office who have retired into oblivion!' What he wanted to do was to call back to life those slave-owning states so that the slave-owning aristocracy which had been sentenced to death, could reclaim the leadership. This was a thoroughly reactionary political slogan to re-establish the old and that which had been sentenced to death.[80]

The connection with the rehabilitation, as pursued particularly by Chou En-lai, of leading cadres who had been purged during the Cultural Revolution were now as hard to overlook as the obvious allusions to Chou's aristocratic origin. So that there could be no doubt about the allusion, the article in several places used the name of the Chou Dynasty and mentioned the 'Duke of Chou'.

For over a week Yang's article received no response in the country. It was only on 15 August that the Fukien Provincial broadcasting station read out an article by a student who in 1968 had been deported to the country 'to be re-educated by the poor and lower middle peasants'. In this article even more than in Yang's the reference to the present was clear:

The class enemies in society *and in particular the chieftain of the opportunist line in the Party [Tang-nei chi-hui-chu-yi lu-hsien-te t'ou-tzu]* have always attempted to revive Confucianism in order to prevent the establishment of the revolutionary line of Chairman Mao.[81]

When on 21 August the Shanghai leadership group added the slogan 'agents of the exploiting classes like Confucius' to that of 'chieftain of the opportunist line in the Party',[82] it demonstrated the form of words that was to be used in the attack on Chou. This terminology sounded similar to 'China's Khrushchev' and the 'pseudo-Marxist swindlers like Liu Shao-ch'i'.

There was, however, one important difference. The epithets with which the respective leaderships of the CCP had criticized Liu Shao-ch'i and Lin Piao referred to the conflict with the USSR and to other confrontations within Marxist-Leninist doctrine. By introducing the name of Confucius into the debate, the Left departed from the area of argument of Marxism-Leninism and instead reached back into China's historical heritage. This process, first pointed out in the area of foreign policy by Marie-Luise Näth,[83] had already become apparent in the New Year's Day article of *JMJP* in 1973. Here a sentence ascribed to Mao Tse-tung was presented as a slogan for the new year: 'Dig tunnels deep, store grain everywhere and never seek hegemony!'[84] *(Shên wa tung, kuang chi liang, pu cheng pa!)* This phrase actually had nothing in common with the authorizing beliefs of Marxist-Leninist ideology, which the Chinese Communists claim to follow. It is much more a paraphrase of the advice given in 1357 by a Taoist hermit to the leaders of the national Chinese revolution against the Mongolians, and the founder of the Ming dynasty, Chu Yüan-ch'ang; 'Erect high walls, store grain everywhere and do not hesitate to pronounce yourself leader!' *(Kao ch'u ch'iang, kuang chi liang, huan cheng wang)*. Here we meet the phenomenon of the 'nationalization' of terminology, which seems to be indicative of the fact that the Chinese Communist leaders increasingly replaced universal by esoteric and indigenous communications.

It also confirmed an important part of the conflict which had begun at the turn of 1972-3 within the Chinese leadership, with the counter-attack of the Left on the designers of the second 'readjustment'. It had taken its first step in July and August 1973 with the publication of Chang T'ieh-sheng's letter and with the introduction of a campaign of criticism against the heritage of Confucius. When on 24 August (and seventeen days late) *NCNA* took up Yang Jung-kuo's article and also published it in English,[85] it had already become clear where the stage of the first round of the new dispute was to be—the 10th Party Congress of the CCP had started the same day in Peking.

REFERENCES

1. Frederick C. Teiwes, 'Chinese Politics 1949–1965: A Changing Mao, Part II', in *CS*, Vol. XII, No. 2, February 1974, pp. 15 ff.

2. See pp. 68 ff.

3. Radio Hupei, 21 February 1972 and Radio Shensi, 7 March 1972.

4. *JMJP*, 4 March 1972.

5. E.g. 'Nan-fang jih-pao', 10 April 1972.

6. 'Hunan jih-pao' and Radio Hunan, 15 April 1972.

7. *JMJP*, 24 April 1972.

8. Reports from refugees and travellers returning from China, interviewed in Hong Kong, 2, 4 and 10 October 1972.

9. *JMJP*, 17 and 26 August, 13 and 17 September 1972.

10. *KMJP*, 6 October 1972. See also *HC*, No. 9, 1972.

11. *KMJP*, 6 and 25 December 1972.

12. Ibid., 18 December 1972.

13. Radio Ssuch'uan, 30 November 1972.

14. See p. 176.

15. *JMJP*, 19 September 1971.

16. Ibid., 16 December 1971.

17. *KMJP*, 10 February 1972.

18. In interviews with British officials in Hong Kong in April 1972.

19. *TKP*, 21 February 1973.

20. *NCNA*, Tokyo, 16 October 1973.

21. Ch'inghai, Fukien, Hunan, Hupei, Kiangsu, Kuangsi and Shensi (*CNA*, No. 826, 19 November 1971).

22. Anhui, Kiangsu, Shanghai and Shantung (ibid.).

23. Chekiang, Kirin, Kuangtung, Liaoning, Shansi, Sinkiang, Tibet and Yünnan (ibid.).

24. HC. No. 1, 1972 and Radio Hupei, 22 January 1972.

25. Radio Shensi, 25 January 1972.

26. Ibid., 28 January 1972.

27. Radio Kueichou, 8 January 1972.

28. *HC*, No. 2, 1972.

29. *Nan-fang jih-pao*, 2 June 1972.

30. *JMJP*, 6 July 1972.

31. *Inter alia:* Radio Lhasa, 11 July and 11 September 1972; Radio Ssuch'uan, 26 August and 8 September 1972; Radio Kuangsi, 29 August 1972; Radio Shensi, 10 September 1972.

32. *JMJP*, 7 September 1972.

33. Ibid., 25 September 1972.

34. See, Domes, *Internal Politics*, op. cit., pp. 52 f.

35. *HC*, No. 8, 1972.

36. *JMJP*, 13 October 1972.

37. *HC*, No. 12, 1972.

38. E.g. Radio Kuangtung, 1 Programme, 17 November 1971; Radio Yünnan, 2 December 1971 and 23 January 1972; Radio Lhasa, 27 December 1971.

39. Radio Anhui, 7 December 1971; Radio Hupei, 22 January 1972.

40. Radio Ssuch'uan, 22 and 30 November 1971, 14 January 1972; Radio Haik'ou, 22 and 24 November 1971.

41. Radio Sinkiang, 25 December 1972.

42. *HC*, No. 12, 1972.

43. *Inter alia:* Radio Kiangsi, 19 December 1972; Radio Ch'inghai, 29 December 1972; Radio Liaoning, 5 January 1973.

44. *Kirin jih-pao*, Ch'angch'un, and Radio Kirin, 9 January 1973.

45. *Nan-fang jih-pao*, 16 January 1973.

46. Radio Ssuch-uan, 30 January 1973.

47. Radio Shantung, 19 January 1973; Radio Chekiang, 20 January 1973; Radio Inner Mongolia, 29 January 1973; Radio Kuangsi, 27 January 1973; Radio Ch'inghai, 2 February 1973; Radio Hunan, 7 February 1973; Radio Yünnan, 16 February 1973; Radio Sinkiang, 18 February 1973; Radio Lhasa, 19 February 1973.

48. Radio Yünnan, ibid.

49. *HC*, No. 3, 1973; *JMJP*, 7 March 1973.

50. Radio Hupei, 27 February 1973.

51. *HC*, No. 3, 1973.

52. Radio Lhasa, 11 March 1973.

53. Radios Kuangsi, Canton and Shansi, all 24 March 1973.

54. At present the only available critical biography of Wang Hung-wên is, Chu Wên-lin, *Wang Huang-wên*, paper, Third Sino-American Conference on Mainland China, T'aipei, 1973, passim.

55. *JMJP*, 1 January 1973.

56. *NCNA*, Peking, 21 February 1973.

57. *NCNA*, Shênyang, 10 March 1973.

58. *NCNA*, Peking, 3 April 1973; *NCNA*, Nanking, 5 April 1973.

59. *NCNA*, Peking, 27 April 1973.

60. Ibid., 5 May 1973.

61. Ibid., 13 May 1973.

62. Ibid., 1 June 1973.

63. Ibid., 29 June 1973.

64. *NCNA*, Lhasa, 2 July 1973; *NCNA*, Peking, 18 July 1973.

65. *NCNA*, Shanghai and *NCNA*, Peking, 23 April 1973.

66. *NCNA*, T'ienchin, 1 JUne 1973.

67. *NCNA*, Peking, 8 and 15 June 1973.

68. Ibid., 28 June 1973.

69. Radio Kuangtung, 1 Programme, 3 July 1973; *NCNA*, Peking, 4 July 1973.

70. *NCNA*, Peking, 2 July 1973.

71. Ibid., 19 July 1973.

72. Ibid., 5 August 1973.

73. *Liaoning jih-pao*, Shênyang and Radio Liaoning, 19 July 1973.

74. Central Radio Peking and Radio Heilungkiang, 9 August 1973.

75. *JMJP*, 10 August 1973.

76. Radios Anhui, Hopei, Fukien, Honan and Inner Mongolia, 10 August 1973.

77. Radio Shanghai, Chekiang and Yünnan, 11 August 1973.

78. *JMJP*, 18 August 1973.

79. See pp. 179 ff.

80. *JMJP*, 7 August 1973.
81. Radio Fukien, 15 August 1973.
82. *CFCP* and Radio Shanghai, 21 August 1973.
83. See p. 215.
84. *JMJP*, 1 January 1973.
85. *NCNA*, Peking (English), 24 August 1973.

12. The 10th Party Congress: A Compromise and A New Conflict

The calling of a new Party Congress of the CCP had become necessary before the end of the five-year time limit provided by the Party constitution because after the fall of Lin Piao his name had to be removed from the constitution. Furthermore, decisions about personnel had to be made in order to replenish the top leadership group, because ever since the Lin Piao crisis there had been a rump Politburo at the head of the Party with only thirteen members and three alternate members.[1] These decisions seemed to have caused considerable difficulties particularly in connection with the new disputes within the leadership which had become apparent since the Left's counter-offensive during the spring of 1973. Finally, however, it seems that an understanding was reached within the Peking leadership as T'aiwan intelligence sources reported on 6 July 1973 that the Politburo of the CCP had decided at the beginning of June to call the Party Congress for the end of August or beginning of September, and the 4th National People's Congress (which had been overdue ever since the beginning of 1969) for the first ten days in November.[2]

In fact the 10th Party Congress of the CCP met in strictest secrecy from 24 to 28 August 1973. Although the 8th Party Congress of the CCP in September 1956 had been accompanied by extensive daily reports in the Chinese media, and there had been reports at least at the beginning and after fourteen of twenty-four conference days of the 9th Party Congress in April 1969, the first report on this Party Congress appeared only after it had ended.[3] The Congress thus met in strict secrecy. None of the numerous foreign diplomats and journalists in Peking had been informed before or during the sessions, and the first indications of the Congress appeared on 26 August in a Hong Kong newspaper.[4] Again there are only a few documents available on the work of the Party Congress: a press communiqué from *NCNA* on 29 August 1973 with the lists of members of the Presidium of the Party Congress, and of the members and alternate members of the 10th Central Committee;[5] the text of the report given by Chou En-lai on behalf of the Central Committee;[6] the report given by Wang Hung-wên on the revision of the Party Constitution, and the new text of this constitution.[7]

The communiqué stated that Chou's Political Report, Wang's Report on the Constitution, and the election of the 10th Central Committee had been the only points on the agenda of the

Congress. At the same time it reported a Party membership of 28 million, and included the information that the delegates had been 20% women and 67% 'Workers, Peasants and Soldiers' and that Taiwanese residents had participated in the Congress for the first time. After almost two years of covert attacks under various different epithets, Lin Piao and Ch'en Po-ta were now finally named in person as Party enemies and their expulsion from the Party was officially publicized. The Party Congress was attended by 1,249 delegates, a number lying between the 1,026 of the 8th Party Congress and that of the 9th which had 1,512 delegates, and which was thus quite conventional.

Chou En-lai's Political Report concentrated primarily on an extensive repetition of Peking's official account of the course of the Lin Piao crisis, which in this way was officially made public for the first time. A large part of this report was also occupied by Chou's remarks on the situation in foreign policy,[8] in which he started from the basis of the proposition that 'détente was a temporary and superficial phenomenon' whereas 'a great deal of disorder would remain'. This 'disorder' was 'a good thing for the people'. In a spirited argument Chou defended the policy he had introduced, of an opening towards the West and of détente with the United States. The energy which he put into this leads one to suspect that this policy had given rise to disputes within the Party leadership even after Lin's fall. On the other hand, the part of his speech dealing with domestic policy was kept extremely short. Here Chou adopted some Cultural Revolutionary rhetoric, often using quotations from Mao Tse-tung, and he equated the importance of the slogans of the Great Leap Forward and the principles of the first 'Readjustment' period. On the other hand, the only parts of this report dealing with questions of practical policy were, after a 'revolutionary' introduction, kept at a very pragmatic level:

In order to learn from Tach'ing and to learn from Tachai in agriculture, we must persist in putting proletarian politics in command, vigorously launch mass movements and give full scope to the enthusiasm, wisdom and creativity of the masses. On this basis planning and co-ordination must be strengthened, rational rules and regulations improved and both Central and local initiatives further brought into full play. Party organizations should pay close attention to questions of economic policy, concern themselves with the wellbeing of the masses, do a good job of investigation and study and strive effectively to fulfill or over-fulfill the State plans for development of the national economy, so that our socialist economy will make still greater progress.[9]

Much tougher language was used by Wang Hung-wên, the second Central figure next to Chou, at the Party Congress in his report on the revision of the Party constitution. At the centre of his exposition were harsh attacks on 'revisionism' and the repetition of a quotation from Mao Tse-tung that it was a 'Marxist-Leninist principle' to 'swim against the tide'. Wang clearly appealed for a return to the Cultural Revolution. In this he strongly criticized all tendencies to repress criticism within the Party. In view of the distribution of power in the Chinese provinces, it can hardly be doubted that Wang was speaking against a continuation of the persecution of the Cultural Revolutionary Left when he informed the Party Congress that,

There are still after all a small number of cadres, *especially some leading cadres*, who will not tolerate the differing views of the masses inside or outside the Party. They even suppress criticism and retaliate, and it is quite serious in some individual cases.

Wang's attack was obviously based on a judgement of the situation, in which the forces of the Left saw themselves as a minority in the Party. However, he suggested that they represented the correct view even though they were in a minority:

We must have the revolutionary spirit of daring to go against the tide ... When confronted with issues that concern the line and the overall situation, a true Communist must act without any selfish considerations and dare to go against the tide, not fearing either removal from his post, expulsion from the Party, imprisonment, divorce nor guillotine.[10]

With these words the spokesman of the Left advertised further conflicts within the new Party leadership.

However, this announcement apart, the Party Congress took place at a time when new fundamental conflicts within the Chinese Communist leadership had begun to emerge. For the first time in the history of the CCP since 1949, there were three obvious contradictions apparent between the two Central Party Documents.

(1) In the foreign policy section of his report, Chou En-lai clearly distiguished between the two world powers; 'We must maintain high vigilance and be fully prepared against any war of aggression that imperialism may launch, particularly against a surprise attack on our country by Soviet revisionist social-imperialism'. According to Chou, the USA is also fundamentally capable of starting a war of aggression against China; but the real danger to China lies in the USSR. This was quite different to Wang Hung-wên, who started from a policy of simultaneous conflict with the two super-powers: 'We must without fail prepare well against any war of aggression and guard against surprise attack by imperialism and social-imperialism.'

Chou's policy of détente with the United States therefore remained a matter for dispute within the Peking leadership, and one has to assume that in any new conflict this question will again be under discussion.

(2) In the part of Chou's report dealing with domestic policy, Chou attacked not only Lin Piao but also Ch'en Po-ta. Wang, on the other hand, limited his attacks on Lin, and did not mention Ch'en Po-ta at all in his speech. It seems that, as far as possible, the Left exercises a limited degree of solidarity with its purged leaders.

(3) Chou and Wang both emphasized that in future there will again be disputes within the Party. However, the Prime Minister referred to 'struggles' *(tou-cheng)* between the two lines and declared: 'Such struggles will occur ten, twenty or thirty times.'

Wang, on the other hand referred to the Cultural Revolution as such: 'Revolutions *(kê-ming)* like this will have to be carried out many times in the future.' The battle lines in the new confrontation within the leadership were thus clearly drawn. The bureaucrats, development-oriented politicians and diplomats around Chou En-lai, while prepared for further intra-Party conflicts, obviously wanted to continue on the New Course, and had a low opinion of mass mobilization in the style of the Cultural Revolution. The Left, on the other hand, announced a further attempt to return to just that policy of mobilization which had already on three occasions brought about serious domestic political crises.

There are, however, some indications that the first attempt at a Left counter-offensive against the New Course had failed at the Party Congress and that a certain uneasy and as yet uncertain compromise between the groups had been achieved. Even though the *NCNA*'s publication of Yang Jung-kuo's article about Confucius on the first day of the Congress[11] had been an obvious affront to Chou En-lai, immediately after the end of the Party Congress the media began to connect the campaign to criticize Confucius, which fully developed during the autumn and winter 1973-4, with Lin Piao. Obviously Chou and his followers had succeeded, at least temporarily, in diverting the impact of the new movement.

A compromise was also basic to the alterations on the April 1969 Party Constitution agreed by the 10th Party Congress. On the one hand, the revised version accepted Wang Hung-wên's phrase that 'revolutions' such as the Cultural Revolution would 'have to be carried out many times' in the future.[12] The text also contained the provision that it was 'absolutely forbidden' to 'suppress or fight back any criticism'.[13] On the other hand, in some places in the new version the emotional term 'masses' *(Ch'ün-chung)* was replaced by the more neutral term 'non-party members' *(Fei-tang-yüan)*.[14] Of greater importance, however, were the decisions made in personnel policy, which indicate that the Left was incapable of asserting itself fully. Before the Party Congress, Chiang Ch'ing had vehemently demanded a larger representation for women in leadership organs. On the first day of the Congress, women in fact occupied thirty -two or 21·6% of the 148 seats in the Praesidium of the Party Congress. Of the 195 members of the new Central Committee elected on 28 August 1973 by the Party Congress, only twenty or 10·3% were women. The proportion of members from the PLA, on the other hand, rose from forty-three or 29% on the Praesidium of the Party Congress to seventy-five or 39·5% of Central Committee members. Of the 148 members of the Congress Praesidium, only fifteen did not become either members or alternate members of the new CC. Of these, six were women and seven were male representatives of mass organizations. Particular attention should be given to the fact that among the latter was Mao Yüan-hsin, the Party leader's nephew who, particularly during the Cultural Revolution, had been closely associated with Mao's wife.

The character of compromise also became apparent in the composition of the 10th Central Committee,[15] determined on 28 August 1973 by the Party Congress. There had been many fewer changes than at the 9th Party Congress in April 1969. Among the 195 members of the new CC, there were 122 or 62·6% who had already been members, and eighteen or 9·2% who had been alternate members of the 9th Central Committee. Fifty-five members or 28·2% were new entrants to the leadership, although among these were twenty officials who had been purged during the Cultural Revolution and who had now been rehabilitated. Of the 124 alternate members nominated by the 10th Party Congress to the CC, sixty-three or 50·8% had already been alternate members on the 9th Central Committee, two had been members of the 9th CC and fifty-nine or 47·6% were new entrants, nine of whom came from the group of rehabilitated cadres.

Although a socio-political analysis of the composition of the 10th Central Committee shows that, in comparison to its predecessors, the CCP's leadership had not fundamentally changed, nonetheless appreciable changes had occurred. The following analysis of Central Committee membership has been carried out according to the same criteria which have already been applied to the 9th Central Committee in Chapter 2.[16] The four members who died between the end of August 1973 and 1 June 1974, have been disregarded.[17]

In investigating the age structure of members of the 10th CC, the ages given refer to age on 31 December 1974. On this there is reliable data for 137 or 71·7% of the 191 persons who are relevant to this study.

While the average age of members of the 9th CC at the end of 1969 was 61·4 years, it was 63·1 years at the end of 1974 for members of the 10th CC. By comparison ninety-two members of

Table 12/1

AGE STRUCTURE OF THE 10th CENTRAL
COMMITTEE OF THE CCP

Age group	Number	Percentage of 137 members	Percentage on 9th CC	Percentage on the 8th CC at end of 1968
Under 40	5	3·6	—	—
40–49	6	4·4	3·4	—
50–59	22	16·05	37·3	9·8
60–69	75	54·7	42·4	56·5
70–79	22	16·05	13·5	27·1
Over 80	7	5·1	3·4	6·5

the 8th CC in December 1968 had an average age of 65·8 years, and at their election in September 1956 an average age of only 56·4 years. Again it is true that the average age of the 10th CC would be marginally lower if the missing information on the remaining forty-four members became available. However, since there are still, as in 1969, many elderly representatives of mass organizations and elderly officials among them, one has to expect that even so there will be an average age of about sixty years. Even the 10th Party Congress could not bring about a real rejuvenation of the Chinese leadership.

The process of a further differentiation in the regional origin of the members, which had already begun with the election of the 9th CC, continued with the election of the 10th CC. As a result twenty-five of the twenty-nine major administrative units are represented in the CC, as compared to seventeen on the 8th CC and twenty-one on the 9th CC. Nonetheless the CCP's leadership is marked by a majority of Southern Chinese. This remains true despite the fact that the proportion of members from the Southern provinces (which have 54% of the population) has declined from 73% on the 9th CC to 67·5% on the 10th CC. There was hardly a change in the proportion of CC membership from the inland provinces—it sank from 68·9% to 68·0%.

One remarkable change was in the proportion of natives of the four inland provinces of Hunan, Hupei, Kiangsi and Ssuch'uan on the 9th Central Committee, which had been 52·3% and was now only 42%. This cannot be explained merely by the fact that the proportion of Mao Tse-tung's countrymen from Hunan, which had been 29·3% on the 8th CC and only 19·9% on the 9th CC, was now only 17·7%. There was a clear reduction in the membership from Lin Piao's home province, Hupei, which instead of the 17·2% on the 9th CC, was only 10·1% on the 10th CC and had thereby sunk even lower than its 10·9% on the 8th CC. Once again, it was plain that political group formation in China was determined by regional associations. The rise of Lin Piao as the appointed successor of the Chairman brought about a rise in the proportion of CC members from Hupei by 57·8%; his fall reduced this share by 41·3%. At present there is data available on the regional origins of 169 or 88·5% of the members of the 10th CC, as shown in Table 12/2.

In addition to the renewed change in the relation between Hunan and Hupei, special attention should also be paid to the fact that the city of Shanghai had a much stronger representation on the 10th Central Committee than previously. Here the effect of the Cultural Revolutionary Left's gain in influence was clearly demonstrated.

An analysis of the educational background of CC members reveals that those changes which had already become apparent on the 9th CC continued. In this area there is information on 145 or 75·9% of the 191 members (see Table 12/3).

Once again the proportion of college graduates remained at about three-quarters of the 145 members of the 10th Central Committee for whom there is relevant data available. However, it had fallen marginally since the 9th Central Committee. The changes in the relative proportions of University graduates and graduates from military academies which had already become apparent on the 9th CC were confirmed by the 10th Central Committee. At the same time the proportion of both groups rose marginally, whereas that of graduates from teacher training institutes fell substantially. In addition, the trend of a falling proportion of members with foreign experience during education continued to fall markedly (Table 12/4).

The total here does not equal the sum of individual entries since, as with the 9th CC, a number of members had studied in more than one foreign country. The decline in the proportion of CC members with foreign educational experience in the selection of the 10th CC was, however, balanced to some extent by the fact that eleven members of the new leadership had experiences as diplomats, whereas there had only been three of these latter on the 9th Central Committee.

The greatest change in the composition of the 10th CC was in the members' degree of Party seniority. Here (Table 12/5) it is quite clear that the quantitative influence of old revolutionaries has now become extremely limited, even if they still command a clear majority in the CC. The year of joining the Party is known for 182 or 95·3% of CC members.

It can be seen that only 63·2% of members of the 10th CC came from those generation-groups who had joined the Party before the

Table 12/2

REGIONAL ORIGIN OF MEMBERS OF THE 10th CENTRAL COMMITTEE OF THE CCP

Province	Percentage of Chinese population	Number	Percentage of 169 members	Percentage on 9th CC	Percentage on 8th CC
Hunan	5·6	30	17·7	19·9	23·3
Hupei	4·8	17	10·1	17·2	10·9
Ssuch'uan	10·5	13	7·7	7·3	10·9
Kiangsi	3·3	11	6·5	7·9	7·6
Shansi	2·7	10	5·9	4·6	5·4
Shanghai	1·3	8	4·7	—	
Honan	7·5	8	4·7	4·0	3·3
Hopei	4·8	8	4·7	6·0	4·3
Kiangsu	6·5	7	4·1	4·6	4·3
Kuangtung	6·0	7	4·1	6·0	6·5
Shensi	2·7	7	4·1	2·0	6·5
Shantung	8·6	6	3·5	5·3	3·3
Anhui	4·5	5	2·9	0·65	2·2
Fukien	2·1	5	2·9	4·6	5·4
Kansu	2·0	2	1·2	0·65	—
Liaoning	3·6	4	2·4	2·6	1·1
Chekiang	4·7	3	1·8	2·0	1·1
Inner Mongolia	2·0	3	1·8	1·3	1·1
Peking	1·4	2	1·2	—	—
Sinkiang	1·2	2	1·2	—	—
T'ienchin	0·3	2	1·2	—	—
Heilungkiang	3·1	1	0·6	0·65	1·1
Kueichou	1·8	1	0·6	—	—
Tibet	0·6	1	0·6	—	—
(from Taiwan)	—	2	1·2	—	—
Coastal Provinces	42·6	54	32·0	31·1	26·1
Inland Provinces	57·4	115	68·0	68·9	73·9
North China	46·3	55	32·5	27·2	29·4
South China	53·7	114	67·5	72·8	70·6

end of the 'Long March'. However, the proportion of the members who had joined the CCP only after the foundation of the PRC rose from 7·7% to 21·4%. Here it is clear that a generation change is developing. However, this has not fully taken effect on the 10th CC, because still today almost four-fifths of the CC membership have belonged to the Party for more than twenty-five years. Probably only the next Central Committee of the CCP, or even the

Table 12/3

EDUCATIONAL BACKGROUND OF MEMBERS OF THE 10th CENTRAL COMMITTEE OF THE CCP

Last educational establishment	Number	Percentage of 145 members	Percentage on 9th CC	Percentage on 8th CC
University	38	26·2	23·8	44·3
Teachers' Training Institute	14	9·7	16·7	13·4
Military Academy	56	38·6	35·7	15·5
Total Higher Education	108	74·5	76·2	73·2
Secondary School	13	8·9	10·3	7·3
Primary School	12	8·3	11·9	6·2
No formal education	12	8·3	1·6	4·1
All Other	37	25·5	23·8	17·6

Table 12/4

FOREIGN EXPERIENCE OF MEMBERS OF THE 10th CENTRAL COMMITTEE OF THE CCP

Country	Number	Percentage of 145 members	Percentage on 9th CC	Percentage on 8th CC
USSR	29	20·0	27·8	39·2
France	8	5·5	6·3	13·4
Japan	6	4·1	4·8	4·1
Germany	4	2·8	2·4	3·1
USA	2	1·4	—	2·1
Great Britain	1	0·7	0·8	1·1
Turkey	1	0·7	0·8	—
Total	39	26·9	32·5	46·4

one after next, will bring about the decisive change from the rule of the old revolutionaries to that of the post-revolutionary generation.

An important change of emphasis also occurred in the institutional background of members of the 10th CC. Data available on 190 or 99·5% of the CC members (Table 12/6). The Lin Piao crisis

Table 12/5

PARTY SENIORITY OF MEMBERS OF
THE 10th CENTRAL COMMITTEE OF THE CCP

Date of entry to Party	Number	Percentage of 182 members	Percentage on 9th CC	Percentage on 8th CC
1921–7	47	25·8	39·8	87·6
1928–31	43	23·7	28·7	7·3
1932–5	25	13·7	11·9	4·1
Entry before the end of 'the Long March'	115	63·2	80·4	99·0
1936–7	7	3·8	4·2	—
1938–45	14	7·7	2·8	1·0
1945–9	7	3·9	4·9	—
Entry before the foundation of the PRC	143	78·6	92·3	100·0
Entry since 1949	39	21·4	7·7	

Table 12/6

INSTITUTIONAL BACKGROUND OF MEMBERS OF THE
10th CENTRAL COMMITTEE OF THE CCP

Group	Number	Percentage of 190 members	Percentage on 9th CC	Percentage on 8th CC
State and Party Cadres	76	40·0	28·2	59·0
Academics	5	2·6	2·9	3·1
Total of 'Revolutionary Cadres'	81	42·6	31·0	62·7
Commanders	51	26·9	35·3	26·4
Political	24	12·6	14·7	11·5
Total PLA	75	39·5	50·0	37·9
Mass Organizations	34	17·9	17·7	—

has, without any doubt, brought about a considerable decline in the proportion of the PLA on the CC which now stands only marginally above its level on the 8th CC. This change is particularly to the advantage of the civilian Party cadres, who now once again form the strongest group in the CC, while the proportion of representatives of mass organizations as compared to the 9th CC has remained almost unchanged.

This change also becomes apparent in an analysis of the present areas of activity of CC members. If one uses their predominant occupation as the base for analysis, then the statistical pattern shown in Table 12/7 appears for 189 or 99% of the members of the 10th Central Committee.

The tendency for a 'regionalization' of the leadership, which had clearly emerged as a result of the Cultural Revolution in the composition of the 9th CC in April 1969, was also confirmed. The proportion of representatives of Central organizations continued to decrease. At the same time, the Lin Piao crisis put an end to the trend of militarization. The proportion of representatives of military organizations in the CC declined in comparison to that of the 9th CC by 21·9%, and evened out mid-way between the levels of the 8th CC (25·3%) and of the 9th (47·5%).

A limitation of the PLA's influence occurred even in an area where its representation had still been comparatively strong: with the members of the Secretariats in the Provincial Party Committees. Here, by the end of 1973, the members of the armed forces had lost the absolute majority which until then they had managed to retain in these groups.[18] By 31 December 1973, of 181 Provincial Party secretaries, only eighty-eight or 48·6% were military men, whereas eighty-one or 44·8% were civilian cadres and twelve or 6·6% representatives of mass organizations. Even so, their representation in the Provinces is today still considerably higher than it was before the Cultural Revolution (Table 12/8).

The weakening of the position of the Army in the elections of the 10th Party Congress and its associated effect in the Provinces is due particularly to the fact that the PLA did not manage, even after the fall of Lin Piao, to appear as a monolithic unity. Although there was increasing evidence of the start of a process of dissolution in the traditional loyalty groups, nonetheless at the 10th Party Congress these differences within the military system still played an important role. This becomes evident when comparing loyalty group representation on the 9th and 10th CCs, as in Table 12/9. While the 4th Field Army loyalty group, which Lin Piao used in order to become leader, had lost more than half its CC membership, the membership from the 3rd and the 2nd Field Army continued to rise. This was doubtless due to the important participation of Generals Hsü Shih-yu and Ch'ian Hsi-lien in the purge

Table 12/7

AREA OF ACTIVITY OF MEMBERS OF THE
10th CENTRAL COMMITTEE OF THE CCP

Area of Activity	Number	Percentage of 189 members	Percentage on 9th CC	Percentage on 8th CC
Central Civilian	43	22·7	20·4	46·1
Central Military	26	13·8	21·0	23·1
Regional Civilian	76	40·2	32·0	28·6
Regional Military	44	23·3	26·6	2·2
Total Centre	69	36·5	41·4	69·2
Total Regional	120	63·5	58·6	30·8
Total Civilian	119	62·9	52·5	74·7
Total Military	70	37·1	47·5	25·3

Table 12/8

INSTITUTIONAL ORIGIN OF PROVINCIAL
PARTY SECRETARIES

Group	1965	1971	1973
PLA	10·5	62·0	48·6
Civilian Cadre	89·5	32·9	44·8
Mass Organization	—	5·1	6·6

Table 12/9

FIELD ARMY GROUPS ON THE 9th AND 10th
CENTRAL COMMITTEE

Group	1 FA	2 FA	3 FA	4 FA	FA
9th CC	7	15	13	39	7
10th CC	11	17	19	17	7

of Lin Piao. In this context one can also understand the strengthening of the proportion of members from the 1st Field Army. Its former leaders, Marshals P'eng Tê-huai and Ho Lung, had previously been purged due to Lin's influence. They were not personally able to bring about their rehabilitation—and in the case of P'eng, who had openly opposed Mao, this was hardly to be expected—but some of their former subordinates were after all re-admitted into the leadership group. In this way the anti-Lin coalition obviously attempted to expand its base within the Armed Forces.

Our understanding of the changes in the leadership structure of the People's Republic of China as a result of the 10th Party Congress of the CCP would certainly become clearer if we could but proceed with a similar examination of group categories as was carried out in Chapter 2 regarding the leadership structure before and after the Cultural Revolution.[19] Unfortunately this is not yet possible as it requires a longer period of continuous observation to identify who can be counted as part of the leadership strata, the leadership forces, and the decision-making body. Such an analysis will have to wait until the activities of members and alternate members of the CC and the provincial Party secretaries make it possible reliably to establish the positions of members of the leadership.

On the other hand, it is now possible already to analyse more closely the composition of the 10th Politburo of the Central Committee, which held its 1st Plenum on 30 August 1973.[20] There were twenty-one members and four alternate members.[21]

(1) Mao Tse-tung (81), Chairman of the CC, member of the Standing Committee of the Politburo, member of the Politburo since 1935.

(2) Chou En-lai (76), Prime Minister, 1st Vice-Chairman of the CC, member of the Standing Committee of the Politburo, member of the Politburo since 1927. Died January 1976.

(3) Wang Hung-wên (41), 2nd Vice-Chairman of the CC, member of the Standing Committee of the Politburo, Secretary of Shanghai Municipal CCP Committee, Political Commissar of Shanghai Garrison, newly elected.

(4) K'ang Shêng (75), 3rd Vice-Chairman of the CC, member of the Standing Committee of the Politburo, member of the Politburo 1949-56 and again after 1966, Alternate member of the Politburo 1956-66. Died December 1975.

(5) Marshal Yeh Chien-ying (76), member of the Standing Committee of the Politburo, 4th Vice-Chairman of the CC, 1st Vice-Chairman of the CC Military Committee, member of the Politburo since 1966.

(6) General Li Tê-sheng (60), 5th Vice-Chairman of the CC, until 31 December 1973 member of the Standing Committee, Director of the General Political Department of the PLA, Chairman of the Revolutionary Committee and First Secretary of the Provincial Party Committee of Anhui; from 1 January 1974, Commander of Shênyang Military Region, alternate member of the Politburo since 1969. In January 1975 demoted to regular membership of the Politburo.

(7) Chang Ch'un-ch'iao (63), member of the Standing Committee of the Politburo, First Secretary of Shanghai Municipal CCP Committee and Chairman of Shanghai Municipal Revolutionary Committee, 1st Political Commissar of Nanking Military Region, member of the Politburo since 1969.

(8) Marshal Chu Tê (88), member of the Standing Committee of the Politburo, Chairman of the Standing Committee of the NPC, member of the Politburo since 1935.

(9) Tung Pi-wu (88), member of the Standing Committee of the Politburo, Acting Chairman of the PRC, member of the Politburo since 1945. Died April 1975.

(10) General Ch'en Hsi-lien (61), until 31 December 1973 Commander of Shênyang Military Region, Chairman of the Revolutionary Committee and First Secretary of the CCP Provincial Committee of Liaoning; since 1 January 1974 Commander of Peking Military Region, member of the Politburo since 1969.

(11) Ch'en Yung-kuei (66), Secretary of the Shansi CCP Provincial Committee, Leader of the Agricultural Model Brigade Tachai, newly elected.

(12) Chi Teng-k'uei (?), 1st Political Commissar of Peking Military Region, alternate member of the Politburo since 1969.

(13) Mme. Chiang Ch'ing (60), wife of Mao Tse-tung, Adviser to the Culture and Education Group under the State Council, member of the Politburo since 1969.

(14) General Hsü Shih-yu (68), Vice-Minister of Defence, until 31 December 1973 Commander of Nanking Military Region, Chairman of the Revolutionary Committee and First Secretary of the CCP Provincial Committee of Kiangsu; since 1 January 1974 Commander of Canton Military Region, member of the Politburo since 1969.

(15) Hua Kuo-fêng (63), Chairman of the Revolutionary Committee and First Secretary of the CCP Provincial Committee of Hunan, newly elected. In April 1976, appointed First Vice-Chairman of the CC, member of the Standing Committee of the Politburo, and Premier of the State Council.

(16) Li Hsien-nien (69), Vice-Premier, member of the Politburo since 1956.

(17) Marshall Liu Po-ch'eng (82), Vice-Chairman of the Standing Committee of the NPC and of the Military Committee of the CC, member of the Politburo since 1956.

(18) General Wang Tung-hsing (?), Commander of the Guard Regiment Peking, Director of the General Office of the CC, alternate member of the Politburo since 1969.

(19) General Wei Kuo-ch'ing (68), Chairman of the Revolutionary Committee and First Secretary of the CCP Regional Committee

of Kuangsi, 1st Political Commissar of Canton Military Region, newly elected.

(20) Wu Tê (64), Leader of the Cultural Group under the State Council, Chairman of the Revolutionary Committee and 1st Secretary of the Peking CCP Committee, 2nd Political Commissar of Peking Military Region, newly elected.

(21) Yao Wên-yüan (51), 2nd Secretary of Shanghai CCP Committee, member of the Politburo since 1969.

Alternate members of the Politburo:

(1) Ni Chih-fu (60), Model worker, Chairman of the Peking General Council of the Federation of Trade Unions, newly elected.

(2) Saifudin (62), Chairman of Sinkiang Revolutionary Committee and First Secretary of Sinkiang CCP Committee, 1st Political Commissar of Sinkiang Military Region, newly elected.

(3) Admiral Su Chen-hua (65), Vice Commander of the PLA Navy, newly elected.

(4) Mme. Wu Kuei-hsien (39), Secretary of Shensi Provincial Committee of the CCP, Textile worker, newly elected.

Those twenty-three members and alternate members of the Politburo whose date of birth is known have an average age of 66·3 years, whereas the average age of the preceding Politburo at the end of 1969 was 64 years. The date of entry into the Party is known for twenty-two members and alternate members. Seventeen had joined the CCP before the end of the Long March, four joined the Party between 1936 and the founding of the People's Republic of China in 1949: these were Ch'en Yung-kuei, Chiang Ch'ing, Yao Wên-yüan and Saifudin. The younger post-revolutionary generation is represented in the Politburo by Wang Hung-wên and Mme. Wu Kuei-hsien.

A reduction in the influence of the PLA within the Politburo also became apparent by comparison to 1969. Only nine (eight members and one alternate member) of the twenty-five had had a primarily military career. By comparison fourteen (thirteen members and one alternate member) have to be considered civilian Party cadres, and two alternate members as representatives of mass organizations. At the time of their election, seven members were still primarily active in the Central Civilian system, while three members and one alternate member were active in the Central military system. Seven members and three alternate members came from regional civilian units, two members from the regional military, while one member was active both in the Central military and in the regional civilian and military *apparats*. Since the appointment of the Politburo, two or even three representatives of the regional civilian *apparat* have apparently been transferred to the Centre.

The nomination of members and alternate members of the Politburo was apparently made on the basis of a compromise between different institutional and opinion groups who, in the dispute with Lin Piao, had joined together in a coalition. However, this coalition had from the start to bear the burden of differences between the diplomatic and administrative *apparats*, and the regional military commanders on the one hand and the representatives of the Left on the other. These differences became apparent in the attacks of the Left on the New Course after the spring of 1973 and in the contradictions which marked the 10th Party Congress. Whenever such contradictions within the leadership become apparent, the question that is uppermost is whether the institutional and opinion groups within the Party leadership take clearly identifiable positions in the recognized areas of conflict, to the extent that the formation of factions—i.e. coherent groups with extensive alternative political programmes—becomes possible.

An analysis of the organizational associations and the political positions of members and alternate members, as seen during the Cultural Revolution and also the Lin Piao crisis, makes possible a distinction between at least five such institutional and opinion groups:

(1) The group of those cadres of the diplomatic and administrative *apparat* who, in spite of some attacks during the Cultural Revolution, were able to keep their positions. This group is clearly led by Prime Minister Chou En-lai. Its most prominent representatives are now Li Hsien-nien, Wu Tê, Saifudin and probably Wei Kuo-ch'ing. On the 10th CC it had about 40-45 members. Closest to them is the second group—

(2) of *rehabilitated cadres* of the anti-Maoist faction in the civilian Party *apparat* during the early stage of the Cultural Revolution. From 1973 to 1976, its most prominent representative was Teng Hsiao-p'ing, who returned to the Politburo in January 1974, was appointed First Vice-Premier and Vice-Chairman of the CC in January 1975, and was again entirely purged in April 1976. To this group belong a number of provincial leaders, who since the autumn of 1971 have once again returned to their old positions. At least fourteen members of the CC have to be attributed to this group. After the purge of Teng, the future leverage of this group appears at least severely reduced.

(3) The group of the Cultural Revolutionary Left headed by Chiang Ch'ing and Yao Wên-yüan. It relies most heavily on the theoreticians of the inner circle around the Chairman and on those former officials of Maoist mass organizations who in the meantime have gained access to the Party *apparat*. These include Ch'en Yung-kuei, Ni Chih-fu and Mme. Wu Kuei-hsien. In the CC there are 35-40 members who should be counted in this group. Linked

to the Cultural Revolutionary Left in the person of the Shanghai Party Leader Chang Ch'un-ch'iao is another group, which is understood by most observers of Chinese politics to be part of the Cultural Revolutionary Left, but which in reality has begun to come into conflict with it increasingly. This is

(4) the Secret-Police-Left, whose position since the beginning of 1973 has become noticeably stronger. Under the leadership of Hua Kuo-fêng, and Wang Hung-wên, it also includes Chi Teng-k'uei and General Wang Tung-hsing, and at least fifteen other CC members. This group also has close contacts with the Political Department of the PLA due to its good relations with General Li Tê-sheng.

(5) The representatives of the Armed Forces in the leadership do not make up an exclusive group. The old Marshals Yeh Chien-ying, Chu Tê and Liu Po-ch'eng have for a long time been working closely together with Chou En-lai. The regional military is represented in the Politburo by Ch'en Hsi-lien, Hsü Shih-yu and Wei Kuo-ch'ing. The rehabilitated commanders are represented by alternate member Su Chen-hua. Li Tê-sheng may be included in this group, but he seems to have maintained his contracts with the Cultural Revolutionary Left. This group accounts for about seventy of the CC membership. This figure suggests that in future disputes the PLA could have a key role to play if its leading representatives were in the position to return to a united front.

Such a survey leads to the conclusion that the representatives of the New Course provide seven members and one alternate member to the Politburo, to which must probably be added four members and one alternate member from the PLA. They certainly have the support of 55-60 CC members. The two groups of the Left are represented in the Politburo by eight members and two alternate members, and among the CC members again 55-60 can be reckoned as of this group.

The intensification of the campaign of criticism against Confucius, the attacks on the social policy of the New Course (which since the beginning of February 1974 had become evident, particularly in the central media), and the extensive re-location of regional military commanders at the turn of the year (1973-4), leave doubts as to whether the new conflict which had been emerging since 1973 would continue after the 10th Party Congress. Apart from the disputes over Chou En-lai's foreign policy, which had been apparent at the Party Congress, four areas of conflict were also noticeable in domestic policy.

(1) New attempts at mobilization in a Cultural Revolutionary manner are in opposition to the efforts for a continuation of the stabilization policy of the New Course during 1971-2.

(2) There is a clear dispute over the question of promotion of

young cadres. Here the demands of the Left were to give the newcomers promotion guarantees, whereas the Party veterans and military men emphasized the need to gain experience and to practise discipline.

(3) It would be as inappropriate today as in 1971 simplistically to construct a contradiction between the Army and the Party, but there are many indications that in China there are intensive confrontations over the question of whether the Party and the State administration in the Provinces was in future to be led by civilian cadres or by the military.

(4) The dispute between the demands for recentralization and the tendency to de-centralize was reactivated in the spheres of economic planning and economic management and also in the area of education policy, which in the Lin Piao crisis had already gained considerable importance.

Until now it had seemed that opinion groups and conflict areas overlapped so much that a clear pattern of confrontation within the Chinese leadership was not yet discernible. This apart, the priority given to ensuring national security, resulting from Peking's perception of Soviet pressure, had the effect of inhibiting conflict. It encouraged compromise, which despite all disputes still determined the pattern of Chinese political development after the 10th Party Congress.

However, one cannot ignore the fact that since the spring of 1973, and increasingly since the 10th Party Congress, there has been a return to the doctrines and terminology of the Cultural Revolutionary Left. A renaissance of the Left-wing has also been discernible in the area of personnel policy. The Left had reinforced its positions in the secret police system, and had gained new organizational strength from the reconstruction of the official mass organizations, in particular from that of the Communist Youth League and the trade unions. However, because of its connections with the secret police and the trade unions, it too began to change in character. Stalinist and Cultural Revolutionary organizational doctrines are today effective side by side. One cannot exclude the possibility that in future they might come into conflict with one another.

Despite the renaissance of the personnel and the policies of the Left, in most of the provinces the New Course (with its orientation towards pragmatic development) was continued in rural social policy, industrial planning and management, and also in large areas of the education system. As a result, an increasing contradiction is developing between the requirements of the Central media and everyday socio-political reality.

The People's Republic of China is on the brink of a new internal political conflict. The substance of this conflict remains the same as it was in the Cultural Revolution and in the Lin Piao crisis: once again the forces of the Left are attempting a return to the Maoist development concept of 1958. This time however, the position of the Chairman is not quite clear. Ever since the Cultural Revolution Mao Tse-tung has withdrawn increasingly from decision-making in everyday politics and has confined himself to the role of 'Legitimator'. However, Hong Kong observers of the Chinese political scene noted some important differences between the Chairman's role in the Lin Piao conflict and that which he had taken in the dispute with the majority of the Party *apparat* in the early phases of the Cultural Revolution.[22] While in August 1966 he had become involved in the factional struggle with a slogan 'Bombard the Headquarters',[23] he had since the autumn of 1971 not openly attacked Lin Piao. Before 1 May 1971 he had appeared repeatedly in public with Lin Piao. Since the fall of his second appointed successor, he did not appear in person either at the celebrations for the national holiday or at those on 1 May. Even though Mao seemed to support the policy of the then leadership around Chou En-lai, Chou was never termed the Chairman's 'closest comrade-in-arms', whereas Lin Piao was given this title as early as August 1966.

Finally, it should be emphasized that Mao did not give explicit and specifically formulated orders to sentence Lin Piao. The central slogan in the campaign against Lin Piao, published in *JMJP*'s New Year's Day editorial in 1972, and incorporated in August 1973 into the first chapters of the revised Party constitution, did not originate with the Chairman himself:

Practise Marxism and not Revisionism, unite, and don't split, be open and aboveboard and don't intrigue and conspire! *(Yao kao ma-k'ê-ssu-chu-yi pu-yao kao hsiu-cheng-chu-yi; yao t'uan-chieh pu yao fên-lieh; yao kuang-ming cheng ta, pu yao kao yin-mou kuei-chi!)*[24]

This slogan was put together from three different previous Mao sayings, none of which had any reference to Lin Piao. The first part had already appeared as a quote by the Chairman on 1 July 1970 in the central organ of the CCP.[25] In the 1972 New Year's article the *People's Daily* had published it in large letters but without the quotation marks, which every other Mao-quote in this article carried. The slogan was only identified as a Mao quote in May 1972, and was at the same time termed 'The Three Principles' *(San-ke chi-pên yüan-ts'ê).*[26]

This practice leads to a suspicion that the anti-Lin coalition, during the period when the New Course developed, manipulated the Chairman's orders so as to justify their own policies. If this is true, then one cannot exclude the possibility that in any further conflict Mao would side with the Left, which promoted his doctrines and his concept of development. The question whether his being involved in the conflict would bring about a decision in favour of the concept of mobilization and thus against the New Course cannot be answered with certainty. However, one projection of China's political development does seem reliable. A study of the last fifteen years of Chinese domestic politics leads one to the conclusion that attempts to return to the policy of the 'Three Red Banners' were subject to the law of diminishing marginal returns. The original idea of the Cultural Revolution failed because of long-drawn-out disputes which badly damaged the Chinese political system. Lin Piao's socio-political offensive was at no time able to reach all the Chinese provinces, and it collapsed after just one year and a half. Nonetheless, there will probably be many more attempts to return to 1958, in addition to that which has just begun. However, these will also be followed by new periods of 'Readjustment' until the followers of a pragmatic and development-oriented course have finally asserted themselves against the doctrines of social utopia. The Chinese Revolution stepped into the 'Period of the Directory' when it introduced the 'Readjustment' in the early 1960, and even more so with the New Course of 1971-2. This path is difficult and will suffer more than one interruption. However, today the signs have already become more frequent that in the end it will lead to a society where the demands of the élite on the population will be increasingly limited and will therefore become more human.

REFERENCES

1. Mao Tse-tung, Chou En-lai, K'ang Shêng, Chang Ch'un-ch'iao, Ch'en Hsi-lien, Chiang Ch'ing, Chu Tê, Hsü Shih-yu, Li Hsien-nien, Liu Po-ch'eng, Tung Pi-wu, Yao Wên-yüan and Yeh Chien-ying (all full members); Chi Teng-k'uei, Li Tê-sheng and Wang Tung-hsing (alternate members).

2. *Chung-yang jih-pao*, T'aipei, 6 July 1973.

3. *NCNA*, Peking, 29 August 1973. A first analysis of the 10th Party Congress can be found in Thomas Scharping, *Die Volksrepublik China nach dem X Parteitag*, Berichte des Bundesinstituts für ostwissenschaftliche und internationale Studien, No. 12, 1974, Köln, 1974, pp. 1-11.

4. *Hsing-tao jih-pao*, 26 August 1973.

5. *NCNA*, ibid.

6. Ibid., 31 August 1973.

7. Ibid., 1 September 1973.

8. See also, pp. 249-53.

9. *NCNA*, Peking, 31 August 1973.

10. Ibid., 1 September 1973.

11. See p. 180.

12. Chapter 1, Section 6 of the revised Party Constitution of 28 August 1973.

13. Ibid., Chapter 3, Article 5, Section 3.

14. *Inter alia:* ibid., Chapter 6, Article 12, Sections 1 and 2.

15. The information for the following investigation is taken from the same sources as referred to in footnote 2, Chapter 2.

In addition: Hsiao Yeh-yün, *'Chung-kung tsui-kao ling-tao-ts'eng-te ch'üan-li chieh-kou chi ch'i wei-lai tou-cheng-te ch'ü-hsiang'* (The structure of the top leadership group of the CCP and the direction of the future struggle) in *CKYC*, Vol. 7, No. 9, September 1973, pp. 5-9; Fang Chün-kuei, *Chung-kung shih-chieh chung-yang wei-yüan-hui-te fên-hsi* (An analysis of the 10th CC of the CCP), ibid., pp. 16-33. See also: Wolfgang Bartke, 'Das neue Zentralkomitee der KPCh', in *China aktuell*, Vol. 2, No. 8, September 1973, pp. 574-80; Bartke, 'Die 195 Mitglieder des 10. ZK der KPCh' in ibid., No. 9, October 1973, pp. 656-73. Bartke's conclusions differ at some points from those presented here because his criteria of organizational origin refer solely to the position/function occupied at the time, and also because in some rare instances he does not present any data at all.

16. See pp. 29-45.

17. Chang T'i-hsüeh, Ch'en Yu, Wang Chia-hsiang and Wang Shu-shêng.

18. See p. 143.

19. See pp. 37 ff.

20. *NCNA*, Peking, 31 August 1973.

21. The members of the Politburo are listed from position 10 onwards in alphabetical order. The data on age are calculated as at 31 December 1974.

22. See *CNS*, No. 468, 24 May 1973.

23. *JMJP*, 5 August 1967.

24. Ibid., 1 January 1972.

25. Ibid., 1 July 1970.

26. Ibid., 3 May 1972.

PART FOUR

THE FOREIGN POLICY OF THE PEOPLE'S REPUBLIC OF CHINA: TALLEYRAND REDIVIVUS?

Marie-Luise Näth

13. Evolution and End of an Independent World Policy

In attempting to analyse Chinese foreign policy after the Cultural Revolution one is led back, as with domestic policy, to 1958.

In the course of that year decisions were taken not only about the introduction of a specifically Chinese path of development, but the first steps were also taken towards a specifically Chinese foreign and world policy. However, China's departure from the strict guidelines of Stalinist development policy and the simultaneous attempt to increase its room for manoeuvre in foreign policy did not yet at that time serve the end which more clearly emerged in the 1960s; namely of bringing about a total break with its Soviet ally. The change of direction in both areas of Chinese politics arose at that time from different sets of motives. However, in the perception of the Soviet leadership it soon appeared as a challenge in terms of both domestic and foreign policy to the alliance.[1]

Until the autumn of 1957 the alliance between China and the Soviet Union in terms of foreign policy—i.e. both states' policy towards the non-Communist countries—had functioned smoothly. This relationship may not always have been without its differences of opinion and temporary difficulties. However this is precisely what distinguishes this relationship from those of other Communist countries with the Soviet Union. China's dependence on Moscow, despite its economic and technical basis, expressed itself primarily in the foreign policy sector.[2]

Stalin had already had to accept Mao Tse-tung's ideological self-determination.[3]

Khrushchev, for the sake of a reconciliation with the Yugoslav

Head of State, Tito, had been prepared to make extensive concessions on the question of individual roads of domestic development to Socialism and even on that of the cooperation of 'Socialist' states with 'Imperialism', so he could not have had any objections in principle to the introduction of a new path of development in China.[4] However, even before China had begun on the new 'Maoist' path of development, the Peking leadership had called into question this very preparedness of Khrushchev to make concessions. In the toleration of a Socialist Yugoslavia, with its neutral foreign policy between the Socialist and Imperialist camps, China's leadership recognized the first irreversible step whereby Khrushchev was hoping to transform the policy of peaceful coexistence, which Stalin had introduced for tactical reasons, into a long-term strategy of détente towards the West.[5] These prospects contradicted all the ideological convictions of the CCP leaders,[6] and furthermore all the interests of practical policies in China.

A long-term policy of détente assumes the recognition of the *status quo* as the basis of ongoing compromises in power politics between the Soviet Union and the USA. It also assumes the renunciation of the need to protect one-sided Chinese interests like, for example, its interest in re-integrating T'aiwan into the mainland state system. It therefore meant at the same time the exclusion of China from all important decision-making in international politics. The extent to which these apprehensions were justified is shown not only in a series of tactical manoeuvres which the Soviet Union undertook, without regard to the sensitivities of its Chinese ally, during the Middle East crisis in the summer of 1958,[7] but also in the growing preparedness of the Soviet leadership (in liaison with the Western atomic powers) to bring about consultations on the cessation, under international control, of atomic tests.

This preparedness implied the danger that Moscow would retract previous concessions made to the People's Republic of China,[8] in order to withhold from the Peking leadership those means of power where by, despite all American attempts at containment, it could acquire its independent weight in international relations.

As a result, the first serious differences of opinion between China and the USSR occurred in 1958 on questions of foreign and international politics, and over the first Chinese attempts to prevent a policy of détente towards the USA from developing at their expense.[9]

In the spring of 1958, for the first time, the then Chinese Foreign Minister, Ch'en Yi, declared that China intended to become a nuclear power.[10] Khrushchev's visit to Peking in early autumn 1958, which seemed to have been arranged at the last minute, ended with the signing of a joint communiqué announcing the intensification of all-round coordination between China and the Soviet Union, and confirmed their 'totally identical opinions'. Only three weeks after Khrushchev's visit, China started to bombard the Nationalist Chinese island of Quemoy.[11]

One can only speculate as to whether this event occurred with the consent of Khrushchev;[12] it does seem rather unlikely that he would have agreed to the creation of a Far East crisis. There is much to be said for the assumption that the paths of the two countries had already divided before this crisis, which was probably intended to provoke Moscow's support for China's foreign policy aims.[13]

With this forceful advance the Peking leadership, which since August 1955 had held regular talks at ambassadorial level with the American government and had apparently supported the Soviet Union's policy of détente, renounced its part in the policy of peaceful coexistence.

A few months later there were serious incidents on the border between China and India. Furthermore, only a few months later, on the ninetieth anniversary of Lenin's birth (20 April 1960), the CCP started its first large-scale propaganda attack on the Soviet leadership.[14] At the 22nd Party Congress of the CPSU in October 1961, Khrushchev started a massive counter-attack against the Chinese Party, whose leaders left the Party Congress prematurely after having ostentatiously laid a wreath on the grave of Stalin, whom the First Secretary of the CPSU had denigrated.[15]

When in the autumn of 1962 Khrushchev found himself locked in a test of strength with the USA over the Cuban crisis (the dramatic nature of which remains uncontested up to this day), the Chinese Communists not only refused Moscow verbal support, but even tried to undermine and weaken Moscow's policy.[16] At just that time, a true Sino-Indian border war developed, which was soon decided in favour of China and which forced Moscow into making a choice between the two contestants.

Although the Soviet Prime Minister initially tried to evade this pressure, openly criticizing the Chinese attack on India,[17] and even though the Chinese tactics of disturbance during the Cuba crisis became the subject of serious dispute among Communist states and within Communist world front organizations, nonetheless in spring 1963 the CPSU and the CCP united to agree on the need for a Summit Conference. Here all differences of opinion could be discussed and, if possible, cleared up.

In July 1963 this summit conference actually took place. However, while it came to an end after only a short session without issuing any communiqué on its content or its conclusions, on 5

August 1963 the Soviet Union, together with the governments of Great Britain and the USA, signed the first nuclear test ban treaty.

The Peking leadership arrived at the conclusion that it could not come to an agreement with the Soviet Union under Khrushchev's leadership. Even so, it remained interested in negotiations at some later time. This time seemed to have arrived when, on 14 October 1964, Khrushchev fell and a new coalition of forces led by Leonid Brezhnev and Alexei Kosygin took over the inheritance of this man, who had been personally despised in China.[18]

Premier Chou En-lai came to Moscow to attend the October Revolution anniversary celebrations the following month. But Chou came not only as a representative of the world's most populous state (which was passionately concerned over the purity of Marxist-Leninist teachings) but also as a representative of the youngest and only nuclear power among the developing countries in the world. On 16 October 1964 the first nuclear test in China had proved successful. This was to symbolize the will and the ability of Chinese Communists to become an independent world political power.

Chou En-lai returned to Peking without any encouraging news. The Soviet leadership had not been prepared to come to any agreement on the basis of the conditions laid down by Peking. This journey of the Chinese Premier still remains the last sign of Chinese willingness to come to an agreement. However, this willingness not only excluded the possibility that China would unilaterally submit itself to Moscow's conditions, but also positively presumed that Moscow would recognize the validity of Peking's politico-ideological stance, which in the meantime had gone far beyond the arena of foreign and international politics.[19] The Chinese Communists have never really offered their Soviet comrades any real compromise. However, the reverse is also true.

In many parts of Western Europe and probably also in some sectors of the USA the obstinacy and impenetrability of the Chinese leadership *vis-à-vis* the Soviet Union had rightly aroused some admiration. This admiration, however, should not blind us to the sources of Chinese intransigence. A misunderstanding over this point could quickly lead to a false assessment of the then distribution of power in international relations.

Neither in the early 1960s nor at any later time has the Peking leadership been in a position to rely absolutely upon its 'own' often praised 'strength', and on the strength of the Chinese people, in its opposition to the Soviet Union. While the political line of 'relying on one's own strength' in the sphere of development expressed the legitimate wish for total independence and sovereignty,[20] it remained of extremely dubious importance in the area of foreign policy.

In the first years of conflict with the Soviet Union, the leaders of the People's Republic of China took advantage particularly of the long-term political and psychological crisis which Khrushchev's policy of de-Stalinization had left within the 'Socialist camp' and in the whole of the international Communist movement. Initially the Sino-Soviet dispute was itself part of this crisis, which had a debilitating effect on the Soviet Union.[21]

The hope, expressed both inside and outside China, that the Sino-Soviet conflict would lead to a decentralization of power in the Eastern alliance, accompanied by a similar erosion within the Western alliance, that would finally lead to a decentralization of power in the whole world, remains unfulfilled. On the contrary, the cracks in the Eastern bloc and in the West have not prevented the further accumulation of power by the Soviet Union and the USA. In the 1970s these two world powers still maintain control over all essential decision-making in international politics. It is they who in reality rely on their own strength and hardly at all on the loyalty of their allies.[22]

However, in Khrushchev's last months of office, China's leaders had already started to bring to an end these two powers' 'conspiracy' of détente, and were strengthened in their resolve after their first meeting with the new Soviet leaders.

After the end of the 22nd Party Congress of the CPSU, the Chinese Communists initially concentrated on the attempt to call Soviet policy in the East European bloc and the international Communist movement into question, in order to form a majority and, if possible, isolate the Soviet Union.

In the course of 1963 China's efforts were directed towards gaining a diplomatic base from which an independent Chinese world policy could be conducted. According to the statement published by the CC of the CCP on 14 June 1963—the 'Proposal on the general line of the International Communist Movement'—the platform of China's world policy was to be: the establishment of a broad united front of all anti-imperialist forces to take up the active struggle against the USA and at the same time to isolate the revisionist Soviet Union and its allies; and a struggle against both the world's super-powers on the diplomatic and revolutionary fronts.[23] In other words, the Peking leadership had decided to lead a struggle against both world powers simultaneously and to fight, both by diplomacy and by revolutionizing its environment. For this strategy of simultaneous conflict they proceeded to search for comrades-in-arms, wherever these could be found. The united front which it sought was to be an alliance of all militant anti-American governments and of all active revolutionary forces with which these governments were basically in direct conflict at the domestic political level.[24]

China found two 'natural' partners in its immediate neighbourhood: Pakistan, which was in conflict with India, and Sukarno's Indonesia, which was in conflict with Malaysia. Together with these two countries—Pakistan at that time treading an anti-Soviet path due to fear of a close collaboration between India and the Soviet Union, and Indonesia with a strong anti-American sentiment—Peking attempted to organize an Afro-Asian solidarity conference following the example of the Bandung Conference of April 1955.

Apart from the long-term goals already mentioned, this Conference was intended to mobilize a large front against the nuclear test ban treaty of the three great powers, and Peking probably also intended to make sure of the international support of the 'small and weak' countries in Asia and Africa for its own claim to be the fifth nuclear power. After all, China had made this claim in order to break the political monopoly of the 'white' powers.[25]

At the turn of the year 1963-4, Chou En-lai started on a diplomatic mission which was to take him to ten African and three Asian countries, as well as to Albania. However, the results of this journey remained unsatisfactory.[26] The reports of a talk between Chou and the Tunisian Head of State, Habib Bourguiba, provide evidence of the results of his visits and of the effect of China's solitary gambit in world politics on the governments which had been seen as the PRC's potential partners.

President Bourguiba reported:

I told him what shocked us in his manner, style and conceptions. I said, 'You come to Africa as the enemy of the capitalist states, of the West, of the neutralists and the non-aligned, of India, of Tito, of Khrushchev—of everybody. You have not chosen an easy policy.... Others won't tell you straight out but I will—you won't get far in this continent.'[27]

In fact, the Chinese Communists did not 'get far' in Africa or in Asia with their policy.[28] The intolerance with which it was pushed forward, and the dangers that any non-Communist government which allied itself with Peking would certainly encounter, were obvious major reasons for this lack of achievement. But it also proved that the Soviet Union would make it very difficult for some countries (such as Egypt, Algeria and Indonesia) to opt for Peking.[29]

The more intense the Chinese leaders' insistence on excluding the Soviet Union from the planned Solidarity Conference and the more unambiguous Moscow's indication that Soviet participation was a matter of principle, the more the whole project was endangered.[30] It was finally to fail completely in the summer of 1965.[31]

The start of the American bombing of North Vietnam in

February 1965 (which came as a great shock to most Asian governments) also comes within this context. The first Afro-Asian Solidarity Conference at Bandung had been called out of a deeply-felt need for security and with the declared aim of halting the expansion of the Cold War on to the Asian continent. Now they were to experience the way in which, from Peking, the new pioneers of the Afro-Asian Solidarity Movement responded to the dangerous intensification of the Vietnam War—not with suggestions of détente, but rather with enthuiastic declarations of solidarity with Hanoi and the Vietcong.

The first reactions of the Soviet leadership to the American bombing were interpreted by Peking as a willingness to capitulate. Subsequently, it categorically rejected Moscow's suggestion that all socialist forces should join a single united front for action—even if confined to the Vietnam problem.

In the autumn of 1965, two further events were to supplement the catalogue of China's foreign policy failures: the outbreak of the Indo-Pakistan war[30] and the fall of Sukarno after a Communist insurrection had been put down by the Indonesian Army. In both cases Peking felt completely deprived of its sphere of influence; it had lost its most important partners in foreign policy.

China's foreign policy débacle in the second half of 1965 has to be seen particularly against a background of long smouldering tensions within the Chinese leadership, which were now breaking into the open. From the officially declared *weltanschauung* of Communist China one can deduce that throughout the entire development of its foreign policy there has been a strong tendency for the leadership to project their own experiences from domestic policy and contemporary history, and in certain cases even from the history of the Chinese empire, upon the world about them. Now this tendency began to become even more pronounced.

Lin Piao's speech on 3 September 1965 marking the twentieth anniversary of the end of the last Chinese-Japanese war gave occasion to construct an international revolutionary strategy after the example of the Communist revolution in China. To quote from this speech:

Taking the entire globe, if North America and Western Europe can be called 'the cities of the world', then Asia, Africa and Latin America constitute the 'rural areas of the world'. Since World War II, the proletarian revolutionary movement has for various reasons been temporarily held back in the North American and West European capitalist countries, while the people's revolutionary movement in Asia, Africa and Latin America has been growing vigorously. In a sense, the contemporary world revolution also presents a picture of the encirclement of cities by the rural areas.[33]

Lin Piao always pointed to the example of the Anti-Japanese War in China to prove that the most important revolutionary war in the world was the 'People's War' and that in such a war victory was certain:

In other words, you [the enemy] rely on modern weapons and we rely on highly conscious revolutionary people. You give full play to your superiority and we give full play to ours.... Only by relying on our own efforts can we in all circumstances remain invincible.[34]

Lin's explanations aroused attention particularly because at that time they were associated with a clear declaration of China's attitude to the Vietnam war. China would make use of this instrument of People's War, of the unleashing of such People's Wars, to avert a potential attack from the USA. It would use the method of pre-emptive strikes through third countries who would have to rely primarily on their own strength in their fight against imperialism; and it would not attempt the obvious—a return for its own safety's sake to the side of the Soviet Union. The Minister of Defence thereby confirmed China's strategy of conflict in foreign policy towards the two world powers.[35]

However, by pointing back to the historical experiences of the Chinese Communists, he had chosen the most unsuitable example. The Anti-Japanese War had been led not by Mao Tse-tung but rather by Chiang Kai-shek, under whose command the Communist armies had placed themselves after the Japanese attack.[36] Japan's downfall had not been achieved in China, but rather on Japanese soil, and it certainly did not come about because of the 'revolutionary awareness' of the Chinese people, but with the help of the most modern weaponry available at that time, namely the first atom bomb, developed and applied by the USA.[37]

Lin Piao had therefore either deliberately distorted history, or he had indulged in self-deception.[38] Whatever the truth, his exposition had made the increasing Cultural Revolutionary atmosphere of combat inside China consistent with the dangerous war activities in China's immediate neighbourhood. Similarly, the decision to launch a massive revolutionary mass movement against 'China's Khrushchev', as he was called (President Liu Shao-ch'i), and at the same time the willingness to push the conflict with Moscow up to a new level, were both reconciled.

On 11 November 1965 an editorial in *JMJP* declared the Soviet Union to be an enemy who stood in antagonistic contradiction to the People's Republic of China.[39]

As a result China seemed to be totally master of a situation which was continuously pushing the country into unprecedented isolation.

However, Foreign Minister Ch'en Yi no longer seemed to be in control of the situation. In his press conference on 29 September 1965 he gave vent to his feelings. He ended the press conference with the following words:

We do not have any illusions about US imperialism. We are totally prepared for US aggression. If the US imperialists are determined to open a war of aggression against us then we will welcome it if they come sooner, similarly even if they come as soon as tomorrow. Let the Indian reactionaries, the British imperialists and the Japanese militarists come with them. Let the modern revisionists coordinate their efforts with them from the North! In the end we will always win.... We have been waiting sixteen years for the US imperialists to attack us. My hair has gone grey with waiting. Perhaps I will not be so lucky as to see the invasion of China by the US imperialists.... But my children will live to see it and they will continue the struggle wholeheartedly.[40]

In 1967 Foreign Minister Ch'en Yi was severely attacked on several occasions by the Red Guards, but without being purged. He died at the beginning of January 1972 and was given a full State funeral, attended by Mao Tse-tung personally.[41] His son, however, was executed in 1967. Against the background of Ch'en's words, which have just been quoted, this was particularly tragic.

During the years of the Cultural Revolution the People's Republic of China became almost totally incapable of action in foreign policy. The intra-Party purges left behind only a rump of a government, and even the position of Chou En-lai, who in all previous CCP crises had remained untouched, seemed at times so endangered that even he could no longer be trusted as an anchor of Chinese politics.[42]

In the course of 1967, all ambassadors were recalled from abroad to Peking. The one exception was Ambassador Huang Hua, who was able to continue in his position in Cairo.[43]

In August 1967 the Foreign Ministry in Peking was for a short while under the control of the Red Guards who, in a wave of protest notes, multiplied China's conflict with the rest of the world. Red Guards also laid siege to a number of foreign embassies, and mishandled some diplomatic personnel,[44] and thereby made the worsening relationships with foreign countries still worse. Among the beleaguered embassies was that of the Soviet Embassy, but Moscow answered the mass terror against their diplomats only with notes of protest, and the expulsion of the last remaining Chinese students in the Soviet Union.

Only when an element of moderation re-asserted itself in China's general attitude towards foreign relations did the Sino-Soviet relationship acutely deteriorate to the extent that—as it seemed to some Western observers—direct armed confrontation seemed a possibility.

The 9th Party Congress began on 1 April 1969 against this background. In order to understand this Party Congress as a change of direction and as the end of a totally independent Chinese world policy, we need to provide a brief overview of the pattern of international relations, on which China had had practically no influence since the autumn of 1965. This should make it possible for us to assess the real effects of the Peking government's independent foreign policy in the years 1963-9.

During this period it had not been possible for Peking to 'encircle' 'US imperialism' with a large combat-ready united front of all the anti-American forces in the world. However, the political and psychological effect of attrition which the Chinese leadership had hoped for from the long-lasting US engagement in Vietnam had come about. The Western super-power had become tired of war. It had become entangled in a deep domestic political crisis, and its foreign policy had stagnated. Nothing could make America's compulsion to reorientate itself in world politics more obvious than Lyndon B. Johnson's resignation from the Presidential Election race in March 1968.

So the notion of the almost unlimited power of a people decided on a revolutionary struggle against an enemy which was materially far its superior but psychologically and morally was weak, had been confirmed even without China directly contributing. But even though the then Chinese leadership around the minister of Defence, Lin Piao, may have tried to deny it, this notion had been confirmed at the expense of China and its national security. In fact, the fighting power of the Vietnamese Communists played a relatively secondary role in the struggle on the Indochinese battlefield, which was being determined particularly by the testing of ever new weapon systems by the two super-powers. From this struggle it was not China but the Soviet Union that benefited, just as the United States had lost in political fighting power and moral fibre.

This recognition seems to have become accepted in the autumn of 1968 and spring of 1969, at least in those circles of the Chinese leadership that had foreign experience and had become acquainted over many years with the complicated pattern of events in world politics—i.e. in the group around Chou En-lai and his associates in the diplomatic corps. These post-Cultural Revolutionary bearers of Chinese foreign policy must have become aware, when the Moscow government decided on intervention in Czechoslovakia, and when, a few months later in March 1969, it started a massive military attack on Chinese troops stationed on the Ussuri river, of how the Soviet Union had consolidated itself in world politics after Khrushchev's fall and of how much the self-cleansing process of the Cultural Revolution and its shock effect on all other countries had benefited the new Soviet leaders and handicapped the political security of China.

The intervention of Warsaw Pact troops in Czechoslovakia and the heavy fighting on the Ussuri island of Ch'en-pao (Damansky), which according to Western correspondents was originally started on 2 March 1969 by the Chinese attacking Soviet border troops but had then led to a Soviet counter-attack on 15 March, undoubtedly gave a severe shock to the whole Peking leadership. Chinese propaganda had much earlier envisaged the possibility of a Soviet attack, but now the Soviet Union's physical threat to China had become a reality.

Peking had every reason to take the Brezhnev Doctrine seriously. Formulated shortly after the invasion of Czechoslovakia, it was a theory of the limited sovereignty of 'Socialist' states and the fraternal responsibility of other such states to intervene in cases of direct threat to a governing Communist Party. At the time of the Hungarian crisis in 1956, Mao Tse-tung and his followers had themselves sanctioned this thesis.[45] Certainly it had not been fully formulated at that time; it had been understood solely as a logical consequence of so-called 'Proletarian Internationalism', the apparently higher form of relationship between 'Socialist' states, which could only be fulfilled by governing Communist Parties and consequently gave precedence to securing the rule of the Party over guaranteeing independence and self-determination to states and peoples.

China's support for the Soviet intervention in Hungary had set a precedent, and it carried little conviction when Peking condemned intervention in Czechoslovakia so heavily, calling the Soviet leaders 'Social Imperialists',[46] and at the same time criticized Alexander Dubcek's reformist course.

Peking's protest resulted clearly from Mao's awareness that the Cultural Revolution had created ideal circumstances to justify a Soviet intervention in China. The victory of the Maoist faction in this domestic political conflict had been achieved at the price of an intact leadership by the Party over the nation.

Here arguments based on ideology had to remain ineffective. In fact, the term 'Social Imperialism', which the Chinese Communists used to describe the Soviet Union after the autumn of 1968, has been exaggerated by Western observers. However, what was really new, in the sense of a real perceptual change in the Chinese assessment of the Soviet Union, was the formula 'New Czars', first used in the spring of 1969.[47] With this formula the Peking leadership not only attacked a renegade from the correct path of Communist theory and practice but also a historical behavioural trend of its Russian neighbour, the politics of a country which tenaciously aspired to world rule and was notorious for its expansionism.[48]

This new realization certainly did not spring solely from the recent events of the autumn of 1968 and the spring of 1969. These events only suddenly made obvious the extent of Moscow's political expansion since the autumn of 1964. The most important landmarks of the Soviet Union's world political advance were:

(1) The successful peace negotiations between India and Pakistan in the winter of 1965-6, after which until 1970 it was possible for the Soviet Union to build up an advantageous diplomatic position for itself in both countries;

(2) The strengthening of Soviet influence in the Arab world after the Six Day War of June 1967;

(3) The start of a détente dialogue in Europe, which gained increased impetus with the nomination of Willy Brandt as Foreign Minister of West Germany in the winter of 1966, and with the gradually increasing readiness of Bonn to recognize 'the realities consequent upon the Second World War'; and finally

(4) A gradual but steady development over the years, without spectacular events, of a rapprochement between Japan and the Soviet Union, which finally went to the length of Moscow selecting Tokyo as the place where, in November 1969, the first details of a Soviet plan on collective security in Asia were to be developed.

The Chinese Government—given its foreign policy and diplomatic presence in the second half of the 1960s—could not have had much effect upon Moscow's successes in détente in Europe and in the consolidation of its influence in the Middle East. However neither with regard to the Indian subcontinent nor towards Japan was China objectively predisposed to total inactivity.

Towards India, Peking had systematically preserved a policy which served to confirm exactly what the Chinese alleged of its neighbour: its inability to prevent interference by foreign powers and its tendency to serve as a starting-point for any attack from the West or from Europe on China.[49] In fact, only when faced with the increasing threat from China did the Indian government get pulled into the sphere of the Soviet Union.[50]

Peking's deep distrust of Japan was emotionally understandable[51] and had rational justification so long as China felt itself threatened by the US and interpreted the American-Japanese defence pact as being directed primarily towards itself. Even so, the extent of Chinese irreconcilability towards Japan was based primarily on an irrational transference of an enemy image of America on to the latter's East Asian ally. This 'total enemy' perception can be understood only in the context of China's ever-increasing politico-ideological rivalry with the Soviet Union in the 1960s. A continuous activator of this rivalry was Peking's greater readiness to fight imperialism and concern for fundamental principles when representing the interests of the world revolution.[52]

Peking had been informed of the limited aims of Washington's military involvement in Vietnam via Chinese-American talks at ambassadorial level in Warsaw.[53] After the difficult domestic political conflicts of the Cultural Revolution, when the then continuous fears of an invasion by Chiang Kai-shek's troops aided by the US had not been justified, there was one rational explanation less for Chinese animosity towards the USA.

It remains to be noted that by presenting itself as 'everyone's enemy', China had blocked itself in terms of foreign policy and had thereby given the Soviet Union a greater chance to expand its diplomatic influence. China's attempt at an independent world policy had led to its own paralysis in foreign policy.

Defence Minister Lin Piao should actually have come to this conclusion in his report at the 9th Party Congress. But his picture of the world, which he systematized into a catalogue of contradictory relationships,[54] was only to serve the purpose of characterizing international relations as a battle of 'all against all' and thereby to justify the continuation of a strategy of simultaneous conflict.[55]

Lin's exposition remained incoherent. He declared his government's willingness to start relations with all the world's non-Communist countries on the basis of peaceful coexistence. At the same time, he declared it an honour for China to be exposed to the two super-powers' continuous attempts at blockade. He mentioned that China needed at all times to be prepared against a military attack by 'US imperialism' as well as by 'Soviet revisionism', and that it had to be equipped for both a conventional and a nuclear war. Even so, he was of the opinion that the two super-powers' policy of isolation could do no harm to the People's Republic, as it was a challenge to the people's determination to uphold China's independence and keep the initiative in its own hands, to rely on its own powers and to work for the wealth and power of the nation. All this he justified with the argument that it was not 'imperialism', 'revisionism' or 'reaction' that determine the fate of the world, but rather the proletariat and the 'revolutionary people' of all countries.

Lin Piao announced that the general line of Chinese foreign policy would also in future be determined by the invisible trinity of Proletarian Internationalism towards the Socialist countries, Peaceful Coexistence towards states of different social systems, and Revolutionary Solidarity with the world's revolutionary forces.

He put forward a whole list of the world's movements and forces which were to be supported. In mentioning some countries by name where the revolution was to be continued (Laos, Thailand, Burma, Malaya, Indonesia and India) he took the risk right at the start that his offer of international relations with non-Communist states in China's immediate neighbourhood would be considerably restricted.

Lin therefore remained convinced that China would be able to preserve its autonomy in the three constituent areas of foreign policy: in national security and defence, defining the foreign interests of the nation, and the manipulation of the world's nations.

More than four years after the 9th Party Congress of CCP it had become apparent that the end of an independent Chinese world policy in this sense had already come about, even though the Minister of Defence once again swore to the unchangeable continuity of his policy before the victors of the Cultural Revolution.

REFERENCES

1. On the significance of the internal and economic policy measures of the CCP in the autumn of 1958 for the Sino-Soviet conflict, see Donald S. Zagoria, *The Sino-Soviet Conflict 1956-1961*, Princeton, N.J. 1962, p. 77-141.

2. This is pointed out particularly by Richard Löwenthal in *Chruschtschow und der Weltkommunismus*, Stuttgart, 1963, passim; and 'Chinas Perzeption der internationalen Konstellation und seine nationalen Interessen', in *Die Aussenpolitik der VR China-Entscheidungsstruktur—Stellung in der Welt—Beziehungen zur Bundesrepublik Deutschland*, published by the German Society for Foreign Policy, München-Wien 1975, pp. 139-61.

3. An essential document in this context is Mao's essay *On New Democracy*, 1940. See: *Selected Works of Mao Tse-tung*, 4 vols., London 1954-6, Volume III, pp. 106-56.

4. See particularly Khrushchev's Report at the 20th Party Congress of the CPSU.

5. See Löwenthal, *Chruschtschow*, op. cit., pp. 119-24; Zagoria, op. cit., pp. 145-221.

6. See China's explanation of the Policy of Peaceful Coexistence in 1963: 'Peaceful Coexistence—Two Diametrically Opposed Policies', Sixth Commentary on the Open Letter of the CC of the CPSU of 30 March 1963 (commentary); Chinese reset in *JMJP*, 12 December 1963; English in *Peking Review*, Peking *(PR)*, No. 51, 20 December 1963.

7. See Löwenthal, *Chruschtschow*, op. cit., pp. 126-9; Zagoria, op. cit., pp. 195-9.

8. According to the Chinese, the Soviet Union renounced on 20 June 1959 a secret treaty of 15 October 1957, in which the People's Republic of China was promised a sample atom bomb and technical data on the production of atom bombs. See *PR*, No. 33, 16 August 1963.

9. See Zagoria, op. cit., pp. 172-99.

10. *Die Welt*, Hamburg, 12 May 1958.

11. The Soviet Prime Minister was in Peking from 31 July till 3 August 1958. Text of the Sino-Soviet communiqué in *Pravda*, 4 August 1958.

12. Löwenthal is of the opinion that the firing on Quemoy was agreed upon by Peking and Moscow. Zagoria's documentation (op. cit., pp. 206-17), however, seems to suggest that the Chinese leadership took action on its own. This approach was recently taken up by the Soviets. See Ernst Henry, *What is Peking After?*, pamphlet, Moscow, 1974, p. 24.

13. In this way it could be interpreted that the firing on Quemoy was from the start a limited affair. The Chinese leadership did not at that time intend to lead a real campaign of liberation against Nationalist China. According to the Soviet Union (see fn. 12), Peking at that time did seek a confrontation, possibly even between the super-powers.

14. The attack was carried out in disguised form and without mentioning the Soviet Union by name.

15. The Soviet leadership used Albania as an excuse for its attack. However, the Chinese delegation demonstrated its solidarity with Albania.

16. See for greater detail Ernst Kux, 'Die feindlichen Brüder', in the German edition of Zagoria, *Der chinesisch-sowjetische Konflikt, 1956-1961*, München 1964, pp. 451-4.

17. As in his speech before the Supreme Soviet on 12 December 1962, in *Pravda*, 13 December 1962. Neville Maxwell (*India's China War*, London, 1970) has attempted to prove that it was not China, but India which was guilty of causing the border war. His point of view has, however, remained much disputed. Some useful expositions on this event from the Indian side are the following: A. G. Noorani, *Our Credulity and Negligence*, Bombay, 1963; and Noorani, *Aspects of India's Foreign Policy*, Bombay, 1970.

18. See Kux, loc. cit., pp. 481-6.

19. See the Chinese argument in: 'A proposal concerning the general line of the international Communist movement', *JMJP*, 14 June 1963; English in *PR*, No. 25, 21 June 1963.

20. This train of thought, which can be found already in Mao's early writings on military strategy and which even in the years of the Sino-Soviet alliance had never disappeared entirely, became more prominent in Chinese propaganda particularly during the 'Great Leap Forward'. However, it was not a matter of a typical Maoist idea, but of a typical Chinese one, originating in old Chinese philosophy.

21. See Löwenthal, *Chruschtschow*, op. cit., pp. 44-64.

22. This has been clearly proven in the latest international crisis, namely the Middle-East conflict of October 1973.

23. See 'A proposal concerning the general line ...', loc. cit.

24. The most prominent example of this was to be Indonesia, where the Communist Party attempted a *coup* in September 1965. China's involvement in this *coup* soon became apparent, which is why the victory over the PKI was immediately followed by a violent persecution of the Chinese.

25. This was a time when the Chinese leadership consciously reflected on its common political stance with the continents of Asia, Africa and Latin America, the non-white continents.

26. See William E. Griffith, *Sino-Soviet Relations, 1964-1965,* Cambridge, Mass. 1967, passim; W. A. C. Adie, 'Chou En-lai on Safari', in *CQ,* No. 18, April-June 1964, pp. 174-94; W. A. C. Adie, 'China and the Bandung Genie', in *CS,* Vol. 3,—15 May 1965.

27. Quoted from the *Jewish Observer and Middle East Review,* 3 April 1964, in Adie, 'Chou En-lai', loc. cit., pp. 186-7.

28. Ibid.

29. At that time the Soviet leadership developed a lively travel activity and offered generous credits to a number of countries. The Algerian President Ben Bella, who was to be the host of the conference, was even awarded the title 'Hero of the Soviet Union' in May 1964.

30. In the summer of 1964, Khrushchev had given up the demand for the participation of the Soviet Union. This is why it only became a matter of principle when the new Soviet leaders restated this demand after Khrushchev's fall.

31. The immediate cause for the change of date was the fall of Ben Bella in June 1965. However, after this most of the respective governments had become tired of conferences, which meant that no other date was ever made for this conference.

32. This was a double failure for the PRC. First, Peking's project of an Afro-Asian Solidarity Conference faded into the more distant future; and secondly, because of the anti-war politics of the super powers, the Chinese leadership felt incapable of giving massive support to its Pakistani favourites. Most probably the Chinese leadership was actually actively discouraged by the two super-powers.

33. See Lin Piao, 'Long Live the Victory of People's War', English in *PR,* No. 36, 3 September 1965, (pp. 9-89) p. 24.

34. Ibid., p. 19 and 22.

35. See Helmut Dahm, *Abschreckung oder Volkskrieg: Strategische Machtplannung der Sowjetunion und China im internationalen Kräftverhältnis,* Olten and Freiburg-im-Breisgau, 1968, and Hartmut Fackler, 'Aussen- und innenpolitische Aspekte der Strategie-diskussion in der Volksrepublik China von 1949 bis 1969', Ph.D. thesis, Berlin, 1972.

36. The Anti-Japanese war was actually led by Chiang Kai-shek, in propaganda and in reality, as a war of resistance *(k'ang chau),* which is how it was celebrated by Lin Piao. Chiang was the first to refer to it as a 'protracted war'. Mao's writing 'on the protracted war' actually took up the General's slogan. Until Lin's speech, the 'People's Liberation War' *(jen-min chieh-fang chan-cheng)* played the leading part in the glorification of their military tradition. It was that war which had led to the banishment of Chiang Kai-shek.

37. The victor's pride of the Chinese is certainly understandable and is shared by the Nationalist Chinese. After all, Japan was the first Asian power to win a victory in 1905 over a white power, viz. Russia. That after the Second World War the Chinese had claimed a victory over Japan seems a most understandable correction of historical reality.

38. It is probably a matter of self-deception. Mao Tse-tung had never designed an anti-imperialist military strategy, and the leaders of the Nationalist movement were never suspected of this because they had always negotiated with imperialist powers. The later theories of the 1960s

seem to suggest that the CCP itself was inclined to avoid a physical confrontation with 'Imperialism'.

39. See the English version in *PR*, No. 46, 12 November 1965 ('Reputation of the new leaders of the CPSU. On "United Action" ').

40. See *NCNA*, London, 6 October 1965.

41. See *PR*, No. 2, 14 January 1972, pp. 3–5.

42. See Daniel Tretiak, 'The Chinese Cultural Revolution and Foreign Policy', in *CS*, Vol. 8, No. 7, 1 April 1970.

43. In the autumn of 1971, Huang Hua was head of the Chinese delegation to the United Nations.

44. Among others, diplomatic staff at the Indian Embassy and their families, who according to eye-witnesses, were ordered into the Embassy building so that their safety could be guaranteed. It was precisely these people who were exposed to massive and planned terrorism by the Red Guards.

45. After his talks with the representatives of the CCP on the occasion of the 3rd Party Congress of the Communist Party of North Vietnam in September 1960, the Indian Communist Hare Krishar Konar reported that the Chinese were proud of their attitude on Soviet intervention in Hungary, even in opposition to Khrushchev, who was still hesitating. See Zagoria, *The Sino-Soviet Conflict*, op. cit., p. 337–8.

46. See *JMJP*, 23 August 1968, and the article on the Centennial of Lenin's Birthday in *JMJP*, *HC* and *CFCP*. English text in *PR*, No. 17, 24 April 1970, pp. 5–15—'Leninism or Social-imperialism?'

47. See *JMJP* and *CFCP*, 4 March 1969.

48. See 'Leninism or Social-imperialism?', loc. cit., passim.

49. One could call this the trauma of the Opium War of the Chinese—the fact that India had been the stepping-stone of the English invasion into China. This is probably what Ch'en Yi was referring to in his press conference of 29 September 1965.

50. See, *inter alia*, Harish Kapur, *The Embattled Triangle: Moscow, Peking, New Delhi*, New Delhi, 1973, pp. 118–27.

51. The Japanese war crimes in China weighed heavily, even though in 1945 the Chinese Nationalist government and in 1972 the Chinese Communist government forgave the Japanese people, not holding against them the suffering of the Chinese people during the Japanese occupation.

52. See particularly the 4th commentary ('Defenders of Neo-colonialism'), *JMJP*, 22 October 1963; English in *PR*, No. 43, 24 October 1963, pp. 207–45.

53. Besides, the Chinese government was informed of this by the American government's public statements and by public discussion in the USA—where, other than at the time of the Korean War, the re-establishment of the *status quo* was mentioned as the only aim of war.

54. Lin Piao distinguished between four contradictions in the world: (1) the contradiction between the suppressed nations and imperialism and social-imperialism; (2) the contradiction between the proletariat and the bourgeoisie in the capitalist and revisionist countries; (3) the contradictions between the imperialist and social-imperialist countries and between the imperialist states, and (4) the contradiction between the socialist countries and the imperialist and social-imperialist countries. See, *The Ninth*

National Congress of the Communist Party of China (Documents), Peking, 1969, Lin Piao's speech, (pp. 3–108), pp. 83 ff.
    55. See ibid., pp. 79–108.

14. Advances to the Western Super-Power

The American journalist Edgar Snow, who from the early 1930s had a close personal relationship with the CCP and Mao Tse-tung and who even after the Communist seizure of power in China continued to act as a medium for the Chairman's political declaration to the Western world, made an interesting prognosis on Peking's foreign policy in this context during July 1969. Snow did not exclude the possibility that the Chinese leadership already perceived the Soviet Union as the more dangerous of the two world powers. However, he still stated that it was almost unthinkable that in Mao's lifetime there would be a détente between China and the USA which would go much beyond the automatic weakening of the conflict between the two countries after the end of the Vietnam war. He said:

Mao is feeling no pain, as some imagine, from any sense of isolation. With de-escalation of the Vietnam conflict, removing the immediate threat of an American war, and with a major domestic campaign [the Cultural Revolution] lagging behind, Chairman Mao is in no mood to yield concessions of important principles in order to make his terms of peaceful coexistence more attractive. Chairman Mao does not intend to accept any seat in the United Nations under its present charter, even if T'aiwan were unseated.[1]

This prognosis does not seem totally atypical of interpretations of Chinese politics made by some Western observers, particularly those who claim intimate knowledge of China and the Chinese. It can at least be put down to the nature of their understanding of their own political culture and its main dynamism, namely the competition for political power: that game which seems to be monopolized by dark and secret forces against which the thinking individual is powerless although not exposed to them unwillingly. To this individual a China which in fact was often tormented by the world around it,[2] and whose leaders had taken on the sisyphean task of demolishing power structures wherever they had begun to gain control of the people, must appear as a desirable counter-world. Understandable expectations of such a counter-world thus become descriptive categories of reality.

For Snow's prognosis to have come true, it would have required the Peking government to abandon any politics at all. The question whether one could expect this from any government answers itself. There is no convincing evidence in the fields of domestic and foreign policy that the Chinese leaders had ever had a distant relationship to political activity, whether in their fight for or in their use of power.

Those who, after the end of the Cultural Revolution, made predictions about Chinese foreign policy based on the policy expressed by Lin Piao at the 9th Party Congress cannot be reproached for not having predicted the fall of the Defence Minister two years later. Their misjudgement, however, rested on premises which had been proved illusory in the latter half of the 1960s: the suppositions that Chinese foreign policy could be carried on essentially as a continuous sequence of one-sided sovereign acts of political will and declarations (which had only led to total isolation), and that the People's Republic of China could in its isolation live through severe conflicts of its own making with both super-powers simultaneously.

The latter was already a question of mere risk-taking willingness and actually no longer a question of *raison d'état*, which of course has to be answered by a Communist government like any other, particularly if the existence of international plurality is perceived as a major threat to the politico-ideological fundamentals of Communism.

Today one can say with some certainty that in the three years following the autumn of 1968 the post-Cultural Revolutionary leadership in China was divided into two factions over questions of foreign policy: one which was quite willing to take risks and the other consisting of *realpolitik* politicians, oriented by *raison d'état*. The protagonists of these two factions were, respectively, Lin Piao (until his fall) and Premier Chou En-lai.

Actual developments finally proved Chou En-lai to be the protagonist of the cause of reducing the conflict with one of the super-powers, namely the USA. The campaign which was to expose Lin Piao as a traitor after his fall insinuated that he had held essentially the same ideas, with the difference that he had allegedly sought détente with the Soviet Union.[3]

At least outside China, there are no grounds for the allegation that Lin was intending to turn back towards the Soviet Union. However, there is more to support the assumption that the discussion of alternative directions in foreign policy was manipulated by the representatives of the *realpolitik* faction, so that it appeared to be only a question of towards which side the dialogue of détente was to be directed. Being faced by the hypothetical choice of either returning with Lin Piao to the side of Soviet Union or seeking security and political relief with Chou En-lai in the West, it may have been easier for Chairman Mao Tse-tung to come down in favour of the policy which he was finally going to legitimize: that of détente with the USA.[4]

When analysing the practice of China's foreign policy between the autumn of 1968 and September 1971, the paradoxical picture that emerges is one of two contradictory political directions acting together, though at times acting one against the other: policies directed simultaneously towards both revolution and anti-imperialism, and towards the normalization of diplomatic relations.

Hardly any of the generally accepted indicators of trends—the declarations in the Chinese press on 1 May, 1 August (Army Day), National Day (1 October) or New Year's Day—had pointed to a fundamental change in China's foreign policy by the summer of 1971. Above all, it appeared totally normal that from May 1969 onwards the ambassadorial posts which had been vacant since 1967 should gradually be re-filled. The Minister of Defence and his colleagues also saw this as a precondition for the reactivation of foreign policy. As before, Peking now also answered its obligations of revolutionary solidarity with the Communist rebels in Malaysia, Thailand, Indonesia and the Philippines and Burma, to name only the most important examples.[5]

When at the end of March 1970 the Cambodian Head of State, Prince Norodom Sihanouk, while on a diplomatic tour to Paris, Moscow and Peking, was deposed by the pro-Western leader of his government, Lon Nol,[6] he was willingly given asylum in China. In the famous 20 May 1970 declaration of solidarity with Sihanouk, Mao Tse-tung called upon the 'Peoples of the World' to stand up once again against 'US imperialism and its running-dogs'.[7]

In August that year a remarkable event occurred in Chinese foreign policy. After twelve years of bitter animosity, the People's Republic of China announced the resumption of diplomatic links with Yugoslavia. At the time this news was of much greater importance than the resumption of diplomatic relations with Canada, Italy and Ethiopia that was soon to follow. In the first phase of the Sino-Soviet dispute, Yugoslavia had been the starting-point of discussions on the strategy and tactics of Communist foreign policy. It had then been the main target for Peking's more or less veiled criticisms of the Soviet Union. Within the 'socialist camp' Yugoslavia had been declared the most important enemy, and later it was also to be attacked by the Chinese for being the spokesman for the neutralist movement. Apart from the criticism of Tito's domestic policy, Yugoslavia's deadly sin had always been its willingness to cooperate with the West, and in particular its attitude of reconciliation towards the USA.

In August 1970 the Chinese Communists revoked none of their criticisms of 'Yugoslav revisionism'. However, the fact that China had made contact and had invited the then Yugoslav Foreign

Minister indicated not only the Chinese interest in all countries threatened by the Brezhnev Doctrine, but also a changed attitude in Peking towards Socialist countries having diplomatic contacts with the West. At the same time, this indicated a mellowing of China's own attitude towards diplomatic relations with the West.

This perspective also seems important in the context of the intensified cooperation between China and Romania observed during 1970. Both countries had cooperated quite well with one another since 1962. However, the Romanian Party leadership was generally presented in the West as the mediator between China and the Soviet Union. In fact, Romania had had the best possible contacts with the West for a number of years, and in August 1969 it received the first visit by an American President to an East European country.

The connection between this visit by President Nixon and the détente between China and the USA was to become apparent only two years later, when the *NCNA* published on 16 July the rather sensational news that Nixon had been invited as President of the USA to visit the People's Republic of China.

In the years that have passed since President Nixon's visit to Peking in the spring of 1972, it has come to seem as natural as the visit of an American President from time to time to Moscow. Nixon himself, with his sense of history, described his visit to Peking as a week which had changed the world.[9] The European observer, however, cannot take comfort in the trivializing or in premature historical judgement of the Sino-American summit meeting. Chinese foreign policy has at all times certainly been far less hectic than for example Soviet foreign policy in Khrushchev's day, when summits were called off at short notice and dramatic crises almost fell out of the bright blue sky of détente. But this was only finally confirmed by the successful arrangements for the Nixon visit.

There is no doubt that this visit had some connection with the fall and death of Lin Piao. Even if this drama took place without the knowledge of the public, it does justify some of the apparent scepticism before the Presidential aeroplane actually landed at Peking Airport on 20 February 1972. It still seems somewhat doubtful whether the Peking summit did actually change the world, because a world without the total involvement of China in international decision-making cannot be considered changed. The American administration certainly took a very big step in this direction, but it was essentially left to the decision-makers in Peking to decide whether this involvement would prove successful. We will have to return to a discussion of this question at the end of this account of China's post-Cultural Revolutionary foreign policy.

The major aspects, from Peking's point of view, which led to the détente with the USA have already been considered: the awareness of an ever more direct threat from the Soviet Union; a situation of isolation which in the face of the Soviet threat seemed, at least to some leaders within the Peking government, to be increasingly unbearable; and the determination of Chinese politicians and diplomats to give the principles of *realpolitik* priority over a 'Socialist country's' missionary principles.

The historical uniqueness of the Sino-American détente seems to lie in the fact that, at the same time as preparations were being made within China for a totally new orientation in foreign policy towards détente, it met in the USA a similarly-minded partner.[10]

Already during his election campaign in the autumn of 1968 Nixon had mentioned the need to revise America's China policy.[11] His new approach towards China had scarcely resulted from a general re-evaluation of the People's Republic, but instead was closely linked with his determination to solve the Vietnam conflict. Chou En-lai had something similar in mind. Here too the pressure to revise China's policy towards America developed out of a quite different need, namely the necessity to have a secure defence against the Soviet Union. It is thus superfluous now to consider on which side there was the greater interest in détente. The history of Sino-American relations ever since the Korean War shows clearly that if the desire for détente had only come from one side, it would not have proved enough to ensure a relaxation of tensions.[12]

The 'Winning back of China'[13], a country and people for which the Americans had felt extremely strong emotional ties, had been necessary for the Nixon administration both with the view of solving the Vietnam problem and in order to revive American foreign policy, which at that time was stagnant. It had also become necessary in view of the USA's image of itself, consciously accepted by Nixon more than by any previous President, as one of the two super-powers, if not the world's only real super-power.[14]

For Chou En-lai the deciding factors were certainly not only aspects of security policy, but also interest in Western technology and in the development of trade with the USA. Finally, one also has to understand Chinese preparations for a dialogue with the USA as the logical development from an increasing feeling of alienation towards the Soviet Union. As this alienation became ever less ideological and more existential, it became ever less possible to maintain the ideologically rationalized alienation from the USA. After a Soviet–American policy of détente and a consequent atmosphere of ideologically neutral power compromises had been in existence for years—as far as the Soviet Union was concerned, of non-ideological acquisitions of power[15]—ideology could no longer explain the reality of world politics.

However much one may be able to say about Sino-American

détente, the observer still seems very much in the dark about the reality of the process. It took place between personalities whose major abilities were in the area of secret and cabinet politics. Chou En-lai owed his entire political and Party career to his ability for intrigue, negotiation and compromise. Henry Kissinger, at that time special security adviser to the American President, had to develop these abilities in his specific office.

There had been 134 meetings between the Chinese and the American Ambassadors in Warsaw when, after a break of several months,[16] a proposal was initiated by the Chinese for a meeting on 20 November 1968. The date was then changed to 20 February 1969 and was finally postponed indefinitely. On 20 January and on 20 February 1970 the 135th and 136th meetings took place. No joint public statements were made on these meetings.

There had been a delay in the talks for the simple reason that the post of Chinese Ambassador in Warsaw was only filled again at the beginning of 1970. Nonetheless, it seems doubtful whether Warsaw was the central switch-board for the Sino-American détente. It seems more likely that the visit of President Nixon to Romania in August 1969 was an important step in its preparations.

In July of that year the President announced his doctrine of the Vietnamization of the Vietnam War, i.e. the 'Asianizing' of the defence efforts for Asian countries. According to this, the USA was in future to give material aid only, and to leave the actual tasks of defence to its Asian allies themselves.[17] Nixon had therefore given notice of his military retreat from Vietnam and advance warning of his disengagement from other South and East Asian countries.

On 21 July 1969 the government in Washington unilaterally decreed the easing of restrictive regulations on trade and travel with the People's Republic of China. A Hong Kong press report of 29 July stated that Chou En-lai had told a Pakistani delegation that China would be prepared for a dialogue with the USA on matters of peaceful coexistence, if the USA's 7th Fleet were withdrawn from the Straits of T'aiwan as well as the US forces from T'aiwan itself.[18] On 26 December 1969 Secretary of State Rogers announced a reduction in the patrols of the 7th Fleet between Quemoy and the Chinese Mainland.[19]

Between these two dates came not only Nixon's visit to Bucarest, but also at the beginning of September, the visit of the Romanian Prime Minister, Gheorge Maurer, to Peking and a stop-over in Peking at short notice by the Soviet Prime Minister Kosygin.[20] Three weeks later the Chinese government accepted the Soviet demand (made at the end of March) to convene a negotiating committee to discuss mutual border problems.

Until late August there had been repeated military incidents all along the border. According to Soviet sources, in the period from June until mid-August alone 448 'border violations' had occurred—all 'obviously' started by the Chinese. A larger military confrontation was reported on 13 August from the border in Sinkiang.[21] On the question of starting negotiations, the Chinese had insisted on their demand that the Soviet government recognize all the border treaties made between the Russian Tsar and the Imperial Chinese government as 'unequal' or of an imperialist nature.[22] Their view was that on this basis there should be negotiations with the aim of working out new and equal contracts. Peking pointed out that the Soviet Union was occupying about 1·5 million km.[2] of Chinese territory, but declared that it would renounce its claims on the territory in favour of an acceptable border agreement based on the nineteenth-century unequal treaties.[23]

The Soviet government rejected such preconditions and insisted on the introduction of consultative negotiations. To emphasize this request, the Soviet Union not only took open measures to strengthen the Soviet armed forces on the Chinese border, but also used the subtler methods of political terror: the dissemination of rumours of a Soviet pre-emptive attack on the Chinese nuclear centre in Lop Nor, Sinkiang,[24] and Moscow's supposed attempt to win the support of the government in Washington for this operation;[25] the pretence of a détente between the Soviet Union and T'aiwan as the result of a then much publicized visit by the Soviet journalist Victor Louis to Nationalist China;[26] and the public consideration, by precisely this journalist, of whether the Soviet Union could find an anti-Maoist leader in China who would ask the Socialist countries for fraternal help in the struggle with the Peking leadership.[27]

Kosygin's visit to Peking on 11 September lasted only an hour. The Chinese and Soviet Prime Ministers meeting at the airport could not have discussed much. From this one can conclude that on 8 October Chou En-lai accepted the Soviet offer of negotiations without any preconditions, because the possibility of a dialogue with the USA had already opened up, giving him the assurance that negotiations with the Soviet Union would result in nothing against the wish of his government.[28] In fact the Sino-Soviet negotiations petered out in the autumn of 1973.

In the course of 1969 there were, on the American side, increasing press comments, declarations by the Secretary of State and his colleagues, and statements by leading politicians and diplomats on the question of Sino-American détente. The Americans, for whom since the start of the Korean war T'aiwan had been represented as their country's Chinese partner, were now prepared for the dialogue with Peking.[29] One probably has to start from the assumption that the American government was already certain enough of the possibility of entering into a dialogue with the Chinese leadership in Peking systematically to pursue such preparations.

Similar preparations were not made on the Chinese side. On the contrary, when the Nixon–Sato communiqué on the return to Japan of the American military base at Okinawa was publicized in November 1969, Chinese criticism of the USA became harsher than usual. Even though this communiqué clearly announced the reduction of the American combat forces facing the People's Republic of China, Chinese propaganda interpreted the agreement very differently: i.e. as an American-Japanese conspiracy to reinstate Japanese imperialism and militarism.[30] Peking demanded instead that Japan should be neutralized, which alone would give some guarantee against Japan becoming self-sufficient as both a military and a political power.

After the end of the 136th Sino-American meeting in Warsaw in the spring of 1970, all progress in matters of détente seemed to the outside world to have crumbled. The fall of the Cambodian Head of State, the spontaneous solidarity of Mao Tse-tung with Prince Sihanouk and the beginning of the civil war in Cambodia seemed to entail a further hardening of the external positions of Peking and Washington. Today we know that there was actually no interruption in negotiations between them. In fact the venue of the ambassadorial meetings was only changed from Warsaw to another European capital. It was certainly not by chance that this capital, Paris, was outside the Soviet area of control.

The Chinese side was represented in Paris by Ambassador Huang Chen, the only Chinese representative at the time who was a member of the CC of the CCP. Huang had therefore been given special authorization. In the spring of 1973 he was to be nominated Director of the newly-established Chinese Liaison Office in Washington.

The year 1970 brought no obvious changes in the Sino-American relationship, as far as the rest of the world was concerned. In the spring of 1971, however, the Chinese government introduced a policy soon to be known, with reference particularly to the Sino-American relationship, as 'ping-pong diplomacy'. A number of foreign sports organizations were invited to international table-tennis events in China, and Peking allowed its own table-tennis champions to take part in sporting events abroad. As a result, in April an American group of sportsmen and journalists entered China. The group was given a friendly reception on 14 April by the Premier in person.[31] On the same day President Nixon announced in Washington a further easing of restrictions for tourism, trade and foreign exchange between China and the USA. On 10 June

1971 the trade regulations towards China were adapted to those that were valid for the Soviet Union.

One month later, on 9 July, Kissinger left for his first, at that time secret, visit to Peking. The American Special Adviser had spent some time in Pakistan to discuss the political events which, since the spring of 1971, had been threatening to develop into an international crisis.[32] Islamabad at the same time came to be the terminal station on the path of Sino-American negotiations which was to lead the American President to the People's Republic of China.

On 16 July the Chinese news agency announced Chou En-lai's invitation to President Nixon. The news came as a surprise to all the world's governments. In Particular, America's Asian allies, who were doubtless immediately affected by a fundamental change in America's China policy, became bitterly aware that they had not been consulted.[33] In Japan the announcement of this change in policy was actually termed the 'Nixon-shock'. In fact, it was in this way that the assumption was abandoned that Japan—as China's East Asian neighbour with the closest personal and economic ties with Peking of any Western ally—would as a matter of course be the mediator and peacemaker in any Sino-American détente.

However, it was not only Washington that had problems with its totally astonished allies. Chou too had not informed his Communist partners (Albania, North Vietnam and North Korea).[34] After 16 July both sides consequently made every effort to appease their allies who had been shattered in their belief in the reliability of the super-powers and to re-convince them of their fidelity.[35]

Even though with the beginning of the Sino-American dialogue there had been a real landslide in favour of accepting Peking as a UN partner, Washington continued to insist that the Western governments should continue to take the American point of view on the question of Chinese representation in the UN. It was only a few weeks before the annual vote in the United Nations on this question was due to take place.

At American instigation, Japanese diplomats in particular now made extensive efforts in the United Nations to keep the People's Republic of China outside this organization if possible, or at least to safeguard the seat of Nationalist China.[36] Even so in the autumn of 1971 the plenary session of the United Nations decided with a majority of exactly the same size that, each year since 1961, had rejected Peking's claim for sole representation, to replace the Nationalist Chinese representatives by representatives of the People's Republic.[37]

There had been much discussion at that time as to whether the acceptance of the People's Republic in the United Nations had been one of the prices which President Nixon had been willing to pay for his visit to Peking. There was some evidence to suggest this: the choice of the date for making known to the public the process of détente; the fact that the USA did not request the United Nations, as in previous years, to treat the question of representation as an 'important matter'; and Kissinger's second stay in Peking at the time when the vote on the question of China's representation in the UN was taken.

President Nixon angrily took note of the result of the vote taken by the plenary session, and the jubilant outburst from some of the delegates at the exodus of the Nationalist Chinese UN delegation. It was doubtful whether his anger was real, but it is of some interest that the Nationalist Chinese representatives in New York at that time still insist today that the outcome of the vote came as an unwelcome surprise for the Nixon administration.[38]

In fact it was just these representatives who had for some time been criticizing Nationalist China's permanent seat on the Security Council of the UN. On this point, as generally on the question of the possible reconquest of mainland China by Chiang Kai-shek's troops, the T'aiwanese foreign propaganda had not for some time been reflecting the true thinking and understanding of leading personalities in T'aipei politics.[39] In the opinion of the latter, the vote of the United Nation's plenary session in favour of Peking in the autumn of 1971 came about not because of a direct or indirect compromise between Chou En-lai and Kissinger. but rather as the result of an acute disintegration of the West then beginning, which resulted from the risk taken by the American government when, in the interests of a successful dialogue with Peking (and in the interest perhaps also of the Chinese leaders, who entered into this dialogue against the resistance of their political enemies at home), it had decided to keep this process of détente secret.

Seen today in retrospect, this idea makes sense. The foreign policy of both Nixon administrations had brought about not only impressive successes but also disintegration and lack of orientation among American's allies in Europe and Asia. These were the logical consequences of secret diplomacy, which by its nature denies the principle of consultation which is implicit in any alliance and, as an equally natural consequence, calls into question any international consensus in the pursuit of secret interests.

The Chinese government may have counted on just this advantage in its secret negotiations. This was not only its right, but also legitimate in its struggle for sole representation in the face of a super-power pursuing the obviously contradictory aims of at once achieving reconciliation with China and supporting China's isolation from the organizational forum of world politics.

Peking's representatives not only entered the Security Council to observe China's continuous membership in the Council, but they also joined the United Nations' sub-organizations. The Nationalist Chinese representatives had to give way to them everywhere. This alone remains questionable, right up to the present time, and—being in mind that T'aiwan is equal in size of population to East Germany, which has been represented in the UN since 1973—seems an intolerable side-effect of the enforcement of China's representation in the international organization. This remark, however, should be understood only as an expression of sympathy with a country whose post-war development seems to have had a history of long-lasting national self-paralysis. China's partition had not been forced upon it by any foreign power, and none could have prevented a reunification and certainly none would have prevented the leadership of Nationalist China from achieving national self-sufficiency. But this leadership insisted on its claim of sole representation and its goal of re-establishing its sole rule over Mainland China, just as the Peking government did with regard to T'aiwan. Both sides sought continuous confirmation from the world for their demands to be the one and only China. On this and on one last point the Chinese leaders in Peking and T'aipei had achieved more accord with one another over more than twenty years than with any of their respective allies. The question of the one and only China was advocated on both sides by representatives of a mainland irrendentism which stemmed not only from domestic political power struggles, but also from the wish to remove all encroachments of colonial power and to revive the modern Chinese nation-state if possible within the borders of the last pre-colonial dynasty.[40]

This is clearly confirmed by the fact that the two Chinese governments agreed not only that the island of T'aiwan (which had been occupied for more than fifty years by Japan) was an integral part of China, but also on the demands made by Peking on Indian and Soviet territory. There may have been a disparity in their selection of methods of enforcing these demands;[41] however, there was never any doubt on the part of T'aipei that, for example, Tibet was an integral part of China, and that the recognition of the sovereignty of Outer Mongolia could only be valid so long as it was enforced by China's Russian neighbour.[42]

When President Nixon visited Peking, American diplomacy not only saw itself confronted with the problem of how to defend T'aiwan's vital interests before the People's Republic of China, but it had to come to terms with the apparent paradox of how this could be accomplished, while at the same time respecting the national self-awareness of a divided whole China. The formula which was found in the communiqué at the end of the summit meeting on 27 February 1972 seems an artistic achievement in its simplicity and in its plausibility:

The United States acknowledges that all Chinese on either side of the T'aiwan Strait maintain there is but one China and that Taiwan is a part of China. The United States Government does not challenge that position. It reafirms its interest in a peaceful settlement of the T'aiwan question by the Chinese themselves.[43]

This formula in fact only described the actual state of affairs. With it Washington may have renounced all attempts to create an independent T'aiwan, or to bring about an international solution to the T'aiwan problem. However, the American government did not comment on the question of what was to happen if the uniform idea 'of all Chinese on both sides of the Straits of T'aiwan' were to collapse. The very real problem that would face an independent T'aiwan if there were a change in the national self-awareness of those Chinese living there was not mentioned. None of the points of view specified by the Chinese Communists in the closing communiqué of their claim on T'aiwan was confirmed by the Americans. These points of view were the following:
(1) 'The Government of the People's Republic of China is the sole legal government of China' [consequently the T'aipei government had to be regarded as illegal].
(2) 'T'aiwan is a province of China which has long been returned to the mother-country' [consequently it is only being occupied at present by American troops].
(3) 'The liberation of T'aiwan is China's internal affair in which no other country has the right to interfere' [consequently the defence alliance between T'aipei and Washington had to be seen as an interference], and finally
(4) 'All US forces and military installations must be withdrawn from T'aiwan.'
In that part of the American statement relating to the fourth point, it was stated that the final aim of the American government was the withdrawal of all armed forces and military installations from T'aiwan. A similar statement could at any time be made by Washington with regard to West Germany. Here, as in T'aiwan, the stationing of troops should probably be understood as a necessity of political security rather than as an end in itself. This attitude is reflected also in the last sentence of the American statement regarding the problem of T'aiwan:

In the meantime it [the American government] will progressively reduce its forces and military installations on T'aiwan as the tension in the area diminishes.[45]

Whereas this sentence leaves room for different interpretations, the possibilities of a lessening of tensions 'in this area' seem quite limited: a voluntary return of T'aiwan to the mainland; T'aiwan's independence being accepted by Peking; and a quasi-German solution, where in China's case both sides accept a 'united nation' as a solution which is neither re-unification nor partition, but is based principally on the priority of safeguarding peace.

T'aiwan was one of the most important points of discussion at the Sino-American summit meeting in Peking, and the USA's diplomatic relations with T'aipei have continued to prevent the realization of Chou En-lai's demands, made as long ago as the beginning of the Nixon visit, for the establishment of diplomatic relations between Peking and Washington.

As already pointed out, there were two fundamental peculiarities of the American state visit to the People's Republic: the lack of any type of formal contact, and the unity in conflict which was documented in the form of the communiqué. The so-called Shanghai communiqué was made up of seven parts: a formal statement of the Nixon visit; a joint appreciation of the contacts; a one-sided declaration by the USA on foreign and international policy, in particular on the strength of its alliances with Japan and South Korea; a one-sided statement by China on this question and on the question of its alliances with North Vietnam and North Korea; a joint statement on the principles of foreign policy held by both sides; a summary of the different points of view on the T'aiwan question; and a joint announcement that the contacts that had been made should be continued, and expanded in the areas of politics and of science, technology, culture, sport and journalism.[46]

In the spring of 1972, the Shanghai communiqué was examined by Western observers, in particular with regard to the question of what progress the USA could make in the solving of the Vietnam conflict and what concessions had been offered in return.

In fact President Nixon probably made only a minimal profit, if any, from his Peking visit over the Vietnam problem. The People's Republic of China simply was not the place where this question could be decisively clarified. This also explains why, such a short time after the Sino-American summit, the situation in South-East Asia became more tense when Washington ordered the mining of harbours and the river delta in North Vietnam.[47] Other aspects of the communiqué have in the meantime proved to be important long-term results of the Presidential visit:

(1) The resolution to continue and intensify contacts;

(2) The resolution to expand the content of discussions, in particular in the areas of technology and trade. Here Nixon had already made an offer to the Chinese government by leaving behind the satellite station which had been specially installed for his visit and which was of great importance from the point of view of China's strategic defence system.

(3) The agreement on both sides to fight any attempt at hegemony

by a foreign or even regional East Asian power. China and the United States themselves renounced such attempts and at the same time turned against those powers still in the position to pursue them—namely the Soviet Union and Japan.

For us there is a further matter of importance. The People's Republic of China admitted to renouncing threats of violence or the use of violence. It declared, with the American government, the intention to avoid international military conflicts and expressed its attitude that the normalisation of Sino-American relations was not only in the interests of the two negotiating countries 'but also contributes to the relaxation of tension in Asia and the world'.

With this the Chinese government had accepted new values with priority over the struggle against 'imperialism' and against the USA as the major driving force of imperialism: the priority of the interests of a pluralist world state system and of détente as an internationally acknowledged aim of foreign policy. Chou En-lai and his colleagues had introduced a policy which has to be understood not only by reference to their choice of new foreign political partners, but also by their basic understanding of foreign policy as a policy of Western orientation.

REFERENCES

1. Snow in an interview on 7 July 1969. Quoted in *Asian Almanac, Singapore (AA)*, Vol. 8, No. 12, 21 March 1970, P. 3859.

2. The leaders of the People's Republic of China have often had to submit to the pressure of a nuclear threat. However the long-term USA trade embargo and the sudden withdrawal of all development aid by the Soviet Union in the summer of 1960 are also relevant in this context.

3. See Chou En-lai, 'Report to the 10th National Congress of the CCP', in *PR*, No. 35/36, 7 September 1973 (pp. 17–25), p. 20.

4. See Issue 7/8 of *Peking Review*, 25 February 1972, under the heavily printed title of 'Chairman Mao Meets President Nixon'.

5. See Lin Piao's report to the 9th Party Congress of the CCP, loc. cit., pp. 100 ff.

6. Prince Sihanouk at that time was on a tour, which was to further the protest in Paris, Moscow and Peking against the increasing occupation of Cambodia by North Vietnamese Troops. See also Douglas Pike: 'Cambodia's War', in *South-East Asian Perspectives*, New York, No. 1, March 1971, passim.

7. See *PR*, special issue, 23 May 1970, pp. 8–9, also the speech of the Chief of the General Staff, Huang Yung-sheng on the 23rd anniversary of the 'Democratic People's Republic of Korea' on 9 September 1971. Three days before his fall, Huang directed a massive attack upon the USA. See *NCNA*, London, 10 September 1971.

8. In November 1970 Romania was promised credit by the People's Republic of China estimated at almost US$300 million. See Wolfgang

Bartke, *China's Economic Aid*, London, 1975. From April 1971 until May 1972 thirteen delegates were sent from China to Romania, and in the same period fifteen delegates went to North Korea. In the meantime China received eighteen groups of visitors from Romania. See also 'China in the Communist World', in *CNA*, No. 922, 8 June 1973.

9. See *The President's Trip to China*, a pictorial record of the historic journey to the PRC with text by members of the American Press Corps, New York, 1972.

10. With the beginning of Nixon's presidency, the element of missionary dogmatism disappeared from American politics. In the negotiations with the Soviet Union the new president, however, clearly accepted the principle of peaceful coexistence as put forward by Moscow.

11. See also Nixon's fundamental reflections on America's Asia-policy: Richard M. Nixon, 'Asia after Vietnam', in *Foreign Affairs*, New York, Vol. 46, No. 1, Oct.-Dec. 1967, pp. 111-25.

12. During 1955-8, when the Chinese People's Republic demonstrated its willingness to negotiate with the USA, this one-sided desire was obviously not sufficient for a real détente. The Chinese leadership was at that time also not convinced of Détente for its own sake and it did without further efforts at détente with the USA, until the USA's determination to preserve the status quo in East Asia became apparent.

13. See the provocative book title of Anthony Kubek (*How the Far East was Lost: American Policy and the Creation of Communist China 1941-1949*, Chicago, 1963).

14. Henry Kissinger's continuous mediation and travelling—which led to a new style of US foreign policy and is still accepted as the expression of conscious American power politics, especially in countries where Soviet influence had long been dominant, i.e. in the Arab world and East Asia—can be so interpreted.

15. This is in fact what the slogan 'Social-Imperialism—socialist in words, imperialist in deeds' was intended to express.

16. The last talk had taken place on 8 January 1968.

17. See, *inter alia*, Frank N. Trager, 'The Nixon Doctrine and Asian Policy', in *Southeast Asian Perspectives*, No. 6, June 1972, PP. 1-34; William E. Griffith, *Peking, Moscow and Beyond: The Sino-Soviet American Triangle* (6: The Washington Papers), Washington, 1973.

18. Cited in *AA*, Vol. 8, No. 12, 21 March 1972, p. 3857.

19. See ibid.

20. Kosygin had attended the funeral of the North Vietnamese leader Ho Chih Minh, and was on his way back to Moscow, when he was informed on his stop-over in Calcutta of the Peking government's sudden willingness to talk. As a result the Soviet plane took the route to the People's Republic of China.

21. On the border dispute see *AA*, Vol. 7, No. 20, 17 May 1969, pp. 3329 ff. and No. 50, 13 December 1969, pp. 3689-97, also Harold C. Hinton, *The Bear at the Gate: Chinese Policy-making under Soviet Pressure*, Washington D.C., 1971, passim.

22. See Shao-chuan Leng, 'Legal Aspects of the Sino-Soviet Dispute', in *AS*, Vol. 12, No. 6, June 1972, pp. 493-509.

23. For the Peking government it was not a matter of enforcing a real

claim to territory, but rather a matter of establishing in principle that the border between China and Russia had come about illegally. Just as a matter of prestige, Moscow could not seriously consider this question. Quite apart from this, the Soviet leadership had to prepare for the future in which a powerful China could possibly refer back to an oral commitment by the Soviet Union, in order to enforce its territorial claims.

24. The possibility of a Soviet preventive attack was commented upon by the Soviet journalist Victor Louis on 16 September 1969 in the London paper *The Evening News* with the few words: 'Whether or not the Soviet Union will dare to attack Lop Nor, China's nuclear site, is a question of strategy, and so the world will only learn about it afterwards!' *AA*, Vol. 7, No. 50, 13 December 1969, p. 3692.

25. Probably referring to this rumour or to a similar Chinese insinuation, on 13 August the US Department of State vehemently rejected the idea that the USA could take sides in the Sino-Soviet conflict. See ibid., p. 3694.

26. This journey took place in May 1969. The Nationalist Chinese denied the reports that Louis had had talks with the eldest son of Chiang Kai-shek, Chiang Ching-kuo.

27. Ibid., p. 3692.

28. See the PRC's declaration of 7 October 1969 in *NCNA*, 8 October 1969. Here the Chinese referred for the first time to the conversation between Chou and Kosygin on 11 September.

29. See *AA*, Vol. 8, No. 12, 21 March 1970, p. 3857.

30. See *JMJP*, 28 November 1969. Translation in *PR*, No. 49, 5 December 1969, PP. 14-16.

31. See ibid., No. 17, 23 April 1971, PP. 4-5.

32. This refers to the Bangladesh crisis. See William J. Barnds, 'Der innere Zerfall Pakistans', in *Europa-Archiv*, Vol. 26, No. 16, 25 August 1971, pp. 551-63; see also the exposition published soon after the Indo-Pakistani War by D. R. Mannekar, *Pakistan Cut to Size*, New Delhi, 1972; and Dilip Mukerjee, *Zulfiqar Ali Bhutto: Quest for Power*, New Delhi, 1972.

33. The Chinese Nationalist government was particularly embittered. The governments of Singapore and Thailand reserved their judgement and the Foreign Ministers of Indonesia and the Philippines welcomed Nixon's willingness for détente. However, some of the media in the South-East Asian countries allied with the USA hesitated, although this was not mentioned at governmental level. A survey of Asian and European reactions can be found in *AA*, Vol. 9, Nos. 48 and 49, 4 and 11 December 1971.

34. Whereas the announcement of the Nixon visit was interpreted by the North Koreans as a bankrupt statement of American imperialism (see *Nodong Sinmun*, 8 August 1971), the central newspaper in North Vietnam, *Nhan Dan*, noted on 19 July that President Nixon intended to cut a rift between Communist countries. Prince Sihanouk stated on 30 July that the Lon Nol government had expectations from the Nixon visit, which he himself obviously feared: i.e. a détente at the expense of his attempt to reconquer Cambodia from his Chinese exile.

35. See also the Sino-American communiqué at the end of the Nixon

visit, where the People's Republic of China and the USA promised their respective partners their continuing full support. See *PR*, No. 9, 3 March 1971.

36. See the statement by Secretary of State William Rogers on 2 August 1971 on the question of the USA's China policy in the UN. Excerpts in *AA*, Vol. 9, No. 48, 4 December 1971, p. 4914.

37. On the way the vote was taken see, ibid., Vol. 10, No. 1, pp. 4961–2. Also excerpts from the Japanese intervention on behalf of T'aiwan, p. 4963.

38. This point of view was also taken by the then Foreign Secretary of Nationalist China, Chou Shu-k'ai, in an interview with the author on 6 October 1972.

39. After the autumn of 1968, and the consolidation of the Peking government, the attitude that a return to the mainland could no longer be expected became accepted by the population and leadership of T'aiwan. This became apparent to the foreign observer generally only in confidential conversations and by the increasing integration of the mainland and T'aiwanese population on the island.

40. This clearly lies behind Peking's demand for a revision of the supposedly 'imperialist' border treaties with the Soviet Union and India, even if the Chinese leadership had from the start abandoned the idea of claiming the return of large areas which it counted as its own territory.

41. The Nationalist Chinese government obviously condemned the military dispute between the People's Republic of China and these two countries. But this says little about what action it would have taken in place of the government of Mao Tse-tung.

42. In the Sino-Soviet treaties of 1945 and 1950 the Nationalist Chinese government and also the Communist government were forced to recognize the sovereignty of Outer Mongolia.

43. See the text of the communiqué, loc. cit., p. 192.

44. Ibid.

45. Ibid.

46. Ibid.

47. This happened on 8 May 1972, two months after Nixon's visit to Peking and two weeks before the visit of the American President to Moscow. See the statement of the Chinese government on 11 May 1972 in *PR*, No. 20, 19 May 1972, p. 6.

15. Western-oriented Policies

Up to President Nixon's visit to Peking China's post-Cultural Revolutionary foreign policy had passed through three different phases: Phase I, which began in May 1969, was characterized mainly by the reactivation of already existing Chinese diplomatic relations with other countries. During 1970 efforts to extend diplomatic contacts gained priority in Peking's foreign policy—this was Phase II. The Spring of 1971 and the beginning of open détente between China and the USA marked Phase III, which was concluded with the signing of the Shanghai Communiqué in the spring of 1972. If one counts the period between the spring of 1972 and the 10th Party Congress of the CCP in August 1973 as Phase IV, this phase is marked less by the quantity of Peking's newly-emerging foreign political partners and more by their quality. Apart from the contacts which the Peking government managed to make with the developing countries, this period saw a reconciliation with Japan, the simultaneous normalization of relations with West Germany, and at least the institutionalization of relations with Washington. While the United Kingdom closed its Consulate in T'aipei as early as March 1972 and raised its representation in Peking to ambassadorial level, Australia and New Zealand established diplomatic relations with the People's Republic of China in December 1972. Amongst China's many visitors were the Foreign Ministers of France, West Germany, Britain and Italy, Japan's Prime Minister and, at the beginning of September 1973, the French President. One thing was common to all these countries sending visitors to the People's Republic of China, namely their political and military alliance with the United States. Today one can easily prove that this common factor was not a coincidence but rather that it played a positive part in the foreign policy considerations of the Chinese leadership. During negotiations on the normalization of relations with Japan in September 1972, Chou En-lai waived the old demands that Tokyo should disengage from its close relationship with the USA and that China's island neighbour should become neutral ground. Peking's publications meant for abroad, such as *Peking Review* and the *NCNA Bulletin*, suddenly and almost as a contrast to the emergence of a number of crises within Western Europe, put a large amount of faith in the

European Economic Community. Moreover, they began even to show positive interest in the meetings of the NATO Council.[1]

Peking's support for Japan's territorial demands on the Soviet Union dated back to 1964,[2] but after the normalization of relations between the two East Asian countries, Chinese propaganda stood up even more for the re-integration of the four contested South Kurile islands into Japan. At the time of the visit of the West German Foreign Minister Scheel to Peking in October, the Chinese Foreign Minister Ch'i P'eng-fei went so far as to describe the division of Germany as 'abnormal'.[3]

Even though we have no ground for believing that Ch'i thereby expressed sympathetic concern for a united and free Germany, he did in principle express unambiguous support for the idea of German reunification.

In Phase IV after the end of the Cultural Revolution, China's foreign policy served a double aim: the development of relations with the West as a system of political unions and military alliances and, simultaneously the reactivation of its combative attitude towards the Soviet Union. The latter accounted not only for China's support for the political and territorial demands of Western countries on the Soviet Union, but also for China's massive criticism of the Conference for Security and Cooperation in Europe. From the start, Vice-Foreign Minister Ch'iao Kuan-hua called this conference an 'Insecurity Conference',[4] and in the autumn of 1973 it was to be the centre of a serious but unsuccessful discussion between Prime Minister Chou En-lai and President Pompidou.[5] China's policy of orientation towards the West had a well developed anti-Soviet component. This, of course, did not pre-empt Peking's interest in cooperating with the industrialized countries within the Western alliance. On the contrary, this interest has become apparent in a number of cultural exchange programmes, which will make it possible in future for Chinese students to pursue regular studies at Western universities, and will give Chinese scientists in particular the opportunity to keep in touch with their Western colleagues. Whereas the establishment of diplomatic relations has hardly affected China's already good economic relations with Japan and West Germany, its economic contacts with the USA have expanded tremendously. Without a doubt they are a good indication of China's independent interest in the Western world. On the other hand, the anti-Soviet component in the new policy of orientation to the West was not by itself an expression of another independent offensive. It was rather a largely impotent reaction to the new Soviet advance which occurred almost simultaneously with China's return to international politics. It was this that in 1971 encouraged the rapprochement with the West to develop its own dynamic.

The new Soviet offensive became apparent at three different levels:

(1) At the military level, Moscow endeavoured not only to extend its positions along the border with China, but also to create a permanent naval presence in the Indian Ocean.[6] By sending a naval unit through the Straits of T'aiwan, the Soviet Union demonstrated in the spring of 1972 that it intended to surround China by sea from Vladivostok to the Indian sub-continent. Moreover, a territorial link between the Soviet Union and the Indian Ocean via Afghanistan and Pakistan had been established in the autumn of 1970.[8]

(2) At the level of Asian diplomacy, Moscow began in the second half of 1969 to develop its own plans for a collective security system in Asia, which was to serve the dual aim, first, of enforcing the general recognition of the Soviet Union as an Asian power[9] and, secondly, of forming an alliance based on the Soviet Union, India and Japan against the People's Republic of China.[10]

Even though the outbreak of the Bangladesh crisis does not at first sight seem to fit into this concept at all, Moscow in the end succeeded in gaining considerable advantage from this situation. In spite of all its efforts, the Soviet Union did not succeed in binding India *and* Pakistan to itself in a form of contract. When, however, after the summer of 1971 the Indian government felt affected by the internal political crisis in Pakistan and considered the possibility of intervening, the time had come for a Soviet-Indian treaty of 'peace, friendship and cooperation'.[11] The Indian intervention in December 1971, which led to the secession of East Bengal from Pakistan, came about with the unambiguous support of Moscow against China's massive protests, and with great misgivings on the part of the American government.[12] The Soviet Union, however, had implicitly proved that it was playing a key role in maintaining the security of Asian countries and peace in Asia.

(3) At the level of international diplomacy, Moscow's Asian initiative meant the prolongation of the Soviet policy of détente, with the European Security Conference at its centre. Both security initiatives overlapped with efforts towards an agreement with the USA over the limitation of strategic rearmament by both world powers. The first so-called SALT agreement was signed in Moscow in may 1972.[13]

At none of these levels was Soviet policy directed solely against China. However, only China was directly threatened by a new Soviet attempt of containment, even if not—as Peking claimed—by encirclement. Considering the obvious reversal of roles of the two super-powers in their attitude towards the People's Republic of China, the Soviet Union having become the pioneer of a policy of containment and the USA the forerunner of a policy involving China in the international system, it was only to be expected that Peking should change its foreign policy considerations accordingly.

Japan, particularly because of its alliance with the Western super-power, was seen as a desirable partner and offered the People's Republic of China, at least for the period of the Soviet offensive, more security than a neutral Japan would have done.[14] During the phase of Chinese–Japanese détente, Peking was to draw considerable benefit from the emotions of a large part of the Japanese population, who could not get over the solitary nature of US policy towards China. A barely controllable China-euphoria[15] in Japan gave rise to a situation where the Chinese leadership could almost determine the pace of reconciliation unilaterally.

Chou En-lai rejected negotiations with the Sato Eisaku government. In June 1972 Sato was replaced as Japanese Prime Minister by Tanaka Kakuei, and the latter did everything possible to be accepted in China.[16] The Chinese–Japanese communiqué of 30 September 1972 contained the strongest formula of recognition with which any government had so far shown its recognition of Peking's demand for sole representation. Tanaka also allowed himself to be forced into annulling the peace treaty of 1952 between Japan and the Chinese Nationalist Government. This humiliation was made even worse by the fact that Japan was once again violating the vital interests of that China which it had attacked in the last phase of imperialist rule.[17]

But the East Asian daily papers were in the position to report an interesting detail about Tokyo's dramatic turning away from the Nationalist Chinese Government. Apparently it was Mao Tse-tung who on this occasion uttered some friendly words about his embittered rival, Chiang Kai-shek, and who declared his respect for the inexorability and single-mindedness with which he had always pursued his aims, however unacceptable these were.

Japan in fact only sacrificed its political honour in favour of a rapid normalization of its relations with Peking. In the end Peking did not press its former demand that Japan should break off all its economic relations with T'aiwan and South Korea.[18] It was only on the question of a massive Japanese share in the economic opening up of Eastern Siberia that the Peking government cast its veto.[19]

The détente between China and West Germany came about without any pre-conditions on either side. As the Bonn government had no diplomatic relations with T'aipei, the relatively short communiqué merely expressed the resolution to exchange ambassadors. This resolution, in fact, implied the contradictory position of the West German government renouncing its claim of sole representation, but at the same time recognizing that very claim on the part of the Chinese.

The Bonn government could only have accepted this position with the clear intention of using its relations with the People's Republic of China in its own foreign policy interests. For example, it would have been in its interest to invite the Peking government to participate at the European Security Conference, in order thereby to bring about the participation of China as of the other four permanent members of the Security Council in the shaping of a European system of peaceful coexistence. This should have been in the interests of China itself and of all those countries which were seeking Peking's involvement in the global system of détente. However, the West German government did not take this initiative, which seems symptomatic of the fact that, despite the Chinese policy of orientation towards the West, there was no coherent China-policy in the West itself.

Whereas the United States government fulfilled expectation by defending its policy of détente towards China to the Soviet Union with the assurance that it intended not to make use of the Sino-Soviet conflict, but to expand the détente process in international relations, the Bonn government obviously refrained from making such a declaration of intent. This was because West Germany could not on any account give the impression of collaborating with China in any way that would be directed against the Soviet Union; it thus gave clear priority to concern for Soviet sensibilities instead of attempting to work towards peace and détente in Europe and in global power relations simultaneously.

This is why it was only consistent that the Chinese government should pursue its policy of normalization with Western Europe through the argument that the Soviet Union was trying to create the impression that China was its main enemy against which it had to be on guard. Actually, however, the Soviet Union's intentions were directed primarily against Western Europe.[20] Peking therefore recognized that the negotiation by the Western states of compromises with Moscow was based on the false hypothesis that Soviet willingness to compromise had expanded considerably because of the Chinese threat.

In fact the idea was hardly ever expressed in Western Europe that the Soviet Union was manipulating itself through propaganda into the role of being threatened, in this instance by China (in the 1950s and 1960s the threat was from West Germany), in order to be able to sell its willingness to compromise as a policy of appeasement. The Chinese expressed this view very clearly in their observation that Western Europe still played a far more important part than China in the Soviet Union's concept of foreign policy, and that therefore in spite of all the successes of détente in that part of the world, there was an essential community of interest between Europe and China against the Soviet Union's notorious expansionism.

This view was accepted by neither West Germany nor France, whose President was allowed in September 1973 to have the most extensive talks that any foreign head of state had had till then with Mao Tse-tung. Georges Pompidou explained unambiguously to his Chinese hosts that Sino-French friendship was not to be at the expense of a third partner.[21] At the political level the Peking leadership thereby had to recognize the limits of Sino-European cooperation. Symptomatic of the position of the Western states, these limits were fixed not at those points where existing differences between China and the USA were also bound to strain China's relationship with Western Europe, but rather where the thin ice of Soviet-West European understanding could break again at any time.

Hence the possibilities of development in Chinese foreign policy actually remained confined to relations with the USA and to problems in its own region in the fourth phase after the Cultural Revolution, which was publicly characterized by Peking's détente with the USA's allies in Europe and with Japan. Here, however, Peking was in a position to gain some success. On his fifth visit to the People's Republic of China, Henry Kissinger came to an agreement with Chou En-lai that, as long as full diplomatic relations could not be established because of Washington's diplomatic ties with T'aipei, liaison offices would be set up in both countries.[22] As has already been mentioned, Peking sent one of its top diplomats, Huang Chen, to the Peking liaison office in Washington. President Nixon in turn chose in David Bruce an elderly but nonetheless excellent representative of the American government to manage the USA's office in Peking.

At the end of February 1973 Foreign Minister Ch'i P'eng-fei took part in the final international conference in Paris on the conclusion of the Vietnam War. In Peking this conference was celebrated not only for reasons of propaganda but also, apparently, because of quite pragmatic considerations.

The outcome of the Paris negotiations on the Vietnam problem were certainly unsatisfactory for all the parties involved. Not one of the powers directly or indirectly involved in the Indochina dispute had reason to celebrate a victory in the spring of 1973. However, the Chinese leaders may have seen a considerable advantage in the disinvolvement of the two super-powers from Vietnam. A series of three educational tracts for the troops in the Military Region of K'unming, which found their way to the West in April 1974 and the authenticity of which has since been proved, gives some information on this point.[23]

The first of these papers was concerned with the question of why the Vietnam armistice treaty of 27 January 1973 should be seen as a victory, and particularly as a success for China. One of the answers which was elaborated in this context seems of particular interest to us: apparently the Soviet Union had pursued the goal of engaging as many US troops as possible in Vietnam in order to weaken the American government's ability to compete in power politics in other parts of the world. The truce consequently cut across Soviet intentions as it put the Western world power back into a position of being able to act and compete. In other words, it was now insinuated that the Soviet Union had the same intentions which China had propagated for years. It was admitted at this point that in foreign policy terms the Vietnamese war of attrition had not been to China's advantage but rather to that of the Soviet Union.

It was in fact conspicuous that although during the Nixon visit in February 1972 the government of the People's Republic of China verbally demanded the withdrawal of all American troops from East and South-East Asia,[24] it did not continue to press this demand in its negotiations with the USA's South-East Asian allies. Nor were the presence of American troops in Thailand or the Philippines and even the membership of these two countries in the SEATO alliance a handicap to the process of détente.[25] The governments of Thailand and the Philippines had developed an interest in détente at a quite early stage, as had Malaysia, the only country in the ASEAN group[26] which (in May 1974) had normalized its relations with the People's Republic of China. In the diplomatic foreplay of give and take, it was clearly these states which had made demands on China: for Peking's unconditional recognition of the independence, sovereignty and integrity of the South East Asian states; for the discontinuation of all aid to the Communist rebel movements in the individual countries; and for an end to a type of interference in the internal affairs of South East Asian states particularly common in this area, namely the mobilization of the overseas Chinese.[28]

The relationship between the region's non-Communist countries and the People's Republic of China was so strained in every way that the problem of close relations between these countries and T'aiwan was only of secondary importance.

In the more or less secret negotiations which, since the spring of 1972, the representatives of Bangkok, Manila, Kuala Lumpur and Djakarta had been conducting with Chou En-lai, the Chinese declared that they were ready to revise their previous policy fundamentally.[29] Agreement had already been in sight by the spring of 1971 on the question of recognition. Malaysian traders reported on their return from the People's Republic that Peking would recognize the name 'Malaysia' as the official name of the state. They also reported that the Chinese point of view towards the Overseas Chinese had changed.[30] Thereafter, Peking actually repeatedly and publicly renounced pretentions of authority over the Chinese-born population outside the country, and went so far as to encourage them to show loyalty towards the governments of the individual host-countries.[31] On the question of aid to revolutionary movements, Chou En-lai expressed his view personally, though his words were not officially confirmed; according to reports from his South-East Asian negotiating partners, he confirmed that China had discontinued every form of aid to Communist 'terrorists' and all deliveries of weapons to Communist countries.[32]

Even so, except in the case of Malaysia, détente did not proceed beyond the phase of ping-pong diplomacy.[33] There were not even sporting contacts between China and Indonesia. The reasons for this hesitancy can be summarized in one sentence: the strain on the relationship between China and the South-East Asian states stems from the abnormality of a regional super-power which does not exert hegemony over a sphere of influence and which in its own security interests can only seek such a sphere of influence at the expense of its South-East Asian neighbours.

The fact that China was interested in gaining a strategic sphere of security became apparent at almost the same time as contacts were developing between the South-East Asian countries and Peking. The Chinese government tolerated the resolution of the ASEAN states seeking to bring about an international guarantee for the neutralization of the entire South-East Asian region.[34] However, it claimed for itself the sole possession of the islands and coral reefs in the South China seas. As this claim was contested by the Philippines, both states of Vietnam, and Malaysia, Peking had to rely on the comparatively weak legal evidence which the old Chinese Empire had bequeathed to the leaders of modern China.[35]

But this was not the only factor which put an added strain on China's relations with the South-East Asian states at the time when tensions in the region were gradually being relaxed. The representatives of the People's Republic of China used the very first session of the UN Asian Economic Committee (ECAFE) which they attended, in the spring of 1973, to stand up relentlessly for the interests of their special allies. The official ending of the Vietnam war and the increasing efforts at détente by both Korean governments after 1971 certainly justified Peking's request that North Vietnam and North Korea should be admitted to the Economic Committee. However, China did not let matters rest there: it supported the inclusion of the South Vietnamese provisional government (the Vietcong) and Prince Sihanouk's Cambodian Liberation Front (NUFK), demanding at the same time the immediate exclusion of the government of Lon Nol.[36] This could

not have been acceptable to any Asian government, but particularly not to those who had had to deal with Communist rebel
movements. The Chinese government here attempted to create the
precedent for self-appointed Communist authorities in other countries replacing legal governments.[37]

The situation was different in South Asia, where Chou En-lai
had twice clearly detached himself from attempts at revolutionary
insurrection and from a people's liberation war against the legal
government. This had happened first in the spring of 1971, when
there had been a rebellion of the radical Left in Sri Lanka.[38] The
second case was the rebellion of the East Bengalis the same year.
The People's Republic of China had had good relations with the
governments of Sri Lanka and Pakistan, and if only for that reason
it was not in its own interests to support the rebellious movements
in either country. Another probable reason why the Bengali
secession movement had to do without Peking's moral support was
that it was a non-Communist movement and probably did not
have the right, in Peking's eyes, to claim self-determination and
independence. Apart from that, the Awami League had cooperated
with India and with the Soviet Union. This was one point which
weighed heavily against the not unthinkable possibility that the
People's Republic of China should adopt a neutral position in the
Bangladesh crisis.

In a detailed analysis one would have to consider whether the
Chinese and, naturally, the USA too, when confronted by the
developments on the Indian subcontinent in 1971, were as lacking
in concepts as they had been in previous crises in the region, and
whether they actually provoked the Bengali secession movement's
association with Moscow.

By inclination its leader Sheikh Mujibur Rahman was certainly
more pro-Western than pro-Soviet. On the question—by no means
unimportant for Peking—of a collective security system. he
detached himself (after the establishment of Bangladesh) from
following the Soviet line, as far as this was possible while
remaining isolated from the West and from China.[39]

By openly siding with the Pakistani central government, Peking
in any case risked all the progress it had made in détente with
India.[40] This time the People's Republic of China had to see
demonstrations on the steps of its Embassy in New Delhi. The
Chinese government showed little understanding over this incident,
even though it had itself introduced mass terror as an instrument in
disputes over foreign policy.[41]

As a result China's relations with India remained unclear during
1972-3. Whereas the Indian government had openly stated its
interest in a settlement with China, there were only a few indications in Peking of readiness for reconciliation: a more objective

reporting of domestic political events in the neighbouring country, similar to reporting on all other parts of the world except the Soviet Union and Eastern Europe; support for the ideas of India and Sri Lanka on regional security in South Asia;[42] and finally, Peking's declared readiness to adopt a more pragmatic policy towards Bangladesh.[43]

Regarding South and South-East Asia, the People's Republic of China was in the midst of a process of détente when in the last days of August 1973 the 10th Party Congress of the CCP began in Peking. For this reason the question of the extent to which the Party Congress would confirm Chou En-lai's policies was of particular importance.

Stating one's own conclusions first—the Party Congress did not answer this question unequivocally. This impression stems partly from the fact that the 10th CC of the CCP had, if only in the interests of continuity in its inner-Party policy, to confirm the guidelines in foreign and domestic policies presented by Lin Piao at the 9th Party Congress. Only Lin Piao personally could be attacked and not his statement, which Chou En-lai reported as having been presented by Lin Piao unwillingly, since it was at variance with the ideas of the former Minister of Defence.[44]

At the 10th Party Congress, however, differences of opinion once again became apparent between Wang Hung-wên, who reported on the revision of the Party Constitution, and Chou En-lai—which seemed to revive the conceptual contrast between Lin Piao and the Prime Minister. Whereas Wang's argument was based on the view of China's present position of conflict *vis-à-vis* both the two super-powers simultaneously, Chou represented the argument of China having positions *vis-à-vis* the USSR and the USA that were different from one another, but which had in common the fact that they were positions of conflict.

Finally, the statements made at the 10th Party Congress by the Chinese Prime Minister on questions of foreign and international politics were supplemented to a considerable degree by aspects which he, contrary to all expectations and experiences, did not mention. As the report of the CC of the CCP at the 9th Party Congress, which had been delivered by Lin Piao, was confirmed, one cannot exclude the possibility that for certain sections of the Chinese leadership it filled in the gaps which Chou En-lai had left vacant. However, this presumes that the Prime Minister was still confronted with resistance by such sections within his own leadership.

In fact any analysis of the thoughts presented by Chou on questions of foreign and international politics has to start off from this point. What was most striking about his report was the fact that it was delivered from a defensive position. In line with the

Cultural Revolutionary analysis of the world situation, he started with the remark that there was widespread unrest. The Prime Minister described this as proof of Lenin's thesis of contradictions in the imperialist epoch, but he refrained from defining and systematizing these contradictions in detail. Chou started from Lenin's fundamental remark that the epoch of imperialism was determined by the rivalry of a number of great powers over hegemony. He then concentrated totally on the power-struggle of the two super-powers. Theoretically what was new was the fact that the Soviet Union was declared a constituent power in the historical era of imperialism. Chou En-lai then faced the question of how China was to behave in this situation, and his first answer to the question already contained a remarkable detail. Chou started out from the thesis that compromises between revolutionary and imperialist countries were a necessity. These compromises, so it was argued, were to be distinguished from secret collusion and from compromises between 'Soviet revisionism' and 'US-imperialism'. As Lenin had already suggested, each situation and every condition and variety of compromise had to be analysed. In other words, the compromises which the People's Republic of China had agreed to with the USA were seen as being different from those into which the Soviet Union had sought to enter with the Western world-power. The nature of the differences were only defined by the assertion that the compromises of the People's Republic of China had been necessary.

The historical example upon which Chou drew to clarify this difference emphasizes to the Western observer the force of the argument. He pointed out that the Brest-Litovsk Peace Treaty belonged to the category of necessary compromises between revolutionary and imperialist countries, but that on the other hand the policies of Khrushchev and Brezhnev amounted to a betrayal of Lenin's policy. In the Brest-Litovsk Peace Treaty, in which the young Soviet power had in fact had to submit to far-reaching compromises, it had essentially been a question of whether the war with Germany was to be continued, or whether broken off because of the priority given to the consolidation of the new Soviet government. Here it was a question of *raison d'état* versus the willingness to take risks. But in this case *raison d'état* was represented by Lenin alone. In the Council of the People's Commissars he was initially in a minority of one.

Did this historical example support China's situation and Chou En-lai's position at the time of the introduction of détente with the USA? Did the advice of the Prime Minister on the double-edged nature of compromise mean that some influential leadership personalities were not yet convinced of the correctness of the policies towards the West?

Such a conclusion seemed to suggest itself, and was also partly confirmed by the differences which appeared between Chou En-lai and Wang Hung-wên's speeches. If one begins with the assumption that it was necessary, in order to come to decide on a policy towards the West, to understand first that the People's Republic of China was threatened more by the Soviet Union than by the USA, then one of these differences certainly played a critical role. It was Wang Hung-wên who maintained that the People's Republic of China had to be prepared for an attack from the Soviet Union *and* the USA.[46] Chou En-lai demanded defence measures against 'any war of aggression, that imperialism may launch' and 'particularly against surprise attack on our country by Soviet revisionist social-imperialism'. For Chou the Soviet Union was undoubtedly the more dangerous of the two super-powers and China's main enemy.[47]

This appraisal did not, however, dissolve the ideological animosity against the USA. Chou also demanded, as Lin had done before him, that a united front should be established against imperialism, colonialism and neo-colonialism. In particular, however, he did not demand united action to 'bring down Soviet-revisionism and US-imperialism', as Lin had done at the 9th Party Congress, but rather a united front 'against the hegemonic aspirations of the two super-powers, the USA and the USSR'.[48]

The Prime Minister therefore did not represent the line of an offensive struggle against two total enemies, but rather that of a defensive position against the expansion of power of two enemies in the power-politics situation.

We now get to those points which Chou En-lai left unmentioned:

(1) He did not mention at all the trinity of proletarian internationalism, peaceful co-existence and revolutionary solidarity, as the general line of 'socialist' foreign policy.[49] At one point in his report the principle of proletarian internationalism did appear, which considering that this principle could only be fulfilled by the Party, was doubtless in line with his general reasoning. The politics of peaceful co-existence, however, were not mentioned at all, having obviously lost some of their declamatory power after the People's Republic of China had entered diplomatic relations with most of the non-Communist countries in the world.

(2) In Chou's report the usual enumeration of Communist rebel movements that were assured of China's support was also absent. Chou declared China's solidarity only with the 'Palestinian people' and the 'peoples of Indochina'. The Communist movements in Somalia, Thailand, Malaysia, the Philippines, Burma and Indonesia were no longer mentioned.[50] Instead of providing a list of fighting movements, Chou stated that the awakening and growth of the

'Third World', i.e. a combination of states and not a world of revolutionary fighting units,[51] was an important event in present international relations. It was this that was put forward by way of demands for a 200-mile coastal limit or for economic zones, and in its efforts to defend its national independence.

(3) Chou did not mention at all those South and South-East Asian countries which, because they had remained unnamed as theatres of revolutionary struggle, now had a changed role to play in the foreign policy of the People's Republic of China. Here the Prime Minister, in pointing to a policy of peaceful co-existence, could have shown the fundamental change in the relations between China and its immediate neighbours. An opportunity for such a gesture arose in June 1973, when the Malaysian Prime Minister Tun Abdul Razak announced the start of formal negotiations with the People's Republic of China. The fact that Chou managed without conciliatory gestures towards China's Asian neighbours can be explained by the explosive impact of China's détente, in which the revolutionary spirit which had determined Peking's policy in South and South-East Asia for more than twenty years was sacrificed. This may appear understandable, but at the same time it also reflected the political possibilities open to Chou. Particularly in relation to the leadership groups within his own Party, these political possibilities seemed to be limited to methods of secret diplomacy. However, China's Asian negotiating partners did not keep the fact or the content of their negotiations with Peking secret.[52]

Whether these Western-oriented policies would be confirmed, therefore, remained a practical problem for the future. Ten months after the end of the 10th Party Congress this practice began to show new traits of militancy, although at the same time there was a continuation of the Sino-American détente. The Peking government reacted strongly to the outbreak of the war in the Middle East in October 1973 and to the efforts by both super-powers to bring it to an end as soon as possible. China's verbal support for the 'just struggle of the Palestinians' characteristically resulted not in an argument with the Western super-power supporting Israel at the UN, but in an extensive political-ideological dispute with the Soviet Union. The imminent visit to Peking by Henry Kissinger, now nominated Secretary of State, was postponed until November 1973, not because of an estrangement between the People's Republic of China and the USA, but because Kissinger's negotiating ability had become necessary in the Middle East. The Chinese government willingly accepted this delay.

One sign of a new militancy was certainly the Chinese attack on South Vietnamese troops on the Paracel Islands in January 1974. This was followed in April by a restatement at the ECAFE meeting of China's exclusive claim to onwership of the islands in the South China Sea, threatening force against any foreign power which attempted to call this claim of ownership into question.[53]

However, the outcome of the sixth Kissinger visit to Peking on 10-14 November 1973 pointed to a moderation on the part of the Chinese government which had the effect of strengthening bilateral contacts. The final communiqué dealt particularly with questions of bilateral cooperation.[54] Particular attention was paid to the T'aiwan question. Whereas the Americans repeated the formula of the Shanghai communiqué, Peking declared that 'the normalization of relations between China and the United States can be realized only on a basis of confirming the principle of one China'.[55]

Kissinger declared during his visit to Peking that the significance of the visit could only be partly revealed by the then still incomplete communiqué, but at a Press conference on 21 November, he categorically excluded the possibility of entering into diplomatic relations at the expense of T'aiwan.[57]

The Chinese declaration of Peking's claim to sole representation for the whole of China, therefore had to appear in a different light. Any progress at all towards the normalization of relations[58] had occurred during Kissinger's sixth visit and was due to Peking's acceptance of the American declaration of principles and to the renunciation of its demands for an ending of relations between the USA and Nationalist China. Again one will have to wait to see the actual final developments. However, a minor event, considered quite unusual in the United States, seems quite important in this context.

Kissinger assured his Chinese guests, at a banquet given by him on 13 November in Peking, that friendship with the People's Republic of China was a constant factor of American foreign policy, no matter what might occur in the USA in the years to come. This was repeated in another sentence during his short talk. With this Kissinger may have been alluding to the Watergate affair and to the increasingly loud demands for the resignation of the joint guarantor, together with Mao Tse-tung, of the Sino-American détente—President Nixon. But Kissinger would probably not have been prepared to give such an obvious guarantee of the continuity of American foreign policy had the Chinese not asked him to do so. That it was of great importance to the continuity of Chinese foreign policy seems quite obvious.

The continuity of Chinese foreign policy after the 10th Party Congress was manifested particularly by the Prime Minister's further confirmation in office. Without a doubt, Chou En-lai can be closely identified with every phase of current Chinese foreign policy. If ever there was continuity in Peking's foreign policy, then it can be most readily put down to the continued presence of this personality in the foreign policy decision-making process. After the end of the Cultural Revolution and with the beginning of such a rigorous change of policy towards the USA, Chou En-lai may in fact have lost some room to manoeuvre within his own Party leadership: he was more than ever dependent on the success of his policy, as China's Western orientation did after all shake the basis of this 'revolutionary country'.

If the success of Chinese foreign policy (i.e. the effective balance between the foreign policy threat from the Soviet Union and the security diplomatically guarded by the USA due to its interest in an independent China) cannot guarantee its continuity of Peking's foreign policy should Chou's opponents in internal politics gain control and problems of *realpolitik* in foreign policy again be disregarded, then a number of questions still remain unanswered which in the 'long run must weigh rather heavily upon a success-oriented foreign policy.

Essentially foreign policy after the Cultural Revolution united the propaganda of an independent Chinese path of simultaneous struggle against both super-powers with the practical cooperation with one super-power against the other. Both the Soviet Union and the USA were alleged to be striving for hegemony. In the case of the USA, China accepted a declaration, contained in the Shanghai communiqué, stating its renunciation of all attempts to gain hegemony, as the basis for détente with the USA. Everywhere it was possible for the USA to set limits to Soviet expansion, China favouring the American side. But in the last four years there has been no example of a similar procedure being used to limit American expansionism. This is only logical, as long as for reasons of security China has no alternative to a policy of positive neutrality towards the USA. There would in fact be only one alternative if relations with the Soviet Union were like those with the USA, examined in terms of considerations of *realpolitik*. Only then could China's self-identification as an anti-super-power in foreign policy become credible and possibly even politically important. At present, China's claim to be an anti-super-power is based solely on a statement, quite irrelevant politically, that the Chinese People's Republic will never make itself into a super-power[59]—the Chinese will leave a judgement on this to be made by other countries. The equally incredible statement that China would never be the first to use atomic weapons was to underline the moral infallibility of this anti-super-power.[60] But how would the Chinese leadership discharge its responsibility if it saw itself hopelessly confronted, even in conventional terms, by the far greater strength of the Soviet aggressor? What could justify the development of Chinese nuclear power if not the possibility of using it as a defensive weapon, even if the aggressor counted on a victory in conventional warfare?

China could therefore only become an anti-super-power if it developed enough world political influence to stand up to against the hegemonic strivings of the super-powers at the conference table. But even then the precondition for this would be that the Peking leadership got on speaking terms with the Soviet Union and attempted to bring about a balance of power not only between itself and Moscow and the USA respectively, but of the two super-powers in their relationship with one another. The People's Republic of China cannot at present influence Soviet-American relations because this problem is actually of an exclusively 'power-politics' nature. If this is true from the start, then the attempt to carry on a policy of Western orientation on the basis of anti-Sovietism is contrary to all practical insight. The anti-Soviet factor will in the long run, and increasingly if China is tending to force her negotiating partner into her own position, be a disturbing element in the progress of Sino-American cooperation. It is impossible to discern the value of this anti-Soviet factor unless the talks between Peking and Washington were to serve as preparation for a formal alliance.

This possibility does not seem to be on the cards today, even though in a prognosis of Chinese foreign policy it should be considered as much a possibility as the alternative of a total (i.e. also ideological) reconciliation with the Soviet Union. However, it can be said that, within the foreign policy framework itself, the decision over the continuation of Western orientation will be dependent on the development of relations with the Soviet Union. The continuation of a policy of conflict, in its present form or even harsher, must lead to stagnation in the policy of Western orientation and to disappointment, because American willingness to support the People's Republic of China must itself be limited. Chou En-lai and his closest colleagues were certainly aware of this. However, even if one insinuates their awareness of the point that détente with the Soviet Union will have to be sought, one should still not expect such spectacular statements and measures as in the process of détente with the USA.

One indicator of the gradual normalization of Sino-Soviet relations will undoubtedly be China's reconciliation with India. If this should happen in the foreseeable future, then we could conclude that China's leaders have finally accepted India's desire for independence and are willing to support this claim in relation with the Soviet Union. Because India had (from among its possible partners in foreign policy) at all times given emotional preference to China before the USA and the Soviet Union, and because after the detonation of its first atom bomb it has gained in self-esteem in its relations with China, there is a real possibility here for Peking to break its actual or supposed encirclement by the Soviet Union. This would in fact create a favourable basis for a Sino-Soviet dialogue.

REFERENCES

1. See, Fritz von Briessen, 'China und die EWG: Eine neue Differenzierungsstrategie in Westeuropa', in *China und die Welt*, edited by Marie-Luise Näth, Hannover, 1972, pp. 79-89; Dick Wilson, 'China and the European Community', in *CQ*, No. 56, October-December 1973, pp. 647-66.

2. In his much noticed interview with representatives of the Japanese Socialist Party on 10 June 1964, Mao had demanded among other things the return to Japan of the four Southern Kurile Islands, occupied by the Soviet Union. See Dennis J. Doolin, *Territorial Claims in the Sino-Soviet Conflict, Documents and Analysis*, Stanford, 1965, p. 42; and Heinrich Bechtoldt, *Die Allianz mit der Armut—China's Revolutionsstrategie gegen Russland und Amerika*, Freiburg, p. 226.

3. See the Foreign Minister's speech at a banquet in honour of the West German Foreign Minister on 11 October 1972. English translation in *PR*, 42, 20 October 1972, p. 7.

4. See the Deputy Foreign Minister's speech at the 27th Plenary Session of the United Nations on 3 October 1972, ibid., No. 41, 13 October 1972 (pp. 4-10), p. 8.

5. See ibid., No. 37, 14 September 1973, pp. 8-12.

6. See Wolfgang Höpker, 'Der Indische Ozean im Visier des Kreml' in *Aussenpolitik*, Hamburg, Vol. 23, No. 6, June 1972, pp. 355-64; A. M. Rendell, 'Russia's Power in Indian Ocean' in *The Times*, London, 15 September 1970, p. 11; Oskar Weggel, 'Zur Lage im Indischen Ozean (Peking und die Pläne um Diego Garcia)', in *China aktuell*, Vol. 3, No. 4, May 1974, pp. 240-8.

7. See *Asia Research Bulletin*, Singapore *(ARB)*, Vol. 1, No. 12, May 1972, p. 861 A.

8. See: Rendell, loc. cit.; Dieter Braun, 'Perspektiven Sowjetischer Südostasienpolitik', in *Osteuropa*, Stuttgart, Vol. 23, No. 5, May 1973, pp. 366-75.

9. Since 1969 on different occasions Soviet politicians have pointed out with some determination that two-thirds of the Soviet territory was in Asia and that Moscow was thus as closely linked to Asia as to Europe: e.g. Nikolai Podgorny on his visit to Hanoi in October 1971.

10. See: Justus M. van der Kroef, 'Sowjetische Sicherheitsstrategie in Asien', in *Aussenpolitik*, Vol. 21, No. 8, August 1970, pp. 402-503; Dieter Braun, loc. cit.; Joachim Glaubitz, 'Die Politik der Sowjetunion gegenüber Japan', in *Osteuropa*, Vol. 23, No. 5, May 1972, pp. 323-36; Dieter Braun and Joachim Glaubitz, 'Kollektive Sicherheit also Konzept sowjetischer Asien-Politik' in *Europa-Archiv*, Bonn, Vol. 29, No. 1, 10 January 1974, pp. 22-30.

11. English text in *AA*, Vol. 9, No. 50, 18 December 1971, p. 4937-8.

12. See, for a comparison, the Sino-American communiqué of 27 February 1972 which contained similar statements on the Indo-Pakistan conflict of December 1971.

13. See the Soviet-American communiqué at the end of the Nixon visit to Moscow (22-30 May 1972) in *ABR*, Vol. 2, No. 1, June 1972, pp. 981-3; *NCNA*, London, 21 April 1972, published in advance a bitter commentary in which the two super-powers were labelled 'super-criminals' taking into slavery 'the small and weak nations'.

14. After the visit to Japan of the Soviet Foreign Secretary Gromyko at the end of January 1972, the Peking leadership watched the development of Soviet-Japanese relationships very closely. The neutralization of Japan would certainly leave the USSR room for greater influence than it has at present.

15. For reasons of convenience and also because of a genuine China-enthusiasm, most of the larger daily newspapers in Japan chose not to discuss the Lin Piao crisis.

16. Tanaka, who had been elected the new Prime Minister on 6 July 1972, accepted (a few days later) Chou En-lai's three preconditions for normalizing relations: (1) the recognition of Peking's claim to sole representation; (2) the confirmation that T'aiwan was an integral part of Chinese territory; and (3) the annulment of the peace treaty with T'aiwan. Prime Minister Sato had only accepted the second condition and had suggested that Tokyo would recognize the Peking government only as 'a legitimate one'. Sato also insisted that such questions should be resolved at governmental level and that they could not be accepted before negotiations had begun. See *ARB*, Vol. 2, No. 2, July 1972, pp. 1074-5.

17. Text of the Chinese-Japanese communiqué, translated in ibid., No. 5, October 1972, pp. 1227-8.

18. In April 1970 Chou En-lai had put forward the four following principles: China would not cooperate with those companies which (1) were trading with T'aiwan and South Korea, (2) were investing in both areas, (3) were sending weapons for the USA to Vietnam, Laos and Cambodia and which (4) were American companies in Japan. See *SWB/FE*, No. 3359, 22 April 1970, p. A 3/3.

19. As through Liao Ch'eng-chih, the Chairman of the Chinese-Japanese Friendship Society, who in the spring of 1973 mentioned to the Japanese paper *Yomiuri*, that a closer Soviet-Japanese cooperation could raise 'bitter feelings' in China and could lead to counter-measures. Cited in Glaubitz, loc. cit., p. 335.

20. This argument was also put forward by Chou at the 10th Party Congress of the CCP. See 'Report to the Tenth National Congress of the Communist Party of China', loc. cit., p. 22.

21. See *PR*, No. 37, 14 September 1973, p. 11.

22. See the background report, 'A Milestone in Sino-American Relations' in *ARB*, Vol. 2, No. 10, March 1973, pp. 1606-9.

23. English translation in *Background on China*, New York, 11, 12 and 13 April 1974. The directives originated in April 1973. They followed shortly after the Paris Conference on Vietnam.

24. See the Sino-American communiqué of 27 February 1972, loc. cit.

25. See the report by Benjamin Romualdez, who in February 1972 visited Peking at the request of the Philippine President Marcos. Excerpts in *AA*, Vol. 10, No. 17, 29 April 1972 and also the report of the then Thai Minister of Defence, Air Marshal Thawi Chunlasapya, on his conversation with Chou En-lai in February 1974, in *SWB/FE*, No. 4531, 20 February 1974, pp. A 2/2 f.

26. Indonesia, Malaysia, the Philippines, Singapore and Thailand.

27. The first possibilities for making contact with the People's Republic of China emerged in the autumn of 1971 on the occasion of the 26th Plenary Session of the United Nations. In the first few months thereafter, from November 1971 until January 1972, there were increasing suggestions of a possible rapproachement with China. But then there also were counter-arguments by those politicians who were concerned specifically with the internal security of their countries.

28. See, *inter alia*, the statement by the Malaysian Premier to the Parliament in Kuala Lumpur in June 1971; excerpts in *AA*, Vol. 10, No. 7, 19 February 1972.

29. Informative in this respect is in particular the late Thai Minister of Defence's report on 16 February 1974. According to accounts given by the Philippine President, Chou admitted to his aide Romualdez in the spring of 1972 that 'Lin Piao elements' had trained the cadres of the Philippine rebels. However, the Prime Minister had given an assurance that such activities had been discontinued by the Chinese. See footnote 25; and: ARB, Vol. 3, No. 1, June 1973, p. 1842, A.

30. See *UPI*, Kuala Lumpur, 23 May 1971.

31. See among others the speech given by Marshal Yeh Chien-ying to welcome more than 700 'Countrymen from Hong Kong, Macao and Taiwan, and Overseas Chinese and foreigners of Chinese origin', on 29 September 1972, *NCNA*, London 30 September 1972.

32. Thawi and Romualdez, see footnote 25.

33. In September 1972 Malaysia, the Philippines and Thailand sent for the very first time teams of table tennis players to the People's Republic of China to participate in the first Congress of the Asian Table Tennis Union (ATTU). See communiqué of the 1st Congress of the ATTU, 13 September 1972, in, *PR*, No. 37, 15 September 1972, p. 8.

34. This resolution originated from the initiative of Tun Abdul Razak who shortly after his nomination as Prime Minister of Malaysia in November 1970, developed his neutralization plans. In November 1971 his initiative was accepted by all ASEAN states. See *ARB*, Vol. I, No. 7, December 1971, p. 490 A.

35. On the island dispute in the South China Sea, see ibid., Vol. 1, No. 3, August 1971, pp. 169–171 A.

36. See *ARB*, Vol. 2, No. 12, May 1973, p. 1750 B.

37. In December 1973 the Malaysian representative argued against the attempt by the People's Republic of China to push through the exclusion of the Lon Nol government from the United Nations, on the grounds that this would set a dangerous precedent. See ibid., Vol. 3, No. 8, 31 January 1974, p. 2367 B.

38. See Chou En-lai's note to the Sri Lanka Prime Minister, Mrs. Bandaranaike, 26 April 1971. Cited in *AA*, Vol. 9, No. 26, 3 July 1971.

39. In May 1973 an 'Asian Peace Conference' was held in Dacca under Soviet aegis, which was to deal in particular with questions of a collective security system in Asia. The government of Bangladesh, however, clearly detached itself from these activities.

40. This at least was declared by the Indian Prime Minister, Mrs. Gandhi, at a press conference immediately after the end of the Simla Conference in July 1972. See ibid., Vol. 10, No. 37, 16 September 1972.

41. See the Chinese report of the siege of the PRC's Embassy; English version in *PR*, No. 16, 16 April 1971, p. 3.

42. See, ibid., No. 50, 15 December 1972, p. 8.

43. See the speech of the Head of the Chinese delegation, Huang Hua, to the United National Plenary Session on 29 November 1972, in Ibid., 8 December 1972, pp. 10-12.

44. See 'Report to the 10th National Congress of the CCP', loc. cit., p. 17.

45. See ibid., pp. 17-25.

46. See 'Report on the Revision of the Party Constitution', ibid. (pp. 29-33), p. 33.

47. See 'Report on the 10th National Congress of the CCP', loc. cit.

48. Ibid., p. 25.

49. See Chapter 12, p. 186.

50. Against this, see Lin's speech to the 9th Party Congress of the CCP, loc. cit.

51. After the entry of the People's Republic of China into the United Nations, the term 'Third World' was used increasingly by members and representatives of the Chinese government. Since the spring of 1973 the *Peking Review* has at irregular intervals contained a news column under the heading of 'Third World'.

52. See footnote no. 25. The content of such conversations is obviously not fully revealed.

53. See *PR*, No. 15, 12 April 1974.

54. Full text in *ARB*, Vol. 3 , No. 7, December 1973, p. 2346.

55. Ibid.

56. Kissinger during the banquet on 13 November 1972, see ibid., p. 2281 A.

57. Cited in ibid., p. 2281 A.

58. See Kissinger's Speech of 13 November 1973.

59. See Deputy Foreign Minister Ch'iao Kuan-hua's first speech to the 26th Plenary Session of the United Nations on 15 November 1971, English in *PR*, No. 47, 19 November 1971, pp. 8 ff.

60. Ibid.

CONCLUSION

REVOLUTIONARY LEADERSHIP AND CRISIS

Without doubt the Lin Piao crisis was another shock to the PRC's political system after the Cultural Revolution, although it was very different in character. It is a considerable political and organizational achievement that in the course of the four-and-a-half years between the 9th and the 10th Party Congresses, while the leadership group of the CCP changed in composition, it still managed to arrive at an extensive consolidation of the governmental system. This achievement seems even greater since there was a simultaneous stabilization of economic growth, at least as far as the foreign observer can tell. If one remarks on this achievement, then one must also question what it meant for the development of the country in terms of those aims which the leadership had set itself.

In the first years of Communist rule in China there was wide-ranging agreement among the Party's leaders that the transformation of Chinese society via a Socialist to a Communist system could not be divorced from the country's material development. However, Mao Tse-tung's experiments with a concept of development through mobilization, which were implemented in 1958, led to a conflict over priorities which has still not been resolved. Political developments in China ever since have demonstrated that whenever an interest in the mobilization of the 'new men' for the 'new society' became more prominent, then material development was handicapped and left to stagnate. Those forces within the Chinese leadership which feel particularly committed to material development are most probably of the conviction that they are serving in their own way the goal of the development of a Communist society. However, despite all the correctives which have emerged since the summer of 1973 in the return to Cultural Revolutionary terminology, development and growth-oriented policies have shown a growing tendency to become detached from the revolutionary vision of the future.

A similar process has also been apparent in foreign policy, where after the end of the Cultural Revolution—although the verbal obligation to support a world revolution has not been renounced—it quite obviously had to give second place to measures to secure China's national existence, particularly in the conflict with the Soviet Union. Corresponding to the apparent tendency since 1970-1 to reduce the political demands on the population and to emphasize principles of material development on the home front, a foreign policy has emerged which has striven to consolidate China's position as a member of the international states-system.

These two trends are certainly called into question by those forces committed to the continuation of the revolution at home and abroad. For this reason it would be premature to consider them as constant factors for the future of Chinese politics. But in spite of various dangers threatening their existence, their continuity seems to have proved itself stronger than the doctrine of permanent revolution.

China's development since the Cultural Revolution seems to indicate that here too, despite continued revolutionary rhetoric and the temporary return to mobilizatory policies, Communist rule is subject to the same laws as have been confirmed in the course of other revolutionary movements.

Max Weber has indicated the importance for political systems of the transition from charismatic to institutionalized leadership, of the *Veralltäglichung des Charisma* (routinization of charisma). This idea has been taken up by Richard Löwenthal with the suggestion that the securing of the transition from charisma to institutionalization poses a significant problem for any ideologically-based one-party system. Such a system develops, where it has not been introduced into a country by military force, through a *revolution*. Not just any change of leadership can be regarded as such a revolution: it has to be a change in *political power and social structure* by violent means, resulting from a change of leadership. Such a change is brought about by alternative élites who are committed to a certain doctrine and who use this doctrine to create a new base for the legitimization of rule. With this, transition from charisma to institution is already prescribed. The experience of the development of Communist rule in the Soviet Union since the October revolution of 1917 and the observation of political developments in China since 1958 lead us to conclude that political leadership in Communist states has to pass through three consecutive stages of development:

(1) The stage of *charismatic leadership*, as in the Soviet Union under Lenin and in China under Mao Tse-tung until the end of the 1950s;

(2) The stage of *transitional leadership*, which took the form of one-man rule in the Soviet Union under Stalin, and which in a

totally different manner has determined China's political system since 1959; and

(3) The stage of *institutionalized leadership*.

In every one of these three stages political decision-making is accompanied by intra-Party conflicts. Such conflicts are observable because of certain signs. One-party systems, particularly those which cling to a doctrine claiming to be of a consistent and rational character, are under the pressure of a totally uniform outward appearance. Because Lenin was fully aware of this, he enforced the prohibition of fractions within the CPSU(B), a system that has been adopted by most other Communist parties. Ever since, differences of opinion within ruling Communist parties have usually made their first appearance only through changes in the terminology used in the media.

For this reason content analysis is seen to be a necessary instrument when studying the politics of Communist countries. *Differences in terminology* are in many cases the first sign to the foreign observer of the development of an intra-Party conflict. Even in cases where these differences of terminology are indicative of changes of political direction pursued without the appearance of further signs of conflict, then these changes were mostly preceded by a severe dispute within the leadership.

Differences in terminology are therefore necessary but not sufficient signs of an intra-Party conflict. There are four further signs which also indicate the increasing intensity of a dispute. However, they do not necessarily have to follow the same order as presented here.

(1) The *removal* from office of Party leaders in influential positions in the State and Party system. This, however, does not necessarily have to result in the expulsion of dissidents from the Party, so that as a rule it does not prejudice the impression of monolithic unity which the Communist Party seeks to present to the outside world.

(2) The *expulsion* from the Party of some leading cadres, still so designated to sustain the outside world's picture of a united leadership.

(3) An *open rift* which becomes apparent because the media no longer conceal it within the active leadership group. So far this has only happened when a collapse of the consensus over procedure has followed a collapse of the consensus over the content of the intra-Party debate. Without a doubt, a dramatic example of such an open rift was the start of the Cultural Revolution.

(4) A *blood purge*, preceded in many instances by the dissident's removal from office and expulsion from the Party; the latter may, as in the Soviet Union in the 1930s, occur years before the actual 'blood-purge'. However, 'blood purges' have taken place without any such preliminary symptoms where leaders of the armed forces

or state security systems in Communist countries were involved: in the Tuchatschevsky crisis of 1937, the fall of Yezhov in 1938 and that of Beria in 1953, as well as in the Lin Piao crisis.

The present character of Communist rule in China and its prospects can be more clearly identified if we categorize the signs of intra-Party conflict and the identifiable types of group formation and allocative processes in terms of the three stages of development.

The stage of charismatic leadership is characterized by the obviously dominant position of the Party leader, who at the head of the Party ensures the victory of the revolution. The most prominent organizational feature of this stage is the Party's undoubted control, more as a political body than as a bureaucratic *apparat*, over all other pillars of the political system. If at this stage intra-Party conflicts arise, they are manifested mainly by differences in terminology and in removals from office, but very rarely in expulsions from the Party. 'Blood purges' are generally confined to non-Party enemies. The only exceptions have been the death of Camilo Cienfuegos in Cuba and the liquidation of the Stalinists in Yugoslavia in 1948. Intra-Party group formation remains at the level of opinion-groups, and the allocative process depends on the majority constructed by the Party leader.

The course of China's political history since 1955 has shown that the stage of transitional leadership does not necessarily take the form of one-man rule. In China since 1959, a second type of transitional leadership has developed—in effect a *transitional crises system*; a series of factionally determined crises plus a gradual pressure pushing the previously charismatic leader into the role of legitimator. In the case of one-man rule, the political system is determined by the balance between the bureaucratic competition of different governmental sectors, maintained by the leader's personal secretariat. The second type of political system is determined by political competition between majorities and minorities in the different governmental sectors. In the case of one-man rule, the signs of intra-Party conflict are removal from office, expulsion from the Party and, in particular, 'blood purges'. In the case of a series of factional crises, the signs are mainly differences in terminology, removals from office, expulsions from the Party and an open rift. However, 'blood purges' occur less frequently. These latter have to be understood as specific phenomena of one-man rule, and not as phenomena of the struggle between majorities and minorities.

Under one-man rule, opinion groups are generally broken up in their early stages and the consolidation of factions is not at all likely. This is so because the lone ruler's paranoia detects the emerging groups and identifies them as coherent factions with an alternative political programme, and consequently has them liquidated.

A 'transitional crises system', however, is based on the interplay of opinion group formations and their consolidation into factions. If the charismatic leader is forced into a position as legitimator without the simultaneous permanent securing of institutions, political initiative 'is suppressed', it tends to be parcelled and paralysed with regard to long-term decisions.

Under one-man rule there is no allocative process in the sense of our definition. In a transitional 'crises system', such a process serves both the creation and the growth of majorities. As the Party leader becomes more and more resigned to his role as legitimator, this type of majority formation becomes more prominent. In these circumstances the intra-Party conflict takes on the form of a conflict over power and direction.

The stage of *institutionalized leadership* leads to stable competition based on compromise between *apparats*. Its characteristics are those defined by Graham Allison as comprising 'bureaucratic politics'. Governments act through negotiation and compromise, since different sub-systems of the political system have different political aims and different perceptions of their requirements.

Differences in terminology and removals from office are, as usual, signs of intra-Party conflict, and while there are sometimes expulsions from the Party, there are no longer any 'blood purges'. The balance between bureaucratic sub-systems frequently has to be restored, as a minority which is in an inferior position at one point could, in the next round of compromises, be of use again. If only for these reasons physical liquidations are not allowed.

Functional groups and historical loyalties become of greater inportance than pure opinion-groups. The compromise-ridden nature of the political decision-making process makes the consolidation of opinion groups into factions less likely. The allocative process is clearly one of majority formation.

The Soviet Union has already reached the stage of institutionalized leadership, and the same is true of the majority of the East European countries, in which there never has been a charismatic leadership. In these countries institutionalized leadership succeeded a special transitional form of leadership, and was limited purely to executive functions because they developed only from one-man rule in the Soviet Union.

In all such cases where Communist tule emerged from a violent internal revolution, charismatic leadership came at the beginning of such developments. This was succeeded by a transitional period, characterized on the one hand by a system of one-man rule, and on the other by a transitional 'crises system'. Succeeding one-man rule there has been a third and so far final stage of development, that of institutionalized leadership.

In the early stages of discussions on the theoretical principles of the Communist movement first developed by Lenin in 1902, Trotsky uttered the following warning: 'These methods lead, as we shall see, to the following: the Party organization takes the place of the Party, the Central Committee takes the place of the Party organization, and finally the "Dictator" takes the place of the Central Committee.' Trotsky's premonition has obviously come true only in the medium term, as it is a characteristic of the third stage of development of Communist rule that the bureaucratic *apparats* take the place of the 'Dictator'.

At the stage of institutionalized leadership the character and content of intra-Party conflict change fundamentally. The programmatic disputes of the transitional phase have receded, their place being taken by competition among the *apparats*, and the place of struggles over political power and direction being taken by the rivalry between bureaucratic subsystems. The content of conflict is less and less determined by the desire for political change, and increasingly determined by the interests of independent-minded *apparats* in changing the emphasis of bureaucratic influence. The depersonalization of conflicting forces is equalled by the depoliticization of the content of conflict.

If it were at all useful, in an analysis of the development of Communist rule, to apply Marxist thought, one would be most likely to find such thinking among the critics of the reality of Communist-ruled states such as Milovan Djilas, Jacek Kuron, Karol Modzelewski and the unknown authors of the documents of the Left Red Guard opposition from 1968. One thought is common to all the thinkers of the opposition despite all differences, namely that political change comes about not through the cooption of leaders but by a change of leadership. However, such a change in the leadership of these political systems, where the instrument of election is unknown, can be brought about only by two routes: by a succession of generations of administrative bureaucrats, who do not change the system; or by revolutionary change.

In this way, principle of Mao and his closest followers of a continuous revolutionary process gains a significance which the leadership of the CCP would hardly have envisaged: that in the long term there is a possibility of replacing Communist rule by political forces which are not determined by different interpretations of a Marxist–Leninist vision of the future.

However, the question still remains whether the transformation of leadership which stemmed from revolution into institutionalized government is historically inevitable. At present, there is insufficient evidence for such a projection into the future. Even a comparison between Communist-inspired revolutionary movements and the French Revolution hardly brings us much further forward.

First of all, this revolutionary movement lacked the instrument of a cadre Party. The Clubs are hardly comparable to such parties as sociological organizations. The period of the rule of terror under the Committee of Public Security cannot be unequivocally identified as charismatic leadership, nor with any certainty can Robespierre's one-man rule. There were traits of both forms of rule in a system of government not solely determined by one person. On the other hand, the period of the Directory showed all essential characteristics of a 'transitional crises system'. However, it was obviously succeeded not by a clear transition to institutionalized government but by the phase of Bonapartist one-man rule, which was not ended by internal political change but by foreign influence.

The course of the French Revolution therefore differs considerably from the revolutions in Russia and China. In order to determine the causes of these differences one would need an extensive comparative examination going far beyond the scope of this study. Here it can only be suggested that the absence of a revolutionary cadre Party had a considerable impact on these differences.

However, it was just this revolutionary cadre Party which was temporarily paralysed during the crisis of the Cultural Revolution. One still cannot predict with certainty whether it will regain its full organizational force. Should this not occur, then one-man rule, as perhaps a new period of charismatic leadership, could easily follow the period of the 'transitional crises system' in the PRC. However, it is not possible at present to identify any political forces or personalities who could ensure any such forms of leadership.

For this reason, the prospect of a change in China towards institutionalized leadership seems very likely. Should this view prove correct, competition among functional bureaucratic *apparats* would in future gain prominence over fundamental political disputes. In the framework of such competition these functional groups deserve particular attention: that is the civilian Party *apparat*, the diplomatic and administrative systems, and the Army. (Already in the past fifteen years, and especially since the Cultural Revolution, they have asserted considerable influence over the political decision-making process.) The damping of the armed forces' political potential since the Spring of 1973 should not convince us that there is no possibility that the military will again have an opportunity, particularly in a succession crisis, to assert considerable influence on intra-Party conflicts.

Already today we can see with some certainty the possibility that within the PLA in the next decade the importance of the competition between loyalty groups will take second place to the competition among the different regional *apparats* and auxiliary service arms. However, these conflicts within the armed forces will probably decline in personal intensity, and as a result the position of the Army as a whole will again become stronger.

The prospects seem to indicate that—after a transitional phase in which there will be several failed attempts (after initial partial successes) to return to the mobilizatory concept of development—the political system in the People's Republic of China will be determined by the interaction of bureaucratic competition and compromise with elements of military federalism. In the sphere of foreign policy such a system of government will retain the priority given to national security, and will finally recognize too the equal status of the country in relations between states.

These projections into the future do not answer the questions whether the content of the Chinese Revolution may expand to include the effective participation of large sections of the people in the process of political decision-making, and whether a larger area of individual freedom may be permitted. Contrary to still widespread clichés, these two elements have been part of the content of the Chinese Revolution's development process ever since the beginning of this century. This has remained true since 1949: we find it in the intellectual revolt of the 'Hundred Flowers Movement' in 1957, in the criticisms of the Maoist concept of development by leading Party intellectuals since 1961, in the political ideas of the Red Guard movement and the resistance of large groups of the rural population to Lin Piao's socio-political experiment, and in the dramatic uprising of the masses in Peking in early April 1976. This fact sets limits to the prospects for the development of Communist rule in China, even though its continuation seems certain for the coming two decades.

Epilogue to the English Edition

Habent sua fata libelli—when the page-proofs for the German edition of this book had been revised, the PRC, at the Fourth NPC in January 1975, completed the reconstruction of the leading organs of State power. Hence, the results of this meeting could not be taken account of in the German edition.

When the English translation was completed, a new deep and far-reaching confrontation beset the Chinese leadership élite. It reached its first climax in the purge of Teng Hsiao-p'ing as well as in unprecedented popular rebellion right in the centre of the PRC's capital and was then further complicated by the death of Mao Tse-tung. Readers may wonder why these events, and also developments in 1974 and 1975, are not discussed in this book.

There are three reasons for this omission: first, with the 10th Party Congress in 1973, a new stage of political development in China has begun, which needs adequate academic analysis in a separate study. Secondly, for such a study a systematic scrutiny of documentary sources and data has yet to be made. For the developments of early 1976, this study could only begin in about half a year. Thirdly, it has not been the intention of the present study to offer an up-to-date account of developments in China since the 'Cultural Revolution', but rather to analyse the period from 1969 to 1973, with major emphasis on the Lin Piao crisis and its immediate aftermath.

Yet the author believes that the present study will still be helpful to the understanding of current developments in China. While the process of factionalisation seems, again, to have reached the stage of open conflict—i.e. direct confrontation between factions among the élite—the major issues are the same as they were in the period dealt with in this book.

Shall China follow the road of development through mass mobilization and enthusiastic austerity, the road of 1958? Or shall her future be mapped out by leaders who adhere to more conventional economics, and who stress modernization rather than revolutionization?

Shall leadership demands on the Chinese peasants be tightened or loosened? Shall the level of agricultural collectivization be raised or lowered? Shall the education of the next Chinese generation be dominated by indoctrination or by instruction?

These are the issues at stake, and I repeat what I said in the present study when its German page-proofs were finished around New Year 1975: this will by no means be the last clash between these different approaches to China's future. More such confrontations—probably even more violent and critical ones—are bound to follow.

But the Peking rebellion of April 1976 has brought to the surface a new aspect of Chinese politics. Beyond the lines of intra-élite conflict and confrontation—which are continuing—much more basic contradictions in Chinese society have again come to the fore. Today we do not yet know to what extent they will shape the immediate future perspectives of politics in the PRC. But, in the long run, these contradictions may well lead to the final completion of the Chinese revolution: China's definite entry into the modern world. *This* revolution, however, may go beyond the capacity of Communist leadership. And in *that* long run, we may still not all be dead.

Saarbrücken, 1 October 1976

Index